IP in Wireless Networks

Basavaraj Patil
Yousuf Saifullah
Stefano Faccin
Srinivas Sreemanthula
Lachu Aravamudhan
Sarvesh Sharma
Risto Mononen

PRENTICE
HALL
PTR

PRENTICE HALL
Professional Technical Reference
Upper Saddle River, New Jersey 07458
www.phptr.com

ISBN 0-13-066648-3

94999

9 790130 666481

Library of Congress Cataloging-in-Publication Data

IP in wireless networks / Basavaraj Patil ... [et al.].
    p. cm.
Includes bibliographical references and index.
  ISBN 0-13-066648-3
  1. TCP/IP (Computer network protocol) 2. Wireless Internet. 3.
Wireless communication systems. I. Patil, Basavaraj.
  TK5105.585 .I65 2003
  004.67'8—dc21

                            2002153606

Editorial/production supervision: Jessica Balch (Pine Tree Composition, Inc.)
Cover design director: Jerry Votta
Cover designer: Nina Scuderi
Art director: Gail Cocker-Bogusz
Interior design: Meg Van Arsdale
Manufacturing buyer: Maura Zaldivar
Executive editor: Mary Franz
Marketing manager: Dan DePasquale
Editorial assistant: Noreen Regina
Full-service production manager: Anne R. Garcia

©2003 by Pearson Education, Inc.
Publishing as Prentice Hall Professional Technical Reference
Upper Saddle River, NJ 07458

Prentice Hall books are widely used by corporations and government agencies for training, marketing, and resale.

For information regarding corporate and government bulk discounts, please contact: Corporate and Government Sales (800) 382-3419 or corpsales@ pearsontechgroup.com

Other company and product names mentioned herein are the trademarks or registered trademarks of their respective owners.

Printed in the United States of America

10 9 8 7 6 5 4 3 2 1

ISBN 0-13-066648-3

Pearson Education Ltd., *London*
Pearson Education Australia Pty. Limited, *Sydney*
Pearson Education Singapore, Pte. Ltd.
Pearson Education North Asia Ltd. *Hong Kong*
Pearson Education Canada, Ltd., *Toronto*
Pearson Educación de Mexico, S.A. de C.V.
Pearson Education—Japan, *Tokyo*
Pearson Education Malaysia, Pte. Ltd.

About Prentice Hall Professional Technical Reference

With origins reaching back to the industry's first computer science publishing program in the 1960s, Prentice Hall Professional Technical Reference (PH PTR) has developed into the leading provider of technical books in the world today. Formally launched as its own imprint in 1986, our editors now publish over 200 books annually, authored by leaders in the fields of computing, engineering, and business.

Our roots are firmly planted in the soil that gave rise to the technological revolution. Our bookshelf contains many of the industry's computing and engineering classics: Kernighan and Ritchie's *C Programming Language*, Nemeth's *UNIX System Administration Handbook*, Horstmann's *Core Java*, and Johnson's *High-Speed Digital Design*.

PH PTR acknowledges its auspicious beginnings while it looks to the future for inspiration. We continue to evolve and break new ground in publishing by providing today's professionals with tomorrow's solutions.

PRENTICE
HALL
PTR

CONTENTS

The wireless market is already a huge market, with over 1 billion active mobile wireless users worldwide. The wireless operators' revenues passed $300B mark in 2001 and are continuing to grow. Wireless voice, in particular, has been a huge success for the industry. Driven by the increased mobility of society, as well as the convenience, simplicity, competitive rates, and attractive offers from the wireless operators, there has been a significant shift in voice minutes from fixed wireline networks to wireless networks.

Wireless data has had a limited success up until recently. SMS (short message service) has been a huge and unexpected success, especially with young consumers. Today, more than 1 billion SMS messages are sent worldwide per day, contributing around 10–12% of operators' revenues. Encouraged by the SMS success, as well as the i-Mode success in Japan, wireless operators have been deploying 2.5G GPRS and cdma2000 packet/IP based networks in order to get into the wireless data market in earnest.

Building on the proven and profitable model of SMS, wireless operators are busy today rolling out MMS (Multimedia Messaging Service), utilizing their packet/IP-based networks. Even though the success of MMS is far from guaranteed, there are various positive projections for significant revenues from such services. MMS could be the next big mass-market opportunity for wireless data, provided that the industry players get it right!

In fact, wireless operators have recognized recently that it is the services and applications that will deliver future growth for them. As a result, there has been significant increase in investment and attention placed on the development and deployment of services and applications that are considered compelling to attract and retain subscribers and that help with the average revenue per user (ARPU) growth. Almost all the operators around the world are busy building service and application infrastructures to offer services, as well as to stimulate the growth of third-party applications. However, wireless operators will have a small percentage of these services and applications hosted within their networks (as low as 5–10%); for the rest of the services and applications, they will have to rely on third-party applications hosted and offered from outside of their networks. The Application Programming Interfaces (APIs), primarily revenue sharing, charging, and security, will be critical for the success of these third-party applications. Today, around 85% of revenues are voice-related, but most operators are projecting 30–40% of their revenues to come from various wireless data applications in the coming years. Thus, data services and applications are going to be very critical for wireless operators growth in the future.

The next major wireless network build-out will be based on 3rd generation (3G) radio and network technologies. Some wireless operators have paid huge sums of money for 3G spectrum licenses, especially in Europe. These 3G networks will enable much more capacity, as well as higher speed data rates for mobile wireless applications, enabling wireless operators new revenue streams. However, the pace of 3G network deployments will be tied to the success of wireless data applications such as MMS in the near term.

The wireless operators are facing major challenges for different parts of their wireless networks today. For radio networks, the top issue is cost, from site acquisition and site preparation to actual hardware and software that needs to be deployed at each and every site. More sites are needed to accommodate increasing traffic, new features, and new technologies. Another big pain point is adequate or appropriate coverage, which is very much tied to the number, type, and location of sites. Coverage is also tied to the quality of service and dropped call rates, especially in hand-over situations (e.g., driving on the highway).

For radio access networks (RANs), the top issue is again cost, but this time it is mostly operational expenditure (OPEX) that may concern the operators, who do not own wireline infrastructure. Considering that there are thousands, if not tens of thousands, of cell sites that need to be connected to BSCs/MSCs, this cost could be as much as 30–40% of the total OPEX for the wireless operator.

For the circuit switched part of the core network, the major pain point remains cost, but this time it includes capital expenditure (CAPEX) and OPEX. Circuit switches (i.e., MSCs) are both costly and difficult to offer new services on, and wireless operators would like to cap their investments in MSCs as they move to all-IP networks. However, there are several major challenges for the packet switched part of the core network as well. As more packet/IP based networks are being deployed, the emerging challenges are primarily in scalability, security, addressing, new charging paradigms, and quality of service.

As the wireless operators are faced with these challenges mentioned above, they are developing and implementing strategies to cope with them. They are extending the life of their 2G/2.5G networks, getting more out of them, such as launching more wireless data services with GPRS. They are announcing infrastructure sharing for 3G deployments with other operators and better timing their 3G investments and deployments, tying it with adequate device and market demand availability.

Wireless operators are also evolving their networks towards end-to-end all-IP networks, driven by three fundamental factors:

- *Significant cost reduction* There is a strong expectation that significant cost savings, in the range of 30+% can be achieved in terms of CAPEX and OPEX by implementing various IP technologies through-out the wireless infrastructure.

- *Significant new revenue generation There is a strong expectation* that significant new applications and new revenue sources would be enabled, and in particular third-party application development be facilitated by utilizing IP technologies on an end-to-end basis.
- *Shorter time to market* All-IP networks will most likely enable new service launches with much shorter time to market.

Wireless operators, as well as the infrastructure suppliers, have been working on the definition of standards for the evolution of both GSM networks and the CDMA networks toward this end-to-end all-IP target architecture. Standards that enable smooth evolution have already been defined and some products are already commercially available, and the rest are projected to become available by mid-2004.

The key enabling technologies for this evolution will be SIP (session initiation protocol), IPv6, IP over-the-air optimization, as well as QoS, security, and other IP-related enhancements. IP would become the overriding transport technology, definitely capping TDM and potentially capping and/or replacing the ATM technology at both radio access networks (RANs) as well as in the core networks.

Since significant voice traffic growth is still expected for wireless networks, the business case for VoIP, with the use if SIP, is not based on replacement of existing TDM networks, but rather on capping such networks and putting the growth as well as new services, such as "rich call" services on such real-time IP networks. "Rich call" is a type of real-time multimedia service that will be enabled with the use of SIP, SIP application platforms, and opening up the services layer to third parties through APIs.

There are several potential paradigm changes or discontinuities that may take place in the wireless operators' networks as a result of all-IP network direction. The key technical paradigm shifts could come from the separation of the signaling and bearer channels, for all multimedia services, even for IP services. Also, the multimedia services, starting with MMS, combining voice, data and image, not to mention video clips, will create key requirements and we should expect some disruptive technologies in this space. Also, the core networks will evolve to MPLS-enabled, mobility-enabled, IPv6-based routing environments, and thus today's routers will need to undergo a relatively major overhaul.

Wireless local area networks (WLANs) based on 802.11 standards have experienced significant growth as extension of enterprise networks. However, there are several challenges such as security, cost, and seamlessness, for WLANs in the enterprise market. The availability of WLANs for public hot spots has drawn the attention of the wireless operators, and they have been evaluating them for such deployments. Cost economics for WLANs vs. GPRS/3G are such that it would be orders of magnitude cheaper to provide high speed access for wireless operators in hot spots using WLAN technologies, if they can be somehow integrated into the wireless operators' infrastructure. In fact, the WLANs and GPRS/3G are very complementary if they are deployed and interoperated effectively. In return, wireless operators are a good choice for public WLAN offerings for mobile professionals, since they already have the customer/billing relationship and cater for broader mobility requirements of these users.

I strongly believe that this exciting field of wireless networks, and their evolution to all-IP networks, is full of many challenges and opportunities. This book, authored by well-recognized industry experts, provides a comprehensive explanation of the field, and will serve as an informative reference for those of us working in this industry.

Dr. Mehmet S. Unsoy
Former VP, Chief Wireless Architect
mmO2 (formerly BT Wireless)
munsoy@yahoo.com
November 2002

The Internet Protocol (IP) has had a tremendous impact on network communications in the last decade. Although IP itself has been around for a much longer time, its relevance and impact on other networks have been felt the most since the 1990s. Before IP became the dominant protocol, a number of networking protocols proliferated. There was IBM's SNA, Appletalk from Apple Computers, Netware from Novell, Xerox Network System from Xerox and others from Digital Equipment Corporation and Microsoft. The success of the Internet and the internetworking protocols that make this possible has made IP the de-facto protocol for existing networks and also as the protocol to be used in the design and architecture of next-generation networks. Wireless networks, which hitherto have been built around protocols and architectures developed within the realms of ITU, ETSI, TIA and others, are now adopting the Internet model and protocols.

The 1990s also saw the rapid growth of wireless networks. Two major wireless technologies, GSM and CDMA, have taken center stage. The wide area cellular networks deployed so far provided primarily voice-based services. Data services were limited due to bandwidth constraints, and performance was poor due to the nature of the air interface designs, which have been built with emphasis on voice quality and capacity. However, with the evolution of cellular networks towards 3G, packet data services have been a major focus in terms of providing higher bandwidth and overall accessibility to the Internet. Vast improvements in radio technology, as well as the need to provide access to the Internet, has driven the evolution of cellular to support packet data. Since the 3G wireless networks are viewed as an extension to the Internet, there is significant emphasis in ensuring that IP operates in a manner very similar to the wired Internet today. Hence, protocols and network architectures for the wide area cellular networks are designed and built to support IP in as efficient a way as possible. Wireless networks are expected to become more data-centric in the next few years, rivaling voice as the "killer" application. The deployment of new data services will have a ripple effect on the wireless networks and the end user devices and terminals; they will change to better support these new applications. The wireless information society that is being created now will continue to grow. The technology enablers such as 3G-and-beyond packet data networks and services will allow this to thrive.

This book captures the essential elements in this convergence path of wireless networks and the Internet protocols resulting in the new paradigm of "Wireless IP." It covers all the important 2G cellular technologies that we have seen in the past decade, along with 3G and other important wireless technologies that will be deployed in the near future. The book extensively discusses the aspects of IP that affect the wireless medium and how it must be modified to guarantee the fullest use and deployment of Wireless IP. This includes the modifications required in protocols, architectures, and framework in virtually every area such as QoS, security, mobility, and so on. The book can be viewed in four different sections. The first section, Chapters 1 to 3, is preliminary introductory chapters. The second section, Chapters 4, 5, 6 and 7, describes second-generation (2G) wireless networks and the support for packet data in these. Chapters 8, 9, 10, 11, 12 and 13, which constitute the third section, are focused on third-generation (3G) wireless networks as well as other technologies such as 802.11 and WAP. The fourth section of the book, Chapters 14, 15 and 16, describes the type of future applications as well as a view on evolution and the role that standards bodies play. The book is written such that it is not required to read chapters in a sequential manner. The split across the 4 sections can be referred to separately.

Since the focus of the book is on the Internet Protocol (IP), Chapter 1 focuses on the history and the current view of the Internet. It is important to understand the nature of the Internet in order to realize the impact that it has had and continues to have on other networks. Chapter 2 is a primer to the key protocols of IP. This chapter describes protocols at the network layer, transport layer, and application layer. It is intended to serve as a quick reference for readers to refer to an IP protocol, and not as an exhaustive description of any one protocol. Chapter 3 provides an introduction to the concepts of wireless networks as well as a brief history of the same. GSM networks span the globe and GSM technology is the predominant wireless technology today. Chapter 4 discusses circuit switched data services including high-speed circuit switched data offered by GSM. Applications such as short message service (SMS) and also email connectivity are described. Chapter 5 looks at circuit switched data in IS-136 networks. Since second-generation networks in North America have been based on this technology it is important to understand support for circuit switched data services in these networks as well. While circuit switched data has not been a great success, SMS has definitely been a tremendous success. The other major wireless technology is CDMA, IS-95. Circuit switched data services in IS-95 networks are covered in Chapter 6. Wireless networks offer a set of different challenges to IP than the wired networks in the last two decades. Mobility issues, the nature of retransmissions over the air interface developed, and other challenges are covered in Chapter 7.

GPRS, which is the evolution of GSM to support packet data, is covered in Chapter 8. GPRS is the first wireless network (not considering CDPD or other variants such as Mobitex) that offers packet data services without having to rely on the circuit switched network and radio technology. 3G UMTS networks provide high speed packet data access. The interfaces, protocols and concepts of UMTS are presented in Chapter 9. cdma2000 networks and the approach to packet data in these are covered in Chapter 10. cdma2000 is the evolution of IS-95 networks. 802.11 technology, which has been developed by IEEE for wireless LAN, is described in Chapter 11. Chapter 12 looks at Bluetooth, which is a personal area networking technology. WAP has been the initial approach taken by wireless networks to emulate the World Wide Web. I-mode is a service that originated in Japan and is now slowly being deployed in other parts of the world. WAP and I-mode are covered in Chapter 13. With the availability of wireless data networks, the technology enabler is in place. It is now up to the types of services that are deployed which will decide success. Chapter 14 looks at the types of future applications that we may see in these networks. The evolution of wireless networks including GSM, CDMA, and 802.11 are captured in Chapter 15. Standards bodies have a huge impact on the technologies that are developed. The role of the major standards bodies that impact wireless data networks and IP are presented in Chapter 16.

The audience for this book is anyone interested in the potential in the convergence of the wireless and IP networks. From a technical point of view, engineers and application developers, who need to understand how packet data services and IP work in the wireless world, may find this text useful. It is also useful to people who do not have a technical background, but who work in the telecommunications or device-manufacturing industry in the fields of sales, marketing, and operations. They may find this book very informative for gaining insight into various wireless technologies available and the promise of convergence of the circuit switched voice and packet switched data networks. Other potential readers include those who may not be in the wireless industry but see the potential of wireless networks and technology and need to realize the basics of the operations of packet data in these. Students of engineering will also benefit from this book as it provides a complete description of the major wireless technologies today and the roadmap to the future.

This book has been written based on the current capabilities in the technologies described in this book and the general direction in the industry towards the wireless Internet. For this reason, this book mostly represents the views and opinions of the authors, based on their technical understanding, experience and the significant amount of research in these areas and does not necessarily represent the views of their employers.

Acknowledgments

We would like to thank Mary Franz for her patience in dealing with us during the entire process. Her enthusiasm and encouragement are what enabled us to complete this book. We would also like to thank Jessica Balch at Pine Tree Composition for the detailed reviews and feedback she provided us.

We would like to acknowledge various people within Nokia who reviewed the chapters and helped with discussion and suggested improvements. Especially, we wish to convey our deepest thanks to Harri Holma, Mario Cardona, Christopher Clanton, Markku Hollstrom, Shavantha Kularatna, Jersey Lai, JuhaPekka Niemi, Craig Rhoades, Bill Sellers, Jonne Soininen, and Curt Wong.

Special thanks are due to our employers for supporting and encouraging us in this venture. We would like to thank our managers, Riku Pirhonen and Khiem Le, for being patient with us while we spent time on the book.

We are extremely thankful to our families for their patience and support. Many a long hour has been spent on this book while our spouses and kids have accepted the late nights and weekends away from them.

The authors welcome feedback and corrections to the book. You can contact them via email at ipinwls@mindspring.com.

Introduction to the Internet

The Internet Protocol (IP) has changed the networking landscape in the last few years and is being adopted as the de facto networking protocol. The success and explosive growth of the Internet in the last few years have led engineers and designers of networking protocols to embrace IP. The fact that IP is an open source protocol and is easily available in all the major operating systems has ensured its success among a very large community of developers, designers, and testers. A large knowledge base and strong development skills make IP a viable networking protocol.

What is it about IP that makes it such a powerful force? There is no single answer or explanation. Economics are obviously a strong force, and the fact that IP reduces the cost of building networks is a clear advantage. The multitude of applications and services that have been developed over IP is another.

Email, the Internet, and numerous applications based on Web technology have become an integral aspect of business and everyday life. The Internet has spawned an entire industry commonly referred to as *e-commerce*. Use of the Internet, as well as applications and services that run over it, is constantly growing.

What constitutes an IP network? In short, networks that are built using the Internet Protocol as the network layer protocol can be loosely defined as IP networks. However, a network that operates using the Internet Protocol does not necessarily become a part of the Internet. There are many private networks, such as networks that run in enterprises, that operate on IP but may not be a part of the Internet. This chapter discusses primarily the Internet, which can be considered the largest IP network in existence.

1.1   What is the Internet?

Although many consider the Internet a recent phenomenon, in reality it has existed and grown since the early 1980s. Above all, the Internet is a communications medium. It has transformed the way information is disseminated or exchanged, is changing the way we do business, access information, and view entertainment today, and holds the promise of becoming as indispensable as the telephone network.

The Internet is a global network of heterogeneous networks enabling computers of all kinds to directly and transparently communicate and share services throughout much of the world. Over 100 million hosts are connected to this network. The Internet is a constantly growing, evolving, and changing network. It is extremely difficult to define the structure of the Internet or explain its characteristics. Some have even referred to it as a living organism that constantly keeps growing at its edges, and as such has a life of it's own. The graph in Figure 1–1 shows the growth of the Internet through 2001 in terms of the number of hosts connected.

What started off as a research network with a few limited hosts has grown into a global-scale commercial network. The Internet has created a

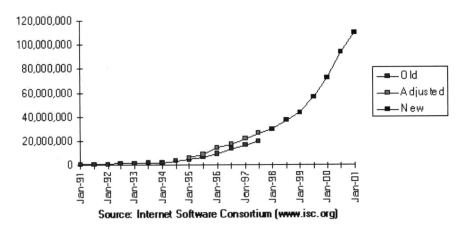

Figure 1–1   *Host count of nodes attached to the Internet.*

class of network operators called Internet service providers (ISPs). Over 6000 ISPs exist around the world today. Some of the bigger ISPs that offer services on a global scale include America Online, with about 30 million subscribers; UUNet, IIJ, NTT/Verio, Cable and Wireless, Earthlink, and Terra.

Fortunately, nobody really owns the Internet. There is no centralized control, and no one can turn it off. Since the Internet is formed by a collection of networks spread across the globe, there is no single company or government that has authority over it. As a result, we have a collection of networks that comprise university and research networks, commercial networks owned and operated by ISPs, networks belonging to governments, and non-government organizations (NGOs) as well.

1.2   History of the Internet

The Internet that exists today is the unintended outcome of the initial research objectives set by the Advanced Research Projects Agency (ARPA) of the United States Department of Defense (DOD) in the late 1960s.

The origins and history of the Internet go back as far as the early 1960s, and the ideas for the Internet as we know it today can be gleaned from memos written in August 1962 by J.C.R. Licklider, who discussed the concept of a "Galactic Network." Leonard Kleinrock of the Massachusetts Institute of Technology (MIT) published the first paper on packet-switching theory in July 1961.

In the mid-1960s ARPA formulated a research interest in computer networks. ARPA is essentially an organization that does not directly do research by itself, but funds research work based on topics defined by it and manages these projects. In 1965 ARPA funded a study through Lawrence Roberts at MIT's Lincoln Laboratory, largely as a result of Kleinrock's earlier work at MIT. The study report, "A Cooperative Network of Time-Sharing Computers," proposed to establish an experimental three-computer network. This proposal was successfully implemented a year later by Roberts and Thomas Merill when they connected the TX-2 computer at MIT to the Q-32 in California through a low-speed dial-up telephone line. A third computer located at ARPA was later connected to this network as well. This experimental network generated a great amount of interest in the computer research community and accelerated further developments. In late 1966, Roberts went to the Defense Advanced Research Projects Agency (former name of ARPA) to develop the computer network concept and came up with a plan for the ARPANET and published it in 1967. In 1968, ARPA invited prospective suppliers to build the network and in 1968 awarded the contract for ARPANET to Bolt Beranek and Newman (BBN). On September 1, 1969, the first Interface Message Processor (IMP) was shipped to the University of California at Los Angeles

(UCLA) and the first host computer was connected. The IMP at UCLA was connected to IMPs subsequently shipped to the Stanford Research Institute (SRI), the University of California at Santa Barbara (UCSB), and the University of Utah. In December 1970, Steve Crocker finished the initial ARPANET host-to-host protocol, called Network Control Protocol (NCP), and ARPANET sites completed implementing NCP during 1971–1972. In October 1972 a large successful demo of the ARPANET took place. Electronic mail was also introduced in 1972. Soon the ARPANET grew to include packet radio networks (ALOHAnet), packet satellite networks, and others.

The refinement of the ARPANET networking model was undertaken by Robert Kahn in 1972. The model of the ARPANET was to connect heterogeneous hosts via a homogeneous network. The concept that Kahn introduced was to allow the network itself to be heterogeneous. After joining DARPA and initiating the Internet program, Kahn enlisted Vinton Cerf of Stanford University to work with him on the detailed design of the protocol. Cerf, who had been involved earlier in the design of NCP, was already knowledgeable about interfacing to existing operating systems. Kahn and Cerf teamed up and came up with the specification for the Kahn-Cerf protocol, which was later named the Transmission Control Protocol/Internet Protocol (TCP/IP). The paper "A Protocol for Packet Network Interconnection," published in May 1974, described TCP and provided all the Internet's transport and forwarding services. The design intent was to have TCP support a range of transport services ranging from sequenced, in-order reliable delivery of data to a datagram service that was less than robust (lossy) and did not guarantee in-order packet delivery. Initial TCP implementations resulted in essentially a protocol that emulated virtual circuits. This model was fine for applications such as file transfer and remote login, but other applications such as packet voice demonstrated that it is not always necessary for the transport protocol to correct errors. That is best left to applications that obviously have their own requirements. This resulted in some changes to the initial proposal, and the outcome was two transport protocols: TCP and User Datagram Protocol (UDP). UDP was added as an unreliable datagram transport protocol for applications that did not need error correction, retransmissions, and congestion management.

DARPA funded Stanford (Cerf), BBN (Tomlinson), and University College London (Peter Kirstein) to implement TCP. Stanford produced a detailed specification from which multiple implementations were produced. Early implementations of TCP were for large time-sharing systems, but David Clark and his research group at MIT proved that the protocol could be adapted as well to small host computers and workstations. The 1980s introduced local-area networks (LANs), PCs, and workstations. Ethernet technology took off on a very large scale. This allowed Internet technology to take hold at the grassroots level. A bigger challenge was to make the technology widely available and have it adapted by multiple people. DARPA supported the University of California at Berkeley, which had developed a version of the Unix operating system. Berkeley developed the TCP/IP code and fit it into the Unix system kernel. Berkeley Software Distribution (BSD) Unix, which was quite popular with the computer science community, adopted the Internet technology and helped foster its growth even further.

TCP/IP was adopted as a defense standard in 1980. The ARPANET was being used by both military and the research community. The ARPANET transitioned from NCP to TCP in 1983, and at the same time the network was split into MILNET (supporting the defense department) and an ARPANET (supporting the research community).

The usefulness of computer networking and applications such as e-mail was recognized by other communities as well, and as a result a host of networks began springing up. In 1985 the U.S. NSFNET (National Science Foundation Network—the Internet backbone in the U.S. which was supported by NSF) program announced its intent to serve the entire higher-education community. NSFNET also mandated TCP/IP for this network. Thus developed the NSFNET backbone. NSFNET, which was funded by federal funds, ended in 1995 and the research network transitioned into a commercial network. In an 8.5-year span the backbone had grown from 6 nodes to 21 nodes. The Internet also constituted more than 50,000 networks on all continents (with 29,000 networks in the United States). The ARPANET was decommissioned in 1990. TCP/IP had spread so vigorously that it made other networking protocols irrelevant or marginal and ensured the success of IP for the future.

1.3 The Internet Architecture

The Internet as it stands today is composed of more than 60,000 constituent networks. Each network is an autonomous network, and the only things that are common across these networks is the use of a common protocol, adherence to a common addressing scheme, and a common name structure. Hence it is hard to visualize the Internet architecture as beginning somewhere or having a center. Over the past 25 years since the ARPANET became operational, the Internet has increased by factors of thousands with respect to backbone speed and by factors of millions with respect to the number of hosts connected to the network. The network can be extended at any point and offer further connectivity. In a way the network is akin to the universe itself, which is ever expanding.

Is there an Internet architecture at all? Many in the Internet community believe that there does not exist any real architecture but instead there exists a set of guidelines. The architectural goal of the Internet is connectivity; the tool for achieving this is the Internet Protocol, and the intelligence is end to end rather than being embedded in the network [RFC 1958].

Important features of the original Internet architecture are as follows:

1. A connectionless packet-forwarding infrastructure (dumb network) that positions higher-level functionality at the edge of the network for robustness (fate sharing)

2. Addresses that are fixed-size numerical with a simple (net, host) hierarchy

The evolution of this architecture over the last 25 years has led to the following architectural features:

1. Subnetting, autonomous systems (AS), and the Domain Name System (DNS). These features were introduced as a direct result of the understanding obtained from deployments and as a measure to address scalability and growth.

2. Congestion control mechanisms were introduced in the late 1980s.

3. IP multicasting developed as a means to disseminate packets from a single node to a number of receiving nodes via an enhanced addressing scheme.

The Internet is structured in a hierarchical manner or at least can be visualized as such. However, it is not a clear hierarchy, but rather a mixed-up one. At the top there exist multiple backbone networks that connect to each other at network access points (NAPs) or exchange points (EPs). Backbone networks of large Internet service providers such as NTT/Verio, Sprint, and UUNet, which span the globe, carry the majority of the Internet traffic. Figure 1–2 shows a network map of UUNet's global network (http://uunet.com/network/maps/) as of June 2001.

Regional networks and ISPs connect to the larger backbones, and smaller ISPs, in turn, are connected to these regional networks. End users obtain connectivity to the Internet via ISPs in general. Peering between ISPs and service agreements between ISPs allow inter-ISP traffic. A model of this hierarchical model of the Internet is shown in Figure 1–3.

In reality, the Internet is not organized as a strict hierarchy. Peering networks could connect to each other and at the same time have connectivity to a larger network. The large backbone ISPs could also be the ones providing end-user connectivity. This type of a model is feasible when you have a relatively small number of ISPs, but as the Internet continues to grow in size and the number of users increases, so do usage and the number of Internet service providers. As a result, ISPs will need to continue to exchange increasing amounts of data traffic. One of the basic underlying mechanisms in the Internet today is the points where various ISPs exchange traffic. These interconnection points are called NAPs or EPs. Exchange points can be defined as

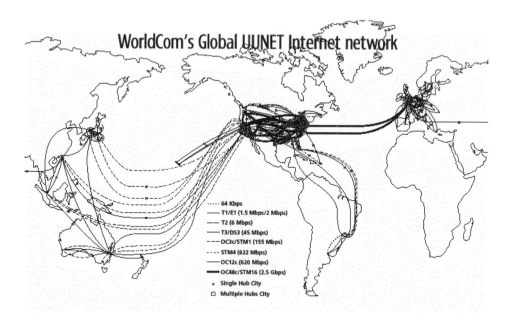

An example global backbone network.

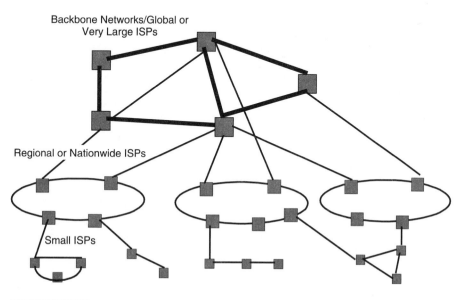

Hierarchical view of the Internet.

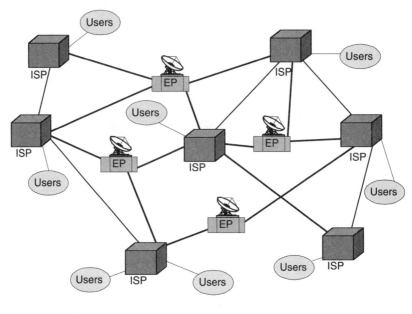

Figure 1–4 *Current view with exchange points.*

multiple-access networks allowing ISPs to exchange traffic and routing information with other ISPs. There are many exchange points across continents today. Some of the larger ones are Sprint NAP, MAE (metropolitan area exchange) East and West, and LINX (London Internet Exchange). A view of Internet architecture taking NAPs/EPs into consideration is shown in Figure 1–4.

The underlying telecommunications and transmission infrastructure that forms the Internet has grown significantly in the last few years. As the processing power of central processing unit (CPUs) of computers and handheld devices keeps increasing, so does the bandwidth of the networks.

1.4 Services on the Internet

There are many different uses of the Internet today, ranging from business communications to information access to entertainment and financial transactions.

Applications on the Internet today can be classified into two types: traditional and new age. Applications such as e-mail, file transfer protocol (FTP), bulletin boards, and Usenet can be considered traditional, while real-time voice, streaming audio/video, instant messaging, and network games can be thought of as the new-age applications.

Let's take a look at a traditional and very widely used application; e-mail or electronic mail. E-mail has become the communication medium of choice. It has become so pervasive that we see it in almost every walk of life today. It is just as common for someone to give their e-mail address as their point of contact as their phone number. The pioneers of the Internet, the ARPANET folks, had probably not envisioned e-mail as a key or "killer" application when the network was created. Another application with a similar scale of acceptance is Instant Messaging, the equivalent of which is Short Message Service (SMS) in the wireless world.

With the advent of faster processors and more bandwidth, the Internet has become a hotbed of innovation, and new applications are constantly coming online. The pace of innovation has been brisk over the last few years, and the future holds even more exciting and interesting applications and use.

1.5   The World Wide Web

Some of the current success of the Internet is undoubtedly because of the emergence of the World Wide Web in the last decade. The phenomenal success of the Web has made the Internet accessible to so many people that it has become synonymous with the Internet. Of course, the Internet itself has been around for a while and was used by mostly engineers, researchers, and technical people before the introduction of the Web browsers and the World Wide Web. For a complete history of the World Wide Web, refer to the W3C Web site (www.w3c.org). W3C (World Wide Web Consortium) is the body that is defining the standards and ensuring the evolution of the Web. But is the World Wide Web the Internet? Not really; the Web is merely an application on the Internet. A good definition of the Web comes from W3C, which defines the Web as the universe of network-accessible information (available through your computer, phone, television, or networked refrigerator).

The concept of the Web originated at CERN (European Organization for Nuclear Research) in Switzerland in 1989 and was the idea of Tim Berners-Lee, who is considered the inventor of the Web. The proposal of using hypertext for information distribution/linking and management was the basis from which the Web was developed. Over the course of the last 10 years, the concept has been refined and has been developed into a global-scale application. Since the Web is essentially an application on the Internet, some of the design principles that have been taken into account are based on the principles on which the Internet has been established:

- *Interoperability:* Specifications for the Web's languages and protocols must be compatible with one another and allow (any) hardware and software used to access the Web to work together.

- *Evolution:* The Web must be able to accommodate future technologies. Design principles such as simplicity, modularity, and extensibility will increase the chances that the Web will work with emerging technologies such as mobile Web devices and digital television, as well as others to come.
- *Decentralization:* Decentralization is without a doubt the newest principle and most difficult to apply. To allow the Web to "scale" to worldwide proportions while resisting errors and breakdowns, the architecture (like the Internet) must limit or eliminate dependencies on central registries.

We can think of the Web as a set of cooperating clients and servers. The window to the Web for most people is via graphical user interface applications known as Web browsers (such as Netscape or Internet Explorer). The World Wide Web is different things to different people. Some think of the Web as a source of information; others think of it as a place to shop or conduct financial transactions; still others think of it as a source of entertainment, including music, audio, and video.

What ties the Web together is the use of a common protocol, which in this case is HTTP. From the stack perspective, HTTP is an application-layer protocol that runs over TCP. HTTP is a text-oriented request response protocol. Another protocol for interacting with the Web has been developed for the wireless industry. The protocol, known as WAP (Wireless Application Protocol), allows wireless devices such as mobile phones and PDAs to access the Internet. WAP is discussed in much further detail in Chapter 13.

The Web and the Internet have become a utility service that is as ubiquitous as the telephone, and the next expansion in this area is essentially in the area of wireless networks and users connecting to the Web via devices that are no longer tethered.

1.6   Internet Registries

Three regional Internet registries are responsible for the assignment of IP addresses and autonomous system numbers globally (other organizations are responsible for the assignment of domain names):

- ARIN—American Registry for Internet Numbers
- APNIC—Asia Pacific Network Information Centre
- RIPE—Réseaux IP Européens

ARIN is a nonprofit organization established for the purpose of administration and registration of IP numbers for the following geographical areas: North America, South America, the Caribbean, and sub-Saharan Africa.

APNIC represents the Asia Pacific region, comprising 62 economies. It is a not-for-profit, membership-based organization whose members include Internet service providers, national Internet registries, and similar organizations.

RIPE is an open collaborative community of organizations and individuals operating wide area IP networks in Europe and beyond. The objective of the RIPE community is to ensure the administrative and technical coordination necessary to enable operation of a pan-European IP network. RIPE has no formal membership, and its activities are performed on a voluntary basis.

1.7   A View of the Future

As voice and data continue to converge, the Internet is becoming the focal point of attention and is taking on the role of the one single global network providing access to information as well as different types of services. But the Internet is not about to replace the existing voice networks, such as the public switched telephone network (PSTN) and other data networks, such as the ATM and frame relay networks, that are deployed on a global scale as well. The one thing that the Internet has yet to achieve is the reliability and security of the PSTN. But it is definitely on its way to achieving that factor of reliability and security. The Internet in its first generation has been mostly connected to fixed and wired end hosts. But as the world becomes increasingly wireless and people are more mobile and need constant connectivity, the Internet as we know it today will change. The Internet will grow in areas that make information access ubiquitous from any place on the earth.

Exponential growth over the years has put some strain on the original design, and as a result a new Internet protocol, IPv6, will be deployed over the next few years. New types of applications, multimedia services, games, and a host of other things will make the Internet an integral aspect of daily life.

1.7.1   Internet2

The Internet was initially a network that was primarily used by research institutes. At one time, use of the Internet by commercial organizations required these organizations to agree to a policy that constrained them to use the Internet only for commercial purposes. The Internet as we know it today is primarily a commercial network.

As a result of this change in philosophy, (i.e., from being a research network to a commercial network), there has been an impact on the network in terms of congestion and availability. Research organizations decided to build a next generation Internet exclusively for research purposes. This initiative resulted in Internet2 (www.internet2.org).

The primary goals of Internet2 are to:

- Create a leading-edge network capability for the national research community.
- Enable revolutionary Internet applications.
- Ensure the rapid transfer of new network services and applications to the broader Internet community.

At the time of this writing, Internet2 has also deployed IPv6 in its backbone.

1.8   Summary

This chapter covered some of the high-level aspects of the Internet. A description of Internet architecture and history, as well as the standards bodies that define the protocols that makes the Internet work, were described. A great amount of information and detail has been omitted because this book focuses mainly on the use of IP in wireless networks. In order to understand the reasons for wireless networks adopting IP and moving toward IP-based architectures in the next generation, it is important to understand the Internet itself.

References

Barry M. Leiner, Vinton G. Cerf, David D. Clark, Robert E. Kahn, Leonard Kleinrock, Daniel C. Lynch, Jon Postel, Lawrence G. Roberts, Stephen S. Wolff, *The Past and Future History of the Internet*.

RFC 1958, *Architectural Principles of the Internet*, B. Carpenter, Editor. Available on-line at www.rfc-editor.org/rfc/rfc1958.txt.

Robert Braden, David Clark, Scott Shenker, and John Wroclawski, *Developing a Next-Generation Internet Architecture*.

Licklider, J.C.R. and Clark, W., *Online Man–Computer Communication,* Aug. 1962.

Roberts, L. and Merrill T., "Toward a Cooperative Network of Time-Shared Computers," *Proceedings of the Fall AFIPS Conference* (Oct. 1966).

Internet Software Consortium (2001). "Internet Domain Survey, January 2001." Available on-line at www.isc.org/ds/www-200101/index.html.

Internetworking Fundamentals

The term Internet, as explained in the previous chapter, refers to a collection of networks that are interconnected. The Internet Protocol makes it possible to build such internetworks. The interesting aspect of IP is that it makes it possible to build networks that can scale on a global basis without relevance to underlying network types of physical media or limitations. In order to understand some of the basic fundamentals of internetworking and IP, we need to take a look at various protocols at various layers in the stack. For the purpose of comparison, the functions that make internetworking possible are compared against the standard seven-layer Open Systems Interconnection (OSI) stack. In addition to understanding IP, Internet Control Message Protocol (ICMP), and ARP, which are network-layer protocols, this chapter looks at transport-layer and application-layer protocols.

Building blocks of the Internet, such as addressing, routing, and naming as well as various protocols at the network, transport, and application layers are described in this chapter. Readers who are already familiar with the Internetworking concepts can skip this chapter and move on to the next.

2.1 OSI Model

The International Organization for Standardization (ISO) and the CCITT (Consultative Committee on International Telephony and Telegraphy), which is now the ITU (International Telecommunications Union), worked on a refer-

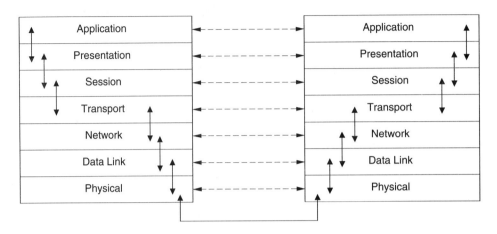

Figure 2–1   *OSI reference model.*

ence model at the same time that DARPA was doing research in networking protocols. The effort resulted in the OSI (Open Systems Interconnection) model (ISO 7498), which defined a seven-layer model of data communication with the physical layer at the lowest layer and application protocols at the upper layer. This model has been widely accepted as the basis for the understanding and design of a network protocol stack. It is also the basis against which other networking protocols are compared. The OSI reference model has seven layers, as shown in Figure 2–1.

The functionality of the seven layers of the OSI model is as follows:

Application: The application layer supports user applications such as file transfer protocol, HTTP, and others.

Presentation: The formatting of data and encryption are performed by this layer.

Session: Manages the establishment and maintenance of sessions.

Transport: Provides the reliable and unreliable end-to-end data delivery protocols.

Network: Performs the packet delivery function and routing of packets in the network.

Data link: Performs the framing of units of information and error checking.

Physical: Does the transmission of bits on the physical hardware.

2.2   Internet Model

The Internet model in comparison to OSI is an optimized version. The functionality of the presentation and session layers is incorporated into the application layer when required and eliminated sometimes. The protocol stack in the Internet model is shown in Figure 2–2.

The suite of protocols at the network, transport, and application layers defined by the Internet Protocol (IP) model provides the basis for building internetworks such as the Internet. Consider, for example, a user surfing the Web and the protocols that are utilized. Figure 2–3 shows a user accessing the Web.

The user connects to the Internet via his or her ISP. As a result of a successful connection, the user's PC is assigned an IP address dynamically. Address assignment may be done using the Dynamic Host Configuration Protocol (DHCP). The user starts a Web browser (e.g., Internet Explorer or Netscape) and requests to connect to the uniform resource locator (URL) www.nokia.com. The browser application uses the HTTP protocol to form an HTTP request. The HTTP request is carried over TCP. Address resolution of the URL needs to be done. A DNS query is sent to the DNS server (the address of which was configured via DHCP). DNS queries are sent over UDP. The DNS response contains the "A" record of the requested URL. The HTTP request is sent to the destination, whose IP address is obtained from the A record. The source IP address is the IP address of the network interface on the PC itself. The Web server receives the HTTP request and sends an HTTP response. The HTTP response contains the data in HTML format. The browser displays the content to the user. What we see from this example is that a number of protocols are utilized in a simple transaction such as requesting a Web page.

| Application |
| Presentation |
| Session |
| Transport |
| Network |
| Data link |
| Physical |

RIP	FTP	SMTP	HTTP	DNS	SNMP
OSPF		TCP		UDP	SCTP
IP and ICMP					ARP
IEEE 802, ATM, Frame Relay, PPP, HDLC etc.					
IEEE 802, T1/E1, Sonet, EIA-232, V.24, V.28					

Figure 2–2   *Internet model.*

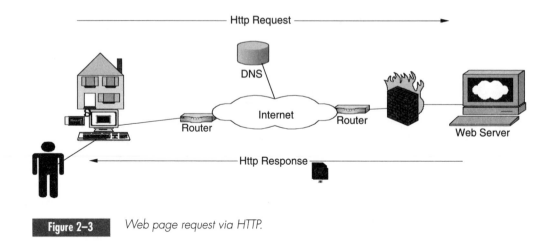

Figure 2–3   *Web page request via HTTP.*

The rest of this chapter looks at the network layer, transport layer, and application layer protocols in more detail.

2.3   Network-Layer Protocols: IP, ICMP, and ARP

2.3.1   Internet Protocol

The Internet Protocol (IP) is defined in RFC 791. RFC 791 provides the detailed specification of the protocol, which provides the guidelines for implementations. IP hides the underlying physical network and creates a virtual network view. This concept enables different types of physical networks to be viewed as an IP network as long as they have IP as their network layer. IP runs over virtually all types of physical media today. This simple and elegant concept has been the cause for the expansive growth of the Internet. IP is an unreliable, best-effort, and connectionless packet delivery protocol. "Best-effort" means that if something goes wrong and the packet gets lost, corrupted, misdelivered, or in any way fails to reach its intended destination, the network does nothing. It does not make any attempt to rectify the error. The Internet Protocol provides for transmitting blocks of data, called datagrams, from sources to destinations, where sources and destinations are hosts identified by fixed-length addresses. The Internet Protocol also provides for fragmentation and reassembly of long datagrams, if necessary, for transmission through "small packet" networks. IP provides two basic functions in addition to the primary task of moving datagrams through an interconnected set of networks:

- Addressing
- Fragmentation

Addressing enables packets to be routed to their destination, and fragmentation allows packets that contain large amounts of data to be segmented and reassembled as they traverse paths that have smaller packet size capability.

Addresses are of fixed length (in the case of IP version 4 (IPv4) it is 4 octets, and in the case of IP version 6 (IPv6) it is 16 octets). The model of operation is that an Internet module resides in each host engaged in Internet communication and in each gateway that interconnects networks. These modules share common rules for interpreting address fields and for fragmenting and assembling Internet datagrams. In addition, these modules (especially in gateways) have procedures for making routing decisions and other functions. The Internet Protocol treats each Internet datagram as an independent entity unrelated to any other Internet datagram. There are no connections or logical circuits (virtual or otherwise).

The IP datagram is fundamental to the Internet Protocol. Every datagram carries sufficient information that allows the network to forward the packet to its correct destination. Like most packets, the IP datagram consists of a header followed by a number of bytes of data. The format of the IPv4 and IPv6 headers is shown in Figure 2–4.

The Version field specifies the version of IP. In the case of IPv4 it is 4, and in the case of IPv6 it is 6.

Hlen specifies the length of the header. IPv6 has a fixed-length header; hence Hlen is not required. Type of Service or TOS allows the packets to be treated differently based on application needs. The TOS field is now called as the DS (Diffserv) field. The Class field was the replacement for the TOS field in IPv6, and the Class field is also now referred to as the DS field (RFC 2474). The Length field specifies the length of the datagram, including the header. The payload length is the equivalent in IPv6, and it does not include the header. Flow label in IPv6 is used to label packets requesting special handling by routers. The Identification field is used in fragmentation and assembly of packets. The flags indicate whether a packet is a part of a fragment and also indicate whether intermediate routers can fragment or not. In IPv6, frag-

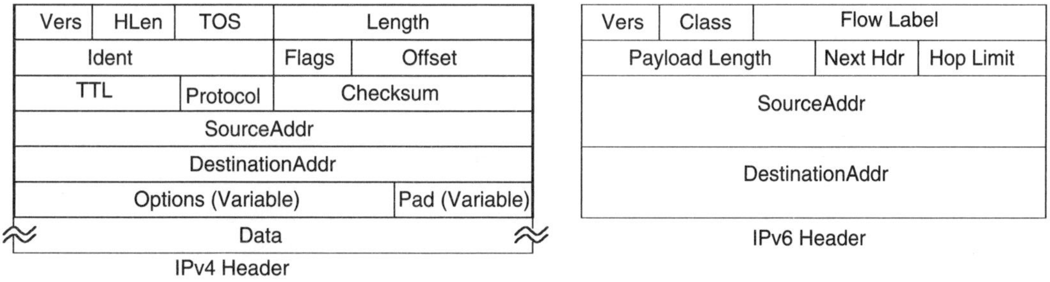

Vers	HLen	TOS	Length	
Ident			Flags	Offset
TTL		Protocol	Checksum	
SourceAddr				
DestinationAddr				
Options (Variable)			Pad (Variable)	
Data				

IPv4 Header

Vers	Class	Flow Label	
Payload Length		Next Hdr	Hop Limit
SourceAddr			
DestinationAddr			

IPv6 Header

Figure 2–4   *IP datagram header.*

mentation is done only at the endpoints, and intermediate routers do not perform fragmentation. IPv6 simplified the IP header by defining a set of extension headers. The Next Header field in the IPv6 header is used to indicate the
type of next header following the IP header. Time to Live and the Hop Limit
fields are used to determine how many hops a packet will survive in the Internet before it is dropped. The current value is 64, and each router along the
way decrements the value by 1. The Protocol field is a demultiplexing key
that identifies the higher-layer protocol. A Checksum of the IP header is calculated by considering the entire IP header. The source address and destination address allow a packet to be routed to/from hosts across the Internet.
Further details of addressing are covered in Section 2.6.

2.3.2   Internet Control Message Protocol

Internet Control Message Protocol (ICMP) is described in RFC 792. ICMP is an
integral part of IP and must be implemented in every IP node. ICMP uses IP
as if it were a higher-layer protocol. ICMP messages are sent in several situations: for example, when a datagram cannot reach its destination, when the
router does not have the buffering capacity to forward a datagram, and when
the router can direct the host to send traffic on a shorter route. The Internet
Protocol is not designed to be absolutely reliable. The purpose of these control messages is to provide feedback about problems in the communication
environment, not to make IP reliable. There are still no guarantees that a
datagram will be delivered or a control message will be returned. Some datagrams may still be undelivered without any report of their loss. The ICMP
messages typically report errors in the processing of datagrams. To avoid the
infinite regress of messages about messages, no ICMP messages are sent
about ICMP messages. Also, ICMP messages are only sent about errors in
handling fragment zero of fragemented datagrams.

There are two simple and widely used applications that are based on
ICMP: Ping and Traceroute. Ping uses the ICMP Echo and Echo Reply messages to determine whether a host is reachable. Traceroute sends IP datagrams with low Time to live (TTL) values so that they expire en route to a
destination. It uses the resulting ICMP Time Exceeded messages to determine
where in the Internet the datagrams expired and pieces together a view of
the route to a host.

2.3.3   Address Resolution Protocol

The Address Resolution Protocol (ARP) is responsible for converting the
higher-level protocol addresses (IP addresses) to physical network addresses.
It is described in RFC 826. The goal is to enable each host on a network to
build up a table of mappings between IP addresses and link-layer addresses.
On a single physical network, individual hosts are known on the network by

their physical hardware address. Higher-level protocols address destination hosts in the form of a symbolic address (IP address in this case). When such a protocol wants to send a datagram to destination IP address wxyz, the device driver does not understand this address. Therefore, a module (ARP) is provided that will translate the IP address to the physical address of the destination host. It uses a lookup table (sometimes referred to as the ARP cache) to perform this translation. When the address is not found in the ARP cache, a broadcast is sent out on the network, with a special format called the ARP request. If one of the machines on the network recognizes its own IP address in the request, it will send an ARP reply back to the requesting host. The reply will contain the physical hardware address of the host and source route information (if the packet has crossed bridges on its path). Both this address and the source route information are stored in the ARP cache of the requesting host. All subsequent datagrams to this destination IP address can now be translated to a physical address, which is used by the device driver to send out the datagram on the network.

ARP is applicable to IPv4 only. IPv6 has developed a concept called as Neighbor Discovery, which is a replacement for ARP. Neighbor Discovery has the same functionality as ARP in IPv6. IPv6 nodes on the same link use Neighbor Discovery to discover each other's presence, to determine each other's link-layer addresses, to find routers, and to maintain reachability information about the paths to active neighbors.

2.4 Transport-Layer Protocols: TCP, UDP, and SCTP

2.4.1 Transmission Control Protocol

Transmission Control Protocol, or TCP as it is commonly referred to, is a transport-layer protocol that runs on top of IP. The best explanation of TCP is from RFC 793:

> TCP is a connection-oriented, end-to-end reliable protocol designed to fit into a layered hierarchy of protocols which support multi-network applications. The TCP provides for reliable inter-process communication between pairs of processes in host computers attached to distinct but interconnected computer communication networks. Very few assumptions are made as to the reliability of the communication protocols below the TCP layer. TCP assumes it can obtain a simple, potentially unreliable datagram service from the lower level protocols. In principle, the TCP should be able to operate above a wide spectrum of communication systems ranging from hard-wired connections to packet-switched or circuit-switched networks.

TCP was specifically designed to be a reliable end-to-end byte stream transmission protocol over an unreliable network. The IP layer does not provide any guarantees that datagrams will be delivered with any degree of reliability. Hence it is up to the upper-layer protocol to provide this reliability. The key functionality associated with TCP is basic data transfer.

- *Basic Data Transfer.* From an application perspective, TCP transfers a contiguous stream of bytes through the network. The application does not have to bother with chopping the data into basic blocks or datagrams. TCP does this by grouping the bytes in TCP segments, which are passed to IP for transmission to the destination.
- *Reliability.* TCP assigns a sequence number to each byte transmitted and expects a positive acknowledgment (ACK) from the receiving TCP. If the ACK is not received within a timeout interval, the data are retransmitted. Since the data are transmitted in blocks (TCP segments), only the sequence number of the first data byte in the segment is sent to the destination host.
- *Flow Control.* The receiving TCP, when sending an ACK back to the sender, also indicates to the sender the number of bytes it can receive beyond the last received TCP segment, without causing overrun and overflow in its internal buffers. This is sent in the ACK in the form of the highest sequence number it can receive without problems.
- *Multiplexing.* Multiplexing is achieved through the concept of ports. A port is a 16-bit number used by the host-to-host protocol to identify to which higher-level protocol or application process it must deliver incoming messages. Two types of ports exist: (1) *Well-known:* these ports belong to standard applications servers such as telnet, ftp, and http. The well-known ports are controlled and assigned by the Internet Assigned Numbers Authority (IANA). Well-known ports range from 1 to 1023. (2) *Ephemeral:* A client can negotiate the use of a port dynamically and such ports can be called ephemeral. These ports are maintained for the duration of the session and then released. Ephemeral ports range from 1024 to 65535. Multiple applications can use the ports as a means of multiplexing for communicating with other nodes.
- *Connections.* The reliability and flow control mechanisms require that TCP initializes and maintains certain status information for each data stream. The combination of this status, including sockets, sequence numbers, and window sizes, is called a logical connection. Each connection is uniquely identified by the pair of sockets used by the sending and receiving processes.

TCP entities exchange data in the form of segments. A segment consists of a fixed 20-byte header and an optional part followed by zero or more data bytes. Figure 2–5 shows the structure of the TCP header.

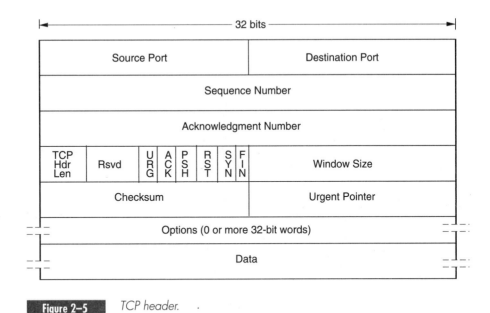

Figure 2–5   *TCP header.*

The fields in the TCP header are desribed as follows:

- *Source Port and Destination Port:* These fields identify the local endpoints of a connection. Each TCP entity decides how to allocate its own ports. A number of well-known ports are reserved for specific applications (e.g., FTP).
- *Sequence and Acknowledgment Number:* Indicate the sequence number of the packet. The ACK number specifies the next byte expected, and not the last byte correctly received.
- *TCP Header Length:* Indicates how many 32-bit words are contained in the TCP header. This is required because of the Options field, which is of variable length.
- *Reserved:* For future use.
- *The six 1-bit flags* are as follows:

  URG—Set to 1 if the Urgent pointer is in use.
  ACK—Set to 1 to indicate that the Acknowledgment number is valid.
  PSH—Indicates PUSHed data. The receiver is requested to deliver the data to the application and not buffer it until a full buffer has been received.
  RST—Used to reset a connection.
  SYN—Used to establish connections.
  FIN—Used to release a connection.

- *Window Size:* This field tells how many bytes may be sent starting at the byte acknowledged. Flow control in TCP is handled using a variable-size sliding window.
- *Checksum:* Provided for reliability. It checksums the header and the data (and the pseudoheader when applicable). While computing the checksum, the Checksum field itself is replaced with zeros.
- *Urgent Pointer:* Used to indicate a byte offset from the current sequence number at which urgent data are to be found.
- *Options:* This field was designed to provide a way to add extra facilities not covered by the regular header.

TCP has been the workhorse of the Internet, and a significant portion of Internet traffic today is carried via TCP. The reliability and congestion control aspects of TCP make it ideally suited for a large number of applications. TCP is formally defined in RFC 793. RFC 1122 provides some clarification and bug fixes, and a few extensions are defined in RFC 1323.

2.4.2   User Data Protocol

User Data Protocol (UDP) is a connectionless transport protocol. UDP is basically an application interface to IP. It adds no reliability, flow control, or error recovery to IP. It simply serves as a multiplexer/demultiplexer for sending and receiving datagrams, using ports to direct the datagrams. UDP is a lightweight protocol with very minimal overhead. The responsibility of recovering from errors, retransmission, etc., is up to the application. Applications that need to communicate need to identify a target is more specific than simply the IP address. UDP provides this function via the concept of ports. The format of the UDP datagram is shown in Figure 2–6.

The following is a description of the fields of the UDP header:

- *Source and Destination Port:* The two ports serve the same function as in TCP; they identify the endpoints within the source and destination nodes.

|←——————————— 32 bits ———————————→|

Source Port	Destination Port
UDP Length	UDP Checksum

Figure 2–6   *UDP header.*

- *UDP Length:* This field includes the 8-byte UDP header and the data.
- *UDP Checksum:* The checksum is computed over the UDP header, the IP header, and the data.

Although UDP does not implement flow control or reliable/ordered delivery, it does a little more work than simply to demultiplex messages to some application—it ensures the correctness of the message via the checksum. UDP uses the same cheksum algorithm as IP. UDP is described in RFC 768.

2.4.3   Stream Control Transmission Protocol

Stream Control Transmission Protocol (SCTP) is described in RFC 2960 and is a recent addition to the transport suite. SCTP is a reliable transport protocol operating on top of a connectionless packet network such as IP. The main services offered by the protocol are as follows:

- Acknowledged error-free nonduplicated transfer of user data
- Data fragmentation to conform to discovered path MTU size
- Sequenced delivery of user messages within multiple streams, with an option for order-of-arrival delivery of individual user messages
- Optional bundling of multiple user messages into a single SCTP packet
- Network-level fault tolerance through supporting of multihoming at either or both ends of an association

SCTP was primarily designed to carry PSTN signaling messages over an IP network. But the protocol is capable of supporting many different types of applications as well. SCTP can be considered as having the properties of TCP while still being lightweight.

The SCTP transport service can be decomposed into a number of functions:

- *Association startup and takedown:* An association is initiated by a request from the SCTP user. A cookie-based mechanism using four-way handshakes ensures security. It provides for graceful close (i.e., shutdown) of an active association on request from the SCTP user.
- *Sequenced delivery within streams:* The term *stream* is used in SCTP to refer to a sequence of user messages that are to be delivered to the upper-layer protocol in order with respect to other messages within the same stream. A user can specify at association startup time the number of streams to be supported by the association (and negotiated with the remote end). The sequencing can be bypassed if required.

- *User data fragmentation:* When needed, SCTP fragments user messages to ensure that the SCTP packet passed to the lower layer conforms to the path Mean Transfer Unit (MTU).
- *Acknowledgment and congestion avoidance:* The acknowledgment and congestion avoidance function is responsible for packet retransmission when timely acknowledgment has not been received. Packet retransmission is conditioned by congestion avoidance procedures similar to those used for TCP.
- *Chunk bundling:* The chunk-bundling function of SCTP is responsible for assembly of the complete SCTP packet and its disassembly at the receiving end. Each chunk may contain multiple messages (or data).
- *Packet validation:* A mandatory Verification Tag field and a 32-bit Checksum field are included in the SCTP common header to ensure packet validity.
- *Path management:* The SCTP path management function chooses the destination transport address for each outgoing SCTP packet based on the SCTP user's instructions and the currently perceived reachability status of the eligible destination set. The path management function monitors reachability through heartbeats when other packet traffic is inadequate to provide this information and advises the SCTP user when reachability of any far-end transport address changes. The path management function is also responsible for reporting the eligible set of local transport addresses to the far end during association startup, and for reporting the transport addresses returned from the far end to the SCTP user

The SCTP packet format is shown in Figure 2–7.

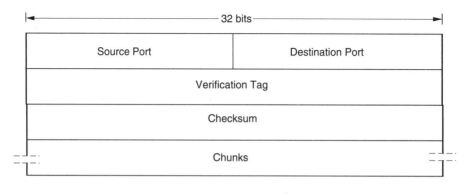

← —————————————— 32 bits —————————————— →	
Source Port	Destination Port
Verification Tag	
Checksum	
Chunks	

Figure 2–7   *SCTP header.*

The fields of the SCTP header are described as follows:

- *Source Port and Destination Port:* These identify the endpoints within the source and destination nodes.
- *Verification Tag:* The receiver of this packet uses the Verification Tag to validate the sender of this SCTP packet. On transmit, the value of this Verification Tag *must* be set to the value of the Initiate Tag received from the peer endpoint during the association initialization.
- *Checksum:* This field contains the checksum of this SCTP packet, which is computed over the SCTP common header and one or more control or data chunks.

SCTP is a relatively new protocol, and its implementation is only now beginning to occur. The implementation of SCTP will probably not be as widespread as TCP and UDP in the next few years.

2.5   Application Layer Protocols: FTP, Telnet, HTTP

2.5.1   Telnet/FTP

Telnet and FTP are two very commonly used application-layer protocols on the Internet. They have been around for over 20 years now.

Telnet is an application-layer protocol and allows a user to connect to an account on another remote mechine. A client program on one machine can connect with a server program running on another machine using this protocol. Users utilizing Telnet interact with the remote machine in the same way as they would with a local machine. Telnet was one of the earliest protocols and in the early days was used primarily to allow users in one location to access accounts or machines in another location.

The Telnet client has two primary functions:

- Interacting with the user terminal on the local host
- Communicating with the remote telnet server

The default port (reserved by IANA) that the telnet client connects to on the server side is port 23. The client/server TCP connection is maintained throughout the telnet session. Since telnet can work across different platforms, telnet assumes that the hosts run a general network virtual terminal, which is a simple character device with a keyboard and printer. Data typed by a user on the keyboard are transmitted to the remote server, and the received data from the server are output to the printer.

In order to differentiate between a telnet control message and user data, each control message is preceded with a special octet, eight bits of 1s. Initial control messages during a telnet setup indicate the capabilities of the two end-points to each other. After this is completed, the server requests an ID and password for logging in. The user types in his or her ID and password, and this is transferred to the server over the TCP connection. Once authenticated at the server, the connection is opened and data start to flow in both directions.

The File Transfer Protocol (FTP), as the name indicates, is used to download or copy files between remote machines connected via an IP network. FTP is also a client/server protocol. One of the interesting aspects of FTP is that it uses separate TCP connections to send control messages and to send data. The default port assigned by IANA for FTP on an FTP server is 21. FTP also uses TCP as the underlying transport protocol. A file is transmitted as a stream of bytes, and the closing of the TCP connection setup indicates the completion of the transmission. The control connection persists across multiple file transfers. But every file transfer requires a separate data connection. FTP is in the process of being enhanced in the IETF by a working group known as FTPext.

2.5.2   HTTP

The Hypertext Transfer Protocol (HTTP) is the request-response protocol underlying the World Wide Web and was proposed by Tim Berners-Lee in March 1990 at the CERN laboratories, as a mechanism to access documents anywhere on the Internet and to help navigate between them via hypertext links. HTTP is an application layer protocol similar to FTP, SMTP, or NNTP. HTTP can use any underlying transport protocol to transmit the messages from the sender to the receiver. However, most known implementations of HTTP today use TCP as the transport protocol. It is important to understand the difference between HTTP and the World Wide Web. The Web itself consists of three parts: HTTP, HTML, and the universal resource identifier (URI) naming scheme. Browsers with graphical interfaces for example are a component of the Web in addition to proxies and servers.

The key propoerties of HTTP are as follows:

- It is primarily a request-response protocol—HTTP requests are sent by clients and result in responses from servers. The direction of the flow is from clients to servers.
- It depends on the global URI infrastructure.
- It relies on the URI naming mechanism. All transactions use URIs to identify the resources on the Web.
- It does not require maintenance of state across requests. No state is maintained by clients or servers across requests and responses. Each pair of request and response is treated as an independent message exchange.

* The notion of metadata is important: Information about the resources is often included in Web transfers and can be used in multiple ways.

HTTP relies on the concept of an URI. This naming mechanism allows resources to reside anywhere on the Internet. A resource can have the same URI associated with it forever, although the contents of the resource or its representation can change over its lifetime. A URI denotes a resource independent of its current location or the name by which it is known. A URI is a combination of a uniform resource locator (URL) and a uniform resource name (URN). The most poular from of a URI is a URL, which is represented, for example, as http://www.nokia.com. A Web request for a resource requires more than one protrocol, such as DNS to look up the host name where the resource resides and TCP to fetch it over a transmission link.

While HTTP was designed as a stateless protocol, there was a need to maintain state for certain applications, such as banking and financial transactions. A transaction-based mechanism using cookies was introduced to enhance HTTP, and with the addition of SSL (Secure Socket Layer) for security, the use of HTTP for banking and other financial transactions (e-commerce) has become successful.

2.6   Addressing

IP addresses are 32-bit (in the case of IPv4) and 128-bit (in the case of IPv6) unsigned binary values. For example, the following shows an IPv4 and an IPv6 address: 199.174.41.5 and 12AB:0:0:CD30:123:4567:89AB:CDEF. IP addressing for IPv4 is described in RFC 116 and for IPv6 in RFC 2373. IP addresses are essentially hierarchical in nature, which provides scalability to the addressing architecture. IP addresses are made up of two parts, a network part and a host part. The network part of the IP address identifies the network to which the host is connected; all hosts attached to a network have the same network ID in their address. The host part identifies each host uniquely on that network. Let's look at addressing in IPv4 and IPv6 networks separately.

2.6.1   IPv4 Addressing Architecture

There are two types of addresses from a uniqueness perspective: globally routable addresses and private IP addresses. Globally routable addresses are unique on a global scale. Private addresses are one of a set of solutions for the diminishing address space in IPv4 networks. These addresses are not globally unique and are usually used by enterprises and small networks that do not directly connect to the Internet. Three ranges have been set up for this: 10.0.0.0, 172.16.0.0 to 172.16.31.0, and 192.168.0.0 to 192.168.255.0.

The hierarchical nature of the address architecture created a class structure, A, B, C, and D as described next. The class of the IP address is identified by the most significant bits (MSBs) in its address.

- If the first bit is 0, then it is a class A address. It has a has a 7-bit network number and a 24-bit local address, thus allowing 128 class A networks to be created.
- If the first bit is 1 and the second is 0, then it is a class B address. It has a 14-bit network number and a 16-bit local address. This allows 16,384 class B networks.
- Is the first two bits are 1 and the third is 0, it is a class C address. It has a 21-bit network number and an 8-bit local address. This allows 2,097,152 class C networks.
- The fourth type of address, class D, is used as a multicast address. The four highest-order bits are set to 1-1-1-0.

2.6.2   Subnetting

Due to the rapid growth of the Internet and as a result of the fast depletion of IP addresses, the principle of assigned IP addresses became inflexible. To avoid having to obtain more IP addresses for networks, subnetting was introduced. Subnetting is a mechanism in which the address structure is subdivided into a second network number and a host number. With subnetting the address now appears as

Network number, subnetwork number, host number

The subnetwork division is visible only to the internal network, and from a routing perspective the network number is still the key to routing packets to a destination. Subnetting is accomplished using a 32-bit subnet mask. Bits with a value of zero bits in the subnet mask indicate positions ascribed to the host number. Bits with a value of 1 indicate positions ascribed to the subnet number. The bit positions in the subnet mask belonging to the original network number are set to ones but are not used. Like IP addresses, subnet masks are usually written in dotted decimal form. Two types of subnetting are in common use: static subnetting and variable-length subnetting.

- In static subnetting the subnets obtained from the same network use the same subnet mask. This is less optimal since it tends to waste address space in small networks.
- Variable-length subnetting allows subnets within the same network to use different subnet masks. It divides the network such that each

subnet contains sufficient addresses for the required number of hosts.

2.6.3   Classless Internet Domain Routing (CIDR)

The rapid growth in terms of the number of hosts and networks in the 1990s made designers rethink the hierarchical class-based address architecture of IPv4. Unless some form of aggregation was enabled, there was a serious possibility of running out of addresses by the mid-1990s. Standard routing was based on class A, B, and C network addresses. Subnetting provides a greater degree of granularity within these networks. However, it is not possible to specify that multiple class C addresses are related. This results in an explosion in the routing table entries in the backbone. If a class B network requires 1 entry in the backbone, an equivalent network of class C address ranges would require 16 entries.

CIDR helps in aggregating routes. It enables a single entry in the forwarding table to reach a set of different networks. It achieves this by getting rid of the class structure of the IPv4 addresses. It is based solely on the high-order bits of the IP address. These bits are termed the IP prefix. CIDR is specified in RFCs 1518, 1519, and 1520. The implementation of CIDR in the Internet is primarily based on the Border Gateway Protocol Version 4 (BGP-4). The mechanism of combining multiple networks via the use of network masks is sometimes refered to as supernetting. With the introduction of CIDR, IPv4 addresses are no longer classified as being of type A, B, or C.

2.6.4   IPv6 Addressing Architecture

IPv6 addresses are 128 bits as compared to the 32-bit IPv4 addresses. This significant increase in address size is expected to be sufficient for a long time. With 128 bits, it is possible to have 340 undecillion addresses as compared to the 4 billion IPv4 addresses. The IPv6 addressing architecture is specified in RFC 2373.

Three different types of addresses can be assigned to an IPv6 interface (note that addresses are assigned to interfaces and not nodes) :

* Unicast address
* Multicast address
* Anycast address

UNICAST ADDRESSES

IPv6 unicast addresses are aggregatable with contiguous bitwise masks similar to IPv4 addresses under classless interdomain routing. There are several forms of unicast address assignment in IPv6, including the global aggregatable unicast address, the Network Service Access Point (NSAP) address, the

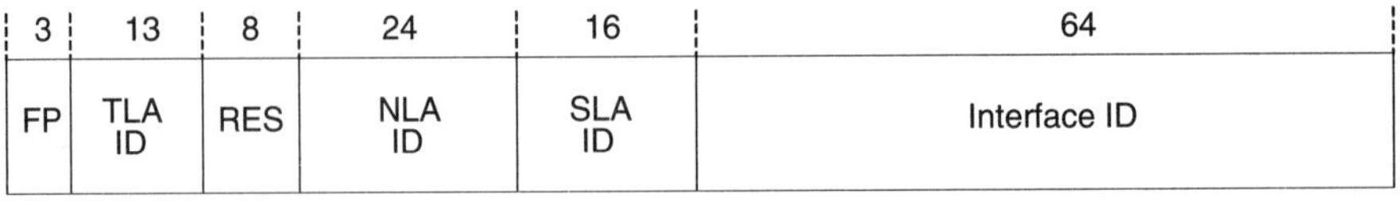

3	13	8	24	16	64
FP	TLA ID	RES	NLA ID	SLA ID	Interface ID

Figure 2–8   *Aggregation in IPv6.*

Internet Packet Exchange (IPX) hierarchical address, the site-local address, the link-local address, and the IPv4-capable host address. The global unicast address can be aggregated; the format of the aggregation is as shown in Figure 2–8.

In Figure 2–8,

001: Format prefix (3 bit) for aggregatable global unicast addresses

TLA ID: Top-level aggregation identifier

RES: Reserved for future use

NLA ID: Next-level aggregation identifier

SLA ID: Site-level aggregation identifier

INTERFACE ID: Interface identifier

ANYCAST ADDRESSES

IPv6 introduces the concept of an anycast address. This is not found in IPv4. An IPv6 anycast address is an address that is assigned to more than one interface (typically belonging to different nodes), with the property that a packet sent to an anycast address is routed to the "nearest" interface having that address, according to the routing protocols' measure of distance. Anycast addresses are allocated from the unicast address space, using any of the defined unicast address formats. Thus, anycast addresses are syntactically indistinguishable from unicast addresses.

8	4	4	112
11111111	Flags	Scope	Group ID

Figure 2–9   *IPv6 multicast address.*

MULTICAST ADDRESSES

IPv6 gets rid of the concept of broadcast addresses since broadcast is a variant of multicast anyway. An IPv6 multicast address is an identifier for a group of nodes. A node may belong to any number of multicast groups. Multicast addresses have the format shown in Figure 2–9.

The first 8 bits set to 1 indicate a multicast address. Flags are a set of four flags. The scope is used to limit the scope of the multicast group, and the group ID identifies the multicast group.

2.7   Routing

Routing of datagrams across the Internet is acomplished by routing protocols. Routers and switches are responsible for making decisions about what path on which to send a packet for it to reach its destination. So how do routers and switches acquire the information that allows them to route and forward packets correctly? Routing is a complex problem, and the fundamentals of this technology are based in graph theory. The basic problem of routing is to find the lowest-cost path between any two nodes. The cost of a path is determined by distance or other factors.

Routing in small networks with only a few hosts can be accomplished easily by configuration of the route tables. This is referred to as static routing. However, when we start scaling, the need for dynamic routing protocols becomes obvious quickly. Routing protocols provide a distributed and dynamic way to solve the problem of finding the lowest-cost path in the presence of link and node failures and changing edge costs. Static routing is useful in some special cases, such as to define a default route that is not being advertised in the network or to supplement an exterior gateway protocol. Dynamic routing protocols can be classified into two groups:

- Interior Gateway Protocols (IGPs)—Examples of these are rowing information protocol (RIP) and open shortest path first (OSPF).
- Exterior Gateway Protocols (EGPs)—An example of this is border gateway protocol (BGP).

Gateway protocols are referred to as interior or exterior depending on whether they are used within or between autonomous systems (ASs). An autonomous system can be viewed as a logical portion of a much larger IP network. The concept of autonomous systems allows the scalability of routing protocols. IGPs exchange routing information within the confines of the AS. EGPs allow the exchange of reachability information between ASs.

Two main classes of routing protocols exist: *distance vector* and *link state*.

2.7.1 Distance Vector Routing

Distance vector routing is based on the concept of each node maintaining the distance from itself to every other node that it is aware of. Distance vector tables consist of a series of destinations and the costs associated with each to reach them. The distance to other nodes is learned via information provided by neighboring routers. Each router transmits its own distance vector table across the shared network. The following steps are generally involved in the setup of a distance vector table:

1. Each router initializes itself with a distance vector table that contains 0 as the distance for itself, 1 as the distance to directly attached networks, and infinity for all other networks.

2. Each router in the network periodically distributes its distance vector table to each of its neighbors.

3. Each router saves the most recent table that it receives and uses this information to compute a distance vector table.

4. Total cost to each destination is computed by adding the cost reported to it by each neighbor's distance vector table.

5. Each router then generates its own routing/forwarding table based on the lowest cost for each destination.

The preceding algorithm produces a stable routing table after a period that is directly related to the number of routers in the network. This stabilization time is refered to as convergence. The route tables are recomputed if a change is received from one of the neighbors or if a link state changes.

2.7.2 Link State Routing

Large networks have demonstrated the inefficiencies of distance vector routing. This has resulted in a different approach to tackling routing. The new protocols that have been designed are based on what is refered to as link state or shortest path first (SPF) algorithms. The principle of link state routing is relatively straightforward and based on Djikstra's algorithm. A very high-level view of the principles and algorithm is as follows:

- Routers are responsible for contacting their neighbors and learning their identities.

* Routers construct link state packets that contain information about the list of networks and their states. These are transmitted to all routers in a network.
* All routers have identical information about available links and the link states in a network, which results in a common topology view in all routers.
* These topology maps are utilized to construct the best routes to each destination.

Routers contact neighbors by sending *Hello* packets on their network interfaces. Hello packets are sent directly to neighbors on point-to-point networks and nonbroadcast networks. On multiaccess networks these packets are sent to a predefined group or a multicast IP address. Neighbors that receive these hello packets respond with their identities. Once neighbors have been contacted, link state information is exchanged via link state packets (LSPs). LSPs are distributed to all routers in a network via flooding mechanisms. All routers must acknowledge the reception of an LSP. Flooding ensures that all routers in a network have the same link state information. Each router in the network uses the information in the LSPs in the SPF algorithm to generate a shortest path tree with itself as the root. LSPs are sent every time a new router is added or deleted, when a link to a neighbor goes down, or when the cost associated with the link changes. In addition, refresh packets are sent on a periodic basis (~30 min.) to maintain sanity of the routing state.

2.7.3 Interior Gateway Protocols

RIP, RIPv2, OSPF, and Inter System-Inter System (IS-IS) are the standard IGPs. RIP is defined in RFC 1058 and is suitable for small networks. Problems that were identified with RIP were addressed in a subsequent release called RIPv2. RIP runs on top of UDP and uses port 520. RIPng is the version of RIP that is defined for IPv6 networks and is documented in RFC2080. RIPng uses port 521 for sending and receiving packets. OSPF is a link state protocol that is widely used in networks today and is the predominant routing protocol in medium to large networks. OSPF incorporates many features that make it the default choice in many cases. OSPFv2 is defined in RFC 2328.

2.7.4 Exterior Gateway Protocols

EGPs are used to exchange routing information between routers in different autonomous systems. EGPs include EGP, which is defined in RFC 904 and is now considered historical; and Border Gateway Protocol, BGP-4, which is described in RFC 1771. BGP is based on the Classless Internet Domain Routing (CIDR) concept. BGP runs over a reliable transport protocol (TCP) between neighbor routes. TCP port 179 is used by BGP speakers. The BGP protocol comprises four main stages:

- Opening and confirming a BGP connection over TCP with a neighboring router.
- Maintaining the BGP connection via keepalive messages.
- Sending reachability information via update messages to its neighbors.
- Notification of error conditions when they occur. This results in the closing of the TCP connection.

Routing protocols continue to evolve as the Internet grows large. The size of the Internet and rapid growth have put a lot of pressure on routing protocols. As route tables increase in size, efficiency of routing tends to go down. These issues and others related to routing are dealt with in the industry on a constant basis and keep the Internet humming.

2.7.5   Routing for Mobile Hosts

As the number of wireless networks that support IP grows, as well as the number of notebook computers, PDAs, and mobile phones with IP capability, the need for supporting mobility in IP networks becomes greater. The Internet protocol, when designed in the early 1970s and 1980s, did not take into consideration the need for supporting mobility. The need to support seamless mobility was felt more in the 1990s. Note that there is a difference between seamless mobility and nomadic mobility.

Seamless mobility: Mobility in which the sessions and the applications on the device are uninterrupted as the terminal changes its point of attachment to the network. An example of seamless mobility is a user making a voice call (via a wireless network) while driving in a car and the call is uninterrupted while it is handed off between base stations.

Nomadic mobility: Mobility in which the sessions and applications are restarted as a result of the user moving from network connectivity at point A to network connectivity at point B. An example of nomadic mobility is a user connected to the corporate network and then traveling to another location (e.g., hotel) and connecting to the corporate network via dialup and restarting the applications.

THE PROBLEM

Most applications today use TCP as the transport protocol. When a TCP connection is set up, the entities on either side know the IP address associated with the other end. The IP address of a node is based on its point of attachment to the network, and routing in the Internet is based on the network addresses. So when a node changes its point of attachment, the IP address associated with the interface changes. As a result, the TCP connection serving an application is torn down as the connection endpoints are identified by the combination of port number and IP address. The connection cannot survive a change in IP address.

THE SOLUTION

Mobile IP was designed in the IETF to address IP layer mobility, specifically to address the problem described in the previous subsection. The specification for Mobile IP is in RFC 3344. Mobile IP solves the problem by introducing a couple of new network elements. The Home Agent and the Foreign Agent enable a mobile host to move across different points of attachment, which results in a change to the interface's IP address. However, the existing connections are maintained. This is accomplished by a little help from the home agent and the foreign agent. The mobile node, when it moves from its home network to another network or point of attachment (which is served by a foreign agent) acquires a care-of address. So the mobile node has its home IP address as well as a care-of address associated with its interface. It registers this care-of address with its home agent, which is a router on its home network. The home agent proxies for the mobile node and intercepts all packets destined for the mobile node. This is accomplished via a process known as proxy ARP. The home agent then tunnels the packets destined for the mobile node to the care-of address. The mobile node always uses its home IP address in any sessions with correspondent nodes. Since the home IP address is always constant, TCP sessions survive the change in network attachment points. The only thing that changes as the mobile moves is the care-of address. However, since the endpoint of the TCP connection is unaware of the care-of address, there is no impact to the session. Packets from the mobile node to the correspondent nodes are directly routed to it. However, packets from the correspondent node to the mobile arrive at the home agent and are tunneled to the mobile via the care-of address. This is commonly refered to as triangle routing.

The IP mobility solution for IPv6 is slightly different from the one for IPv4, which was just described. In IPv6 there is no foreign agent. The problem of triangle routing is also eliminated by a mechanism known as route optimization. The mobile node can inform a correspondent about its care-of address and thus have the session ongoing between itself and the correspondent without any need for the home agent. However, the home agent still exists in IPv6, and the functionality of the home agent is the same as in Ipv4. The mobility protocol for IPv6 is in the process of being standardized in the IETF at the time of this writing.

2.8   Naming

IP addresses are used by routers to forward packets to their destinations. However, IP addresses are not really human friendly. The solution to this problem is to associate a unique, human-friendly name to every host in a network. A mapping between the human-friendly name and the associated IP address is that is enabled by what is known as DNS, or Domain Name System.

The Domain Name System is essentially a distributed database of host information that is indexed by domain names. A domain name is a path in a large inverted tree that is referred to as the domain name space. DNS implements a hierarchical name space for Internet names. The logical structure of the DNS is shown in Figure 2–10.

A domain is simply a subtree of the domain name space. At the very top of DNS is what is referred to as the "root." Domains below the root are referred to as top-level domains. The original top-level domains (TLDs) divided the Internet domain name space into seven domains, as shown in Figure 2–10. Internet Society (ISOC) has approved a few other TLDs in the last couple of years. Some of these are .cc, .nu, .tv, and .bz.

Every node in a tree has a text label (max 63 chars). Only the root has no label. The domain name of any node in the tree is the sequence of labels from that node to the root. If the root nodes label appears in the nodes domain name, it appears with a dot at the end (e.g., www.nokia.com.). An absolute domain name is written relative to the root. An absolute domain name is refered to as a fully qualified domain name (FQDN).

Domain names that are leaves of the tree normally are associated with hosts. These names may point to the IP address and mail routing information among others. Data associated with domain names are contained in resource records.

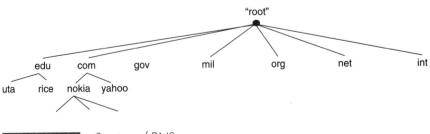

Figure 2–10   *Structure of DNS.*

The following resource record types are the most commonly used:

- A records implement the name-to-address mapping.
- NS records give the domain name for a host that is running a name server.
- CNAME gives the canonical name for a host.
- Mail Exchange (MX) records give the domain name for a host that is running a mail server for the specified domain.

As mentioned earlier, the DNS is a distributed database. The distributed nature of this naming service is achieved via delegation. Delegation refers to assigining the responsibility for a subdomain to another organization. This means that the subdomain nokia.com, for example, is managed by Nokia and has complete control over the subdomain. The .com subdomain merely has a pointer to nokia.com.

What are the elements that make up the DNS? It is primarily comprised of two components: name servers and resolvers. Network nodes that store information about the domain name space are called name servers. These servers have complete information about some part of the domain, which is refered to as a zone. What is the difference between a zone and domain? A domain includes delegated data, whereas a zone, which is bounded, will never include delegated data. Figure 2–11 illustrates the concept of a zone and domain.

Resolvers are the clients that access name servers. Application programs on hosts that require address translation services use the resolver. The primary functions of the resolver are to

- Query a name server.
- Interpret responses from the name server.
- Deliver the info to the appropriate application program that requested it.

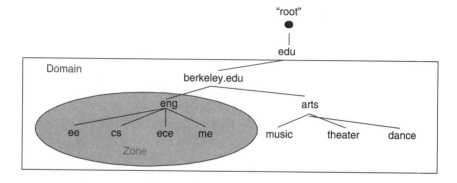

Figure 2–11 *Zones and domains.*

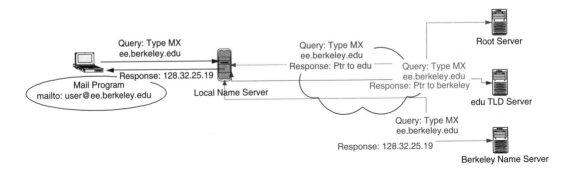

Figure 2–12   *Name resolution operation.*

Do resolvers have to be aware of the root servers in order to resolve names? No. Resolvers are configured with a name server that is commonly in the domain that the node is connected to. Name server configuration can happen as a result of the node acquiring configuration information through DHCP or Point-to-Point Protocol (PPP), for example. Resolvers then send their queries to this name server, which does most of the work on behalf of the resolver. Figure 2–12 shows the modus operandi of name resolution.

In Figure 2–12, the mail program at a host is seeking the MX record of user@ee.berekeley.edu. The application program contacts the local name server that it is configured with. If the name server does not have this in its cache, it will query other name servers, and in the preceding example the querying is initiated from the root server. The local name server may be configured with the address of the root server, or it may contact another name server in its domain.

One final aspect of name server resolution is the inverse mapping of addresses to names. In the Internet's domain name space, the in-addr.arpa portion of the name space is utilized for this purpose. Because any name server only knows about a part of the overall domain, an inverse query is not guaranteed to return a valid response.

2.9   Host Configuration

Internet hosts need to be configured with certain information that allows applications to operate and packets to be routed. Information that is most commonly configured includes the IP address, the gateway, and the DNS server. Configuration can be done manually or can be via an automated process. Manual configuration requires the user to be networking savvy to some extent. The Dynamic Host Configuration Protocol (DHCP) provides configuration parameters to Internet hosts. DHCP is specified in RFC 2131. DHCP is an application-layer protocol that follows the client/server mode. From the client perspective, it can be viewed as an extension to BOOTP, which is used to bootstrap hosts. One thing to note about DHCP is that it is for confguring hosts only and is not intended for routers.

There are primarily two components to DHCP: a client piece of software and a DHCP server. After obtaining parameters via DHCP, a DHCP client should be able to exchange packets with any other host in the Internet. The main services provided by DHCP are to provide persistent storage of network parameters for network clients and to allocate temporary or permanent network (IP) addresses to clients. IP address allocation in DHCP has three mechanisms:

* Automatic—A permanent IP address is assigned to the client.
* Dynamic—An IP address is allocated to the client with a lifetime associated with it.
* Manual—The IP address is assigned by the operator and DHCP is simply the carrier of this information.

Other extensions to DHCP include the concept of a relay agent that can forward DHCP messages to a server that is located elsewhere in the network. Clients broadcast a DHCPDISCOVER message on the local physical subnet and servers on the network respond with a DHCPOFFER message. The client selects one of the offers and sends a DHCPREQUEST message to the server that made the offer. The server responds with a DHCPACK, and initialization is complete.

2.10 Summary

This chapter has provided an overview of some of the important concepts in Internetworking. The fundamental building blocks of the Internet include various protocols at the network, transport, and application layers. These concepts will be useful as we start discussing the use of IP in a wireless/cellular environment in the following chapters.

References

Web Protocols and Practice—Balachander Krishnamurthy and Jennifer Rexford

DNS and BIND—Paul Albitz and Cricket Liu

RFC 2131—Dynamic Host Configuration Protocol

RFC 3344—IP Mobility Support for IPv4

RFC 791—Internet Protocol DARPA Internet Program Protocol Specification

RFC 768—User Datagram Protocol

RFC 793—Transmission Control Protocol

RFC 2960—Stream Control Transmission Protocol

RFC 1945—Hypertext Transfer Protocol—HTTP/1-0

RFC 114—A file transfer protocol

RFC 821—Simple mail transfer protocol

RFC 318—Telnet protocol

RFC 1035—Domain names—Implementation & Specification

RFC 1531—Dynamic Host Configuration Protocols

Overview of Wi

and Technolo

*W*ireless *networks have been an essential part of communica-*
tion in the last century. Early adopters of wireless technology
primarily have been the military, emergency services, and law
enforcement organizations. Scenes from World War II movies, for
example, show soldiers equipped with wireless communication
equipment being carried in backpacks and vehicles.

As society moves toward information centricity, the need to have information accessible at any time and anywhere (as well as being reachable anywhere) takes on a new dimension. With the rapid growth of mobile
telephony and networks, the vision of a mobile information society (introduced by Nokia) is slowly becoming a reality. It is common to see people
communicating via their mobile phones and devices. The era of the pay
phones is past, and pay phones stand witness as a symbol of the way things
were. With today's networks and coverage, it is possible for a user to have
connectivity almost anywhere.

Growth in commercial wireless networks occurred primarily in the late
1980s and 1990s, and continues into the 2000s. The competitive nature of the
wireless industry and the mass acceptance of wireless devices have caused
costs associated with terminals and air time to come down significantly in the
last 10 years. As a result, we now have penetration rates of mobile users reaching almost 100% in countries like Taiwan, Italy, and Finland. Subscriber growth
has been increasing by leaps and bounds; by mid-2002, the number of subscribers already exceeded 1 billion. The exponential growth of mobile subscribers is shown in Figure 3–1.

The service offered on wireless networks today is primarily voice. However, the growth of data via short message services (over 24 billion messages

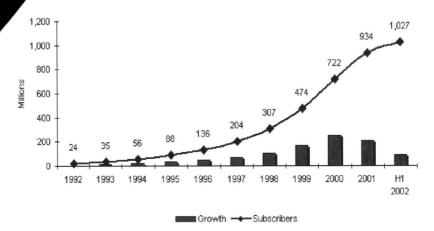

World cellular subscriber growth 1992 - 2002

Subscriber statistics source: EMC World Cellular Database

| **Figure 3–1** | *Subscriber statistics source: EMC World Cellular Database.* |

per month, as per data in the Groupe Special Mobile [GSM] World Congress) in the last few years has been increasing rapidly. Wireless networks have evolved to the point today wherein there are two major technologies deployed today: the TDM-based GSM networks, and the CDMA-based networks. GSM networks account for about 70% of the wireless networks today. CDMA accounts for about 25% of the networks, and the other 5% are networks of other types, such as the PDC network in Japan. Many of the TDM-based IS-136 networks that were prevalent in the Americas are now transitioning to either GSM or CDMA. An example of this is the AT&T Wireless network in the U.S., which is currently rolling out a GSM/GPRS network to replace the IS-136 network; the same is the case with Cingular wireless.

The growth of wireless networks is expected to continue well into the first decade of the twenty-first century, and the number of wireless subscribers is expected to overtake the number of fixed lines within the next three years (by 2006).

3.1 Brief History

At the beginning of the 1950s, the Bell telephone company in the United States introduced a radio telephone service for its customers. This was the first instance of a radio telephony network for commercial use. However, this network was small and could accommodate very few subscribers. As the demand for radio telephony service slowly grew, it forced engineers to come up with better ways to use the radio spectrum to enhance capacity and serve more subscribers. In 1964 the concept of shared resources was introduced. This innovation allowed networks to allocate radio resources on a dynamic basis. As a result, more subscribers could be served by the radio networks.

Spectrum for radio telephony was a scarce resource (and still is), and the need to optimize the available resources to increase utilization has always been a driver in radio networks. In 1971 the FCC (Federal Communications Commission) in the United States allocated a frequency band for radio telephony. The Bell telephone company introduced the AMPS (Advanced Mobile Phone Service) radio network, thereby deploying the first cellular network. In 1982 the United States standardized the AMPS system specification, and this became the radio telephony standard for North America.

In the 1980s several cellular radio networks were deployed around the world. In Europe each country chose its own technology for analog cellular telephony. The UK and Italy chose the American system under the name TACS (Total Access Cellular System). The Scandinavian countries and France chose the NMT (Nordic Mobile Telephone) standard. Germany chose the C-Net standard. All these were analog systems and hence considered as first-generation systems.

In 1982 the Conference of European Posts and Telecommunications (CEPT) created the Groupe Special Mobile (now known as GSM) and mandated the creation of a European standard for mobile radio telecommunications in the frequency band reserved for this purpose. This group produced the GSM standard that is widely deployed today. It also introduced digital radio telephony. Hence the second generation of mobile systems was created. In the United States, the Telecommunication Industry Association has developed two interim standards—the IS-54 standard in 1990, which is based on TDMA, and the IS-95 standard in 1993, which is based on CDMA. The evolution of these networks is covered in Chapter 15.

3.2 Cellular Fundamentals

Some of the basic concepts of cellular telephony include frequency reuse, multiple access techniques, speech coding, mobility, ciphering and authentication and network planning. Cellular networks can also be considered from the perspective of being divided into the radio access network (RAN) and the core network (CN). These are discussed in the following sections.

3.2.1   Radio Access Network

The radio access network comprises of the base transceiver stations (BTSs) and the controller element, which is called the base station controller (BSC). The BTSs are basically the radio elements (RF equipment) on the network side. Mobile terminals connect to the network via the BTSs. The BTS transmits system information over channels defined for broadcastting network specific information, and mobile stations tune in to these channels before performing access functions. A BTS is connected to a cell site, which hosts antennas atop towers or buildings. Cell sites can be of type macro, micro, or pico depending on the coverage radius. The size of a cell site is dependent on the transmit power level of the BTS. Figure 3–2 shows a generic radio access network.

The radio access network is the largest component of the mobile network, and a large number of base stations and cell sites are provisioned in order to provide coverage. Nationwide coverage of mobile networks requires the deployment of thousands of BTSs (coverage of the United States for example). The BTSs provide the channels for use on a dynamic basis to subscribers. Traffic and control channels are defined for the air interfaces depending on the type of technology used. The BTSs are controlled by the base station controller. So from a relationship perspective, a single BSC controls many BTSs. The BSC is responsible for managing the radio resources at the BTSs. The BSC assigns channels to subscribers on a need basis. In addition, it is constantly aware of a mobile station's location and the state that it is in. It measures the signal strength (with the assistance of the BTS and the MS) and makes handoff decisions. In the case of CDMA networks, BSCs are also responsible for performing the macro-

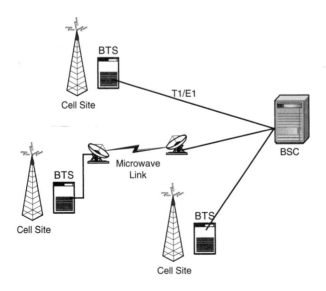

Figure 3–2   *Radio access network.*

diversity-combining function required in spread spectrum systems. In addition, the speech coding function may be incorporated into the BSC in some cases.

BSCs are connected to the BTSs over a wireline network using T1s and E1s. T1s and E1s are physical layer transmission technologies that are widely deployed by telecom operators. T1 is able to multiplex voice and data together in 24 user slots within a frame, as compared to E1, which has 30 user slots within each frame. Microwave links are also used for these connections. BTSs are normally deployed at the cell sites itself and hence are spread out geographically. The network connecting the BTSs to the BSC is referred to as a *backhaul network*. The BSC is normally at a central location such as a central office. The cost of connecting a large number of BTSs to the BSC is a major expense in radio networks.

3.2.2   Core Network

The core network consists of the mobile switching centers (MSCs), the home location register (HLR), visitor location register (VLR), authentication center (AUC), billing servers, operation and support systems (OSS), short message service centers (SMSC), and many other elements. The interface to the public switched telephony network (PSTN) and the packet data network (PDN) is from the MSC in the core network.

The subscriber profile and the services that the subscriber is allowed to access are inserted in the HLR. The HLR is also aware of the mobile station's current location. The BSC interfaces to the core network via the MSC. A single MSC can be serving more than one BSC. Mobility management as well as communication with the HLR, VLR, and authentication centers is done via mobility application protocols such as GSM MAP or IS-41. The core network elements are connected to each other via a signaling system 7 (SS7) network, which provides the transport for signaling messages. The MSC also provides call control and switching functionality. Supplementary services, such as three-way calling and call barring, are also supported by the MSC.

For data services the core network hosts the SMSC as well as modem pools for circuit switched data. The core network is also responsible for authenticating the subscribers before allowing access to the network or access to services. Figure 3–3 shows an example core network.

The Interworking Function (IWF) enables circuit-switched data services in wireless networks. It consists of a modem pool and interfaces to the packet data network such as an ISP. Circuit-switched data in GSM networks is explained in further detail in Chapter 4.

A network operations center (NOC) manages the RAN and the core. An operations support system (OSS) is an element of a telecommunications network that supports the daily operation of the infrastructure. The OSS includes network management equipment, which monitors the state of the network. It also includes billing systems that are responsible for capturing the network usage by subscribers. Call data records (CDRs), which are used to bill the

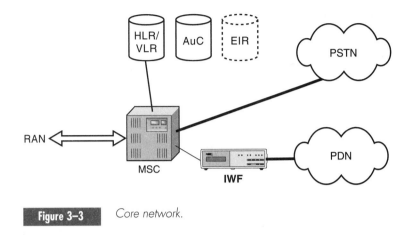

Figure 3–3   *Core network.*

subscriber, are generated based on information received from the MSC by the billing systems.

Core network functionality is an involved topic; for details, please refer to texts that discuss this in detail.

3.2.3   Multiple Access

Any scarce resource that is to be used simultaneously by more than one user needs to be divided into subportions in order to prevent interference in each user's usage of that resource. In telecommunications that resource is a transmission medium and is divided into channels in order to allow multiple users to access the same transmission medium simultaneously. This simultaneous use of channels is called multiple access. A channel can be defined as an individually assigned, dedicated pathway through a transmission medium for a single user's information. The physical medium of transmission, which in our case is the wireless spectrum, can be divided into individual channels based on a set of criteria. These criteria depend on the technology that is utilized to make the distinction between channels.

The three primary technologies used in wireless cellular communication in order to separate the user channels are

- Frequency division multiple access (FDMA)
- Time division multiple access (TDMA)
- Code division multiple access (CDMA)

Figure 3–4 uses the analogy of a room as a transmission resource to illustrate these technologies.

In FDMA, the channel is a specific frequency, and each user is assigned a different frequency for the duration of the call. In our room analogy, this is

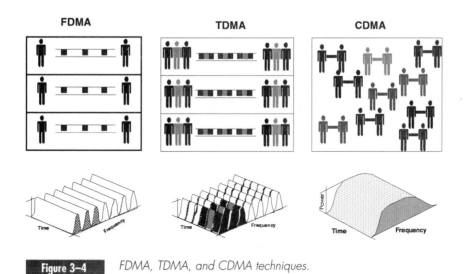

Figure 3–4   *FDMA, TDMA, and CDMA techniques.*

equivalent to partitioning the room and placing users who wish to communicate in each partition. However, due to human speech characteristics, a significant portion of the time that resource is not utilized. In other words, no information is being transmitted. This exclusive allocation results in poor resource utilization.

In TDMA, the channel is a time slot on a specific frequency, and each user is assigned a different time slot on a specific frequency. In our room analogy, this is equivalent to allowing more than one pair of uses who wish to communicate in each partition and limit the time a pair of users can communicate without interruption. Each pair then takes turns to communicate within their allocated time period and then waits till their next turn. In TDMA, this switching between users happens so quickly that the users never perceive that they are sharing their assigned frequency with others.

In CDMA, the channel is a unique code, and each user is assigned a different code. In the room analogy, this is equivalent to breaking down the partitions and allowing all users who wish to communicate to have a conversation simultaneously. However, there is a caveat; each one of these users has to use a different language and each user has highly evolved ears that can tune out conversations that are in a language other than the one that the user understands. Thus each pair of users is able to use the room simultaneously to have a conversation without interrupting other users.

3.2.4   Frequency Reuse

Cellular systems utilize the concept of frequency reuse to provide higher capacity. The core concept of cellular systems is to reuse the same frequency in a network many times over. The ability to reuse the same radio frequency many times is a result of managing the carrier to interference signal levels (C/I). A specific radio frequency is transmitted from one base station at a power level that supports communication within a moderate cell radius. Since the power limit is controlled to serve a limited range, the same frequency can be transmitted simultaneously or reused by another base station as long as there is no interference between it and any other base station using the same frequency.

Several frequency reuse patterns are currently in use in the cellular industry. Each has its own pros and cons. The most commonly used patterns in cellular are the $N = 4$ and $N = 7$ patterns. The frequency repeat pattern determines the maximum number of radios that can be assigned to a single cell site. The $N = 4$ pattern can deploy cell sites with six sectors, whereas the $N = 7$ pattern uses a three-sector cell. Figure 3–5 shows the $N = 7$ pattern reuse.

3.2.5   Speech and Channel Coding

Speech coding is critical to digital transmission systems, and the main use for speech coding has been in wireless networks. The wireline network uses digital pulse code modulation (PCM) at 64 Kbps for voice transmission. Speech synthesis systems such as linear predictive coding (LPC) predict the current sample from a linear combination of past samples. At the expense of poor tone quality, they do achieve high efficiency. The adaptive differential PCM (ADPCM) technique is an alternate method of predicting a speech waveform from past samples.

Another class of speech coding is via algorithms termed vocoders. Vocoders are relatively complex systems and operate at low bit rates (normally 2.4 Kbps). Residual excited linear coding (RELP) is a hybrid coding

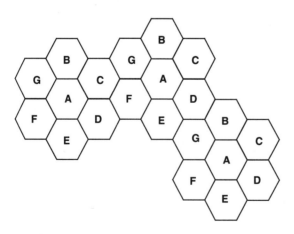

Figure 3–5   *N = 7 frequency reuse pattern.*

scheme for wireline quality speech with a few integrated digital speech processors. CDMA uses a variation of RELP called code-excited linear prediction (CELP). The GSM speech coding scheme is based on regular pulse excitation–long-term prediction (RPE–LTP) at 13 Kbps. Enhanced variable-rate codec (EVRC) is yet another coding scheme that has higher voice quality.

Channel coding is a technique that aims to improve transmission quality when the signal encounters disturbances for reasons such as noise when the reception level is low, intereference, and multipath propogation. The side effect of this is that there is an increase in the number of bits transmitted to compensate for errors. Coding consists of adding some redundant data, which is calculated from the source information. The decoding function makes use of this redundancy to detect the presence of errors or estimate the most probable emitted bits given the received ones.

Channel coding can be classified into block codes and convolutional codes. The codes used in GSM are block convolutional codes; a fire code, which is a conventional linear binary block code; and parity codes, which are linear block codes. CDMA IS-95 systems use convolutional code based on the Viterbi algorithm.

3.2.6   Mobility

Mobility is one of the key factors of wireless networks. It allows users freedom of movement. Depending on the radio technology, mobility can be either limited to pedestrian speeds only or can support communication even at speeds up to 120 Kmph. However, mobility places a few requirements on the network:

- They must have the ability to locate subscribers.
- They must monitor the movement of the subscribers.
- They must enable handoffs seamlessly as the user moves across cells while sessions are kept alive.

The two key concepts of mobility are roaming and handovers.

Roaming can be defined as the movement of the mobile terminal from one network to another. Network operators have coverage that is either limited in scope or is limited to a country. In order to support global mobility, network operators agree to allow subscribers from other networks to roam into their networks and access services. Roaming agreements between operators enable subscribers to roam on a global basis while being reachable all the time.

Handover is the process of switching a call or session that is in progress from one physical channel to another. Handovers can be classified into intra-cell and intercell. Intracell handover is the transfer of a call in progress from a channel in one cell to another channel in the same cell. Intercell handover is the transfer of the call or session to another cell.

CDMA systems are considered as make-before-break systems since the characteristics of spread spectrum allow the system to be connected simultaneously to two or more base stations. In contrast, TDMA systems from a handover perspective are termed break-before-make networks. CDMA also classifies handoffs into soft handoffs, softer handoffs, and hard handoffs.

3.3   First-Generation Mobile Networks

3.3.1   AMPS

First-generation mobile networks are analog systems. Some of the more widely deployed first-generation networks include AMPS and NMT. In this section we focus the discussion on AMPS.

The Advanced Mobile Phone Service (AMPS) is in wide use even today, almost 25 years after it was introduced. AMPS was conceived by Bell Labs in the 1970s, and improvements in the form of digital AMPS (D-AMPS) were made in the late 1980s. The AMPS air interface is specified in EIA/TIA-553. AMPS is based on FDMA.

The FCC allocated a total of 50 MHz (25 MHz on the A side and B side) in the 800-MHz spectrum for AMPS. Each voice channel is allocated a 30-KHz portion of the bandwidth within the AMPS frequency allocations. Because each carrier has 25 MHz of spectrum, this provides a total of 832 (25 MHz/30 KHz) cellular channels (forward and reverse). However, since the same frequency cannot be used in adjacent cells, the 416 duplex channels are a theoretical maximum (actual number of valid voice channels equals 312). AMPS uses the seven-cell frequency reuse method. Control channels are used to set up and clear calls as well as other control messages. Each band (25 MHz) contains 21 control channels. When a mobile station is not in session, it must monitor designated control channels. It tunes and locks into the strongest channel to receive system information. The forward control channel (FOCC) is a data stream from the base station to the mobile, and the reverse control channel (RECC) is from the mobile to the base station. Voice conversation is carried over the forward voice channel (FVC) and the reverse voice channel (RVC).

The identifiers used in AMPS are as follows:

- The mobile station's electronic serial number (ESN)
- The mobile operator's system identification (SID)
- The mobile station's mobile identification number (MIN)

The ESN for a mobile is a 32-bit number that uniquely identifies a mobile and is set up by the mobile manufacturer. System IDs (SIDs) are 15-bit binary numbers that are assigned to cellular systems. One of the uses of the SID is to determine a home network from a roaming network. The MIN is a 34-bit number that is derived from the mobile terminal's 10-digit telephone number.

The network utilizes the IS-41 protocol for mobility and authentication procedures. The MSC provides the capability for call processing, and the HLR and VLRs keep track of the mobile as it moves. The mobile terminal is responsible for updating its location as it moves in the cellular network.

Data services in AMPS are straightforward and analogous to dial-up networking. Because AMPS is an analog technology, it is possible to make use of standard modems directly with AMPS. Data rates are at a maximum of 14.4 Kbps irrespective of the modem protocol (v.90 or others).

3.3.2   D-AMPS

D-AMPS, or digital AMPS, is a hybrid air interface that uses both first-generation and second-generation technology. The D-AMPS specification is detailed in IS-54-B. The primary reason for introducing D-AMPS in the early 1990s in North America was to overcome some of the shortcomings of AMPS technology. The co-channel interference problem of AMPS limited its capacity significantly, and the 30-KHz channel assigned to each user is excess capacity on a per user basis. The hybrid nature of D-AMPS comes from the fact that second-generation TDMA technology is placed on AMPS traffic channels.

The AMPS channels are still used, but the content and formats of the 30-KHz channels are modified. The channels defined for D-AMPS are as follows:

* FOCC—Forward analog control channel; direction: base station (BS) to mobile station (MS) control channel
* FVC—Forward voice channel; direction: BS to MS voice channel
* FDTC—Forward digital traffic channel; direction: BS to MS digital user and control channel
* RECC—Reverse analog control channel; direction: MS to BS control channel
* RVC—Reverse analog voice channel; direction: MS to BS voice channel
* RDTC—Reverse digital traffic channel; direction: MS to BS digital user and control channel

The FDTC and RDTC can be split up into fast associated control channel (FACCH) and slow associated control channel (SACCH), which are used for signaling. One of the improvements that was made in the handoff process was the involvement of the mobile in the handoff procedure. Mobile assisted handoff was introduced in D-AMPS. The MS keeps measuring the quality of the forward channel and sends these measurements to the BS to allow the network to make a more informed decision.

First-generation AMPS and D-AMPS mobile networks continue to exist even today, especially in the United States. They complement coverage of second-generation digital networks such as GSM and IS-95. Most mobile terminals are dual mode (i.e., they incorporate a second-generation (2G) digital radio as well as the analog radio). With roaming agreements in place, 2G network operators can claim nationwide coverage. However, it is expected that the lifetime of these analog networks is coming to an end and will be decommisioned slowly in the next few years. One of the reasons for decommissioning these networks is to reclaim the spectrum for other uses.

3.4   Second-Generation Mobile Networks

Second-generation mobile networks are a step up in technology evolution. 2G networks, as they are commonly refered to, are digital networks. There are several 2G technologies that have been deployed across the world. The most widespread deployment is, of course, the TDMA-based GSM system and the CDMA-based IS-95 system. Other 2G technologies that have been deployed include DECT (Digital European Cordless Telephone), IS-136, and the PDC-based personal handyphone system (PHS) in Japan.

The following sections will take a closer look at the GSM and CDMA networks and technology.

3.4.1   GSM (Global System for Mobile Communication)

GSM is a TDMA-based wireless communications system. Work on the GSM specifications started in the 1980s in Europe as a result of the capacity limits being experienced by analog networks such as NMT.

The GSM 900 system uses two 25-MHz bands for the uplink and downlink, and within this spectrum 200-KHz channels are allocated. The uplink and downlink are separated by a 45-MHz spacing. GSM 1800 uses two 75-MHz bands for the uplink and downlink. Again 200-KHz channels are allocated within those bands and are separated by a 95-MHz spacing. The 1900-MHz systems use two 60-MHz bands for the uplink and downlink using 200-MHz channels within those bands and separated by 80-MHz spacing.

STANDARDS

Europe felt the need for a common mobile telephony standard since different countries had differing analog networks, and as a result roaming of subscribers between these networks was not possible. CEPT (Conference Euro-

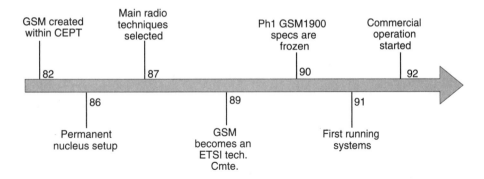

Figure 3–6   *GSM standards timeline.*

pean des Postes et Telecommunications) is a standardization arena in Europe. A new group called GSM (Groupe Special Mobile) was formed within CEPT in 1982 whose task was to specify a unique radio communication system for Europe at 900 MHz. The timeline in Figure 3–6 shows the progress and implementation of the GSM standard.

GSM TOPOLOGY

The topology and network architecture of GSM is shown in Figure 3–7.

The mobile station (MS) is the terminal (phone, PDA mobile unit) provided to the subscriber. It is essentially a GSM two-way radio that conforms to the air interface specifications.

The base station subsystem is functionally subdivided into the base station controller (BSC) and the base transceiver station (BTS). A single BSC normally controls a large number of BTSs. BTSs contain the radio equipment and

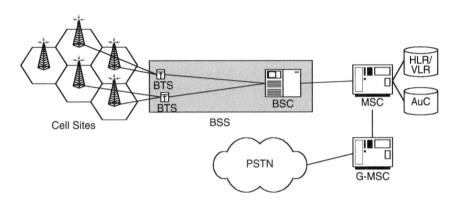

Figure 3–7   *GSM network architecture.*

are connected to cell site antennas. The BTS is essentially a layer two bridge if viewed from a high-level perspective. It provides an entry point for the subscribers who are present in the cell, allowing them to make or receive calls. Some of the base station functions are radio transmission in GSM format, use of frequency hopping techniques, coding and decoding of radio channels, and measurement of quality and received power on traffic channels.

The BSC is a much more complex system. It is responsible for managing the radio resources in the network as well as control handovers. So the BSC has functionality of mobility management, radio resource management, call control, management of intercell handovers, and other housekeeping tasks.

The mobile switching center (MSC) is the centrallized controller of the network. The MSC is a switch that provides call control capability. It also interfaces to the PSTN. An MSC that interfaces to the PSTN is called a gateway MSC (GMSC). The MSC also is responsible for tracking the user as he or she moves between networks. So it plays a role in mobility management as well.

GSM uses two databases, called the home location register (HLR) and the visitor location register (VLR). The HLR contains the subscriber's profile information (which is static) as well as the current location of the subscriber (i.e., it knows the reachability information of the subscriber). The VLR stores the current location or point of attachment to the network and the state of the mobile terminal. For mobile terminated calls, the HLR is the initial signaling contact point in the mobile network, whereas the VLR is the initial signaling contact when the call originates from the mobile.

The authentication center (AuC) is a database that stores confidential information, such as keys associated with valid subscribers. The AuC is responsible for authenticating a subscriber. When subscribers attach to the network, the network performs an authentication procedure for the subscriber. The keys associated with the subscriber are utilized in conconjunction with an algorithm to validate the authenticity. The secret key associated with the subscriber is stored on the subscriber identity module (SIM).

INTERFACES

Four main interfaces are defined in GSM networks:

- Um Interface—Between the MS and the BTS
- Abis Interface—Between the BTS and the BSC
- A Interface—Between the BSC and the MSC
- MAP-x—Between the MSCs as well as between MSC and HLR/VLR/AuC.

The Um interface uses a combination of FDMA and TDMA access techniques. One hundred twenty-four full-duplex channel pairs are defined that operate with different carrier frequencies. Each of these FDM channels uses TDMA slots.

The Abis interface connects the BTSs with a BSC. The Abis interface has normally been implemented as a proprietary interface. The physical layer is defined by a 2-Mbps PCM link, and the datalink uses LAPD.

The A interface is an open interface that connects the radio access network (RAN) to the core network. The A interface links multiple BSCs to an MSC. It is the open nature of this interface that makes it possible to connect equipment made by different vendors. The A interface functions include call control and mobility signaling.

THE SUBSCRIBER IDENTITY MODULE

The SIM is a personalized part of the mobile station and operates along with a memory card. The SIM identifies the subscriber. The mobile station is simply a piece of radio equipment and becomes associated with a subscriber only as a result of the SIM being inserted into the terminal. The SIM provides the security needs of the operator and the subscriber.

With the SIM concept, a subscriber is not tied to any specific mobile terminal. A subscriber can use different terminals. As far as the network operator is concerned, a subscriber is identified by the SIM. It identifies the account owner and can be modified or subscription options changed. The key functionalities afforded by SIM are subscriber authentication, secure location for secret keys at the subscriber end, processing capability for executing the authentication, and ciphering algorithms.

MOBILE APPLICATION PART

MAP is a protocol used in GSM core networks on various interfaces. MAP can be denoted as MAP-x, where x can determines the interface. The interfaces where MAP is used are shown in Table 3–1. Functionalities associated with each of these interfaces are defined in the specifications for MAP in GSM 09.02.

Table 3–1   *MAP Interfaces*

Network Elements Connected	Map-x
MSC-VLR	MAP-B
MSC-HLR	MAP-C
HLR-VLR	MAP-D
MSC-MSC	MAP-E
MSC-EIR	MAP-F
VLR-VLR	MAP-G
AuC-HLR	MAP-H

3.4.2   CDMA IS-95

CDMA is a relatively new technology in the mobile cellular industry. Commercial networks were first deployed in the mid-1990s. However, they are growing rapidly and they account for about 25% of the wireless networks globally.

The CDMA standard referred to as IS-95 is specified by TIA/EIA.

SPREAD SPECTRUM

The wireless spectrum is a scarce resource, with tight regulations in terms of usage and power radiated along with licenses required to operate. This is true for most of the wireless systems in place. Interference is an issue that wireless networks must contend with.

Spread spectrum is one of the techniques employed that inherently is less sensitive to interference. Spread spectrum techniques typically use more bandwidth than necessary to transmit and receive bits.

Spread spectrum techniques inherently offer more privacy than narrowband techniques, as they are more difficult to intercept or spy on. They use a code, which is known only to the transmitter and the receiver. Spread spectrum techniques can also coexist with other technologies as the transmitter and receiver can obtain information as long as they are decoding with the same code.

Frequency Hopping Spread Spectrum (FHSS)

Frequency hopping is one of the spread spectrum techniques used in the IEEE 802.11 standard. This is one of the transmission mechanisms of the physical layer. The technique involves the breakup of a wide band of frequency into smaller bands. Then the transmitter "hops" in each of the smaller bands, in a predetermined pattern. The receiver knows this hopping sequence and can lock on to the frequency to receive information. The transmitter and the receiver constantly change patterns using the agreed-on hop sequence; thus, interference is avoided as the transmitter and receiver keep hopping around the smaller bands of frequency over a wide range of frequencies. Interference from narrowband applications (such as garage door openers) will occur only in a specific band for a certain period of time.

The 2.4-GHz frequency spectrum that is available for use is divided into several 1-MHz frequency bands. The transmitter and receiver hop from one 1-MHz frequency band to another, in a near-random sequence. The transmitter will send data in each of the 1-MHz frequency bands, and if the receiver is locked onto the appropriate 1-MHz band, it should be able to receive the information from the transmitter.

The amount of time spent by the transmitter or the receiver in a 1-MHz band is referred to as the dwell time. Typically, any narrowband interference is limited to the dwell time in each band.

Direct Sequence Spread Spectrum

In DSSS the transmitter and the receiver agree on a digital code. The transmitter takes the typically narrowband input signal and spreads or transforms it into wideband by applying the selected code. Each input bit is replaced by the code, resulting in wideband. The receiver applies the same digital code to the received signal and, when properly synchronized, retrieves the input bits transmitted.

DSSS systems are complex to build and provide inherent security due to the transformations performed (i.e., codes used). They have the ability to provide higher data rates when compared to FHSS systems, as most of the FHSS systems are required to use around 1-MHz of bandwidth at any time. In the IEEE 802.11 DSSS system, an 11-bit code called a Barker sequence is used to transform the original data bits. The resulting transformed bits are modulated to send over a carrier frequency using one of two modulation techniques: differential binary phase shift keying (DBPSK) or differential quadrature phase shift keying (DQPSK).

There are two popular spread spectrum techniques. The first is frequency hopping spread spectrum (FHSS), where the transmitter and the receiver hop in a predetermined sequence through a wide band of frequencies.

The second technique is direct sequence spread spectrum (DSSS), a mechanism in which data bits are transformed by codes, which in turn occupy a wide band of frequencies. This technique is already in use in public wireless networks such as IS-95 (or CDMA, as it is popularly known). DSSS is a technique wherein the carrier is modulated by a digital code in which the code bit rate is much larger than the information signal bit rate.

The DSSS system is a wideband system in which the entire bandwidth of the system is available to the user. The user data is spread using a spreading signal refered to as the code signal. The code signal or the spreading signal has a much higher data rate than the user data rates; for example, the 1.2288 MCPS in CDMA vs. user data rates that are much lower. At the receiving end, despreading is accomplished by the cross corelation of the signal with a synchronized replica of the same signal used to spread the data. In CDMA systems pseduorandom noise (PN) sequences are used to spread the bandwidth and distinguish among various users' signals. PN sequences, as the name suggests, are not random but rather deterministic.

ARCHITECTURE AND CHANNELS

The CDMA architecture is based on the reference model from the cellular standards group TR-45. Structure of the standards organization is discussed in Chapter 16. The main elements of the reference architecture are as follows:

- *Base station*—The base station is the BSS equivalent in GSM networks. The BS consists of the BTS and the BSC. The functionality of the BTS and BSC is similar to the functionality of these elements as described in "GSM Topology" (p. 53).

* *Mobile station*—The mobile station is the terminal that is a transmitter and receiver.
* *Mobile switching center* (MSC)—The MSC is the switch that provides call control functionality, mobility, and the trunking interface to the PSTN.
* *Home location register* (HLR)—The HLR is attached to an MSC and maintains the subscriber's profile information as well as the current location of the user in the network from an attachment perspective.
* *Vistied location register* (VLR)—The VLR is attached to an MSC and stores the subscriber information that is obtained from the HLR on a dynamic basis or as long as the user remains within the area served by that MSC.
* *Authentication center* (AC)—The AC is responsible for maintaining the keys associated with a subscriber and performs authentication of subscribers when they register with the network.
* *Operations support, billing systems, interworking function*—Other elements that have the same functionality as described in Section 3.2.2.

IS-95 channels can be segmented into physical channels and logical channels:

* *Physical channels*—Physical channels are defined in terms of an RF frequency and a code sequence. There are 64 Walsh codes available for the forward link (BS-MS) providing 64 logical channels. On the reverse link channels are identified by long PN code sequences. In IS-95, CDMA carrier band center frequencies are denoted by AMPS channel numbers. One CDMA carrier requires 41 30-KHz AMPS channels to provide a CDMA carrier bandwidth of 1.23 MHz. The 1.23-MHz bandwidth of a CDMA carrier makes the minimum center frequency separation between two carriers at 1.23 MHz.
* *Logical channels*—Logical channels can be further subdivided into control and traffic channels. The control channels and traffic channels in IS-95 are as follows:
  Pilot channel (downlink)—The pilot channel is transmitted continuously by the base station on each CDMA frequency and is used to provide a reference to all mobile stations.
  Paging channel (downlink)—The paging channel is used to transmit control information to the mobile station. In order to terminate a call, the network pages the mobiles in an area on the paging channel.
  Sync channel (downlink)—The sync channel is used along with the pilot channel to acquire initial time synchronization.

Access channel (uplink)—The access channel is used by the mobile to transmit control information to the base station. Many messages can be carried on the access channel. When a mobile originates a call, it uses the access channel to inform the base station. This channel is also used to respond to a page.

Forward traffic channels—These channels are grouped into rate sets. Rate sets identify the voice coding scheme that can be used on any channel.

Reverse traffic channels—User traffic on the reverse channel is identified by a user-specific long code sequence based on the user's ESN.

INTERFACES

IS-95 uses the following interfaces:

* *A Interface (BSC-MSC)*—This interface is between the BSC and the MSC. It supports both the control plane and user plane.
* *Abis Intreface (BTS-BSC)*—This is the interface between the BSC and the BTS. This is an internal interface and generally proprietary.
* *B Interface (MSC-VLR)*—This interface is defined in TIA IS-41.
* *C Interface (MSC-HLR)*—This interface uses IS-41 messaging as well.
* *D Interface (HLR-VLR)*—HLR-VLR signaling is based on IS-41 as well. It sits on top of SS7.
* *E Interface (MSC-MSC)*—Inter MSC signaling is defined in IS-41.
* *H Interface (HLR-AC)*—The interface that is used for authenticating a subscriber is defined in IS-124.
* *L Interface (MSC-IWF)*—This interface allows the ability for circuit switched data in second generation networks.
* *Um Interface (BS-MS)*—This is the air interface between the mobile and the network.

IS-41

IS-41 is standardized by the Telecommunications Industry Association (TIA). Revision C is the latest version of the protocol and is called IS-41C. IS-41 is the core networking protocol that supports mobility, authentication, and roaming. IS-41 allows network equipment to be multivendor. Since the equipment has to conform to the standard interface, it is possible to have an environment wherein MSCs are from vendor A and the BSC/radio network is from vendor B.

IS-41C is an application-layer protocol. IS-41 normally is operated over SS7 networks, which provide the reliability required for signaling.

Roaming between networks that use GSM MAP and IS-41 requires the use of gateway functions that convert messages from one protocol to another. Such gateways can be considered protocol translators.

3.4.3   GPRS (2.5G Network)

General Packet Radio Service (GPRS) is an enhancement to GSM networks with support for packet radio. GPRS overlays a packet-based air interface on the existing circuit switched network. It also introduces a packet core aspect primarily for data applications. Packet switching allows radio resources to be shared efficiently by a large number of users since radio resources are allocated if there are data to send or receive. GPRS network architecture as well as the enhancements to the air interface are covered in Chapter 8.

3.5   Third-Generation Mobile Networks

The development of third-generation (3G) mobile systems began when the World Administrative Radio Conference (WARC) at its 1992 meeting identified the frequencies around 2 GHz that were available. ITU (International Telecommunications Union) has recommended several different air interfaces for third-generation systems, based on either CDMA or TDMA technology. The IMT-2000 standards that define 3G air interfaces are as follows:

*   *WCDMA*—Wideband code division multiple access will be deployed in the Europe and Asia in the 2-GHz frequency spectrum.
*   *EDGE*—Enhanced data rates for GSM evolution improves the spectral efficiency of the existing GSM frequencies.
*   *1XRTT or cdma2000*—This is a multicarrier CDMA system that is designed to be deployed in the same frequency band as IS-95.

The Universal Mobile Telephony System (UMTS) is a third-generation mobile system. Standardization of UMTS has been done in the third-generation partnership project (3GPP) organization. UMTS is the evolution of second-generation GSM systems. The biggest change from second-generation to third-generation systems is that 3G systems will offer support for packet data services. 3G networks are expected to become extensions of the Internet and thereby enable the creation of the wireless Internet. With support for packet data built into the air interface as well as the core network, new types of applications and services for the mobile industry are expected to be developed. 3GPP2 is equivalent to the 3GPP organization and has developed an architecture based around cdma2000.

Third-generation mobile networks are in the process of being deployed now. Operators in Korea and Japan have taken the lead with these deployments. In the United States, cdma2000-based networks are now operational. Docomo in Japan is the first network operator to deploy WCDMA in a network known as FOMA (Freedom of Mobile Multimedia Access).

Descriptions of cdma2000 and UMTS networks are covered in Chapters 9 and 10.

3.6　Summary

This chapter provided a brief introduction to wireless networks and technology. Wireless networks today are primarily based on either TDMA or CDMA technology. Second-generation networks support voice as the main application. However, in recent years, the use of SMS has taken off on a large scale and hence SMS as a data service is becoming synonymous with these networks. It is expected that third-generation networks will offer even greater bandwidth for data applications. While third-generation networks will enhance the capacity for carrying voice, they will also be driven by the need and support for data applications.

3.7　References

Black, U., *Second-Generation Mobile and Wireless Networks,* Prentice Hall.

Garg, V. K., *IS-95 CDMA and cdma2000,* Prentice Hall.

Held, G., *Data over Wireless Networks,* Osborne.

Mouly, M. and Pautet, M-B., *The GSM System for Mobile Communication,* Cell and Sys.

Nokia, *MITA Mobile Internet Technical Architecture,* IT Press.

Tisal, J., *The GSM Network,* Wiley.

Data in GSM Networks

The Global System for Mobile Communication (GSM) is a multi-service cellular network. It provides not only voice service, but a good set of data services as well. This chapter describes the data services offered by a GSM network. It describes the data services before the advent of GPRS and EDGE.

The GSM data services can be categorized in terms of traffic, signaling, and broadcast channel data services. The GSM standard specifies data services on the traffic channel (TCH), which can be utilized by data applications such as fax and Internet service provider (ISP) connection. This is also referred to as circuit switched (CS) data service. The data service on a signaling channel is known as the point-to-point short message service (SMS). Using SMS, a subscriber sends or receives a short string of text (maximum 126 characters) using a signaling channel. There is another type of SMS service called SMS broadcast, which is the only broadcast channel data service. This service transports data on a specially defined broadcast channel to all the subscribers in a cell. The broadcast data applications, such as traffic reports and weather alerts, were anticipated to use this service, but it didn't get much attention in deployment from cellular service providers.

4.1   Architecture Description

Before discussing the details of GSM data services, let's first consider an overview of a GSM network for providing TCH data service. A GSM network consists of several main network elements (Figure 4–1).

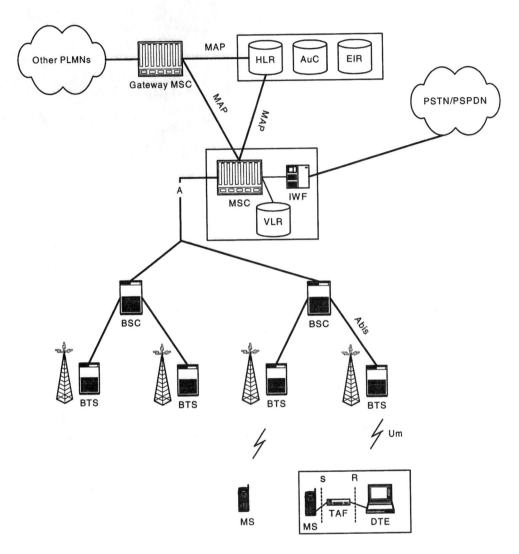

Figure 4-1   *GSM network architecture.*

Home location register: The HLR is a central database for a public land mobile network (PLMN) to store subscription information of users. It keeps information about service profile, location, and activity status of a subscriber. HLR is connected to MSCs and VLRs using GSM MAP protocol.

Mobile switching center: The MSC performs the telephony switching function of the system. It does call control to and from other telephony and data network elements. It also captures billing information from a call. The MSC is connected to the BSS using the A interface protocol.

The Gateway MSC is a gateway to a PLMN and provides call routing to/from other PLMNs and PSTNs.

Visitor location register: The VLR contains subscriber information, which is needed in servicing a roaming MS in a visited network. Although specified as a separate entity, VLR is usually integrated into MSC. When an MS roams into a visited network, its information is transferred from the HLR to the VLR using the location update procedure.

Authentication center: The AuC provides authentication parameters to verify the user's access. It also provides encryption parameters for ciphering over the air interface.

Equipment identification register: The EIR is a database that contains information for preventing calls from stolen, unauthorized mobile stations (MSs). The database maintains this information based on the equipment identifier, IMEI.

Base station controller: The BSC controls a set of BTSs. It provides cellular specific functions, like handover power control.

Base transceiver station: The BTS handles the radio interface. The BTS is connected to the BSC using the Abis interface.

Interworking function: The IWF provides a mechanism for transferring digital data signals from the GSM PLMN to the other type of network (e.g., PSTN, ISDN, or PSPDN). The interworking function also performs any protocol conversion between the two dissimilar networks.

Mobile station: A mobile station has GSM-specified call control, mobility management, and radio interface. It is connected to the network using air interface (Um). As GSM data user equipment, an MS is a logical function complemented by the terminal adaptation function (TAF) and sometimes data terminal equipment (DTE).

Terminal adaptation function: The TAF is used to adapt terminal equipment to connect to an MS. In Figure 4–1, an ISDN DTE is shown that is connected to TAF via an ISDN R interface. The TAF is connected to an MS via an ISDN S interface.

Data terminal equipment: DTE is regular data terminal equipment as used in fixed networks. The DTE, TAF, and MS are all logical functions of user equipment and can be integrated as one device.

4.2   Traffic Channel Data Services

The basic idea in providing TCH data service is to provide a CS conduit for carrying data from the user through the GSM PLMN and vice versa. The conduits are composed of CS bearers in the network and the TCH over the air interface.

The data path establishment procedure is very similar to the voice path establishment. There is also an IWF with the MSC, which serves as a gateway between data signals in the GSM PLMN and other networks, such as PSTN (public switched telephone network) and PSPDN (public switched packet data network). With a TCH-Full rate (TCH/F), the maximum effective data rate possible is 9.6 Kbps. With a TCH-Half rate (TCH/H), the maximum data rate is 4.8 Kbps. The GSM PLMN also provides high-speed circuit switched data (HSCSD), which combines multiple TCH/Fs and can provide a maximum data rate of 56 Kbps.

GSM provides transparent and nontransparent connection for the TCH data services. In the transparent connection, the data services see the path between the IWF and terminal as a constant rate conduit. The GSM PLMN doesn't intercept the data protocol and the data traffic. The radio interface doesn't do any extra processing to safeguard the data from errors. The transparent connection is usually suited for constant rate and fixed delay applications.

In the nontransparent connection, the data protocol and the traffic are intercepted in the GSM PLMN. The data are intercepted to provide reliable transport over the low-bandwidth and error-prone radio link. The GSM specifications have defined link-layer protocols, L2R and RLP, for this purpose. Example applications for nontransparent connections are X.25 LAP-B and character-mode protocols like X.28.

For carrying data through a GSM PLMN, a set of services is defined. These services, called bearer services and teleservices, allow different types of data applications to carry data through the GSM PLMN. We will discuss these services in the next section. The GSM PLMN also interconnects with ISDN, CSPDN, and PSPDN for transparent/nontransparent data services using an IWF. The GSM PLMN performs a set of functions so the data can be carried between the IWF and mobile terminal. These functions are mainly to adapt the data to the circuit switch nature of the transport and the radio nature of the air interface. In this section we will also review those functions.

4.2.1   GSM Bearer Services and Teleservices

A bearer service is subscribed to individually by a GSM subscriber. It is stored as part of the subscriber profile in the HLR/VLR. The GSM PLMN uses the bearer services to provision the capability of transmission of data between two access points (Figure 4–2). It is a network transmission property and is not visible to the end terminal. The service, that is visible to the terminal is called teleservices. The teleservices are complete end-to-end services, including terminal capabilities. For example, Teletex is a teleservice, and a subscriber can use data, circuit duplex, and synchronous as bearer services to carry Teletex through the PLMN. Some teleservices may not have a bearer service (e.g., SMS). This is because there is no need to establish bearers for this service. The GSM bearer services are defined in GSM TS 02.02. The GSM

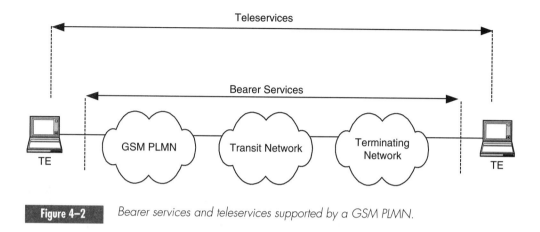

Figure 4–2   *Bearer services and teleservices supported by a GSM PLMN.*

teleservices are defined in GSM TS 02.03. A user can only subscribe to a bearer service and use it for a data application (e.g., IP). In this case, the data application is transparent to the GSM PLMN.

Some examples of teleservices are telephony and emergency call. As the teleservices are subscriber visible and commonly understood, we do not discuss them in detail. Readers can refer to GSM TS 02.03 for further details.

Bearer services are described by a set of attributes. These attributes are described in detail in GSM 02.01. In this book we will try to give a concept of bearer services by discussing a few of the important attributes. An example of a bearer attribute is symmetry; a possible value of symmetry is bidirectional symmetrical transmission. This attribute is mentioned by the user when the same transmission capability is desired in both uplink and downlink directions. In general, the bearer services attributes can be grouped into four categories:

1. **Information transfer attributes:** This category characterizes the network capabilities for transferring information from a user access point in a GSM PLMN to the IWF. This attribute tells whether the data is carried through direct digital transmission or through some analog modem. We will discuss this category in a little more detail.

2. **Access attributes:** This category describes the means for accessing network functions or facilities as seen at the access point in the PLMN. An example in this category is the symmetry attribute.

3. **Interworking attributes:** This category describes the properties of the transit network between the terminating network and the access GSM PLMN. This is an empty set of attributes. The specifications have only defined this category and have not defined any attribute under this category.

4. **General attributes:** This category deals with the bearer services in general. Example attributes under this set are supplementary services provided, such as QoS (quality of service).

Figure 4–3 shows the field of applicability of the preceding attribute categories.

The bearer service category that we use frequently in this chapter is the information transfer category. The following are the bearer services under this category.

- **Unrestricted digital information (UDI):** Unlike the analog modem, where the data is converted to an analog signal and then back to digital again after the modem. UDI is a direct digital transmission into a digital network. This is the bearer service to use when an ISP has a dedicated line to the GSM PLMN.
- **3.1 kHz (external to the PLMN):** This is used to select a modem at the interworking function, which resides at the MSC. This service category is used when interworking with the ISDN or PSTN. "External to the PLMN" indicates that the 3.1-kHz audio service is only used outside of the PLMN, in the ISDN/PSTN. The connection within the PLMN, the user access point to the interworking function, is a UDI connection. This bearer service is used when an ISP is connected to a pool of modem in the IWF.
- **Packet assembler and disassembler (PAD):** This enables PLMN subscribers to access a packet network (PSPDN/ISDN). This service provides an asynchronous connection to a PAD. We define PAD and its use in Section 4.2.5.

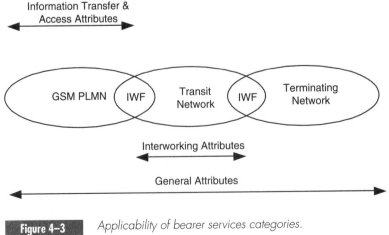

Applicability of bearer services categories.

- **Packet:** This service provides a synchronous connection that enables PLMN subscribers to access a packet network (PSPDN/ISDN).

4.2.2   Rate Adaptation Function

In the GSM PLMN, data traffic goes through different interfaces, and these interfaces support different data rates. For example, air interface supports up to 12.0 Kbps, and A interface supports up to 64 Kbps. Rate adaptation (RA) provides data transmission speed adaptation for different interfaces. For instance, if we hook up a terminal that sends data at 64 Kbps, then for the air interface the RA function will down-convert the data rate to 12 Kbps. For the A interface, the RA function will up-convert the data to 64 Kbps.

The GSM specifications have adapted the RA function from ITU-T V.110, and the details can be found in GSM TS 04.21. The RA functions are described next.

RA0

RA0 is used for converting incoming asynchronous data from the TE to synchronous data and vice versa. The synchronous transmission is needed because of the circuit switch nature of the air interface and the PLMN. The asynchronous data is padded to fit the same or next higher synchronous rate. The nearest higher synchronous rate is defined by 2 to the power n (where $n \leq 6$) times 600 bit/s.

RA1

RA1 is the intermediate rate adaptation function, which turns either the output of the RA0 function or a synchronous user data stream into a data stream at 8, 16, or 32 Kbit/s by bit repetition and frame addition. The resulting data frames also contain control and frame synchronization bits.

RA2

RA2 converts intermediate rates of 8 and 16 Kbps to 64 Kbit/s. This is the final conversion rate. The resulting data can be carried to the terminal equipment or to the A interface. RA2 is usually performed by multiplexing several 8 or 16 Kbps streams.

RA1′

RA1′ transforms data rates from the synchronous user data stream or the output of the RA0 to rates supported on the air interface while adding some control bits. The synchronous data rates of $\leq$2.4, 4.8, and 9.6 become 3.6, 6, and 12 Kbps. The output from RA1′ is used for forward error correction (FEC) on the air interface. FEC allows the receiving end to correct a radio block that contains fewer than a predetermined number of symbols in error.

Figure 4–4 illustrates how the different rate adaptations work together for carrying data traffic.

Figure 4–4 shows the rate adaptation for some transparent data connections. The first case is a DTE supporting the ISDN S interface. The mobile terminal will first apply RA2 to reduce the data rate from 64 to 8 or 16 Kbps, and then apply RA1/RA1′ to reduce the data rate to 6/12. The BSS performs the reverse change, so the user data rate can come back to 64 Kbps for A-interface transmission. In the second case, a synchronous DTE is rate adapted with RA1′ to 3.6, 6, or 12 Kbps. The BSS applies the RA1′/RA1 function to transform the data to the intermediate rate of 8 or 16 Kbps. The RA2 function is used to adapt the data rate for the A interface. The third case of asynchronous DTE is very similar to the second case, except that the RA0 is used to convert asynchronous transmission to synchronous transmission.

Nontransparent data makes use of the RLP function (Figure 4–5). For the first case, RA2 is used to reduce the data rate to 8 or 16 Kbps, and then RA1 is used to reduce the rate to 4.8 or 9.6 Kbps. The choice between 4.8 Kbps or 9.6 Kbps depends on the channel rate that is to be used, which in turn is set by the bearer service. The RLP always uses the highest available rate. For TCH/H the data will be downconverted to 4.8 Kbps, and for TCH/F the data will be downconverted to 9.6 Kbps. The output of RLP is adapted to

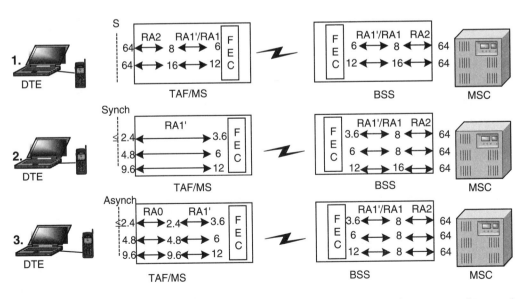

Figure 4–4   *RA examples for transparent data. Reprinted with permission from GSM and Personal Communications Handbook, by Redl, Weber, and Oliphant. Norwood, MA: Artech House Publishing, 1998. (www.artechhouse.com)*

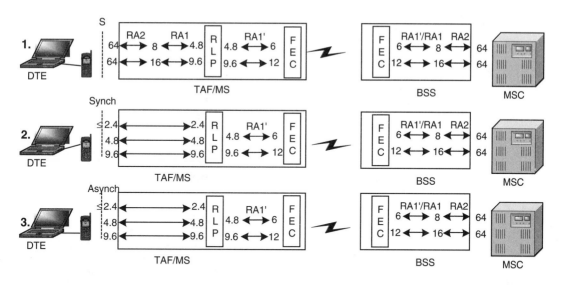

Figure 4–5 *RA examples for nontransparent data. Reprinted with permission from GSM and Personal Communication Handbook, by Redl, Weber, and Oliphant. Norwood, MA: Artech House Publishing, 1998. (www.artechhouse.com)*

the data rates available at the air interface (i.e., 6 or 12 Kbps). For the second and third case (i.e., synchronous and nonsynchronous transmission), the rate adaptations chosen at different points are the same. This is because the RLP doesn't distinguish between synchronous and asynchronous transmission. It uses its own mechanism to deliver data to its peer entity at the IWF.

4.2.3 Layer 2 Relay Protocol

The Layer 2 Relay (L2R) protocol acts as a relay between the user nontransparent protocol (NTP) and the GSM-defined RLP. It provides a reliable transportation of user protocols across the GSM radio interface. The L2R uses the services provided by the RLP to transport the protocol information between the MS and the IWF. It also specifies protocol conversion between the user data structure (e.g., ITU-T defined X.25 Layer 2 frames) and a structure more adapted for the RLP. The L2R functions are located in the TAF and the IWF. Only nontransparent protocols can utilize L2R, because the GSM PLMN does not intercept transparent protocols.

The L2R is comprised of three functional entities: an NTP entity, an L2R protocol entity, and a relay entity (Figure 4–6). The NTP entity interfaces the L2R to the physical layer and provides an interface to the particular NTP. The L2RP entity interfaces the L2R to the RLP entity and provides an interface to the appropriate L2R protocol. The relay entity provides the mapping between the NTP entity and the L2R entity.

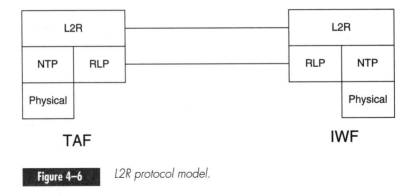

Figure 4–6   *L2R protocol model.*

The GSM standards have specified L2R for two protocols. It has specified L2RBOP for the ITU-T X.25 protocol, which is used for LAPB and for the nontransparent fax. GSM has specified L2RCOP for ITU-T X.28, which is also known as the start/stop protocol. The protocols are very similar, and we give an overview of both.

L2RBOP

For L2RBOP, the NTP entity (Figure 4–6) is called LAPB entity and it terminates the LAPB protocol from terminal or network. The relay entity is called BORE, and it provides the mapping of services between L2RBOP and LAPB. The L2RP entity is called L2RBOP, and it provides the interface to the RLP.

The L2RBOP entity segments and reassembles the LAPB user information fields to fit into service data units (SDUs) of RLP. These segments are transferred between L2Rs in n octet protocol data units (PDUs). The number n depends on the negotiated RLP version and RLP frame size.

The L2RBOP also provides facilities for transferring LAPB connection control information between L2Rs. The LAPB connection control information allows LAPB connections to be established, reset, and released. It also provides a flow control and a mechanism to transfer flow control information between L2Rs.

L2RCOP

This section describes the L2R functionality for nontransparent character-oriented protocols (e.g., ITU-T X.28). In the context of Figure 4–6, the NTP entity for L2RCOP is called character-oriented nontransparent protocol (CONT), the relay entity is character-oriented relay entity (CORE), and the L2RP is L2R character-oriented protocol.

The X.28 information is transferred between L2Rs in fixed-length n octet protocol data units (PDUs). The CORE relays status changes, break conditions, and characters in both directions between the CONTP (X.28) entity and the L2RCOP entity. The L2RCOP entity performs functions similar in scope to

L2RBOP. It provides radio link connection control to establish and release the connection to its peer L2RCOP entity. It also provides assemble and disassemble for data transfer. Data characters are assembled into L2RCOP PDUs until either the PDU is full or the radio link can accept another service data unit. The L2RCOP entity transfers interface status information between L2Rs using the status octets in L2RCOP PDUs. It also provides a flow control and a mechanism to transfer flow control information between the L2Rs.

4.2.4   Radio Link Protocol

The radio link protocol (RLP) provides error control and retransmission mechanisms to increase the chance of delivering data over the air interface. RLP is implemented on TAF and IWF. It is based on layer 2 LAPB and is used by nontransparent data services.

An RLP frame (Figure 4–7) has three main fields: header, information (payload), and frame check sequence (FCS). The header carries the control information to establish or release an RLP link, a sequence number for the in-sequence delivery of the frames, and so on. The information field carries the user data from the NTP. The FCS is used to detect transmission errors in an RLP frame. The GSM TS 04.22 specifies a polynomial, which combines the header and information bits to generate FCS. Based on FCS, the receiving RLP accepts or rejects a frame. In case of frame rejection, the sending entity retransmits the frame. This is also referred to as the automatic repeat request (ARQ) mechanism. We will not go into details of control commands and frame types; they can be found in GSM TS 04.22. RLP frames are sent in strict alignment with the radio transmission. An RLP frame has a fixed length of 240 bits, used when the channel coding is TCH/F4.8 or TCH/F9.6.

Either a terminal or IWF can initiate an RLP link. GSM specifications provide procedural means to deal with contentious situations, should they ever occur. RLP allows simultaneous information transfer in both directions. GSM specifications do not define the transfer of RLP states in handoff. Therefore, inter-MSC/IWF handoff results in RLP reset and may cause data loss.

There are three versions of RLP based on the number and type of supported radio links. The RLP version 0 uses one physical link (i.e., one TCH). The RLP version 1 also uses one physical link but also supports data compres-

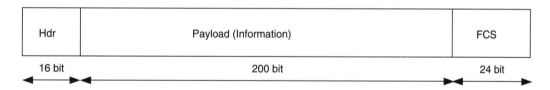

Figure 4–7   *RLP frame structure for TCH/F4.8 or TCH/F9.6.*

sion. The only defined data compression is V.42bis and is used to compress payload of the data packets. The RLP version 2 is designed to support multiple physical links, up to eight. An example application of RLP version 2 is HSCSD.

The RLP has two modes of transmission: asynchronous balanced mode (ABM) and asynchronous disconnected mode (ADM). The ABM is the data link operational mode. In this mode, either RLP entity may send commands at any time and may initiate response frame transmission without receiving explicit permission to do so from the other RLP station. In ADM, an RLP entity is disconnected from the data link and cannot transmit/receive data.

4.2.5   Packet Network Access

A GSM data terminal, in most cases, needs to have a data session with a terminal in another packet network. For this purpose, the GSM PLMN provides access to other packet networks, such as CSPDN, PSPDN, and ISDN. The GSM PLMN is a different network from these packet networks, and for communication with them an IWF is required. The GSM has specified the following access cases:

- GSM PLMN to/from PSPDN
- GSM PLMN to/from ISDN
- GSM PLMN to/from CSPDN

GSM PLMN TO PSPDN

PSPDN is a packet-based network such as public Internet or X.25-based networks. The GSM specifications define access to a PSPDN in GSM TS 09.05. The access is possible either through a packet assembler disassembler (PAD) or a packet handler (PH). The PAD is a protocol converter interfacing asynchronous terminals with a PSPDN. The PAD access is for those terminals that do not support a packet protocol and is only supported in the mobile origination direction. The PAD takes the ASCII streams coming from the terminals and converts them into PSPDN protocols (e.g., IP or ITU-T X.25). ITU-T X.28 defines the control procedures to establish the connections to the PAD and could be used for establishing an asynchronous connection. On the other hand, the PH is accessed by a terminal that has a packet protocol such as ITU-T X.32. The advantage in the PH access is that both mobile originated and terminated data calls are possible.

GSM defines two types of accesses for both PAD and PH, which are basic access and dedicated access. It is a network operators option to provide either or both of these accesses.

BASIC ACCESS • Basic access is an access to a dial-in port in the PSPDN. The dial-in port has an E.164 address, which a subscriber has to dial for access. Therefore, a GSM subscriber has to be a subscriber in the PSPDN to access it.

The subscriber has to dial the access PSPDN port number, followed by the called party number. The called party number is used by the PAD/PH to initiate the call establishment to the called terminal. In this way, a user has to dial in two numbers for basic PAD access. The double numbering also implies that the charging information has to be collected from two networks. The difference between PAD basic access and PH basic access is the protocol between the dial-in port and the terminal. In the PAD case, the protocol is ITU-T X.28, and in the PH case, the protocol is ITU-T X.32 (Figure 4–8).

BASIC ACCESS THROUGH TRANSIT NETWORKS • In this case, the access to the dial-in port in the PSPDN is through a transit network (Figure 4–9). The transit network could be PSTN or ISDN. This can be considered as a special case of basic access. The information transfer in the PSTN case occurs by using modems, and the bearer attribute used is 3.1-KHz audio. The information transfer in the ISDN case occurs by using 64-Kbps digital lines, and the bearer attribute used is unrestricted digital information. An arrangement with the ISDN operator is required for granting access for GSM PLMN subscribers.

DEDICATED ACCESS • The dedicated PAD access provides a direct dedicated link from GSM PLMN to a PAD (Figure 4–10). There is no dial-in for accessing a port in PSPDN. The main advantage compared to the basic access is that

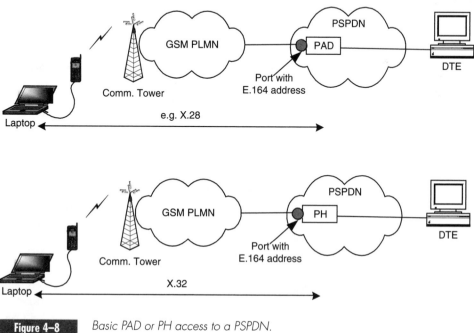

Figure 4–8   *Basic PAD or PH access to a PSPDN.*

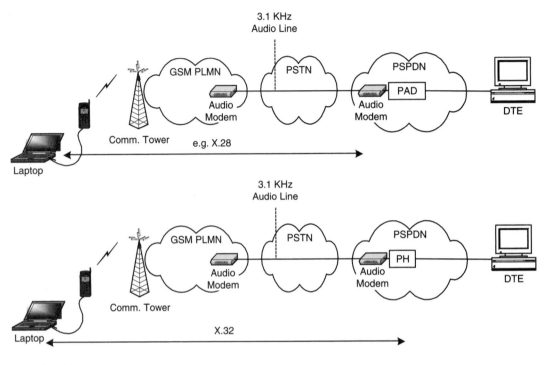

Basic PAD or PH access, through a transit network, to a PSPDN.

there is no double numbering. The mobile only uses the called party number; it does not use any E.164 address to access the PAD. The mobile subscriber needs to have a subscription for dedicated PAD access bearer service. Another advantage is that the subscriber receives all billing information from one operator, the home GSM PLMN operator.

GSM PLMN TO ISDN

The interworking of GSM and ISDN is specified in GSM TS 09.03 (Figure 4–11). The maximum data rate in GSM is 9.6 Kbps, and the minimum data rate in ISDN is 64 Kbps. This mismatch results in inefficient use of digital lines. Therefore, in practice it may not be a commonly used interworking. An ISDN network can be connected directly or indirectly through a PSTN network.

In the direct approach, the GSM PLMN can be interconnected directly via a rate adapter to the ISDN network via a dedicated line. The subscriber subscribes to a UDI bearer service. In an indirect approach, the GSM PLMN is connected to the ISDN network via a PSTN network. From the GSM PLMN

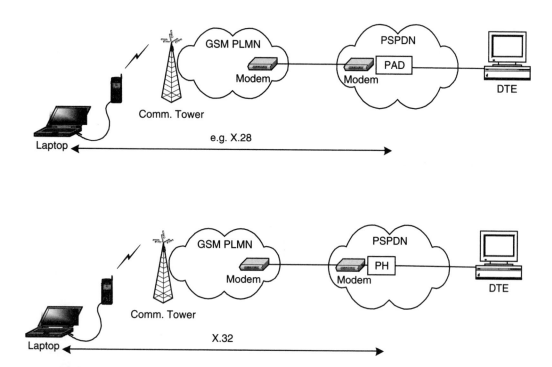

Figure 4–10   *Dedicated PAD or PH access to a PSPDN.*

point of view, the connection to the ISDN network is a PSTN network connection with audio modem. The ISDN network needs to have interworking with the PSTN network, which is comprised of audio modem and rate adapter.

ACCESS TO CSPDN

Circuit switched public data networks (CSPDNs) are general-purpose data networks. Like GSM PLMN, they use circuit switched transmission for transporting data. Interworking between GSM PLMN and CSPDN is defined in GSM TS 09.04 (Figure 4–12). The GSM PLMN provides only synchronous data interworking at the rates of 2.4, 4.8, and 9.6 Kbps. Also, it interworks only transparent data services, since it is not possible to flow control the terminals connected to a CS packet network. There are two ways to interwork with the CSPDN: directly or via the ISDN. In direct interworking, ITU-T defined X.21 is used as a user-network interface. In indirect interworking via ISDN, the user-network interface is according to the ISDN standards, which are defined in GSM TS 09.07.

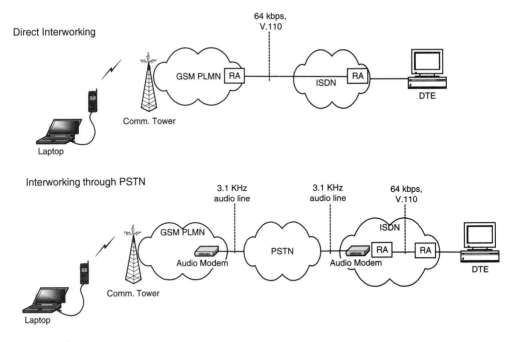

Figure 4–11   *Interworking between ISDN and GSM PLMN.*

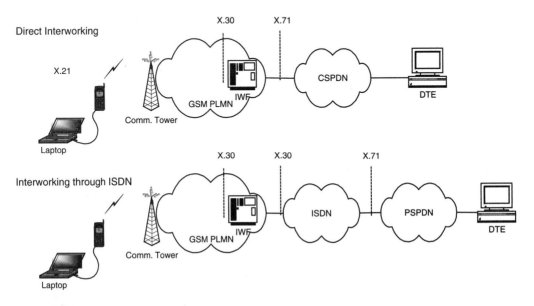

Figure 4–12   *Interworking between CSPDN and GSM PLMN.*

The PLMN is connected to a CSPDN using an IWF according to ITU-T X.300. The interface between the IWF and CSPDN is in accordance with ITU-T X.71 (direct interworking). In GSM, SS7 is used for signaling; therefore, an interworking needs to be defined between X.71 and SS7. If the PLMN is connected to CSPDN via ISDN, the interface to ISDN shall be according to GSM 09.07 and the information rate adaptation is according to ITU-T X.30.

End-to-end transmission is circuit based. Before exposing the air interface to the transmission of user data, an end-to-end terminal synchronization needs to be established. For this purpose, the IWF will send synchronization frames to the mobile terminal. On recognizing frame alignment, the IWF will stop sending the synchronization frames and connect the CSPDN to the terminal.

4.3   Data Application Examples

We have looked at the details of different functions for carrying data on traffic channels. Now let's look at some of the data applications that can be connected using GSM PLMN.

4.3.1   Fax Transmission

GSM technology provides two types of teleservices for fax: alternate speech/facsimile group 3 (TS 61) and automatic facsimile group 3 (TS 62). TS 61 is used when the user wants to switch between the voice call and the fax machine. It uses an in-call modification procedure via the user interface. The fax service can be provided on both transparent and nontransparent connections. Both mobile originated and terminated fax calls are supported. The bearer service information transfer mode for fax is circuit, duplex, synchronous, and symmetric.

For GSM, the group 3 facsimile service is adapted from the fixed network specification defined in ITU-T F.160. This service specification is comprised of two parts: the control protocol described in ITU-T T.30, and the document transmission coding described in ITU-T T.4.

GSM terminal equipment can be connected to a two-wire basic fax machine with the use of the fax adapter function. The fax adapter function converts the analog signals coming from the two-wire fax machine into a serial digital stream having the ISDN-specific R interface as the output. This R interface output needs a standard synchronous TAF (GSM 07.03) to connect to the GSM MS. A personal computer (PC), emulating a fax machine, can be connected directly to a GSM phone with a commercially available PCMCIA fax card supporting GSM phones. In the PCMCIA fax card, the TAF and fax adapter functions are combined.

As shown in Figure 4–13, a fax, either originated from a PC or two-wire fax machine, is sent through the BSS to the MSC. The MSC transfers the data link to the proper IWF. Different types of IWF are possible for the different type of transit networks. The transit network subsequently transports the fax information to the receiving fax machine. Both fax machines communicate with each other using the standard fax protocol defined in ITU-T T.30.

Figure 4–14 depicts an expanded view of the protocols and rate adaptation used for transmitting nontransparent fax through a PLMN. It should be noted that depending on the implementation, the R reference point might not exist explicitly. In this case the LAPB protocol and consequently the LAPB entities operating across this interface may be omitted. L2RBOP and RLP protocol stacks are used at the radio interface. As the fax data is synchronous, RA1′ is used to transform the data rates supported on the air interface while adding some control bits. The air interface rate could be 3.6, 6, or 12 Kbps, depending on the bearer service subscribed by the fax user. The data is sent over the air with FEC. In the BSS, fax data is transformed into the intermediate rates of 8 or 16 Kbps by the RA1 function. The intermediate rate is transformed into an A interface data stream of 64 Kbps by the RA2 function. A similar view can be established for the transparent fax with the absence of L2R and RLP functions.

4.3.2   Internet Connection

A GSM PLMN can provide a circuit switched connection to an IP network or Internet (Figure 4–15). The GSM specifications don't specify a teleservice or bearer service for Internet connection. But the MS can access the Internet by subscribing to any of the data bearer services (e.g., asynchronous PAD access

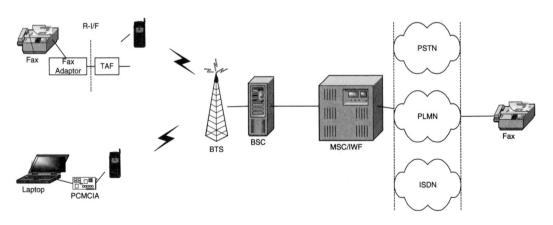

Figure 4–13   *Fax transmission using GSM PLMN.*

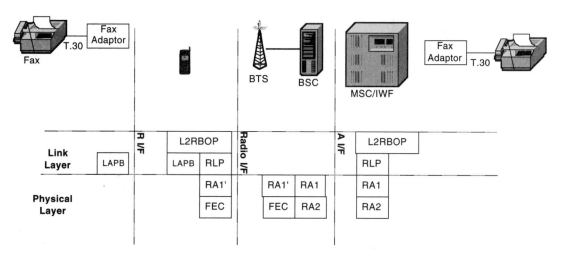

Figure 4–14 *Data protocol and functional view for fax transmission.*

at 9.6 Kbps). Both transparent and nontransparent connections can be utilized. The nontransparent connection provides better protection over the air interface compared to the transparent connection. In this description, we have assumed that an asynchronous nontransparent connection is established to a PAD in the IP network. We will describe both basic and dedicated PAD access to the IP network. In both cases, the GSM PLMN provides a circuit switched bearer to the PAD, and the IP protocol executes transparently on top of this bearer.

Just like any other data terminal of a GSM PLMN, an IP host (e.g., a laptop) needs to be connected to the TAF function of the MS. The TAF function is available on a PCMCIA card, which provides a direct connection from an IP host to the MS.

In the basic PAD access case, the IWF is composed of modem pools to allow modem-based communication across the network. The modem pools allow the users to make calls to the Internet service provider (ISP). The cellular network can be thought of as a big serial cable providing access to the modem in the IWF. The user must first dial the E.164 address of the subscribed port. This address can be configured in the dial-in program so a user doesn't have to input the address with every access. The user sends to the PAD the address of the entity in the IP network to which it needs correspondence (e.g., e-mail server address). The PAD reaches the IP network entity on the user's behalf. This case was represented in Figure 4–9 with only one modem.

Some service providers have dedicated trunks connecting GSM PLMN to an IP network. This is the case of dedicated PAD access. For our example of

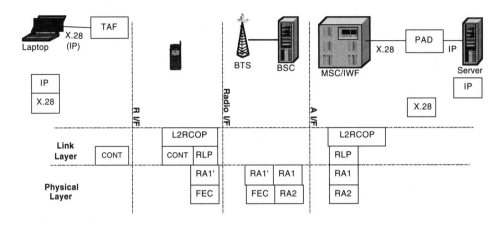

Data protocol and functional view for Internet connection.

e-mail service access, the user only needs to send the e-mail server addresses for establishing connection to the server. The user doesn't need to dial in a port address in the IP network. This case is also represented in Figure 4–10, the modem in that figure is the digital modem used to access the digital line.

For the protocol and functional view, let's assume the most involved case of nontransparent data, as shown in Figure 4–15. The GSM PLMN provides L2R and RLP functions to carry the IP datagrams over the air interface. A simpler view of transparent data can be visualized with the absence of L2R and RLP.

4.4   High-Speed Circuit Switched Data

The HSCSD feature allows subscribers to access higher data rates with multiple TCH/Fs (Figure 4–16). HSCSD has defined mechanisms to make efficient and flexible use of radio resources for HSCSD. Combining/splitting functionality is defined in the IWF and terminal to separate a data stream into n TCH/F, where n ranges from 1 to 8. These n TCH/Fs, carrying a data stream, are referred to as HSCSD channels. The HSCSD channels carry the substreams as if they were independent of each other. However, the HSCSD channels, serving one stream, are controlled as one radio link. Any cellular operation (e.g., handover), treats the HSCSD channels of one stream as a single entity.

Before HSCSD, the air interface user rate in the original GSM data transmission was limited to 9.6 Kbps. The HSCSD made it possible to have user data rates up to 57.6 Kbps, with the same GSM RF equipment. The data rate is limited by the per-channel capacity on the A interface, which is 64 Kbps.

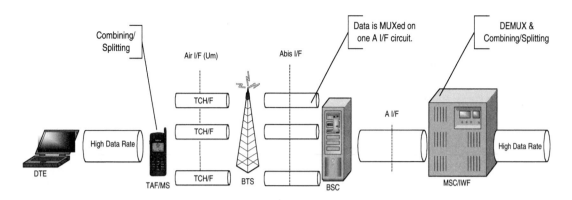

Figure 4-16 Network architecture for supporting HSCSD.

To carry more than 64 Kbps, another split/combine function has to be defined and implemented for the terrestrial circuits on the terminating party. This is not realistic and not needed for circuit switched data.

HSCSD doesn't impose any new requirement for the interconnection with PSTN, ISDN, CSPDN, and PSPDN. The subscriber uses general bearer services as defined in GSM TS 02 series, and the HLR stores the bearer capability information as part of the service profile.

HSCSD serves both transparent and nontransparent connections. In transparent data transmission, the data frames on the HSCSD channels carry data substream numbers to retain the order of transmission between the split/combine functions. Between these functions, channel internal multiframing is also used in order to increase the tolerance against inter-channel transmission delays. A transparent connection may request a data rate that is not a multiple of rates provided by one TCH/F. In such a case the data bits in the nth TCH/F need to be padded with fill bits. In nontransparent connection, the RLP and L2R are modified to support multiple parallel TCH/Fs instead of only one TCH/F. Also, the RLP frame sequence number range is increased to accommodate the enlarged data transmission rate.

HSCSD provides both symmetric and asymmetric connection setup. In the symmetric connections, the number of HSCSD channels is same in both uplink and downlink directions. In asymmetric connections, the number of HSCSD channels is different. The network usually allocates asymmetric connections when the desired air interface user rate requirement cannot be met using a symmetric configuration. The network in this case gives priority to fulfilling the air interface user rate requirement in the downlink direction. This is in consideration that the downlink bandwidth is needed more than the uplink bandwidth for most data applications. Note that the asymmetric connections are only given for nontransparent HSCSD.

4.4.1   HSCSD Call Setup

At call setup, an HSCSD user sends a set of parameters to the network indicating the desired HSCSD characteristics (e.g., number of TCH/Fs). In the case of nontransparent HSCSD connections, the user may also request user initiated service level upgrading and downgrading during the call. The MSC requests the BSC to allocate the channel configuration using parameters derived from the HSCSD-related parameters agreed on in the setup phase. Based on these parameters and operator preferences, the BSC then allocates a suitable number of channels and a suitable channel coding for the connection.

Separate channel activation is applied for each of the HSCSD channels. At assignment completion, the BSS informs the MSC of the chosen HSCSD configuration and the MSC may seize the interworking resources accordingly. The network responds with a set of parameters, indicating the configuration it has prepared to give to the mobile station.

4.4.2   Resource Upgrading, Downgrading, and Configuration Change

Resource upgrading means allocating more channels to the HSCSD configuration. On the contrary, in resource downgrading channels are released. The network or the MS can initiate these procedures. At resource modification completion, the BSC signals to the MSC the new HSCSD configuration, and the MSC may adjust the interworking resources accordingly. These procedures can be applied on both transparent and nontransparent connections. For the transparent connection, the alteration is not allowed to change the air interface user rate, and the alteration is not allowed by a user-initiated procedure.

4.4.3   Air Interface for HSCSD

The number of HSCSD channels used for a session influences the design of a mobile station. Before HSCSD, a GSM phone had a gap of three time slots between transmit and receive channels. Considering that the total number of channels on a carrier is eight, an MS cannot use more than five channels while tuned to one carrier frequency. Therefore, another class of mobile is defined that has RF equipment to do simultaneous receive and transmit. This class of phones is named HSCSD class 2, while the former is HSCSD class 1. The class 2 phones covers from 6 to a maximum of 16 channels, with 8 channels in each direction.

For HSCSD, the channels can be allocated from consecutive or nonconsecutive time slots. Let's see how the TCH/F and the associated signaling channels are used for HSCSD. GSM has defined FACCH and SACCH as the associated signaling channels with a TCH/F. The FACCH carries the signaling messages that cannot be delayed (e.g., handover messages). With multiple TCH/Fs, HCSD designates one bidirectional TCH/F as the main channel. The FACCH of the main channel is used for all fast signaling related to a data session, and the SACCHs of all TCH/Fs are used individually.

The same frequency hopping sequence and training sequence is used for all the channels in an HSCSD configuration. The same channel coding is used for all the channels in an HSCSD configuration. Each of the HSCSD channels is ciphered using separate ciphering keys, but they all are derived from the same subscriber ciphering key (Kc).

4.5   Data Services on Signaling/Broadcast Channels—SMS

The GSM technology is the first in providing data services on signaling and broadcast channels. These services are commonly known as SMS. There are two different types of SMS: SMS point-to-point and SMS broadcast. We will look into both of these services in this section. Data services like SMS are also provided by other radio technologies, such as IS-136 and IS-95.

SMS point-to-point is the data service that uses only the signaling channel (SDCCH) to transport the data over the air interface. In SMS, a short string of text (maximum 126 characters) is carried from one subscriber to another. There is another type of SMS service called SMS broadcast, which is the only broadcast channel data service. As the name implies, the user terminal can only receive the data broadcasted from the network. This service transports data on a specially defined broadcast channel, CBCH, over the air interface. This service is also limited to a short text string based on the carrying capacity of the CBCH. This service was anticipated to be used by the broadcast data applications, such as traffic reports and weather alerts. This service didn't get much attention from service providers because it didn't provide a good revenue generation model.

4.5.1   SMS Point-to-Point

SMS point-to-point (SMS p-p) is a dedicated service between two users. GSM has defined two teleservices for SMS: SMS-MO (mobile origination), and SMS-MT (mobile termination). Using this service, a user sends a short string of alphanumeric characters to another user. SMS can also be used by the network operators to notify a user about certain status (e.g., number of messages waiting in voice mail). SMS is based on the concept that the signaling channel capacity can be utilized for carrying a few bytes of user data. SMS has also opened up GSM PLMN for support of telematics. For example, with a reduced GSM user equipment, a vending machine can become a short message sending entity to send a message to the vendor when a specific supply is needed.

SMS is defined with a store-and-forward mechanism. In this way the message is saved in case the addressee is not reachable and is later delivered based on availability. A subscriber must subscribe to this service, and it is provisioned in the subscriber's profile in HLR.

NETWORK DESCRIPTION

To understand how the SMS works, let's look into the network elements involved in SMS p-p (Figure 4–17).

An SMS message sending/receiving entity is called short message entity (SME). The SME can be a GSM-MS or a computer. SMS has introduced a new NE short message service center (SM-SC). The SM-SC handles all the functions related to SMS p-p. It receives a message and forwards it to the addressee.

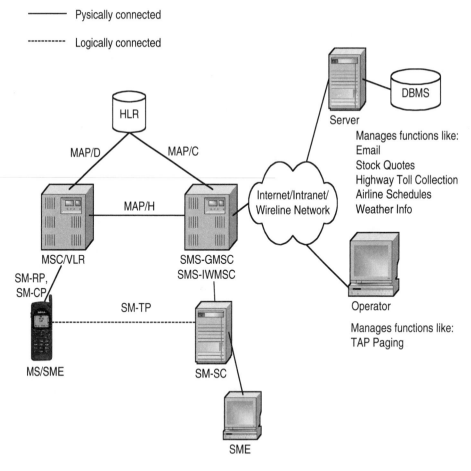

Figure 4–17   *Network architecture for SMS p-p.*

The SME is connected to the SM-SC via the short message transport protocol (SM-TP). The SM-SC allows connection to a computer, which makes SMS possible from e-mails and Web pages. When SME is a GSM-MS, it uses the short message relay protocol (SM-RP) and short message control protocol (SM-CP) to deliver short messages to the MSC/VLR.

The SMS-GMSC is the gateway to a GSM PLMN for SM delivery addressed in the PLMN. The SMS-GMSC interrogates the HLR to locate the subscriber. The interrogation protocol is a generic protocol used also by the GSM call control procedures for locating a called party. The HLR informs about the current location in terms of MSC/VLR, which is used by the SMS-GMSC for eventual delivery of the SM to the MS. In case the MS is not reachable, the HLR sends a response back to the SMS-GMSC.

The SMS-GMSC can be connected to the external servers or terminals to provide SMS application services, such as e-mail, stock quotes, and highway toll collection. These services can be managed with the help of a database management system. Many of the operators provide Web interface to send SMSs to the mobile subscribers.

The SMS-IWMSC is the MSC connected to the SM-SC. It directs the SM originated by an MS in a GSM PLMN to the SM-SC. The SMS-IWMSC functionality might exist together with the SMS-GMSC on one physical MSC.

PROCEDURE DESCRIPTION

The SMS transaction basically consists of two parts. An SME originates a SM, which is delivered to SC. The SC originates a session to deliver the SM to the addressee. In the following procedure description, we consider a generic case of an MS to MS short message delivery, encompassing both SMS-MO and SMS-MT parts:

1. MS originates a short message, with the SM-SC directory number, and uses SM-CP and SM-RP protocols to transfer the message to the MSC/VLR.

2. The MSC/VLR looks at the SM-SC directory number and forwards the SM to the SMS-IWMSC, which in turn contacts the SM-SC and delivers the SM.

3. The SM-SC, based on the terminating party address, contacts the SMS-GMSC. It notifies the SMS-GMSC that there is a short message waiting for an MS in the addressee's network.

4. The SMS-GMSC asks the HLR about the current location of the addressee in terms of visited MSC/VLR.

5. If the addressed MS is reachable, the HLR sends the visited MSC/VLR information to the SMS-GMSC. The SMS-GMSC passes the SM on to the visited MSC.

6. If the addressed MS is not available, the HLR sends that status back to the SM-SC. It also sets a flag to save the information that the attempted delivery was not successful. When the addressed MS becomes reachable, the HLR notifies the MS for the attempted delivery. The MS may contact the SM-SC to retrieve the waiting short messages.

7. The MSC/VLR pages the MS through the BTSs in its registered location area. The currently visited BTS establishes a radio channel and delivers the message to the addressed mobile.

4.5.2   SMS Cell Broadcast

SMS cell broadcast provides a mechanism to broadcast short messages from a radio network to the MSs in a cell area (Figure 4–18). The sources of SMSCB can come from broadcast applications, such as traffic reports and weather reports. The message is limited by the capacity of the broadcast channel that carries it. A single CB message can carry up to 88 bytes. The service broadcasts on a cell level because the SMS-CB uses a specially defined channel called CBCH. The presence of a CBCH is indicated by the system information messages broadcasted for an individual cell on the BCCH. The system information tells the MSs camped on a cell on which frequency and channel CB message are sent.

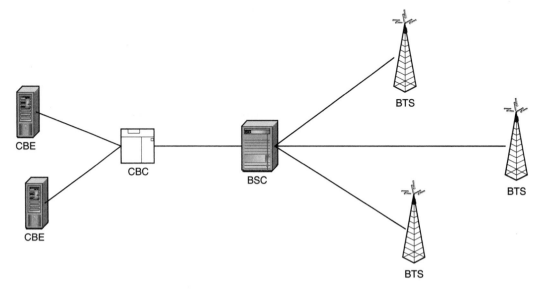

Figure 4–18   *Network architecture for SMS-CB.*

A CB message has a message header and a payload. The CB message header has an identifier, which identifies the source and subject of the SMSCB message. It also has a sequence number, which enables the MS to determine when a new message from a given source is available. SMS-CB messages are not acknowledged by the MS. Reception of SMS-CB messages by the MS is only possible in idle mode.

The SMS cell broadcast service is designed to minimize the battery usage requirements for an MS. An MS can read the first part of a CB message and then decide whether or not to read the rest of the message. In addition, the network may broadcast schedule messages, which provide information in advance about the CB messages that will be sent immediately afterward. The MS may use this scheduling information to restrict reception to those messages the customer is interested in receiving.

The CB short messages are generated in the cell broadcast entity (CBE). The functionality of a CBE is not specified in the GSM standards. The CBE can be understood as a source of SMS-CB, such as a weather information center. It includes all aspects of formatting the CB messages as well as splitting a message into various segments, which will eventually be transmitted on one channel.

The CBC actually handles all the GSM related functions of SMS-CB. It may be getting input from multiple CBEs and could be connected to one or multiple BSCs. The CBC coordinates the formatting and organization of the messages it receives from the CBE into GSM form. It performs functions such as determining the rate at which certain messages must be delivered; setting the language; and determining area where a certain message is to be sent.

The BSS takes care of the radio part of transmitting CB messages. The BSC performs functions such as storing the messages as long as they are to be transmitted; routing the messages to the appropriate BTSs; and scheduling of the CB messages according to the repetition rate. BTS puts the message on the CBCH at the time specified by the BSC.

4.6 Summary

This chapter provides an overview of the data services offered by the GSM wireless network. It describes network architecture and protocol functions required to provide circuit switched data services. It also describes interworking of GSM PLMN with different types of packet networks. It provides an overview of HSCSD. It also explains SMS services (SMS p-p and SMS broadcast) and it describes the architecture and network functions for delivering SMS to a subscriber.

References

Redl, Weber, & Oliphant, *GSM and Personal Communications Handbook,* Artech House Publishers.

Mouly & Pautet, *The GSM System for Mobile Communications.*

GSM TS 02.02, "Bearer Services Supported by GSM PLMN," ETSI.

GSM TS 02.01, "Principles of Telecommunication Services Supported by a GSM PLMN," ETSI.

GSM TS 02.03, "Teleservices Supported by a GSM PLMN," ETSI.

GSM TS 04.21, "Rate Adaptation on Mobile Station—Base Station System (MS-BSS) Interface," ETSI.

ITU-T V.42bis, "Data Compression Procedures for Data Circuit-terminating Equipment (DCE) Using Error Correction Procedures."

ITU-T X.28, "DTE/DCE Interface for a Start-Stop Mode Data Terminal Equipment Accessing the Packet Assembly/Disassembly Facility (PAD) in a Public Data Network Situated in the Same Country."

ITU-T X.25, "Interface between Data Terminal Equipment (DTE) and Data Circuit-terminating Equipment (DCE) for Terminals Operating in the Packet Mode and Connected to Public Data Networks by Dedicated Circuit."

ITU-T X.32, "Interface between Data Terminal Equipment (DTE) and Data Circuit-terminating Equipment (DCE) for Terminals Operating in the Packet Mode and Accessing a Packet-Switched Public Data Network through a Public Switched Telephone Network or an Integrated Services Digital Network or a Circuit-switched Public Data Network."

ITU-T X.300, "General Principles for Interworking between Public Networks and between Public Networks and Other Networks for the Provision of Data Transmission Services."

ITU-T X.30, "Support of X.21, X.21 bis and X.20 bis based Data Terminal Equipments (DTEs) by an Integrated Services Digital Network (ISDN)."

ITU-T X.71, "Decentralized Terminal and Transit Control Signalling System on International Circuits between Synchronous Data Networks."

T.30, "Procedures for Document Facsimile Transmission in the General Switched Telephone Network."

ITU-T V.110, "Support by an ISDN of Data Terminal Equipments with V-Series Type Interfaces."

GSM TS 09.04, "Interworking between the PLMN and the CSPDN," ETSI.

GSM TS 09.03, "Signalling Requirements on Interworking between the ISDN or PSTN and the PLMN," ETSI.

GSM TS 09.07, "General Requirements on Interworking between the PLMN and the ISDN or PSTN," ETSI.

GSM TS 09.05, "Interworking between the PLMN and the PSPDN for Packet Assembly/Disassembly (PAD) Access," ETSI.

GSM TS 03.40, "Technical Realization of the Short Message Service (SMS) Point-to-point (PP)," ETSI.

GSM TS 03.41, "Technical Realization of Short Message Service Cell Broadcast (SMSCB)," ETSI.

GSM TS 03.34, "High Speed Circuit Switched Data (HSCSD); Stage 2," ETSI.

GSM TS 03.45, "Technical Realization of Facsimile Group 3 Service Transparent," ETSI.

GSM TS 03.46, "Technical Realization of Facsimile Group 3 Service Nontransparent," ETSI.

Data in IS-136 Networks

IS-136 networks are commonly referred to as digital personal communications service (PCS) networks or TDMA networks. As described in this chapter, the term IS-136 network refers to the cellular standard defined by the Telecommunications Industry Associations (TIA) for digital PCS networks, called TIA/EIA 136. In this chapter we will use the term IS-136 for simplicity.

IS-136 provides not only voice services but also a set of data services. This chapter describes the family of standards that compose an IS-136 network, the network architecture and protocols, and the data services offered by an IS-136 network. The chapter focuses on the IS-136 data services before GPRS concepts were "imported" in the IS-136 architecture. The enhancements of IS-136 by GPRS concepts are only briefly described in this chapter in the section on evolution of IS-136, since the adoption of GPRS in IS-136 leads to an architecture and services very similar to the GSM/GPRS ones, described in Chapter 8.

IS-136 is the result of the evolution of cellular systems in North America from analog AMPS to digital systems. IS-136 introduces the DCCH (digital control channel), which forms the core of the IS-136 specification, and provides new system functionality and supports enhanced features, including the sleep mode to preserve mobile station battery power, support of multiple vocoders, the ability to acquire seamlessly the same services both in the cellular band (800 MHz) and the PCS band (1900 MHz), and the support of teleservices to transfer application data to and from cellular phones.

The IS-136 standard specifies two types of data services: teleservices and circuit switched data services. An IS-136 teleservice is an application that uses the air interface and network interface as the bearers for transporting a small quantity of bursty information (e.g., short messages) between a server and a mobile station. Circuit switched data services enable data applications, such as fax and ISP connection, to exchange a possibly long flow of information over the digital traffic channel (DTC). The basic idea in providing DTC data service is to provide a circuit switched connection for carrying data from the user through the IS-136 network and vice versa. The establishment of the data connection is very similar to the establishment of a voice call.

In the following sections we describe an overview of IS-136 network architecture and data services. We describe also the protocols and the functions provided by the IS-136 network for carrying data.

5.1   The Digital PCS Standards

The digital PCS standards comprise an interim standard (IS), to indicate that the standard is not yet approved by the TIA/EIA (Telecommunication Industry Association–Electronic Industry Association). However, these standards have achieved the status of TIA/EIA standards but are commonly referred to with their "IS" code (e.g., IS-136).

As described in this chapter, the term *IS-136 network* refers to the cellular standard defined by the TIA for digital PCS networks. In particular, IS-136 identifies a particular part of the digital PCS family of standards and does not identify all the features of digital PCS networks. The IS-136 standard is the result of the evolution of the North American analog cellular systems called advanced mobile phone service (AMPS). Due to the phenomenal success of AMPS networks, the need for a more efficient system and more cellular capacity led to the development of a first digital cellular standard, called IS-54. However, IS-54 drawbacks (higher costs with no clear improvements for the end users) did not allow IS-54 to duplicate the success of AMPS. Therefore, the IS-136 standard was developed to allow for increased cellular capacity and for providing new services to mobile users. IS-136 allowed for a capacity three times larger than the one provided by AMPS, and for new features such as longer battery life, authentication and voice privacy, caller ID, message waiting indication, and short messages. Whereas AMPS systems used analog traffic and control channels, IS-54 introduced a DTC. Full-rate DTC is supported in IS-54 by means of time multiplexing of 30-KHz RF channels, and a mobile user is assigned a full-rate DTC. In addition to the DTC, IS-136 introduced the DCCH, which allows for the new features supported by IS-136 with respect to its predecessors.

The digital PCS standards comprise a set of standards including IS-136, IS-137, IS-138, IS-641, IS-130, and IS-135. Here we give a brief summary of each standard:

- *IS-136: Mobile Station-Base Station Compatibility Standard.* IS-136 describes the channels used in digital PCS from the physical layer to the network layer, focusing in particular on the DCCH.

- *IS-137: Minimum Performance Standard for Mobile Stations.* IS-137 defines the minimum requirements for the mobile station in terms of receiver, transmitter, and environmental requirements. Requirements for the receiver include frequency coverage, acquisition time, demodulation, bit error rate, and signal strength measurement accuracy. Requirements for the transmitter include frequency stability, power output, modulation type and stability, limitation of emissions, and time alignment. Environmental requirements include temperature, power supply voltage, humidity, vibration, and shock. The standard defines the minimum requirements and the method to measure them.
- *IS-138: Minimum Performance Standard for Base Stations.* IS-138 is the companion standard to IS-137 and defines the minimum requirements for the base station in terms of receiver, transmitter, and environmental requirements.
- *IS-641: Enhanced Full-Rate Speech Codec.* IS-641 describes the vocoder adopted in digital PCS.
- *IS-130: Radio Link Protocol.* IS-130 defines the link layer used in digital PCS to support asynchronous data and fax services defined by IS-135 over an IS-136 DTC.
- IS-135: Asynchronous Data and Fax. IS-135 defines a network protocol for asynchronous data and fax transport that described call setup, monitoring, release, user data transport, and other features. IS-135 requires IS-130 as radio link and uses IS-136.

IS-137, IS-138, IS-641, IS-130 and IS-135 are supporting standards for IS-136. This means that they complement the features defined in IS-136 for the support of digital PCS services.

IS-136 standard merges the digital PCS family into a single standard composed of multiple parts in order to allow for easier tracking of standard modifications and for greater flexibility in the development of new features.

5.2   TIA/EIA-136 Architecture Description

Before describing the details of IS-136 data services, in Figure 5–1 we provide an overview of an IS-136 network.

The architecture of IS-136 is very similar to the one of GSM. Several network interfaces have been assigned the same name, even if the protocols over the interfaces are substantially different.

As described in Figure 5–1, an IS-136 network consists of the following main network elements:

Home location register: The HLR is a central database for the IS-136 network to store subscription information of users. It keeps the informa-

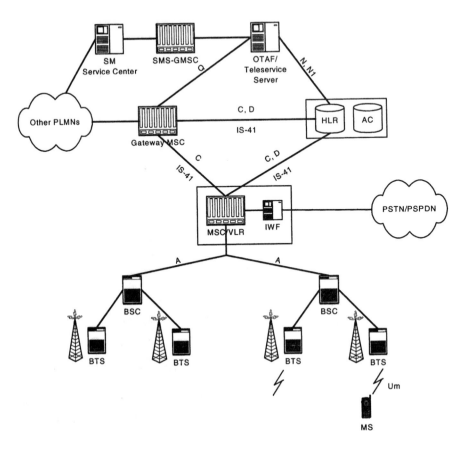

Figure 5–1   *TIA/EIA-136 network architecture.*

tion about service profile, location, and activity status of a subscriber. HLR is connected to MSCs and VLRs using the IS-41 protocol.

Mobile switching center: The MSC performs call control for calls originated or terminated to the mobile station. MSC supports also mobility management and radio resource management. It also captures charging information from the services used by the mobile station to support the creation of billing information. The MSC is connected to the BSS using the IS-136 A interface protocol. The gateway MSC is a gateway to a PLMN and provides call routing to/from other PLMNs and PSTNs. The SMS-GMSC is the GMSC for support of short message service. The MSC contains the VLR function, which contains subscriber information needed in servicing a roaming MS in a visited network. When an MS roams into a visited network, its information is transferred from the HLR to the VLR using the location update procedure.

Interworking function: The IWF performs protocol conversion to allow an IS-136 MS to connect with data networks over PSTN. More details are provided later in Section 5.5. The IWF may be integrated with the MSC or operate independently.

Authentication center: The AC authenticates mobile stations by verifying the authentication information received by the MSC. As a result of a successful authentication, AC also provides encryption parameters for ciphering over-the-air interface.

OTAF/teleservice server: The over-the-air activation function/teleservice server supports teleservices in IS-136 and is also called the message center. Among other services, described later in this chapter, the function supports delivery of short messages to the MS (cellular messaging teleservice, CMT). The OTAF/teleservice server may communicate with other network entities through SS7 or IP. In particular, IS-41 is used to communicate with the HLR and the MSC.

Base station controller: The BSC controls a set of BTSs. It provides cellular-specific functions, like radio resource management and handover power control.

Base transceiver station: The BTS handles the radio interface. In IS-136, the interface connecting the BTS to the BSC in not an open interface. This means that no complete standard exists, and manufacturers implement the interface in different ways.

Interworking function: The IWF provides a mechanism for transferring digital data signals from the GSM PLMN to the other types of network (e.g., PSTN, ISDN, or PSPDN). The interworking function also performs any protocol conversion between the two dissimilar networks. More information is provided later in this chapter.

Mobile station: A mobile station has IS-136–specified call control, mobility management, and radio interface. It is connected to the network using air interface (Um).

5.3   IS-136 Protocol Layers

The IS-136 standards defines three protocol layers.

- Layer 1: physical layer
- Layer 2: data link layer
- Layer 3: network layer

The functionality at higher layers is provided by the teleservices and data services and is described in later sections.

5.3.1   Layer 1: The IS-136 Physical Layer

The physical layer specifies the physical characteristics of the digital PCS air interface such as RF-related parameters, modulation format, power output requirements, and frame and time slot structure. The physical layer also defines hardware requirements for mobile stations and base stations and influences operational parameters of digital PCS networks, such as the number of RF channels possible for each cell or sector, the distance between cell sites, and the frequency reuse patterns.

IS-136 specifies operations of digital PCS in the 800-MHz band and 1900-MHz band, with each band divided in 30-kHz RF channels. IS-136 is a time division multiple access (TDMA) cellular technology that divides RF channels into frames. A single TDMA frame is composed of six time slots and is 40 ms in length. To understand how frames and time slots are used, the examples in Figure 5–2 are provided. A half-rate channel uses only one time slot, whereas a full-rate channel uses two time slots separated by two time slots (e.g., time slots 2 and 5 are paired). A double-rate channel uses four time slots.

The DCCH time-slot structure in IS-136 is described in Figure 5–3. The DCCH is structured in hyperframes of 1.28 seconds of length, composed of two superframes each divided in 16 frames of 40 ms.

The DCCH is divided in logical channels for the forward and reverse directions. The forward DCCH is divided into the following channels:

- *SMS point-to-point, paging, and access response channel (SPACH).* The SPACH channel is divided into SMS channel (SMSCH), used to deliver teleservice messages to mobile stations; the paging channel (PCH), used to deliver pages and other commands to mobiles; and the access response channel (ARCH), used to deliver responses to messages from the mobile station.
- *Broadcast control channel (BCCH).* The BCCH is divided in the fast broadcast control channel (F-BCCH), used to carry time-critical in-

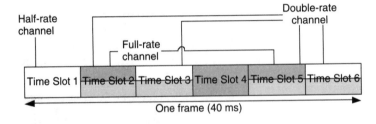

Figure 5–2   *IS-136 frame structure and time slot utilization.*

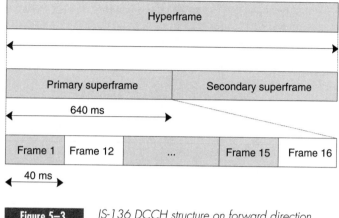

Figure 5–3   *IS-136 DCCH structure on forward direction.*

formation needed by mobile stations to access the network; the extended broadcast control channel (E-BCCH), used to carry less time-critical information; and the SMS broadcast control channel (S-BCCH), used to carry broadcast teleservices.

* *Shared channel feedback (SCF).* The SCF is used to control access of mobile stations to the reverse DCCH to avoid collision. SCF provides information to mobile stations on when to initiate an access attempt, whether the access was successful, and whether the information has been received.

A fixed number of time slots is allocated for each superframe for F-BCCH, E-BCCH, S-BCCH, and SPACH, with the F-BCCH repeated at each superframe.

One logical channel is defined for the reverse DCCH, the random access control channel (RACH). The RACH is a point-to-point channel shared by all mobile stations used to access the DCCH. Mobile stations use the RACH in a contention mode, and collision avoidance is achieved through appropriate information provided on the forward DCCH.

5.3.2   Layer 2: The IS-136 Data Link Layer

The IS-136 data link layer provides the following set of functions:

* Addressing with mobile station ID (MSID).
* Error detection, recovery, and sequencing through monitoring of radio link quality, retransmission control, and CRC generation and verification.

- Media access control: Mobile stations access the network over the RACH in either a contention-based (random access) or reservation-based fashion. The base station controls the access through feedback on shared channels on the forward DCCH and random access on the reverse DCCH.
- Frame delimiting through header formatting, layer 3 message concatenation, layer 2 frame segmentation, and reassembly.
- Flow control on the forward and reverse DCCH.

The data link layer defines service access points and service primitives (i.e., the way layer 3 communicates with layer 2) and protocols for the logical channels on forward and reverse DCCH. The data link layer defines also the DTC in terms of the method of supervising the connection of the DTC to avoid collision between mobile stations on the same channel.

5.3.3 Layer 3: The IS-136 Network Layer

The IS-136 layer 3 or network layer provides a means to establish, maintain, and terminate connections between the mobile station and the network. The layer 3 message set includes messages transferred on both the DCCH and the DTC.

Layer 3 messages include information for registration, paging, DCCH structure, call setup/release, R-data transport for teleservices, and relay of higher-layer information for additional applications. Layer 3 messages are transported in layer 2 packets indicating the type of layer 3 information that is carried.

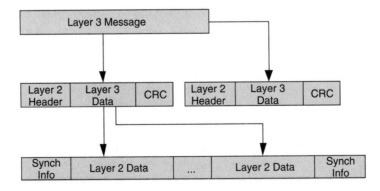

Figure 5–4   *IS-136 control plane layering.*

DCCH

DCCH is used to convey call setup information and to provide the platform for enhanced services through signaling and messaging. Figure 5–4 describes the layering of messages on the control plane.

The IS-136 digital control channel supports the following features:

- The sleep mode to preserve mobile station battery power
- Support of multiple vocoders to take advantage of improvements in voice technology
- The ability to seamlessly acquire the same services both in the cellular band (800 MHz) and the PCS band (1900 MHz)
- The support of teleservices to transfer application data to and from cellular phones
- A hierarchical macrocell-microcell environment providing support for microcellular operation
- Private and residential system identities providing the tools of wireless office service (WOS) operations

IS-136 DCCH occupies a full-rate digital channel (i.e., two time slots out of six). The DCCH is composed of a set of logical channels in the direction from the network to the mobile nodes (forward direction) and a single logical channel in the direction from the mobile node to the network (reverse direction). The logical channels in the forward direction are classified into broadcast channels and point-to-point channels, and the logical channel in the reverse direction is a point-to-point channel. Logical channels are introduced in the DCCH to organize the information flowing across the air interface (Figure 5–5):

1. *Broadcast channel (BCCH):* The BCCH is a downlink channel that provides continuous system information and the rules an MS needs to follow to access the system. The BCCH is divided in fast BCCH and extended BCCH. Fast BCCH is used for time-critical system information that needs to be sent at fixed repetition cycles, such as the system ID (SID) and information needed by the MS to access the system (e.g., network type, protocol version, mobile country code). E-BCCH is used to carry information that is less time critical and does not need a guaranteed rate (e.g., the neighbor cell list for MS mobility).

2. *SMS paging and access channel (SPACH):* SPACH provides MS with paging and system access parameter information. SPACH is divided in paging channel, used to transfer call setup pages to the MS; the access response channel, used to send system responses from the system to the MS (e.g., DTC assignment commands); and the SMS channel, used to transfer point-to-point teleservice data to and from MS.

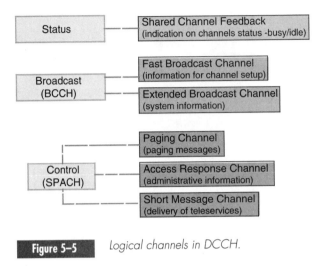

| Figure 5–5 | *Logical channels in DCCH.* |

3. *Random access channel (RACH):* RACH is a shared channel resource used by all MSs when attempting to access the system. RACH is an uplink channel used, for example, for MS response to an authentication request or to acknowledge delivery of a short message. RACH is used by MS to access the system either with a contention-based mechanism (i.e., several MSs try to get access to the system at the same time) or with a reservation-based mechanism (where the system indicates to MS which one is allowed to access and when). The system informs the MS of status of the access through the shared channel feedback.

4. *Shared channel feedback (SCF):* The SCF informs the MS of the status of uplink channels and controls and acknowledges the information sent by the MS uplink.

DTC OPERATIONS

The DTC allows two basic types of time division duplex (TDD) usage of a radio channel: half-rate, which allows six users to share the radio channel; and full-rate, which allows three users to share the same radio channel enabling a user data rate of 13 Kbps. Other channel usage consist of double and triple rate channels (i.e., where one user is assigned four or six time slots, therefore doubling or tripling the data rate available).

The DTC offers two methods of transferring control information: in-band signaling, which replaces user data being transmitted, and out-of-band signaling, also called slow associated control channel (SACCH). SACCH is a continuous stream of signaling information sent besides the user data information. This means that transfer of SACCH information does not affect the transfer of user data since dedicated bits are used. However, transfer of information using SACCH is slow, and for rapid message delivery, the FACCH is used. FACCH implements in-band signaling by transporting FACCH information as a replacement to user data.

DTC performs other operations not described in this chapter, since they are not relevant to wireless data.

5.4 IS-136 Teleservices

IS-136 teleservices are a feature of IS-136 networks that have been developed to speed up the introduction of new services for IS-136 users. A teleservice is an application that uses the air interface and network interface as the bearers for transport between a server and a mobile station. In other words, a teleservice uses the mobile station connection through the cellular network as a "bit-pipe" to exchange information with the mobile station.

Teleservices allow service providers to deliver data units to mobile stations that are connected using either DCCH or DTC. Teleservices are possible both when the user is roaming or in the home network. The data units can contain data for user applications or programming information for the mobile station. Teleservices can be either point-to-point or broadcast.

The following teleservices have been defined and standardized for IS-136:

1. *Cellular messaging teleservice (CMT):* The teleservice used to provide short message service to mobile users. Alphanumeric messages can be sent to and from mobile stations, therefore allowing for a two-way data service. TSAR can be used for CMT to sends messages longer than what IS-136 and IS-41 allow. CMT messages can be carried over DTC, DCCH, or S-BCCH (for broadcast teleservices).

2. *Over-the-air activation teleservice (OATS):* The teleservice used to provide over-the-air activation (OAA); that is, a method to program a mobile station with the home service provider network information (e.g., the identifier of the service provider), the A key for security, the mobile station identity (MSID), and other information. OATS requires the capability to exchange two-way R-DATA, and teleservice segmentation and reassembly protocol (TSAR) may be applied to send messages longer than what IS-136 and IS-41 allow. OATS messages can be carried on DTC or DCCH but not on S-BCCH, since OATS messages are always directed to a single mobile station.

3. *Over-the-air programming teleservice (OPTS):* The teleservice used to provide over-the-air activation (OAA); that is, a method for programming non-NAM (number assignment module) data in the mobile station (i.e., information regarding the intelligent roaming database, IRDB). OPTS is a mobile terminated teleservice between

the network and a mobile station and can be carried over DTC, DCCH, or S-BCCH. TSAR may be used as in the previous cases.

4. *Generic UDP transport teleservice (GUTS):* The application data delivery teleservice that supports the thin client architecture (TCA) for the delivery of text-based information from World Wide Web sites to mobile stations through the cellular network. GUTS is a two-way teleservice that adopts the User Data Protocol (UDP) to identify the port where the data are to be delivered in order to be received by the correct application (e.g., the port for the WAP browser in the mobile station). The WAP browser allows the mobile user to access the Internet from the mobile station through WAP-enabled Web pages. GUTS messages can be carried over DTC, DCCH, and S-BCCH.

5.4.1   Teleservice Delivery

A teleservice is provided above the layer 3 of IS-136 (i.e., it is an application encapsulated in layer 3 messages called R-DATA). IS-41 defines a similar message called short message delivery point-to-point (SMDPP) to carry information for teleservices. A higher protocol layer identifier (HLPI) is used to identify the type of teleservice to the mobile station, whereas a teleservice ID identifies it to servers. Figure 5–6 depicts the protocol stack for teleservices.

For most teleservices, the cellular network takes SMDPP messages received from a server and reformats the content for transmission to the mobile station using R-DATA messages without the need to read or understand the content of SMDPP or R-DATA messages (see Figure 5–7). Teleservices can also be provided over the Teleservice Segmentation and Reassembly (TSAR) protocol defined by IS-136-A, or over the broadcast teleservice transport function.

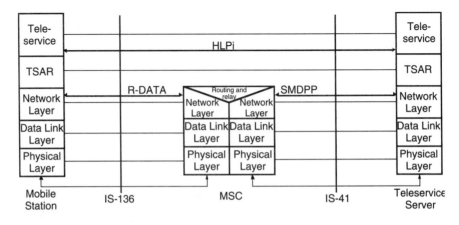

| Figure 5–6 | *Protocol stack for teleservices.* |

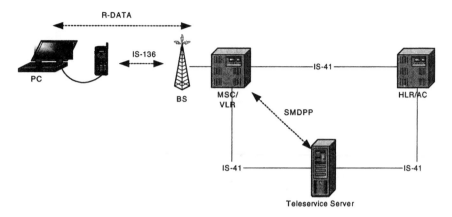

Figure 5–7 *Architecture of IS-136 teleservice delivery.*

Broadcast teleservices are delivered to mobile stations differently. Broadcast teleservices transport allows an efficient way of delivering broadcast teleservices to groups of mobile stations if the same information is of interest of more mobile stations. It allows one to define a zone within a cellular network and to differentiate the services provided in each zone. The transport allows also one to classify broadcast teleservices into categories and service groups and to provide additional information to mobile stations to allow them to discriminate more efficiently between broadcast teleservices to read and broadcast teleservices to disregard. This additional information may indicate to mobile stations what broadcast teleservices are available in the zone where the mobile station is currently located and what channels deliver them.

Figure 5–8 describes transport of broadcast teleservices. When a broadcast teleservices server generates broadcast teleservices information and forwards it to MSCs in SMDPP frames, it includes broadcast teleservice transport information to identify how the broadcast teleservice information is to be distributed. Each receiving MSC uses the broadcast teleservice transport information to determine which cluster of BSs (i.e., which zone) the broadcast teleservice information needs to be delivered to.

5.5 Circuit Switched Data Services

IS-136 provides analog and digital circuit switched data services. Digital circuit switched data services are an enhancement of the analog version and provide higher radio interface capacity and optional encryption over the radio link. In the following subsections, analog circuit switched services are briefly described since their application is very limited. Digital circuit

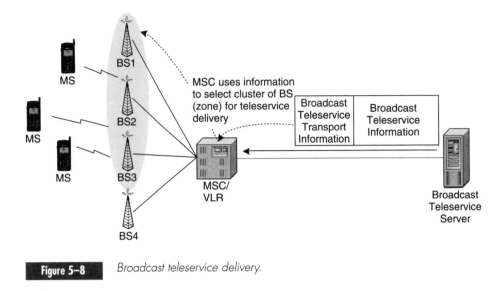

Figure 5–8   *Broadcast teleservice delivery.*

switched services are described more in detail, and examples are provided of how these network services can be used to provide end-user services.

5.5.1   Model for Data Services

IS-136 data services are based on the model described in Figure 5–7. This model foresees that there is a splitting between the terminal equipment (TE) and the mobile terminal (MT). In particular, the assumption is that in the provisioning of data services the MT is used as access equipment that allows the applications residing in the TE to communicate to peers in the network. In other words, the MT is used similar to the way a modem is used by a personal computer to connect to the Internet. Data services in IS-136 have been developed considering that the application using the services resides in a TE such as a laptop computer.

5.5.2   Analog Circuit Switched Data Services

Analog circuit switched data services are provided through the architecture shown in Figure 5–9.

   In order to add extra error control to cope with errors and packet loss over the radio interface, a cellular modem is used in the network through pools of modems connected to the MSC. Cellular modems provide error control and recovery not available in a landline modem, but due to the extra overhead they cannot provide the same data rates as traditional landline modems. Since there isn't a single common cellular analog modem protocol, the MSC has a pool of different cellular modems.

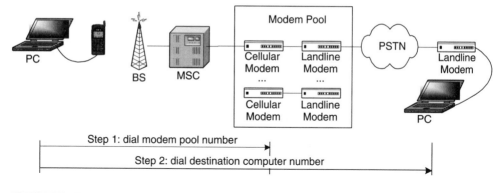

Figure 5—9   *Architecture of IS-136 analog circuit switched data services.*

Analog circuit switched data services are provided through a two-step dial-up process. First, the user dials the access number for the modem pool, requesting a traffic channel (analog voice channel) for circuit switched data; second, when a cellular modem in the network answers, the user dials the number of the destination computer.

Billing for analog circuit switched data services is traditionally the same as for voice calls; since there is no special code used by the user to set up the communication; this allows one to discriminate between a data call and a voice call.

5.5.3   Digital Circuit Switched Data Services

IS-136 digital circuit switched data services are transported over the radio interface through a digital traffic channel (DTC). Cellular modems used for analog circuit switched data cannot be used for digital data services since they do not provide enough efficiency due to the fact they carry data in voice-band tones that are not modeled to a sufficient level of reliability. The data rate that can be achieved over a DTC is 9.6 Kbps uncompressed. It is also possible to have double or triple operations that allow one to achieve uncompressed user data rates up to 28.8 Kbps.

Figure 5–10 shows the architecture of IS-136 digital circuit switched data services. The mobile station is logically divided in a TE where applications reside, and an MT where cellular-specific protocol layers are implemented. Physical implementations in a single unit are possible. The interworking function (IWF) replaces the modem pool used for analog circuit switched data and performs protocol translation between the digital protocols over the radio interface and the modem protocols used in the PSTN. The IWF can be devoted uniquely to a single MSC or shared by multiple MSCs. The IS-136 DTC is implemented in the base station, whereas RLP1 is commonly distributed between the base station and the IWF. Although in Figure 5–11 the IWF

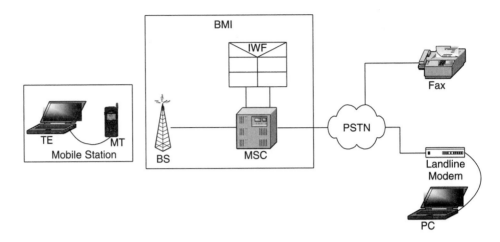

Figure 5–10   *Architecture of IS-136 digital circuit switched data services.*

is connected to PSTN through the MSC, IWF can be connected directly to the PSTN, ISDN, or packet data networks.

PROTOCOL STACK

The protocol stack for IS-136 digital circuit switched data services is shown in Figure 5–11. The data services use the IS-136 DTC L1 protocol described previously. Layer 2 is provided by the Radio Link Protocol 1 (RLP1) defined in IS-130, whereas layer 3 is provided by the IS-135 data part and by the IS-136 layer for the data call setup.

IS-130 "Radio Link Protocol 1" defines the link layer used in digital PCS to support asynchronous data and fax services defined by IS-135 over an

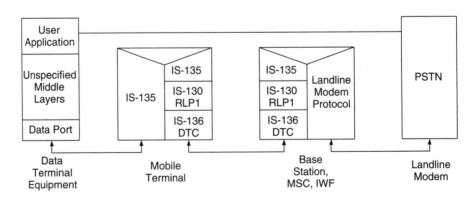

Figure 5–11   *Protocol stack for IS-136 digital circuit switched data services.*

IS-136 DTC. IS-135 "Asynchronous Data and Fax" defines a network protocol for asynchronous data and fax transport that describes call setup, monitoring, release, user data transport, and other features. IS-135 requires IS-130 as radio link and uses IS-136 for call setup, monitoring, and release.

The Radio Link Protocol (RLP1) provides link establishment, link supervision, acknowledged and unacknowledged data transport, data qualification, compression and encryption, and flow control. RLP1 uses a half-rate, full-rate, double-rate, or triple-rate IS-136 DTC to allow for a range of data rates based on user need and mobile and system capabilities. RLP1 supports two multiplexed data links, provided to layer 3 for transport of user data and IS-135 control information, respectively.

IS-135 provides a set of services to the DTE user applications:

1. Call setup, monitoring, and release
2. AT command handling
3. User data transport
4. On-line command signaling, break signaling, and signal leads

IS-135 uses IS-136 call control to perform call setup, monitoring, and release upon request from the user application or the IWF.

In the following we describe how data calls are set up.

MOBILE ORIGINATION OF DATA CALLS

When an asynchronous data call or group 3 fax call needs to be generated from the MS to the PSTN, the TE sends an AT command to the MT. The MT in turn originates a data call on the DCCH and provides the correct service code (for asynchronous data call or group 3 fax call). The MSC, based on the service code, assigns a DTC and connects the call to the appropriate port in the IWF, thus completing the logical links between the MT and the IWF required by IS-130. The MT then forwards the AT commands to the IWF, and the number in the AT command is used to connect the call to the desired destination (Figure 5–12).

MOBILE TERMINATION OF DATA CALLS

For mobile terminated calls, several options are available to deliver data calls:

*   *The MS has one phone number and the call is "prearranged":* In this case, the cellular network cannot detect that the incoming call is a data call and pages the MS with a service code for speech call. The MS needs to know in advance that the call is going to be a data call, and replies to the paging by requesting a data service code. The MSC therefore assigns a DTC and routes the call through the IWF (Figure 5–13).

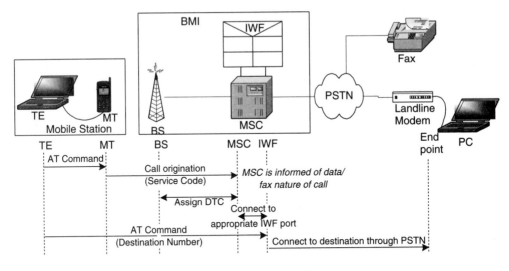

Figure 5–12   *Mobile originated asynchronous data call or group 3 fax call.*

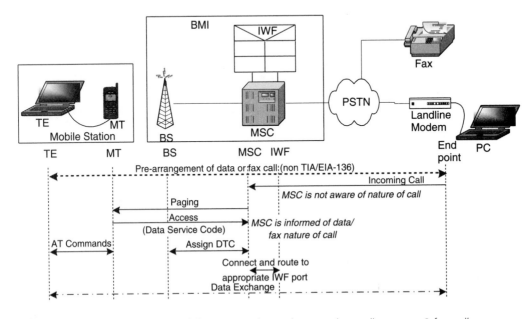

Figure 5–13   *Prearranged mobile terminated asynchronous data call or group 3 fax call.*

- *The MS has one phone number for each service:* This implies that the user has three phone numbers (voice, data, and fax) (Figure 5–14).
- *Two-stage dialing is used:* In this case, the cellular operator or service provider has dedicated numbers for each data service, and the calling party dials first the appropriate number to indicate it is a data call. The calling party then waits for a second dial tone and dials the called party specific number. In this way, the MSC knows in advance it needs to page the MS with a data service code and to route the call through the IWF (Figure 5–15).

APPLICATIONS OVER DATA CALLS

Figure 5–16 describes how Internet access (e.g., for e-mail access and Web browsing) can be supported with IS-136 networks. Two scenarios are depicted: In one case, access to Internet is through the packet data network owned by an Internet service provider (ISP), whereas in the other case access is through the packet data network owned by the IS-136 cellular operator (i.e., the cellular operator acts as ISP).

In this application scenario, the SMTP application is considered for e-mail service for an IS-136 MS, and HTTP is used for Web browsing. In order to run such applications over IP, the MS needs first to set up a connection to the IP network (PDN) by setting up a data call as described in previous sections. This typically allows one to set up a PPP connection between the MN and an access point to the PDN (i.e., a modem) over which IP packets can be carried.

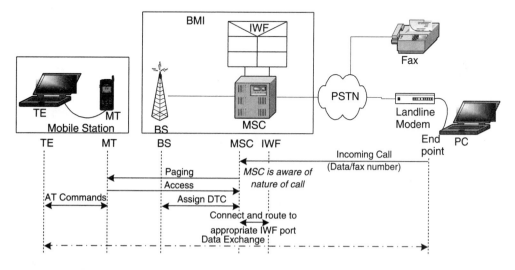

Figure 5–14   *Mobile terminated asynchronous data call or group 3 fax call with multiple numbers.*

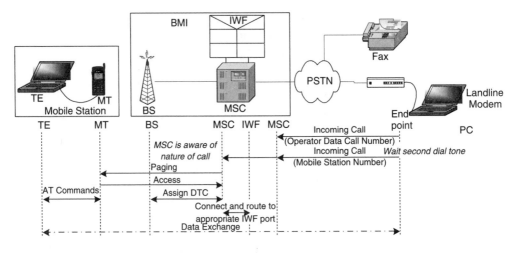

Figure 5-15   *Two-stage dialing mobile terminated asynchronous data call or group 3 fax call.*

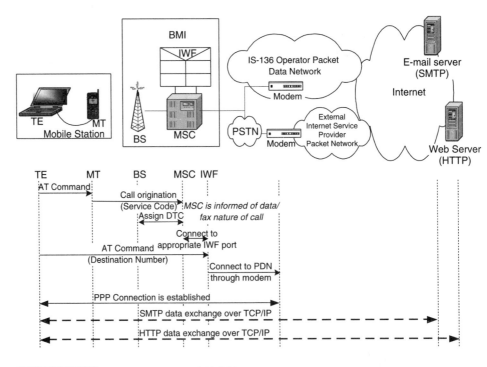

Figure 5-16   *Internet access with IS-136.*

Once the IP connection is available, the user can start the e-mail or Web browsing application in the TE. SMTP and HTTP packets will be carried transparently through the PPP connection between the TE and the modem thanks to the data call, and the MS mobility will not be visible to this connection (i.e., if the MS moves between different BS or even to a different MSC, the connection will not be aware of such mobility).

5.6 Enhancement to IS-136 Standard

To meet the increasing demand and needs of data markets, the IS-136 TDMA community standardized several evolutionary features. In this section these features are briefly described, since to date they have not been adopted or implemented (IS-136 operators have decided to migrate to GSM and UMTS technology for future network deployments).

Several aspects characterize the evolution for IS-136: improved coverage and voice quality, higher spectral efficiency and capacity, indoor services, new data services and application support, and a set of new end-user devices. This evolution addresses a wider market segment and range of use.

A key to the evolution of IS-136 toward third-generation systems is the ability to provide higher data rates by increasing spectral efficiency. The main driver for third-generation wireless communication is the ability to supplement standardized services currently available in GSM and TDMA/136 with wideband services.

The GSM system has been evolving in the last few years with the introduction of improved support for data communications over the air interface (e.g., high-speed CS data, EDGE radio interface) and packet data services (GPRS). For TDMA/136 evolution, similar standardization activities have been taking place. In particular, 136+, 136 HS, and EGPRS-136 have been defined.

5.6.1 IS-136+

IS-136+ is an improvement of IS-136 to support faster data support. IS-136+ uses the combination of multislot operation and a new modulation scheme, 8-PSK (based on the 30-KHz carrier bandwidth), which allow for increased data rates (by approximately four times).

5.6.2 IS-136 HS

IS-136 HS is based on EDGE, a new radio interface technology with enhanced modulation, and increases the data throughput of IS-136 systems to over 473 Kbps per carrier. There are two variants of 136HS in IS-136 systems, EDGE Classic and EDGE Compact. 136HS will be available in both 850 MHz and 1900 MHz IS-136 systems. EDGE Classic is the same as EDGE in GSM systems and is designed for systems with a spectrum of 2.4 MHz or more. EDGE Compact, on the other hand, is designed for IS-136 systems, where the amount of available spectrum for initial deployment of the wireless data solution is limited to 1 MHz. The requirements for 136 HS include flexible spectrum allocation, high spectral efficiency, compatibility with TDMA/136 and 136+, and support for macrocellular performance at high mobile-terminal velocity (in particular, initially this should not require clearance of more than 1 MHz of spectrum). 136 HS is able to coexist with second-generation systems in the same spectrum but without degrading their performance. The introduction of EDGE in 136 HS requires only minor changes to the network elements, mainly in the radio part.

5.6.3   EGPRS-136 HS

EGPRS-136HS introduces the packet-switched GPRS services and provides the same advances in IS-136 systems as that offered by EGPRS in GSM systems, namely higher data rates and "always online" direct Internet connectivity. This enables greater sophistication as end-user services move toward personal multimedia. More information on GPRS is provided in Chapter 8.

The use of the same basic technology, EGPRS, in both IS-136 and GSM systems makes global data roaming possible between these two systems and leads to the possibility of convergence of IS-136 and GSM systems. EGPRS-136HS network elements are overlaid on top of existing IS-136 networks and provide packet data services that add to the circuit switched services currently provided by the IS-136 networks.

IS-136 circuit switched services and GPRS packet switched services over 136+ or 136 HS air interfaces are supported from the same base station; therefore, operators can efficiently reuse existing infrastructure.

5.7   Summary

In this chapter we described IS-136 networks. In particular, we described the network architecture based on the TIA/EIA 136 standard, focusing on the mechanisms adopted in these networks at various protocol levels to provide data services. Two main types of data services are supported and have been described: teleservices and circuit switched data services. Examples of IS-136 teleservices have been provided, as well as the mechanisms and protocols to support them. In the same way, examples of circuit switched data services (in particular, e-mail and Web browsing) have been described. In conclusion, we described enhancements to the IS-136 standard that have been defined for the evolution of IS-136 networks, even if such enhancements have not been deployed by any network.

REFERENCES

TIA/EIA-IS-130-A, "TDMA Wireless Systems—Radio Interface-Radio Link Protocol 1," September 1997.

Boucher N. J., *The Cellular Radio Handbook,* 3rd edition. Mill Valley, CA: Quantum Publishing, 1995.

CDMA IS-95-A/IS-95-B Data Networks

The success of the wireless industry led to the search for new technologies to increase the capacity of wireless systems without requiring additional spectrum. Code Division Multiple Access, or CDMA, was one such digital technology developed to address this need for capacity. It provides increased spectrum efficiency or, in other words, allows multiple users to share the same radio spectrum more efficiently. The actual quantitative improvement over existing analog systems and over competing digital technologies is still a subject of intense debate.

CDMA is a spread spectrum technology, which means that instead of dividing RF spectrum into narrow channels (e.g., 30 KHz each) and assigning one (AMPS) or more (e.g., TIA/EIA/IS-136 TDMA) conversations to each channel, it spreads the information contained in a particular signal of interest over a much greater bandwidth than the original signal.

A CDMA call compresses a digital 64-Kbps stream into a standard rate of 9600 bps (or 14400 bps). This is then spread to a transmitted rate of about 1.2288 Mbps. Spreading is done by applying digital codes, unique to each user, to the data bits associated with users in a cell. The spread signal is transmitted along with the signals of all the other users in that cell over a 1.25 MHz channel. When the signal is received, the codes are removed from the desired signal, separating the users and returning the call to a rate of 9600 bps (or 14400 bps). This primary channel is called the fundamental channel (FCH).

In the United States, the spectrum is divided into two bands: one for ordinary public mobile telephony service in the 800-MHz frequency band and the other for PCS services in the 1900-MHz frequency band. New digital wire-

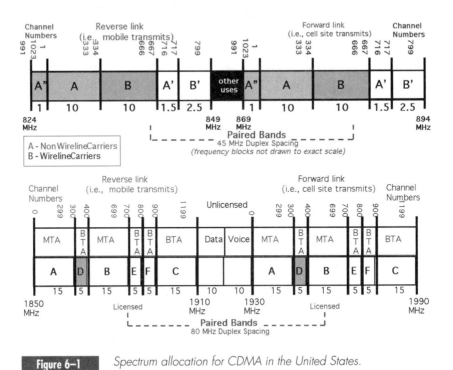

Figure 6-1   *Spectrum allocation for CDMA in the United States.*

less technologies operating in the 800-MHz band are required to be compatible with AMPS. The spectrum allocation for CDMA is shown in Figure 6–1.

The network functionalities for CDMA-based digital systems are specified in the following table.

Network Functionality	Relevant Standard
Intersystem Operations	TIA/EIA/IS-41-D
Mobile Switching Center-Base Station Interface (A-Interface)	TIA/EIA/IS-634
Signaling System 7-based A-Interface	TIA/EIA/IS-651

The radio functionalities for the 800-MHz band are specified in TIA/EIA/IS-95-A and TIA/EIA-95-B and include AMPS compatibility specification. Those for the 1900-MHz band are specified in ANSI J-STD 008. There is essentially no difference in the CDMA-related functionality between the two standards. The service options for wireless data are specified in TIA/EIA/IS-707.

TIA/EIA/IS-95-A was developed primarily to provide increased voice capacity. Support for data was initially limited to circuit-switched (CS) data. CS data requires that a dedicated connection be maintained between the end-points in the network at all times in the duration of the CS data call. This implies that a dedicated radio channel is maintained even if no data is being transferred. However, for most applications, the data traffic is bursty, and this results in an inefficient utilization of scarce radio spectrum with CS data.

Consequently, with the increased development of data services, the standard was enhanced to include support for packet-switched (PS) data. Eventually a superceding revision of the standard, namely TIA/EIA/IS-95-B, was developed that included support for high-speed PS data up to a maximum possible data rate of 115.2 Kbps. This increase in data rate was enabled by introducing a new over-the-air channel called the supplemental code channel (SCH) with a data rate of 14.4 Kbps. Up to seven of these supplemental code channels could be allocated simultaneously to provide a high-speed connection. The following table describes the data capabilities offered by namely TIA/EIA/IS-95-A/B.

Standard	Maximum Data Rate	Data Services
TIA/EIA/IS-95-A	14.4 Kbps (FCH only)	CS, PS, SMS
TIA/EIA/IS-95-B	115.2 Kbps (1 FCH + 7 SCHs)	CS, PS, SMS

PS data works differently from CS data and leverages the bursty nature of data traffic. Instead of continuously maintaining a radio channel, PS data calls occupy the radio channel only for the duration of the data transmission. The radio channel is promptly released after the completion of the data burst. This results in a significant improvement in the spectrum utilization but at the cost of introducing a small delay.

6.1   Architecture Description

The IS-95-A/IS-95-B wireless data network is an adjunct to the IS-41–based voice network. The wireless data network is composed of Mobile Switching Center (MSC), Inter-Working Function (IWF), Public Packet Data Network (PPDN), Public Switched Telephone Network (PSTN), Home Location Register (HLR), Visitor Location Register (VLR), Data Communication Equipment (DCE), Data Termination Equipment (DTE), and modems. The network architectures for CS data and PS data are illustrated in Figure 6–2 and Figure 6–3. The subsequent subsections describe the various nodes that constitute the aforementioned architectures. However, nodes such as the HLR and VLR that are common to wireless technologies are not described.

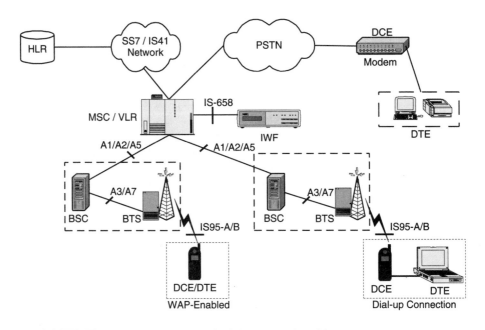

Figure 6–2   *Wireless circuit-switched data network architecture.*

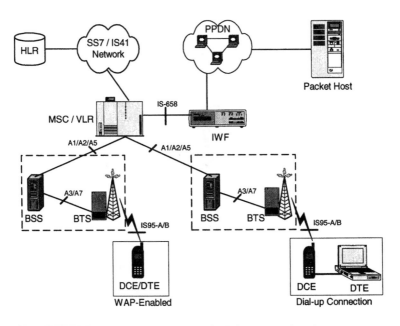

Figure 6–3   *Wireless packet-switched data network architecture.*

6.1.1   Data Terminal Equipment

The terminal equipment acts as a DTE in the standard DCE/DTE relationship. The communication between the terminal equipment and its associated DCE is via standard asynchronous serial input. The terminal equipment uses a set of AT commands (The "AT" sequence is called the "*AT*TENTION COMMAND" sequence) to control the services provided by the DCE. In case of WAP-enabled mobile stations, the MS acts as both the DCE and DTE.

6.1.2   Data Communication Equipment

On the radio side, the mobile station acts as the DCE in the standard DCE/DTE relationship. The data stream received from the DTE is packetized and sent over the air to the cellular infrastructure.

6.1.3   Mobile Switching Center

The MSC for the most part treats the CS data call as a regular voice call. However, it plays a very marginal role in support packet data services, where its primary role is to route the call to the IWF. In addition, the MSC is responsible for controlling intersystem handovers, roaming, and call delivery capabilities that support seamless operation of wireless data services.

6.1.4   Inter-Working Function

The IWF plays the role of a translator between the digital traffic in the CDMA system and the traffic in the connecting wireline voice and IP networks. It translates the protocols, signaling, and transmitted data into suitable forms that are compatible with both CS and PS networks. For a CS or fax data calls, the IWF terminates the air-link protocol suite and converts the data into standard landline modem modulations. In case of PS data for a connection into the PPDN, the IWF terminates the air-link protocol suite and routes the packetized data in the PPDN.

The IWF also plays a role in anchoring a PSTN call for the duration of the data call. This ensures service continuity in the event that a wireless data call is handed off to another MSC. As an example, data modems may drop calls and fax modems may drop calls or cause page errors if a carrier interruption occurs while transferring data through the PSTN. The IWF is located at the anchor MSC for the duration of the call.

6.1.5   Base Station

The Base Station functionality defined in the standard is usually split into two distinct entities: the Base Station Controlle (BSC) and the Base Station Transceiver Subsystem (BTS).

BSC

The BSC contains the radio-link management, cellular mobility management, and data handling (RLP functionalities). In addition, it contains some power control functionality required to provide feedback to the BTS with respect to power control thresholds.

BTS

The BTS provides the TIA/EIA/IS-95 air interface between the MS and the BSS. It is responsible for decoding/encoding the air interface frames and transferring them to the BSS or MS. In addition, it performs power control functionalities by controlling the allocation of power to each channel.

6.1.6   Modem

The modem represents a standard landline modem of the V.x series flavor. Support for V.21, V.22, V.22bis, V.32, V.32bis, V.42bis, V.17, V.27ter, and V.29 is required, whereas support for V.34, Bell-103, and Bell-212A is optional. The modem represents the standard analog and digital fax machines as well as the modem pools that allow users to connect to Internet Service Providers (ISPs).

6.2   Protocol Architecture

In this section we will delve into the layers that constitute the protocol stack for CDMA-based wireless data between the MS and the IWF. The initial CDMA-based wireless data deployment was limited to CS data specified in TIA/EIA/IS-99 followed by support for PS data specified in TIA/EIA/IS-657. Subsequently, these standards were combined into one superceding standard specified in TIA/EIA/IS-707. With the introduction of the TIA/EIA/IS-95-B standard, TIA/EIA/IS-707 was enhanced to include high-speed PS data resulting in a new revision, TIA/EIA/IS-707-A.

The protocol stack architecture can be divided into three distinct categories:

* Async data and group-3 (digital) fax
* Analog fax
* Packet data

For the most part, analog fax is similar to group-3 digital fax. The essential difference is that in case of analog fax, the Rm interface is replaced by an RJ-11 interface, the DTE is a subscriber fax machine, and an analog fax layer is introduced over the application interface layer. For our purposes it is sufficient to describe the Async data and group-3 fax protocol stack architecture.

6.2.1   Async Data and Fax Protocol Stack Architecture

The protocol stack for async data and fax is illustrated in Figure 6–4.

For analog fax, in Figure 6–4, the EIA-232 interface that defines the Rm interface is replaced by an RJ-11 interface and the async or fax layer is replaced by an analog fax layer.

APPLICATION LAYER

The application layer consists of an async data or fax user application on a DTE and the associated application layer interfaces on the DCE and the IWF. The application layer interface provides modem control and AT-command processing functionality in addition to negotiation of air interface data compression and actual data compression.

Data streams entering from the transport layer are parsed by the application layer interface to extract any option negotiation commands. The local AT commands are processed by the application interface layer, and the remaining data is passed to the Rm interface by the DTE or the PSTN data or fax modem by the IWF.

Data streams entering from the Rm interface or the PSTN data or fax modem interface are massaged to insert any in-band commands or option ne-

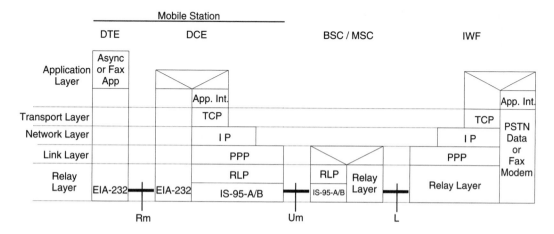

Figure 6–4   *The async data and group-3 fax protocol stack architecture (circuit switched data).*

gotiation commands by the MS and the IWF. In addition, the application layer interface at the MS also does the job of extracting and processing any local time-dependent modem control commands.

TRANSPORT LAYER

The transport layer provides a reliable delivery service to the upper layers and user data exchanges. It is based on the Transmission Control Protocol (RFC 793) with a few amendments specified by RFC 1122. This error recovery functionality ensures data integrity between the mobile and the IWF required to handle intersystem and hard handovers.

NETWORK LAYER

The network layer includes the Internet Protocol (IP), specified in RFC 791, and the Internet Control Message Protocol (ICMP), specified in RFC 792 with a few amendments specified by RFC 1122. A key limitation is that the IP datagrams are not fragmented over the air interface. IP provides global addressability with independence from the type of underlying networks and ICMP control aspects of the IP layers.

Upon the establishment of a CS data call, the IWF assigns a temporary IP address to be used by a user session. This IP address is unique to the MS only for the duration of the call.

LINK LAYER

The link layer provides an end-to-end link management, multiplexings, and framing service. It consists of the Point-to-Point Protocol (PPP), Link Control Protocol (LCP), and the Internet Protocol Control Protocol (IPCP). The link layer connection state machine consists of two states: closed and open. In the closed state there is no established link layer connection. In the open state there is an established link layer connection.

PPP provides framing, CRC checks, and control messaging. LCP provides a mechanism for the MS and the IWF for link establishment and negotiation of various PPP options. IPCP provides a mechanism for negotiating IP addresses and header compression from the IWF at session establishment. The Sub-Network Dependent Convergence Function (SNDCF) does the actual compression of the transport layer and network layer headers.

RELAY LAYER

The relay layer spans across the Rm, Um, and L interfaces. It consists of physical and logical channels required to support the upper layers. The relay layer between the DTE and DCE is called the Rm interface and is defined by a simple EIA/TIA-232-E interface (serial link).

The relay layer between the MS and BS is called the Um interface and consists of the Radio Link Protocol (RLP) layer and the underlying physical layer that provides the medium for data transmission. It is defined by TIA/EIA/IS-95-A/B standard. The RLP is a nak-based protocol and provides segmentation and reassembly functionality to fit frames transmitted over the air. In addition, the RLP layer improves the error characteristics of the wireless link by providing error detection and packet retransmissions. This reduces the need for transport layer retransmission due to lost data. The relay layer also provides call control, multiplex sublayer, and radio link management functionality.

The relay layer between the MSC and the IWF is called the L-interface and uses protocols defined in TIA/EIA/IS-658. It provides a mechanism to transport end-user data between the MS and the IWF via virtual circuits. For CS calls it provides access to the PSTN in order to originate and terminate voice-band modem calls on behalf of modem users. The standard does not describe the PPDN interface to the IWF for PS data services.

6.2.2 Packet-Switched Data Protocol Stack Architecture

For the most part the protocol stack is similar to that for CS data. The key difference is the enhancements in the link layer state and the relay layers. The packet data protocol stack is illustrated in Figure 6–5.

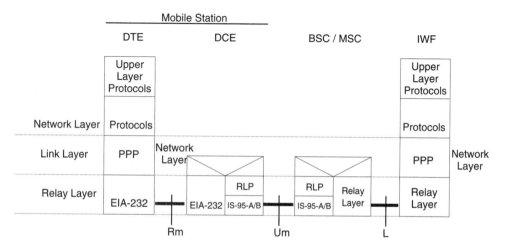

Figure 6–5   *PS data protocol stack architecture (relay layer Rm interface option).*

NETWORK LAYER

Unlike the CS data protocol stack, the support for IP is optional. Alternate network layer protocols are connectionless network protocol (CNLP), specified in ISO-8473, or CDPD, specified in TIA/EIA/IS-732. However, the most common implementation is via IP support.

LINK LAYER

In order to support PS data services, the link layer is enhanced to introduce new substates into the connection state machine. The link layer connection can be in one of two primary states: closed and open. The open state is enhanced to include two substates in order to support PS data: active and dormant.

The Open link layer connection is in an Active substate when data is being transmitted between the MS and the IWF. In this case, there exists on the IWF an L-interface virtual circuit for the MS and the MS is on a traffic channel with a packet data service option. The Open link layer connection is in a Dormant substate when there is no data being transmitted between the MS and the IWF. In this case, the IWF has no L-interface virtual circuit for the MS and the MS is not on a traffic channel. However, the MS, the BS/MSC, and the IWF maintain link connection state information (PPP session information).

While in the Dormant substate, if the IWF or the MS has data to send, then it is not necessary to reestablish any link layer connection (PPP session) or reinitialize any upper-layer protocols. Transition from Dormant to Active state requires simply an establishment of an over-the-air traffic channel between the MS and the BS/MSC.

RELAY LAYER

As in the case of CS data, the relay layer spans across the Rm, Um, and L interfaces. For the Um interface, the relay layer for PS data consists of the Radio Link Protocol (RLP) layer and the underlying physical layer that provides the medium for data transmission. Low-speed PS data support (up to 14.4 Kbps) is provided by introducing a call control state machine for the radio link in the MS and the BS/MSC. However, no enhancements to the physical layer are required.

With the advent of higher-speed data support in competing technologies such as GPRS, the EIA/TIA/IS-95-B standard was introduced, which enhanced the relay layer at the Um interface to provide high-speed data support. A new type of physical traffic channel, called the supplemental code channel, was introduced and had the same characteristics of the original TIA/EIA/IS-95-A traffic channel, now referred to as the fundamental channel. The RLP layer was enhanced to provide allocation and deallocation of this new type of channel and to provide multiplexing of data and control frames between the fundamental and supplemental code channels.

6.3 Data Services

6.3.1 Wireless Internet Access

CDMA-based digital wireless networks provide a ubiquitous and robust wireless data connectivity for browsing the Internet and sending or receiving e-mail. Users simply have to dial up their ISPs and log-on to the network. This is analogous to the wireline dial-up connection via a modem. In a CDMA network, the MS acts as a wireless modem providing connectivity to the data networks. Once on the network, a user can browse the Internet from anywhere and access all Internet applications. A few Internet applications are as follows:

- Electronic mail
- World Wide Web (text, graphics, sound, links, etc.)
- File Transfer Protocol (FTP)
- Remote File Access
- Multimedia Access (sound and video)

For the most part, existing deployments that support wireless Internet access rely on circuit switched data. For the purposes of explaining the process of setting up a call, we have chosen to describe the BSC-MSC messaging as an open interface called "A-Interface," defined in the TIA/EIA/IS-634 standard. However, it is prudent to note that most vendors have proprietary implementations for the BSC/MSC interface. Figure 6–6 illustrates the call flow for a CS async data call.

The user initiates a CS async data call by typing in the appropriate AT commands on the DTE (computer). The DTE forwards the AT command to the DCE (MS) on the Rm interface. Upon receiving the ATD command, the MS initializes the transport layer by issuing an *OPEN* call with the modem server port (380) as the destination port, leaving the source and destination IP addresses unspecified. The MS then sends an *Origination Message* with a data service option requested to the base station in order to set up up the CS data call.

The BSC then constructs a *CM_Service_Request Message* and sends it to the MSC with an async data call service indication. The MSC, recognizing that the request is for a data service, responds with a *SCCP_Connection_Confirmed Message* to complete the establishment of the SCCP connection without allocating any terrestrial PSTN circuit. It then initiates the radio link setup by sending an *Assignment_Request Message* to the BSC.

The BSC and MS then exchange the appropriate messages over the Um interface specified by TIA/EIA/IS-95-A/B in order to complete the establishment of a radio link. Once the mobile successfully arrives on the traffic channel and the appropriate service negotiation is completed, the BSC sends an

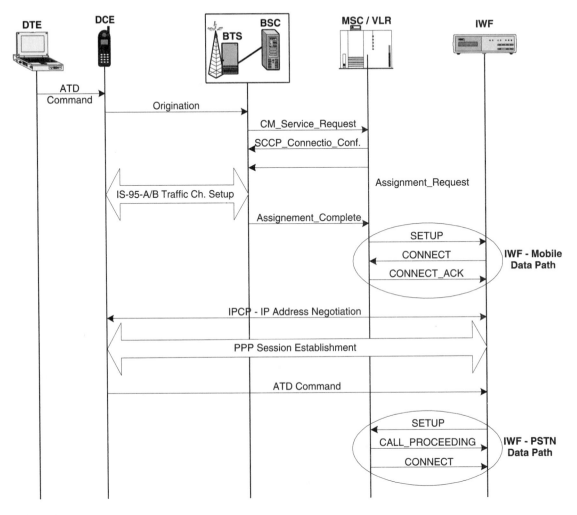

Figure 6–6 *Mobile-initiated async data call setup message flow.*

Assignment_Complete Message to the MSC. During this process the RLP layer is initialized to support CS data service option.

The successful receipt of the *Assignment_Complete Message* is the trigger for the MSC to set up the IWF-Mobile data path. In order to do so, it exchanges messages over the L-interface specified by TIA/EIA/IS-658. It constructs a *SETUP Message* in accordance with ANSI T1.617 and sends it to the IWF.

On receiving the SETUP Message, the IWF responds with a *CONNECT Message* to indicate allocation of a trunk. The MSC responds with a *CONNECT_*

ACK Message and completes the opening and allocation of an L-interface virtual circuit. The IWF relay layer signals this event to the IWF PPP layer. The PPP layer and the IPCP layer in the IWF then carry out self-configuration as per TIA/EIA/IS-707-A.

The IWF then sends an IPCP *Configure-Request Message* to the MS with the IP address parameter set to the address of the IWF. The MS stores this IP address in the destination IP-address field of the transport layer connection (which was left empty earlier). The mobile responds with an IPCP *Configure-Request Message* of its own, with all zeros in the IP address field. This is an indication to the IWF to assign an IP-address to the MS, which it does and includes in the IPCP *Configure-Nak Message* sent to the MS. It then initializes the transport layer by issuing an *OPEN* call with the modem server port (380) as the local source port, its own IP-address as the local source address, leaving the foreign network address and port number unspecified.

The MS extracts the IP address from the received *Configure-Nak Message* and stores it in the source IP-address field of the transport layer connection (which was left empty earlier), thereby completing its transport layer connection and the PPP connection establishment. The establishment of the PPP layer is the trigger for the MS to forward the ATD command to the IWF.

The receipt of the ATD command triggers the IWF into establishing the connection to the data call destination via the PSTN by constructing a *SETUP Message* in accordance with ANSI T1.607 and sending it to the MSC. The MSC responds with a *CALL_PROCEEDING Message* while it initiates the process of establishing a PSTN connection. Once the PSTN circuit is allocated, the MSC sends a *CONNECT Message* to the IWF. This completes the establishment of an end-to-end circuit connection and enables the applications to start communicating with each other.

The connectivity offered by the existing TIA/EIA/IS-95-B CDMA networks is by no means comparable to that offered by the telephone network. The call setup for PS data services mirrors that of CS data services but with enhancements for allocating and deallocating supplemental code channels that facilitate higher data rates. Although the standard allows for speeds up to 115 Kbps, very few manufacturers have chosen to implement that functionality, and data rates for the most part are limited to 14.4 Kbps. The primary reason for this is the quick evolution of the CDMA standard into the third generation, providing true PS capability. The details of this standard, called cdma2000, are provided in Chapter 10.

6.3.2   Short Message Service

Prior to the introduction of wireless data, Short Message Service (SMS) was the only mechanism for transferring data. SMS is the ability to send and receive messages with a limited number of characters directly to your MS's display. SMS allows your phone to behave as an alphanumeric pager. The

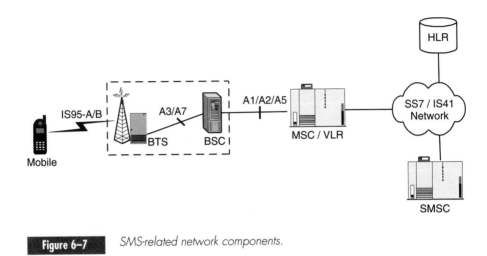

Figure 6–7   *SMS-related network components.*

messages can be transmitted over a common channel, called the paging channel in TIA/EIA/IS-95 networks, or over a dedicated traffic channel.

The SMS network comprises of the SMS Center (SMSC), the MSC, and the access network, consisting of the BSC and BTS. Message entry features, administration features, and message transmission capabilities are distributed between an MSC and the SMS Message Center (SMC). Figure 6–7 shows the topology of a SMS network.

CDMA SMS is defined by the TIA/EIA/IS-637 standard, which is based on the TIA/EIA/IS-95 standards suite. SMS service comprises two types of services: SMS Bearer Services and SMS Teleservices. SMS Bearer Services refer to basic functionality, such as paging, text messaging, and message waiting notification. SMS Teleservices are advanced services, such as broadcast services, scheduled delivery, autonomous delivery, and database information services.

The SMS Bearer Services are provided by the SMS Relay and SMS Transport layers, whereas the SMS Teleservices are provided by the SMS Teleservice Layer. These layers reside on the TIA/EIA/IS-95A link layer for over-the-air transmission and reside on the TIA/EIA/IS-41 link layer for intersystem connectivity. An example of a SMS transaction is illustrated in Figure 6–8.

6.3.3 Secure Corporate LAN/Intranet Access

In wireless networks based on the CDMA technology, the air link is encrypted, providing security for confidential data. This enables solutions for securely accessing corporate LANs. Some CDMA-based service providers leverage this capability to provide virtual private networks (VPNs) to corporate LANs.

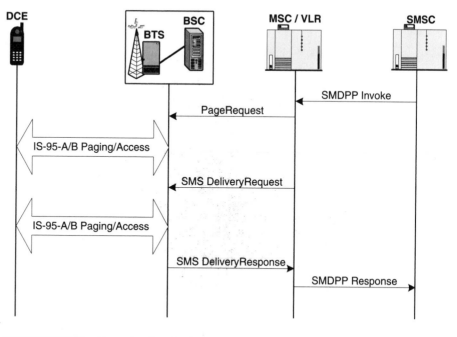

Figure 6–8   *Example of an SMS transaction.*

6.3.4   Digital and Analog Fax

Digital or Group 3 fax service uses the standard CCITT fax protocols to determine the condition of the PSTN connection and capabilities of the endpoint fax unit. The data is carried over a CS connection digitally. Data is packetized over the air interface and then converted into digital PCM before transmission into the PSTN to the destination fax unit. Analog fax service works in a similar fashion.

6.3.5   Wireless Application Protocol (WAP) Applications

One shortcoming of wireless data applications is that a computer or laptop is required for accessing them due to the dearth of processing capability and display real estate on the MS. Moreover, there are problems caused by low bandwidth, high latency, unpredictable availability, and dearth of connection stability. In order to overcome these obstacles, a set of standards was developed that are collectively called Wireless Application Protocol, or WAP.

A constituent of the WAP protocol suite is Wireless Markup Language (WML). This is similar to Hyper-Text Markup Language (HTML) used to lay out Web pages on the Internet but is optimized for wireless networks. Procedural and computational logic is enabled in WML-based Web pages using a scripting language called WMLScript.

Using these and other WAP components, information services similar to Web browsing (micro browser), small downloadable programs, telephony functionality combined with browser, and push services can be provided.

6.3.6   Looking Ahead

In spite of the high data rates made possible by the introduction of the TIA/EIA/IS-95-B standard, most vendors have chosen not to implement this capability. The primary reason is the fixed data rate of the supplemental code channel. Consequently, up to eight separate channels have to be allocated and managed in order to provide a high data rate link. This significantly increases the complexity of implementation. The cdma2000 standard alleviates this by allowing a variable-rate supplemental code channel. A single variable rate supplemental code channel can scale the data rate from 9.6 Kbps to 153.6 Kbps, thereby reducing the complexity of maintaining multiple channels.

In addition, there were other enhancements introduced by the cdma-2000 standard that facilitated true "always-on" packet data session capability, discussed later in the book. These enhancements, along with the short time frame between the releases of the standards, have resulted in most vendors and carriers choosing to leapfrog from TIA/EIA/IS-95-A to cdma2000.

References

TIA/EIA/41-D: Cellular Radio Telecommunications Inter-System Operations, November 1997.

TIA/EIA/IS-95-A: Mobile Station-Base Station Compatibility Standard for Dual-Mode Wideband Spread Spectrum Cellular System, 1996.

ANSI J-STD-008-1995: Personal Station-Base Station Compatibility Requirements for 1.8 to 2.0 GHz Code Division Multiple Access (CDMA) Personal Communication Systems, 1995.

TIA/EIA/IS-95-B: Mobile Station-Base Station Compatibility Standard for Dual-Mode Spread Spectrum Cellular System, 1998.

TIA/EIA/IS-99: Data Services Option Standard for Wideband Spread Spectrum Digital Cellular System.

TIA/EIA/IS-657: Packet Data Service Options for Wideband Spread Spectrum Systems.

TIA/EIA/124-C: Wireless Radio Telecommunications Intersystem Non-Signaling Data Communication DMH (Data Message Handler).

TIA/EIA/634: MSC-BS Interface For Public Wireless Communications Systems, 1999.

TIA/EIA/IS-658: Data Services Interworking Function Interface for Wideband Spread Spectrum Systems, July 1996.

TIA/EIA/IS-707-A.2: Data Service Options for Spread Spectrum Systems: Radio Link Protocol, March 1999.

TIA/EIA/IS-707-A.3: Data Service Options for Spread Spectrum Systems: AT Command Processing and the Rm Interface, March 1999.

TIA/EIA/IS-707-A.4: Data Service Options for Spread Spectrum Systems: Async Data and Fax Services, March 1999.

TIA/EIA/IS-707-A.5: Data Service Options for Spread Spectrum Systems: Packet Data Services, March 1999.

TIA/EIA/IS-707-A.7: Data Service Options for Spread Spectrum Systems: Analog Fax Service, March 1999.

TIA/EIA/IS-707-A.8: Data Service Options for Spread Spectrum Systems: Radio Link Protocol Type 2, March 1999.

TIA/EIA/IS-707-A.9: Data Service Options for Spread Spectrum Systems: High Speed Packet Data Services, March 1999.

TIA/EIA/IS-637 : Short Message Services for Wideband Spread Spectrum Cellular Systems.

Internet Protocol, *RFC791*, September 1981.

Postel, Internet Control Message Protocol, *RFC792*, September 1981.

Transmission Control Protocol, *RFC793*, September 1981.

Braden, Requirements for Internet Hosts—Communication Layers, *RFC1122*, 1989.

McGregor, The PPP Internet Protocol Control Protocol (IPCP), *RFC1332,* May 1992.

Simpson, "The Point to Point Protocol (PPP)", *RFC1661*, July 1994.

Challenges of IP in Wireless Networks

*I*P *has been tried and tested successfully in fixed networks for data services. It has become a de facto standard for data communications on the Internet by connecting universities, businesses, and individuals all over the world. In spite of its technical merit and popularity, it falls short of meeting the demands of wireless networks. In this chapter, the critical limitations of IP applicability to wireless networks are discussed. Aspects related to addressing incompatibilities with the wireless/cellular or PSTN networks and the effects of wireless link characteristics, roaming, and handover are discussed. Further, packet switched networks like IP face challenges with respect to security and guaranteed service quality for certain real-time services. Quality of Service (QoS) offers quality differentiation among various services and users based on their subscription levels. This chapter also covers discussions related to the session and transport issues and transitional support required in the wireless networks for using IP. By the end of the chapter, the reader will have a comprehensive understanding of what is required in the IP suite of protocols to enable IP deployment for wireless networks.*

7.1   Technical Overview

IP in wireless networks plays different roles due to the varying capabilities and applications supported in these technologies. For example, personal area networks (PAN) are concerned with short-range communications within a home or a small office/home office (SOHO) environment for wireless connectivity and for applications like simple file and data transfer. Existing IP protocols with necessary adaptations to specific PAN radio technologies (e.g., Bluetooth, IEEE 802.15) can help achieve those goals.

WLAN, on the other hand, is meant for broadband wireless access in a larger environment, such as airports, hotels, universities, and malls. The intent of WLAN is similar to the Ethernet but provides a link-level wireless solution. Therefore, WLAN, just like Ethernet, can support IP on the network layer and various IP applications that are/have been developed based on the capabilities of the higher-layer protocols over IP.

Current cellular networks (2G and 3G) are some of the most complex network architectures ever deployed on a large scale and provide a complete solution for addressing, security, paging, mobility, accounting, and so on. They are strictly governed by standards developed in standards organizations like ETSI, 3GPP, and 3GPP2 for the purposes of vendor interoperability and transparency of the network services for users roaming to other networks. 2G cellular radios have limited bandwidth and costly radio resources. In 3G cellular, although the bandwidth is higher, the radio resources are still expensive. Cellular networks make use of strict radio admission control to allocate radio resources based on demand and availability. The IP suite of protocols is not well optimized for low-bandwidth and limited resource links.

Cellular networks provide idle mobility, also called roaming, and active call handoff functions to users without any noticeable glitch to allow for seamless mobility within an operator network and across different operator networks. All these features have been tried and tested and are currently in use on a large scale. Toward supporting similar mobility features, IETF is presently defining mobility solutions with IP (versions 4 and 6) that include idle mobility and handover. The IETF also formed a working group to handle internetwork roaming for authentication, authorization, and accounting (AAA) functions for large-scale deployments.

On the services level, cellular networks offer voice communications and an advanced set of call-related supplementary services that include features like call identity, forwarding, and restrictions. Recently introduced 3G cellular networks provide higher bandwidth in their packet core network and offer multimedia applications and Web services as a first step of service integration to the Internet. These IP applications are mainly data centric and work complementary to existing cellular voice services by making use of existing Internet infrastructure support and protocols. But they are not suitable to replace cellular functionality without due enhancements.

The first enhancements include support for real-time call establishments over IP networks leading to the development of an IP-based call/session control signaling (Session Initiation Protocol, SIP) to handle calls and other multimedia sessions. Support for real-time or priority-based traffic is not currently supported by the Internet, since IP treats all the packets the same. Without preferential treatment of packets, it is not possible to provide real-time communications as the service quality suffers significantly. This end-to-end preferential treatment of certain packets opened up a new set of problems: IP must manage, set up and guarantee these desired QoS features, such as delay, jitter, throughput, bit rate, and bit-error rate.

Cellular networks exclusively use the SS7 backbone in the core network to carry signaling. SS7 offers a robust and highly reliable network to carry signaling messages. Cellular networks have been designed to connect seamlessly to the PSTN, which provides landline telecommunication services. This enables mobile users to make calls to landline phones and vice versa. To remain connected to the PSTN network, IP networks must make use of gateways that will perform signaling and media interworking on the border of IP networks and PSTN. A lightweight, reliable transport protocol over IP is under development to be backward compatible with the SS7 protocol stack.

In order for IP to be applied ubiquitously to wireless networks, it must overcome the wireless challenges. The rest of this chapter discusses, at length, the individual challenges of IP applicability to wireless networks.

7.2   The Addressing Challenge

In PSTN, a user is typically identified by a single identifier called a telephone number (e.g., an ISDN number). The ISDN number is a string of digits that can be dialed on any phone in order to reach the user. The ISDN number is used for two purposes: as a public address to reach the user and by telecom operators as an identifier for the user (e.g., for billing purposes).

The deployment of cellular networks has introduced a distinction between the public address and the private address of a user. The public address of a mobile user, also called the mobile number, is the string of digits used by any calling party to reach the mobile user. In general, in cellular networks the mobile number is not used as a private address to identify the user. As a matter of fact, in several cellular networks a mobile user can have multiple mobile numbers (e.g., for different services such as voice, data, and fax). Traditionally, the private address of a mobile user (also referred to as the mobile user identity) is globally unique, and a mobile user is assigned only one private address. The private address is used to identify the user for accounting reasons, for authenticating the user when accessing the networks, and in general for every purpose where the mobile user must be uniquely identified.

Cellular networks have introduced the need to identify separately the mobile user and the terminal the mobile user is using. The reason for the separation is that mobile users need to be able to use multiple terminals and switch from one terminal to another without needing to change the public address. This applies to the case where a mobile user desires to switch to a new mobile phone while maintaining the same subscription and the same public address. Moreover, a mobile phone may get lost or stolen, and mobile users need to be able to maintain their mobile number while using a new terminal.

The adoption of IP in wireless networks, and in particular in cellular networks, introduces a new set of issues regarding addressing. In this section we describe the issues related to addressing in IP wireless networks.

7.2.1   Addressing in Current Cellular Networks

In current cellular networks (e.g., GSM, US TDMA [IS-136], US CDMA [IS-95]), a set of different identifiers is used to address a mobile node.

In GSM networks, addressing is based on three identifiers:

- *IMSI (international mobile station identifier):* The IMSI is the private address of a mobile user. The IMSI is globally unique and is composed of three parts: the mobile country code (MCC), identifying the country to which the mobile user belongs; the mobile network code (MNC), identifying the specific cellular network operator the mobile user has a subscription with; and the mobile user specific identity within the mobile operator. IMSI is used in GSM to identify the user when it registers with the network, to authenticate the user, for mobility procedures, and so on. The IMSI is never used to deliver services (e.g., voice calls) to the user and is not known to calling parties.
- *MSISDN (mobile station ISDN number):* This is the mobile user public address (i.e., the number that can be dialed by a calling party to reach the mobile user). A mobile user can have multiple MSISDN numbers (e.g., for different services such as voice calls, data calls, and fax calls).
- *IMEI (international mobile equipment identity):* The IMEI is a globally unique identifier for the mobile terminal. The IMEI is a string of digits containing the identification of the manufacturer. IMEI is used in GSM networks to identify the terminal a mobile user is using and to avoid usage of stolen or un-authorized terminals.

In GSM networks, a mobile user is given a SIM (subscriber identification module) card that can be inserted into the GSM mobile terminal. It contains the mobile user IMSI and MSISDN, as well as other parameters for security and for the mobile services the user has subscribed to. The adoption of the IMSI and the SIM card allows GSM mobile users to use different mobile terminals by simply moving the SIM card from one terminal to another one, without the need to inform the mobile operator of the change of terminal.

In IS-41 networks (e.g., IS-136 and IS-95 cellular networks), addressing is based on two identifiers:

- *MSI (mobile station identifier) or MIN (mobile identification number):* This is the mobile user public address (i.e., the number that can be dialed by a calling party to reach the mobile user).
- *ESN (equipment serial number):* The ESN is a globally unique identifier for the mobile terminal. The ESN is a string of digits containing the identification of the manufacturer. ESN is used to identify the terminal a mobile user is using and to avoid usage of stolen or unauthorized terminals.

IS-41 networks do not have the equivalent of the GSM IMSI. In fact, in IS-41 networks MSI and ESN are used together to identify the mobile user at registration with the network, to authenticate the user, and so on. Therefore, if a mobile user desires to change terminals, he or she needs to interact explicitly with the mobile operator (e.g., through customer services) to indicate the desire to change the terminal.

7.2.2   Layers of Addressing in IP Networks

The basics of IP addressing were described in Chapter 2. IP hosts traditionally run different applications on top of the IP stack (e.g., e-mail, Web browsers). In addition to these well-known and widespread applications, new applications are being defined. A relevant example is SIP and applications based on SIP that allow an IP host to have multimedia communications (e.g., audio, video) with other IP hosts.

Although a correspondent node can use the host IP address to address the host in applications, the IP address is typically not the most convenient and appropriate address to be used for a set of reasons:

- Memorizing a host IP address may not be convenient, in particular if IPv6 is used.
- An IP host may not have a fixed IP address (e.g., it may obtain a dynamic IP address when getting connectivity with the network and change the IP address every time IP connectivity is reestablished). In such a case, any correspondent node needs first to discover the current IP address of the host.

Therefore, additional addresses have been introduced for IP hosts that allow addressing of an IP host independent of the host IP address and that traditionally have a user-friendlier format (i.e., are alphanumeric strings that are easier to remember). Examples are e-mail addresses, typically in the form username@domain, and URL addresses (e.g., Web site addresses).

When considering IP networks and IP hosts, it is necessary to discriminate between two levels of addressing:

- *Transport level:* Addressing at the transport level allows IP packets to be delivered to the IP host across the IP network.
- *Application level:* Addressing at the application allows delivery to the IP host of IP packets belonging to the service associated with the application level identifier (e.g., e-mail, SIP call).

Traditionally, the IP address assigned to an IP host is considered as the host transport-level address, whereas the host e-mail address and the SIP URL are considered application-level addresses.

The introduction of mobile IPv4 led to the need to identify mobile IP nodes independent from the host IP address. In fact, the foreseen shortage of IPv4 addresses due to the limited IPv4 addressing space brought out the need to have an additional identifier for the mobile node that allows the node to be uniquely identified and receive an IP address dynamically when obtaining connectivity with the network. Therefore, the NAI (network access identifier) was introduced in IP networks. The NAI is a private address for an IP user and, more specifically, for a user having a subscription with a given service provider. An IP host can have several NAIs assigned to it depending on the number of service providers the host has subscriptions with.

In this complex framework, the discrimination between public and private addressing and between addressing and user identification in IP networks is a gray area that depends heavily on the specific type of IP network. In fact, several parties advocate that the sole identifier for an IP host, whether mobile or not, should be the host IP address. Other parties advocate the availability of different addresses and identifiers for IP hosts for usage in different scenarios.

When making a comparison with cellular network, there isn't a clear match between public and private addresses used in cellular networks and addresses of IP networks. The GSM IMSI can be compared with the NAI, and the MSISDN can be compared with the e-mail address or SIP URL. In a similar way, the IMEI can be compared with the identifier of the network interface card the IP host uses to access the network. However, in the case of wireless networks, and in particular in the case of cellular networks, it is not clear what the network interface card identifier is. Finally, in cellular networks there is no clear equivalent for the IP address, since the delivery of services (e.g., voice calls) in cellular networks is not based on any transport-level identifier but on the MSISDN and a set of functionality in the network to keep track of the location of the cellular node corresponding to the MSISDN.

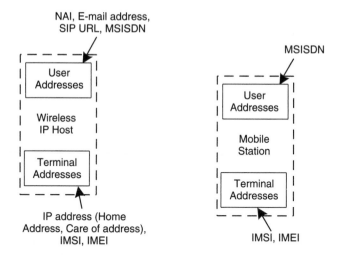

Figure 7–1   *Addressing and identification comparison.*

Figure 7–1 compares a traditional 2G cellular terminal (GSM) with a wireless IP host. The wireless IP host has access to the cellular technology. A terminal has two types of addresses: user addresses and terminal addresses. A user address is visible to a subscriber, whereas a terminal address is internal to the terminal and required by the network for routing or identification. In the figure it can be seen that in addition to MSISDN, IMSI, and IMEI, a wireless IP host needs to have e-mail, NAI, SIP URL, and IP addresses.

With the application of IP to wireless networks, and in particular cellular networks, new addressing issues are introduced. These issues are mainly based on the different types of addresses and identifiers used in cellular networks and IP networks. An issue that is particularly relevant is the need to maintain a clear distinction between transport and application addresses, public and private addresses, and user/terminal addresses as described in the previous sections.

7.3   The Radio Link Challenge

Although IP and its application protocols are designed as link generic to accommodate a very wide range of data link networks, there was an implicit assumption in the designs that the network is a wired network. Now that the wireless is adopting these protocols, it is realized that the radio links have their own characteristics, which impact the performance of the IP protocols. These impacts are more significant in the case of Wireless Wide Area Networks (WWAN e.g., cellular networks) and Wireless Personal Area Network

(WPAN e.g., Bluetooth), compared to the Wireless LAN (IEEE 802.11). This is because WWAN and WPAN offer more latency and limited bandwidth. In this section, we are going to discuss the challenges posed by some of the characteristics of radio links for IP.

7.3.1   Radio Link Efficiency

A radio interface is bandwidth constrained because it is bound to use limited spectrum. Although 3G networks claim to provide bit rates up to 2 Mbps, it is still a far cry from the 52.8 Mbps a very high data rate digital subscriber line (VDSL) can offer on a single twisted-pair copper loop. Similarly, bit rate of 11 Mbps in WLAN is no comparison to 1 Gbps of the gigabit Ethernet (IEEE 802.3). Therefore, it is highly desired to use the available bandwidth as efficiently as possible, so as to give the user a decent performance for IP compared to the wired world. Moreover, cellular operators pay a significant amount of their deployment costs in acquiring a spectrum. Therefore, radio link efficiency is also highly desired for cost savings.

One approach to improving efficiency for some IP protocols is to use header compression. A problem with IP is its large header overhead. This problem is more visible for those real-time applications where a packet is generated at a very fast rate and the payload size is comparable or even smaller to the header size. For example, an RTP (real-time protocol) packet carrying interactive voice conversation could have an IPv6 header of 40 bytes, a UDP header of 8 bytes, and an RTP header of 12 bytes, making the total header bytes equal to 60 bytes. The size of the payload, depending on the speech coding, could be as low as 15 to 20 bytes. In this example the header size is twice the payload size. The Robust Header Compression ROHC working group has developed [RFC 3095] header compression schemes for RTP/UDP/IP. The schemes can reduce the header size down to one or zero byte. The wireless links also need to have robust header compression for the other protocols, such as TCP and SCTP.

Bandwidth efficiency can also be improved by performing compression on IP payloads. The IP Payload Compression Protocol (IPComp) [RFC 2393] defines a framework for payload compression. The 3GPP2 network uses the PPP from the PDSN to the MS and has suggested using the PPP Compression Control Protocol [RFC 1962] for PPP payload compression. Bluetooth LAN access profile also suggests using PPP and PPP payload compression. However, if the encryption is applied to IP datagrams, the compression at a lower layer (e.g., PPP) becomes ineffective. IPComp is especially useful when encryption is applied to IP datagrams. RFC 2757 provides a good analysis of the feasibility of IP payload compression. It suggests that IP payload compression is something of a niche optimization and may not be always useful. It also says that many of the IP payloads are already compressed (images, audio, video, "zipped" files) by the applications or are already encrypted above the IP layer. These payloads will not compress further, limiting the benefit of this optimization. Also, the application-level compression can often outperform IPComp because the applications can use compression dictionaries based on knowledge of the specific data being compressed. Therefore, for payload compression the best bandwidth efficiency can be achieved if application-level compression techniques are used extensively. The challenge is to ensure that all the applications have a compression mechanism and are using them over wireless links.

7.3.2   Radio Delay and Error

Radio links are low-bit-rate links. They can transmit a block of bits, called a radio frame, which is usually much smaller than an IP packet. Therefore, IP packets are usually segmented into much smaller radio frames so they can be transported over these low-bit-rate links. The link layer usually provides queues for the IP packets and the radio frames, to help in the process of segmentation and transmission. This introduces store-and-forward delay and decreases the throughput of IP. The challenge is to reduce this store-and-forward delay to increase throughput. There are new modulation and coding schemes defined for 3G systems that can pack more bits in a radio frame and can reduce the store-and-forward delay to a certain extent. But the increased number of bits usually comes at the cost of error protection.

Another radio delay that adds to the store-and-forward delay is caused by the link-layer error recovery mechanism. The radio links have a relatively high frame loss rate; therefore, an ARQ type of mechanism is used for assured delivery. Retransmission due to the ARQ mechanism adds delay in delivering an IP packet. In addition to the delay, the link-layer ARQ has some adverse effect on applications, which have their own ARQ mechanisms, like TCP. TCP calculates the value for retransmission timeout (RTO) based on the measured end-to-end round-trip time (RTT). When the link layer retransmits radio frames of a TCP packet, link latency momentarily increases. This sudden increase in latency may cause RTO expiry, resulting in an unnecessary retransmission by TCP of a packet that the link layer is still retransmitting. Such spurious end-to-end retransmissions generate unnecessary load and reduce end-to-end throughput.

One can suggest inhibiting link-layer ARQ if the application has ARQ. But link-layer retransmissions are much more efficient than end-to-end error recovery. This is because the end-to-end path could be much longer than the wireless link. As a result, link-layer and application ARQ need to exist together. The challenge here is to establish an efficient interaction between the two layers of ARQ protocols so they will not cause any impairment on the throughput.

Errors on wireless links may result in IP packet loss, which has another implication in TCP. For TCP, a packet loss means that there is congestion in the network. This is because in the wired network, packets are usually lost due to congestion and are rarely lost because of link errors. TCP initiates congestion avoidance or slow start mechanisms; these procedures reduce throughput significantly. While there are mechanisms [RFC 3155] defined for improving TCP performance in such scenarios, the challenge is to optimize the TCP and any other protocols from the assumptions, which are invalid in the case of wireless link layer.

In the cellular world, signaling message sizes are optimized for low bandwidth, so the signaling procedures can be completed with low latency. One such example is the initial access message in GSM [GSM TS 04.08], which is only one byte long. In the IP world, there are text-based protocols, such as SIP, RTSP, and SDP, which are defined without considering bandwidth-limited links. For example, a SIP message can be as big as 2000 bytes. These messages would take a significant amount of time to transfer over the air interface, resulting in a significant delay in session establishment or feature invocation. These protocols need to be optimized for wireless links. The ROHC working group is currently looking into compressing the SIP protocol.

In summary, the challenge is to modify wireless link and/or IP to enhance performance. Wireless links have their own hard limitations, such as bandwidth, which cannot be enhanced further. Also, some enhancements may not be cost effective for commercial use. On the other hand, modifications in IP and its applications are more challenging than wireless links. IP protocols are already implemented in lot of products, and it is not possible to change all those legacy products. Moreover, IP is a layer 3 protocol and it should not be changed because of a specific layer 2 protocol requirement.

The IETF Performance Implications of Link Characteristics (PILC) working group has published documents that provide analysis of link characteristics and set the direction for further research. PILC has also suggested use of performance enhancing proxies (PEPs) for TCP (see RFC 3135 for details). PEP is defined as a function that improves the performance of Internet protocols on network paths where native performance suffers due to the characteristics of a link. So far, the PEP approach is used for TCP, but other application protocols may also like to adopt this approach. However, generalized use of PEPs is discouraged, mainly because they contravene the end-to-end principle of IP. In the long run, wireless link and IP need to be converged in a more substantial way. Future enhancements in one protocol need to be carried out while considering the requirements of the other.

7.4   The Mobility Challenge

Mobility is an important feature in cellular networks and in any wireless network. Hence, it has been a key design element and an integrated part of current cellular network architectures. However, this is not the case with IP networks, and hence mobility can be considered as one of the biggest challenges for IP. This is because IP was initially envisioned as a universal standard for connecting different hosts or computers for data communications. In spite of its great success, application of IP was limited to fixed or stationary hosts. Without support for mobility, the applicability of IP to cellular networks is quite limited and may result in wireless-specific solutions to handle mobility. GPRS is a perfect example on how mobility-unaware IP can be applied to wireless networks. Until recently, there was no initiative to enhance IP to be mobility aware. Mobility in cellular networks is twofold:

1.   Idle mobility
2.   Handover

In the following sections, these two aspects are discussed to show how they are being handled by IP.

7.4.1   Idle Mobility

Cellular networks are operated by different service providers, and each service provider manages the network by dividing the network into manageable network areas in a hierarchical fashion, all the way down to the cell level. Mobile nodes are identified by location based on which cell the user is presently in. Cellular networks perform location management by continuously tracking the location of mobile nodes with the help information received from the mobile nodes. The location information determines the cell (or a larger network area) where the mobile node is currently located. The location information is broadcast to all the mobile nodes in the network or cell area.

When someone calls the user, the network infrastructure, and the mobile switching center in particular, retrieves the latest location information of the mobile node and delivers the call. Mobile nodes periodically update their location information to the network. These location updates are otherwise referred to as idle mobility because they are performed when the mobile nodes are not engaged in any active call or other services. These updates are mainly timer based or event based, in case the mobile nodes may cross the network management areas or even network borders into an area operated by a different service provider (Figure 7–2).

The IETF Mobile-IP Group has defined two different mobility mechanisms for IP, one for IPv4 and another one for IPv6. The fundamental principles are similar, but the protocol capabilities and definitions are quite different. The basic principle is to provide a local care of address (CoA) to the mobile node while it is away from the home network. The mobile node may have a permanent or home address assigned in the home network. The local CoA is provided by the visiting or foreign network where the mobile node is currently present. In IPv6, the mobile node can form its own local CoA through

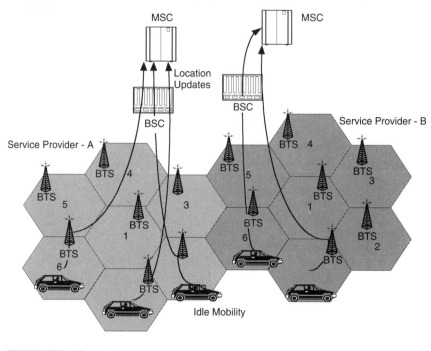

Figure 7–2   *Idle mobility in cellular networks.*

stateless address autoconfiguration by listening to the router advertisement messages from the routers serving that subnet. The mobile node performs a registration or a binding to the home agent (HA) to indicate the local CoA. The HA creates a binding cache between the permanent address and the CoA to tunnel all the packets addressed to the permanent address to the CoA. The same binding is also established at the correspondent node (CN) if there are any active sessions with any nodes. Whenever the mobile node's network point of attachment changes, it obtains a new CoA and performs updates on the binding to the HA and CN. Figure 7–3 shows mobility in mobile IPv6.

If the mobile is far away from the home or CN, it may take a more latency to update the binding. To reduce the frequency of these updates, micro or localized mobility management (LMM) mechanisms are proposed. Cellular-IP, Hawaii, Regional Registration, and heirarchical mobile IP (HMIP) are some of the techniques.

7.4.2 Handover

Another aspect of mobility associated with active calls or sessions is called handover or handoff. When the user is engaged in an active conversation, handovers can be triggered due to movement of the mobile node from one cell to

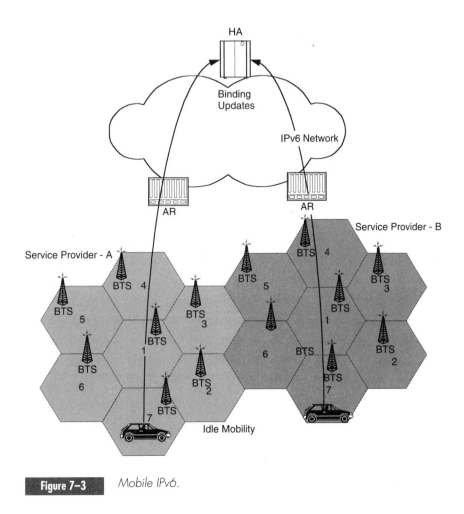

Figure 7-3 *Mobile IPv6.*

another. The network along with the mobile node can monitor radio conditions like signal strength and capacity constraints, which may be the actual reasons for these handover decisions. The handover process results in moving the mobile's current network anchor point to a different one in the target network.

In cellular networks, the mobile, while it is engaged in an active call, provides periodic signal strength information due to neighboring cells to the current radio network. Based on signal strengths and other criteria, the current or the source cell makes the decision to hand over the mobile node to a target cell. It proactively signals the target cell that the handover will be performed so that the target cell can establish the necessary radio channels before the mobile arrives and provide the information back to the source cell. The mobile node is instructed to perform a handover by providing the target cell information. This kind of handover procedure is called a "make before break" mechanism.

In the case of IP networks, without any special handover support, the handover across different network point of attachments (routers) happens in a passive manner. The mobile node loses the network connection at the present router; it later establishes the radio connection at the target cell and obtains the router information and a new CoA at the new router and updates the binding with home agent and CN, assuming there is no micromobility management. This long and cumbersome procedure is not suitable for real-time communications simply because the call break is a long and noticeable break. Cellular-type handovers require that the glitches or break in communications cannot be greater than 150 ms.

Realizing this importance of handover, a fast handover proposal was introduced into the Mobile-IP group in which extensions to base mobile IP protocol were proposed. According to this proposal, the mobile node must make the decision to perform the handover and inform the source router. The source router determines the target router based on information provided by the mobile node and requests to provide a CoA at the target router. When the mobile node loses the network connection at the old router, the packets are tunneled to the target router with the new CoA. The mobile node accesses the target router and is immediately able to configure the new CoA and receive delayed packets. Although this mechanism may work, it may not be practical for the cellular environments. Situations where radio networks can make handover decisions cannot be handled with fast handover. Another mechanism to handle such situations has been proposed. Bidirectional edge tunnel handover (BETH) defines a handover procedure that reduces network-layer signaling in fast handover and performs handover based on triggering from radio link layers.

Another aspect of terrestrial mobility is to allow mechanisms to exchange user subscription, security, accounting, and service information between different networks. The cellular protocols have defined roaming protocols like IS-41 in CDMA and US TDMA networks and GSM MAP for GSM networks to exchange user subscription information related to security and services to allow roaming from one network and another. The IETF has formed an authentication, authorization, and accounting (AAA) working group to address the large-scale deployment of IP-based mobility, security, and accounting mechanisms. AAA developed a Diameter protocol that provides solutions for the roaming functions and intranetwork, internetwork, and interdomain operations.

7.4.3   Access Independent IP Mobility

The previous sections presented high-level mobility aspects of cellular networks. But the details of the mobility mechanisms in each of the cellular networks at the radio level and roaming across different networks are dependent on the protocols used for that specific cellular technology. For example, mobility functions defined for IS-95 CDMA cellular networks are relevant to only IS-95 CDMA terminals. Users can roam only to the networks that support the same IS-95 CDMA technology. In the same way, GSM users can roam only to similar GSM networks. When other noncellular access technologies (e.g., WLAN) are considered, it is even worse since currently there is no common network infrastructure and protocol exchange to support roaming between these dissimilar access networks.

The IP mobility protocol, defined as part of network layer (IPv6) or above (IPv4), can provide an elegant solution to interaccess network roaming. IP-level mobility provides an abstraction to layer 2 access technologies by hiding specific access network protocols. Any mobility functions defined for access-specific technology can be used for micromobility functions that are meaningful only within that specific access network. IP mobility provides macromobility functions to determine the network location of the mobile node on a global scale. From this aspect, IP mobility can enable seamless mobility while roaming and possibly even handovers across different access technologies. Further, it simplifies the mobile terminal by adopting common mobility-level functions above any specific access link protocol stacks.

7.4.4 Dormancy and Paging

Cellular networks support dormancy for mobile nodes that are idle and not engaged in active conversations. Dormant mobile nodes do not perform frequent updates of their network location information at the cell level. Instead, they wake up only when they move across a larger network area. The main benefit of dormancy is to save power on the mobile nodes, since frequent location updates to the network drains the power. The network does not keep track of dormant nodes at the cell level but within a greater network area where the mobile is currently dormant. The mobile nodes remain dormant until there is a need to wake up and update their exact location to the network. When mobile users initiate calls, the mobile node wakes up to perform a cell-level location update, obtain the radio channels for signaling exchange, and then exchange call control signaling to set up the call. For mobile terminated calls, the MSC issues a paging request to all the BSCs in the area where the mobile node was previously registered dormant. The mobile node responds to the page from the BSC and performs wakeup functions; the call is then delivered to the exact location where the mobile is currently located.

Wireless IP networks can be similarly divided into several paging areas. The paging area information can be broadcast with the help of specific radio broadcast capabilities. The mobile node can remain idle within the paging area without needing to perform idle mobility procedures, thus saving power. The mobile node can switch to dormant mode by registering itself as a dormant node to a network element that handles dormancy and paging functions. It needs to wake up only when it crosses the paging area to update its new paging location. Any downstream traffic toward the mobile node triggers a paging request to wake up the mobile node within that paging area.

The benefit of IP-level dormancy and paging is twofold. It offers these power-saving functions to wireless access technologies like WLAN that do not have such capabilities at the layer 2 level. Although all cellular technologies do provide these functions, implementing IP-level dormancy offers transparency between the layer 2 functions and the layer 3 functions. Another incentive to IP-level dormancy and paging is due to its access network independence, as discussed in the previous section.

Paging when combined with mobility management protocols can provide a very desirable solution for dormancy of mobile hosts in IP networks.

7.5   The QoS Challenge

The challenge of QoS is not introduced by wireless networks alone, but it was realized with the introduction of new high-bandwidth applications on the Internet. Normal IP data services, referred to as background or best-effort services, like email, Web browsing, FTP, and telnet sessions can work fine without a need for QoS. As new applications like voice over IP, multimedia streaming, and other bandwidth-hungry applications come into existence, the need to manage, control, differentiate, and guarantee the desired service levels for the duration of the communications has become an important issue. The user perception of quality is determined by end-to-end factors like latency, jitter, throughput, bit-error rate, and bandwidth. QoS management and the associated traffic engineering mechanisms together provide desired service levels.

Providing end-to-end QoS between two communicating endpoints is not a trivial issue as they are separated by networks owned and operated by several operators. There must be common understanding of QoS service levels between the users and the network and across the network borders. One means to achieve this is by establishing *service-level agreements (SLAs)* between users and the network in the form of subscription levels and between network operators to enforce service guarantees (Figure 7–4). Presently, on the Internet, SLAs are established for the aggregated traffic from all users across various ISPs and backbone service providers to provide a guaranteed level of service usually in the form of uptime, bandwidth guarantees, and delays. However, QoS differentiation occurs on an application or service basis or even on per user basis, meaning that all services are treated equally and users cannot request for a higher QoS for a VoIP call to enjoy a better communication experience. There is also an effect due to mobility on QoS. Frequent changes of CoA due to mobility and handover make it difficult to maintain the same QoS levels from one point of attachment to another.

Some current wireless networks, 3G, and future cellular networks are capable of providing high rates over radio connections. Thus, they will have

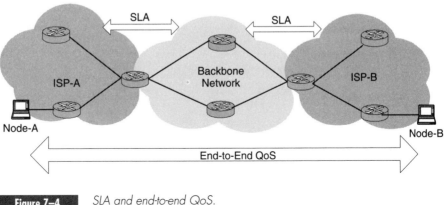

Figure 7–4 *SLA and end-to-end QoS.*

communication bandwidth capabilities similar to the fixed hosts and therefore will be capable of using voice over IP and digital audio and video streaming. 3G cellular networks have already defined QoS classes as part of the radio link layer, but these definitions are limited from the mobile node over the cellular radio up to some core network element that terminates these QoS levels. These networks employ native technology for QoS resource management and admission control to admit or reject any QoS requests from users based on subscription profile and available resources. Additionally, interworking between the QoS classes defined in terms of end-to-end service levels must be mapped to QoS classes over the radio. This QoS link adaptation functions must be performed at the border of the access network and the core (backbone) network.

Over the past years a lot of work has been devoted to understanding, defining, and developing QoS architectures and protocols. The IETF Integrated Services (Inst-Serv) group has developed an integrated service model and QoS framework for QoS provisioning on the Internet. It involves enhancements to network infrastructure to make networks QoS aware and the development of a new protocol, called the Resource Reservation Protocol (RSVP), that end terminals exchange for each direction of communication. The route of the RSVP messages within the network also creates QoS flow-state information for the corresponding session. The benefit of RSVP signaling is realized by its access-independent approach to provide resource management and admission control similar to that of cellular systems but end to end. The Int-Serv model has scalability problems due to establishing context information along the path and therefore may not be suitable for large-scale networks.

IETF has also specified another method for QoS provisioning, called the Diffserv. It offers a scalable solution by not requiring establishment of per-flow states in the network, but by aggregating the flows into predefined service levels. Packet classification and per hop behavior (PHB) are the building blocks of the Diffserv networks. Broadly, two different PHB are defined—expedited forwarding (EF), for delay-sensitive real-time data, and assured forwarding (AF) for noncritical data. There are further four divisions within the AF class. Further, DiffServ does not require prior end-to-end signaling, but the source node can perform packet classification by appropriately marking the IP packets with desired DSCP codes, corresponding to desired QoS levels. Diffserv nodes perform packet forwarding and determine drop precedence in case of congestion based on these DSCP codes.

7.6   The Security Challenge

Traditionally, security mechanisms developed in the IETF for IP networks are meant to provide security features end to end. There is no particular assumption of link-level security functionality. For example, Ethernet, which is one of the most widely used link-layer protocols, does not offer any link-level protection against eavesdropping and spoofing. So a malicious node can gain network access into an Ethernet segment and listen to the broadcasted Ethernet frames on that segment and introduce impersonated frames into the segment. Irrespective of the link-layer security features, IP packets can still be made secure by utilizing security features at the network, transport, or application layers. Without link-level security, unencrypted portions of the packets can be still vulnerable to snooping.

Security Terminology

The following security terms are introduced as defined in *Security Architecture for the Internet* [RFC 2401]:

- *Authentication:* Mechanism to prove or disprove a certain user's or device's claimed identity.
- *Confidentiality:* Privacy protection that the data cannot be viewable by other parties other than the intended recipients.
- *Encryption:* A mechanism commonly used to provide confidentiality.
- *Integrity checking:* Ensuring that the data are not altered along the way from source to destination.
- *Non-repudiation:* Ensuring that the data are originated from a sender to be able to prove for accountability and other reasons.
- *Key management:* Securely distributing cryptographic keys between involved parties.
- *Security association:* A cryptographic agreement between two parties for exchange of data.

While one needs a physical connection to gain access to a wired network, that is not the case for the wireless networks. Therefore, unless there are proper authentication and authorization mechanisms in place, anyone without proper security credentials within the wireless network domain can be a potential security threat in one form or another. Addressing this problem, all the widely accepted wireless standards offer some level of link-level security management. But these security features are limited only to the wireless segment. In addition, complete end-to-end security requires that a network, transport, or higher-level security mechanisms must be used.

7.6.1   Security in Wireless Networks

The handling of security in cellular networks is quite different from that of IP networks. All the security features, like authentication, authorization, encryption (ciphering), and nonrepudiation, are well defined for celullar use and they are handled at the network layer and tied to access-level functions to some extent. For circuit switched cellular networks, the MSC performs user authentication and authorization needed for access to cellular services. Ciphering is done over the radio between the mobile node and the BSC; the core network provides secure circuit switched connections extended to the PSTN.

In UMTS packet networks, the user is authenticated and authorized in a similar fashion at the time of registration. The packet network element in the core network performs the authentication procedures and provides a ciphering key for use to the MN. The packet data traffic is ciphered over the radio and is tunneled in the core network to a gateway element in the core network. There is no security for IP traffic outside the UMTS core network unless an IP-level security mechanism is adopted.

WLAN provides link-level authentication and confidentiality features through wired equivalent privacy (WEP). The authentication mechanism is only to bring the wireless link level to the same assumed physical standards of a physical link. End-to-end or user-to-user authentication may further need to be performed at higher protocol layers. Similarly, WEP provides encryption equivalent to the wired connection for the wireless link. Further, encryption mechanisms are needed at higher layers to guarantee end-to-end data confidentiality.

7.6.2   Security in Wireless IP Networks

Acknowledging the higher risk of security problems in wireless networks opens up new problems due to the inherent mobility functionality associated with wireless networks. While mobility is a great convenience to wireless users, it demands a lot of intelligence and complexity on the network side. Mobility provides that users can establish a wireless subscription with one service provider in their hometown and can roam nationally or internationally. This introduces a connection between roaming and security functionality that the users must be authenticated and authorized for gaining access to network services in the visiting network that they are currently roaming to. The user must provide credentials that are used to identify the home network where he or she belongs, and then the access is provided after performing the security functions. On the flip side, the security function also involves the home network to ensure that the user is a genuine user who has subscribed to its services.

There are numerous security protocols in use on the Internet. Specifically, taking mobility into consideration, IPSec (defined in RFC 2401) provides a robust security framework to satisfy the requirements of the wireless IP networks. It offers access control, connectionless integrity, data origin authentication, protection against replays (a form of partial sequence integrity), confidentiality (encryption), and limited traffic flow confidentiality. These security features are handled at the IP layer, offering protection for IP- and/or upper-layer protocols.

There are two traffic security protocols, the authentication header (AH) [RFC 2402] and the encapsulated security payload (ESP) [RFC 2406], that are used as part of the IPSec. AH provides connectionless integrity, data origin authentication, and an optional antireplay service. The ESP may provide confidentiality (encryption) and limited traffic flow confidentiality. It may also provide connectionless integrity, data origin authentication, and antireplay service. AH and ESP can be used individually or in combination with each other to provide a desired set of security services in IPv4 and IPv6.

A security association is uniquely identified by a triple consisting of a security parameter index (SPI), an IP destination address, and a security protocol (AH or ESP) identifier. Internet key exchange (IKE) is the default automated key management protocol to negotiate protocols and algorithms and to create security associations and generate authentication keys. A security policy database can be used as input data to the IKE.

7.7   Session and Transport Issues

In IP wireless networks a clear separation between session and transport is introduced. Traditionally, a session is a relation between two nodes that is established between the two nodes by means of some protocol and has a limited lifetime.

When the concept is applied to IP wireless networks, the term *session* refers in particular to application sessions (i.e., temporary associations created between two or more IP nodes [e.g., two IP terminals and one server, one IP terminal and one server] in the framework of a given application). Examples of sessions are the relation between an IP node and an e-mail server to support the retrieval of e-mails by the user (e-mail session), and the relation between two SIP nodes and one or more SIP servers (SIP session). In general, *session* refers to the set of services the IP node can access.

A session foresees transfer of IP packets (signaling or user plane) between the nodes in the sessions. Therefore, each session is supported by transport. What is traditionally meant by the term *transport* in reference to a session is a specific flow of IP packets (also referred to as IP bearer) or set of flows that are exchanged between two IP nodes. The transport carries the information to be exchanged between two IP nodes as result of application sessions. Transport can also be unidirectional.

In particular, the following distinctions can be made for transport:

- *End-to-end transport:* Represents IP flows exchanged between two IP nodes, namely the source and the recipient of IP packets in a communication.
- *Wireless access transport:* A wireless access session is a given bearer that supports an end-to-end session. In case of cellular networks, the wireless access session can be a set of radio bearers, or in the case of 3G UMTS packet data networks, a set of PDP contexts and the associated radio bearers.

Figure 7–5 depicts the differences between session and transport.

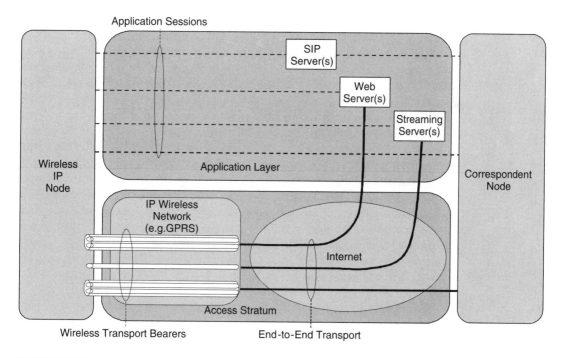

Figure 7–5   *Application sessions and transport.*

In IP wireless networks, session and transport can be considered as separated, as depicted in Figure 7–5, in contrast to the close relation that exists between signaling/control and user plane information in traditional cellular networks. In traditional networks, user plane and control signaling are processed by the same network entities (e.g., BTS, MSC in GSM). The adoption of IP in data networks introduces the ability to carry signaling information and user plane data separately in the network, therefore delivering the information to separate network elements. An example of this is the ability to run SIP services over IP wireless networks (e.g., General Packet Radio Service [GPRS]).

Due to the separation between session and transport, a new set of issues arises. In particular, two issues are relevant and are closely interrelated:

- The control of session and transport
- The ownership of session and transport

The following section describes these issues.

7.7.1 Control and Ownership of Session and Transport

Figure 7–6 describes the relation between the control of session and transport by depicting two examples. In one case, the IP node is involved in an application session where both the control of the session and the transport of IP packets are provided by the same network operator. This scenario is very close to the way services are provided in cellular networks. In the other example, the IP node is accessing services provided by a third party (e.g., Internet service provider) through the transport provided by the network operator. In this case, session and transport are not controlled by the same party.

The separation between session and transport is perceived by several service providers as a threat to their business. In current cellular networks, users access services through the same operator that is providing the connectivity to the network, therefore guaranteeing operators complete control of service provisioning. With the advent of IP and Internet applications and the separation between session and transport, traditional operators are concerned that they will lose control of service provisioning (i.e., lose ownership of sessions and be relegated to the role of wireless ISPs).

In this framework, solutions need to be designed to allow two service-provisioning models:

- Wireless IP operators provide complete services, therefore maintaining control of sessions. To enable this model, operators must be able to control how transport, and in particular QoS, is provided to IP nodes. In fact, IP nodes could request IP transport with QoS to the network operator and access services of third parties.

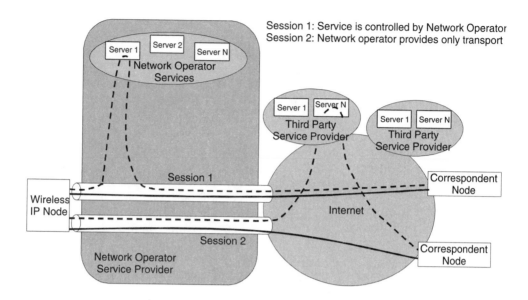

Session 1: Service is controlled by Network Operator
Session 2: Network operator provides only transport

Figure 7–6   *Relation between application and transport sessions.*

- Wireless IP operators provide complete services and simple IP connectivity to IP nodes (i.e., transport with possibly quality of service).

Only the availability of solutions enabling both models would facilitate a successful deployment of IP wireless networks.

7.8   Transitional Support

There are two important aspects to be considered related to the introduction of IP in wireless and cellular networks:

- The introduction of IP services, where IP connectivity is one of the various services provided to the mobile nodes
- The introduction of IP mechanisms for the network infrastructure

IP services have been introduced in cellular networks (e.g., GPRS) as described in other chapters of this book. Provisioning of IP connectivity and IP services is currently supported mostly through mechanisms designed specifically for cellular networks (e.g., for mobility management), and in some cases IP is used as transport (e.g., GPRS).

The introduction of IP mechanisms to support provisioning of IP services and the migration toward more complex IP services (e.g., multimedia services through SIP) in future IP wireless networks represents a significant disruption in the concepts and technology used in cellular networks. An important issue to be considered in this framework is the transition between current networks to future IP wireless networks.

Network operators and service providers have made large investments in terms of network infrastructure, licenses, and service agreements for current cellular networks. Therefore, it is to be expected that the introduction in cellular networks of any IP-based disruptive technology is justifiable only by a high rate of growth in the demand for data and IP multimedia services. A low growth rate for data services will push operators toward the introduction of new services to attract more users while at the same time minimizing the modifications to the network infrastructure. On the other end, a high growth rate for data and multimedia services will lead operators to choose more aggressive solutions to allow more advanced and appealing IP-based services and solutions to optimize provisioning of IP-based services. Network operators will therefore need to develop strategies to cope both with low and high growth rates for data services, allowing both for slow evolution of their networks and aggressive modifications to the network based on disruptive solutions. Smooth evolution and disruptive evolution are transition issues to be considered.

In this scenario, the issue of transition between current networks and future networks is twofold:

- In the case of slow growth of data services, network operators need to maintain backward compatibility between services and network technologies in order to allow for smooth evolution. Revenue from slow growth of data services would not justify large investments in new and disruptive technologies, while at the same time new and more appealing services will be needed to widen the customer base.
- In the case of slow growth of data services, network operators need to maintain some level of backward compatibility in order to support existing terminals. In the case of slow growth, the number of terminals not using the latest technology may be significantly large; therefore, backward compatibility is a must to guarantee that operators maintain a customer base without requiring customers to update their terminals.

In conclusion, particular attention needs to be placed on the technical solutions adopted in IP wireless networks for support of new services and for the evolution to new network architectures in order to guarantee that any evolutionary or disruptive step will allow for backward compatibility.

References

G. Montenegro, "Reverse Tunneling for Mobile IP," *RFC 2344,* IETF, May 1998.

C. Bormann et al., "Robust Header Compression," *RFC 3095*, IETF, July 2001.

A. Shacham et al., "IP Payload Compression," *RFC 2393*, IETF, December 1998.

D. Rand, "PPP Compression Protocol," *RFC 1962*, IETF, June 1996.

G. Montenegro et al., "Long Thin Networks," *RFC 2757*, IETF, January 2000.

"Mobile Radio Interface Layer 3 Specifications," *GSM TS 04.08 v6.7.0*, Release 1997.

S. Dawkins and G. Montenegro, "End-to-end Performance Implications of Slow Links," *RFC 3150*, IETF, July 2001.

S. Dawkins, "End-to-end Performance Implications of Links with Errors," *RFC 3135*, IETF, August 2001.

C. Perkins et al., "IP Mobility Support for IPv4," *RFC 3220*, IETF, January 2002.

B. Adoba and M. Beadles, "The Network Access Identifier," *RFC 2486*, IETF, January 1999.

S. Kent and R. Atkinson, "Security Architecture for the Internet" *RFC 2401*, IETF, November 1998.

M. Handley et al., "SIP: Session Initiation Protocol," *RFC 2543*, IETF, March 1999.

Data in GPRS Networks

*T*he General Packet Radio Service (GPRS) was the first step from European Telecommunications Standards Institute (ETSI) for improving cellular access for packet data networks, such as the Internet. The reason behind GPRS is to introduce packet switching in the GSM network and to optimize radio access for packet networks. GPRS was designed to reuse as many elements of the existing GSM infrastructure as possible, thus optimizing operators' investment in the existing GSM networks. GPRS also allows for later migration to the Enhanced Data for GSM Evolution (EDGE) and the Universal Mobile Telecommunications Systems (UMTS), thus making GPRS a long-term investment for operators.

The EDGE technology is very similar to the GSM technology. It allows data rates of up to 384 Kbps versus 171 Kbps in GSM by using eight time slots of a carrier frequency. The main difference from GSM is the modulation method. EDGE uses 8PSK modulation (3 bits per symbol) instead of GMSK (1 bit per symbol), resulting in increased user bit rates and the possibility for higher coding rates.

This chapter describes GPRS, which was introduced for GSM and is characterized by the Gb interface between the base station controller (BSC) and the core network (CN). This chapter discusses the system architecture, radio, and CN functionalities. It also explains how a GPRS network can be used to transport IP and applications that are based on IP from a user to an external data network.

8.1   GPRS as Compared to GSM CS Data

The data services provided by the GSM circuit switched (CS) network do not fulfill the needs of service providers and users. GPRS has devised a set of mechanisms to transfer user data packets in an efficient way between the user and external packet data networks.

The GPRS packet switched (PS) technology is designed considering commonly used packet protocols (e.g., IP, PPP, and X.25). Therefore, applications based on these standard data protocols are supported much more efficiently than the GSM CS networks. For instance, unlike the CS data there is no need to perform rate adaptation to 64 Kbps on the network interface.

The GPRS system can provide much higher data rates than the current CS data services on the GSM networks. It can achieve a maximum of up to 171.2 Kbps using all eight time slots on a GSM carrier at the same time. This results in supporting much higher bit rate applications. However, it should be noted that most implementations of mobile devices will support either 3 or 4 timeslots on the downlink and 1 or 2 timeslots on the uplink.

The GPRS radio interface provides spectrum efficiency for packet data transfer. It provides mechanisms to compress the header and payload of a packet before it is transmitted over the radio interface. The resulting bandwidth savings are critical since bandwidth is relatively scarce and should be used as efficiently as possible.

GPRS provides PS radio bearers for bursty traffic. A channel is allocated when needed and released immediately after the transmission of the packets. With this principle, multiple users can share one physical channel (e.g., time slot). This results in highly efficient radio resource utilization compared to the dedicated radio bearers in the CS network.

GPRS offers more options for charging packet data usage than that offered by the CS network. In the CS network, billing is based only on the duration of the connection. In addition to duration-based charging, GPRS provides volume and content-based charging. Volume-based charging is more suitable for bursty traffic. A user can be charged based on the data volume exchanged. Content-based charging provides additional flexibility to the operators to price different types of contents.

GPRS provides session setup with a packet session management protocol. In the GSM CS networks, a modem connection on top of a CS connection has to be established before the MS can exchange data with the network. In GPRS, there is no need for a dial-up modem connection, thus reducing the session setup time. GPRS supports concurrent operation with existing GSM services for CS speech, CS data, and SMS.

8.2   Network Architecture Description

The GPRS network has introduced a set of new functions, such as serving GPRS support node (SGSN), gateway GPRS support node (GGSN), border gateway (BG), and charging gateway function (CGF) for a public land mobile network (PLMN). It reuses some existing network elements (NEs) from the GSM CS network, such as home location register (HLR), authentication center

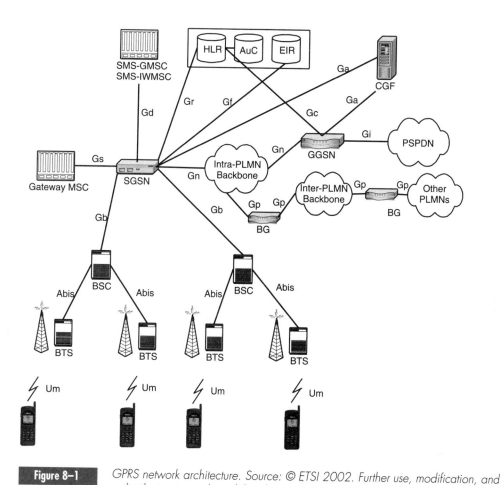

(AuC), and equipment identification register (EIR). The details of the architecture are described in GSM TS 03.60 and are shown in Figure 8–1.

8.2.1   Gateway GPRS Support Node

The GGSN is the gateway to the external packet data networks for the GPRS. It tunnels the packet data units (PDUs) (e.g., an IP packet), to the MS's current point of attachment (i.e., the SGSN). The GGSN may query the HLR of a subscriber to get the current SGSN address. The GGSN also collects the charging information, but based on the usage of the external network resources. A firewall function is needed at the GGSN to filter out unauthorized and unsolicited packets from entering the GPRS network.

8.2.2   Serving GPRS Support Node

The SGSN provides mobility management, performs authentication, and routes packet data. The SGSN collects charging information related to the usage of the network. The SGSN is also connected to the MSC/VLR via the Gs interface. The Gs interface helps in optimizing some CS network procedures by using the GPRS network. For example, the MSC/VLR may initiate paging or collect MS location information through Gs. SMS-GMSC and SMS-IWMSC are connected to the SGSN using the Gd interface. This interface allows GPRS-capable mobiles to send/receive SMS over GPRS radio channels.

8.2.3   Border Gateway

Two intra-PLMN backbone networks can be connected via the Gp interface using border gateways (BGs). The functions for a BG are not specified by ETSI. At minimum, it needs to have a security function for protecting the intra-PLMN network against external attacks. The security functionality is determined based on a roaming agreement between the two PLMNs.

8.2.4   Home Location Register

The HLR contains user subscription data and routing information. The routing information is the current SGSN address. The HLR has SS7-based interfaces with the SGSN and the GGSN. When the MS registers with a new SGSN, the SGSN informs the HLR using the Gr interface and the HLR sends back the user profile. The GGSN may consult the HLR for a user's current location. The HLR from the GSM CS network is enhanced to support GPRS.

8.2.5   Charging Gateway Function

The CGF provides a mechanism to transfer charging information from the SGSN and GGSN to the billing systems (BSs). The CGF can be implemented as a centralized separate NE (CG) or as a distributed functionality resident in the SGSNs and GGSNs. Irrespective of the way in which the CGF is implemented, the functionality of the CGF stays the same.

8.2.6   SMS-GMSC and SMS-IWMSC

The SMS-GMSC and SMS-IWMSC are connected to the SGSN via the Gd interface to enable a GPRS MS to send and receive short messages (SMs) over GPRS radio channels. The SMS-GMSC is the gateway to the GPRS network for the SM delivery to a user homed in the network. The SMS-IWMSC is the MSC connected to the SM-SC. It directs the SM originated by an MS to the SM-SC. Both of these functionalities could coexist in the same physical element.

8.2.7   Packet Control Unit

The radio functionalities introduced by GPRS are required to be an add-on function to the existing GSM BSS network. For this purpose, the packet control unit (PCU) is added to the GSM BSS. The PCU performs the radio link-layer functions for the data packets. If the PCU is remote to a BTS, then the radio frames (PCU frames) are carried in an extension of the Abis TRAU (transcoder rate adaptation unit) frames, which are defined for the GSM voice services. In this way the BSS network doesn't need any modification to handle the PCU frames. The PCU interacts with the channel codec unit (CCU), which performs functions like interleaving and Forward Error Correction (FEC). Any control information between PCU and CCU is carried through in-band signaling.

The PCU is not illustrated in Figure 8-1 due to the flexibility in its location. The specifications have identified three different options for the location of PCU, without mandating any of them: BTS, BSC site, and GSN site (Figure 8–2).

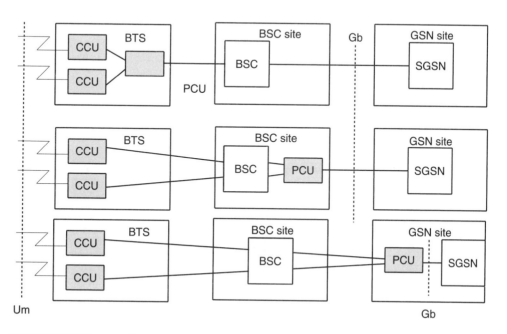

8.3 Protocol Architecture

All the NEs of the GPRS network interact with each other using separate user and control plane protocol stacks. The protocol stacks of the SGSN/GGSN with HLR and EIR are the same as the MSC/VLR with HLR and EIR (i.e., MAP/TCAP over SCCP/MTP). Hence, we do not describe them in this chapter. The protocol stacks among GGSN, SGSN, BSS, and MS are new and are described in this section.

8.3.1 User Plane

The data packets are tunneled between the GGSN and SGSN using the GPRS Tunneling Protocol (GTP) (Figure 8–3). The GTP packets can be carried either in acknowledged (TCP) or unacknowledged mode (UDP) over IP. The SGSN uses the SNDCP (Subnetwork Dependent Data Convergence Protocol) to adapt the network PDUs so they can be transmitted through the radio network. For this purpose, the SNDCP performs functions like compression and segmentation. The segmented and compressed packets are processed by the logical link control (LLC) layer. LLC provides a reliable ciphered logical link from the SGSN to the MS. The user data are transmitted between the SGSN and BSS by using BSS GPRS Protocol (BSSGP). The BSSGP PDUs are transported using a frame relay–based connection called network services (NS). Readers can refer to GSM TS 08.16 for details on NS. Radio link control (RLC) is used over the air interface to provide segmentation and assembly of radio blocks into LLC frames. It also

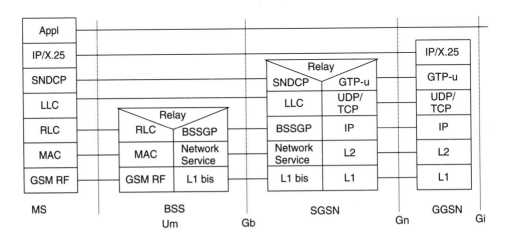

Figure 8–3   *User plane protocol stack. Source: © ETSI 2002. Further use, modification, and redistribution is strictly prohibited. ETSI standards are available from http://pda.etsi.org/pda/ and http://www.ets.org/eds/.*

provides a radio-dependent reliable link. Underneath the RLC is the media access control (MAC) layer, which provides the mapping to the physical channels.

8.3.2   Signaling Plane

The signaling plane consists of protocols for control and support of the user plane functions (Figure 8–4). The GGSN and SGSN exchange control information for managing GTP using GTP-c, which is carried over UDP/IP. For establishing and managing a packet data session, the SGSN and MS use the Session Management (SM) protocol. For managing mobility of an MS, the SGSN and MS use the GPRS Mobility Management (GMM) protocol. The GMM has defined procedures for registering and authenticating an MS in a visiting GPRS network. The LLC provides a reliable ciphered logical link over the radio interface for the signaling plane. The SGSN and BSS use BSSGP for managing the signaling connection between them. The BSSGP is used to convey routing and quality of service (QoS) information between the BSS and SGSN. The RLC is used over the air interface to provide a GSM radio-dependent reliable link. The MAC layer controls the access signaling (request and grant) procedures for the radio channels and provides mapping to the physical channels.

8.3.3   GPRS Tunneling Protocol

GTP is used for both signaling (GTP-c) and data transfer (GTP-u) procedures between the GSNs. It provides a header, which together with the UDP/TCP and IP header identifies the destination GSN and handling of the packet at

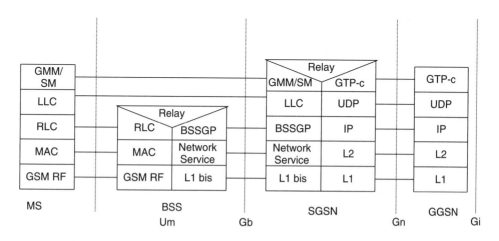

Figure 8–4   *Signaling plane. Source: © ETSI 2002. Further use, modification, and redistribution is strictly prohibited. ETSI standards are available from http://pda.etsi.org/pda/ and http://www.ets.org/eds/.*

the destination. There is another variant of GTP, called GTP′, which is used as a charging protocol. GTP′ is used between GSNs and CGF.

In the signaling plane, GTP-c is a tunnel control and management protocol that is used to create, modify, and delete the tunnels between the GSNs. These signaling procedures are called Packet Data Protocol (PDP) Context Request, PDP Context Update, and PDP Context Delete. These procedures are invoked as a part of session establishment or mobility management between the SGSN and the MS. In the user plane, GTP-u provides a GTP header for the user plane tunneling. In addition to the tunneling, GTP-u provides features like in-sequence delivery and multiplexing of flows.

The GTP header is a fixed-format 20-byte header, as shown in Figure 8–5. The same GTP header is used for both GTP-c and GTP-u. A GTP-c PDU is distinguished from a GTP-u PDU by a unique message type.

The GTP header contains the following fields:

- Version indicates different GTP versions, with the first version as 0.
- PT (protocol type) differentiates between a GTP and a GTP′ message.
- SNN is a flag indicating if SNDCP PDU number is included or not.
- Message type indicates the type of GTP message. For GTP-c, this contains the unique message type for a signaling message.
- Length indicates the length in octets of the GTP PDU, excluding the GTP header.
- Sequence number is used as a transaction identity for signaling PDUs and as an increasing sequence number for user plane PDUs.

Octets	8	7	6	5	4	3	2	1
1	Version			PT	Spare '1 1 1'			SNN
2	Message Type							
3-4	Length							
5-6	Sequence Number							
7-8	Flow Label							
9	SNDCP N-PDU Number							
10-12	Spare 'FF'							
13-20	Tunnel Identifier							

Figure 8–5   *GTP header fields.*

- SNDCP N-PDU number is used at the Inter SGSN movement from the MS to coordinate the data transmission between the MS and SGSN.
- Tunnel identifier (TID) uniquely identifies MM and PDP contexts for an MS. It is based on IMSI and NSAPI.
- Flow label identifies a unique GTP flow. This field distinguishes multiple flows per MS.

8.3.4   GPRS Mobility Management

Mobility is managed by maintaining different MM states in MS and SGSN (Figure 8–6). There are three MM states: IDLE, BUSY, and STANDBY. In the IDLE state, no MS location information is kept in the network. In the BUSY state, the GPRS MS is known to the network at a cell level. In the STANDBY state, the MS is known to the network at a routing area identifier (RAI) level. The RAI is a location identifier and denotes an area represented by a group of cells. The STANDBY state helps in reducing the battery consumption of an MS. This is because the RAI, being larger then the cell size, changes less frequently for an MS. The STANDBY state is reached from the READY state, when there is no activity for an MS for a certain time. The mobility procedures are executed based on the MM states. Some of the important mobility procedures are explained next.

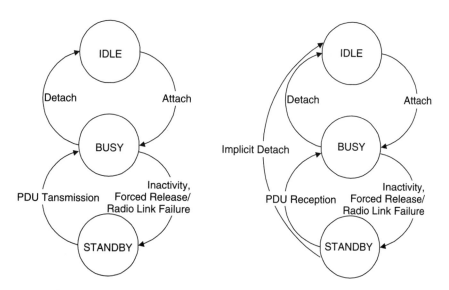

Figure 8–6   *MM state diagram in MS and SGSN. Source: © ETSI 2002. Further use, modification, and redistribution is strictly prohibited. ETSI standards are available from http://pda.etsi.org/pda/ and http://www.ets.org/eds/.*

GPRS ATTACH AND DETACH PROCEDURES

The GPRS attach procedure registers an MS with an SGSN for the GPRS services. It informs the HLR, which SGSN can access the MS. When the MS sends an attach request, the network checks if the user is authorized and copies the user profile from the HLR to the SGSN. The GPRS detach procedure performs the reverse operation; it disconnects an MS from the GPRS services.

LOCATION MANAGEMENT

The network keeps track of the user's current location in terms of a cell or routing area (RA) by executing the cell update or RA update procedures, respectively. A routing area is a geographical location kept by the network to track MS in idle mode. It provides the serving cell information in the system information messages. The MS detects that a new cell has been entered, by comparing the cell's identity with the cell identity stored in the MS's MM context. Similarly, the MS detects that a new RA has been entered by periodically comparing the RAI stored in its MM context with that received from the new cell.

The MS performs the cell update procedure when it enters a new cell inside the current RA and it is in the READY state. The MS sends an uplink LLC frame of any type containing the MS's identity to the SGSN. The BSS, as part of BSSGP, adds the cell global identity to the LLC PDU and sends it as a BSSGP PDU toward the SGSN. The SGSN records this change of cell and directs further traffic toward the MS over the new cell.

A GPRS attached MS initiates RA update when it detects that it has entered a new RA. The SGSN performs intra-SGSN RA update if the old RA is also being served by the same SGSN. In this case, there is no need to inform the GGSNs or the HLR. When the SGSN detects that it doesn't handle the old RA, it performs an inter-SGSN RA update. In this case, the new SGSN interacts with the old SGSN to get the context information. It also updates the GGSN or the HLR about the new MS location. The RA update can also be triggered as a result of periodic RA update procedure, which ensures that regular radio contact is maintained by the mobile. The periodicity of this RA update is determined by the network.

SECURITY FUNCTIONS

One of the important requirements for packet access is security. GPRS builds its security procedure on the already proven GSM security procedures. There are three main security functions provided by GPRS: user authentication, user identity confidentiality, and data/signaling ciphering. The user authentication function is provided to guard against unauthorized GPRS service usage. This is done by performing user authentication and user service request validation procedures. The user identity confidentiality is provided over the air interface by allocating a temporary identity. The ciphering function is for data and signaling encryption over the air interface.

The GPRS authentication procedure is very similar to the GSM authentication procedure. At the time of GPRS attach, the authentication triplets (a random number, signed response, and a key) are stored in the SGSN. The triplets are used in verifying the user access and setting up of the ciphering.

The SGSN also uses a temporary identifier, called P-TMSI signature, for identifying a user. The P-TMSI signature is sent by the SGSN to the MS in attach accept and routing area update accept messages. The MS includes the P-TMSI signature in the next routing area update request and attach request for its identification. If the P-TMSI signature does not match, the SGSN initiates the user authentication functions. The GPRS network also supports the IMEI check procedure for lost and stolen mobile equipments. The IMEI check procedure is the same as in GSM and uses a centrally located equipment identification register (EIR) in the home PLMN.

For the user identity confidentiality, the temporary logical link identity (TLLI) is used for identifying a GPRS user. The relationship between TLLI and IMSI is known only in the MS and SGSN. The TLLI is derived from the P-TMSI, which is usually allocated by the SGSN. The P-TMSI is allocated as part of the attach or RA update procedure. The P-TMSI can also be reallocated by using the P-TMSI reallocation procedure at any time when the MS is in the READY state.

GPRS ciphering is similar to GSM ciphering. It has two main differences from GSM ciphering. First, GPRS ciphering is between the MS and the SGSN as compared to being between the MS and BSS in GSM. Second, GPRS ciphering uses LLC frame numbers in the algorithm as compared to the TDMA frame number in GSM. This is because the TDMA frame number, a radio parameter, is not available in the SGSN.

8.3.5 Session Management

An MS needs to establish a session with the GPRS network before it can exchange packets with the external packet data network. A GPRS user is subscribed to one or more PDP type (e.g., IP, X.121). It establishes a session by activating a context for a PDP type. The GPRS can only support one IP address per PDP context. Therefore, it does not allow multiple IP applications per PDP context. The MS sends the PDP Context Activation request to the SGSN, where the mobile is attached. The GGSN is selected for an MS using Access Point Name (APN). The MS may send a request for a specific APN or the SGSN may choose an APN for an MS. The SGSN queries the DNS to find the IP address of the GGSN corresponding to the APN. The PDP context is created in the MS, SGSN, and GGSN. Session management provides procedures for PDP context activation, deactivation, and modification. The PDP context modification procedure is initiated to modify the parameters, such as QoS and radio priority, of an ongoing session.

A GPRS user uses the subscribed PDP address to establish a session. For each PDP type it can be subscribed to one or more PDP addresses. The PDP address can be allocated to an MS either statically or dynamically. In static address allocation, the home PLMN operator assigns a PDP address permanently to the MS. The MS uses this address in accessing the GPRS services. In dynamic address allocation, either home PLMN or visited PLMN assigns a PDP address to the MS when a PDP context is activated.

A PDP context can either be in an INACTIVE state or ACTIVE state (Figure 8–7). In INACTIVE state, there is no PDP context active and therefore no data can be transferred. In ACTIVE state, the PDP context for the PDP address in use is activated in MS, SGSN, and GGSN. The PDP context contains mapping and routing information for transferring the PDP PDUs for that particular PDP address between MS and GGSN. The ACTIVE state is permitted only when the MM state of the subscriber is STANDBY or READY.

8.3.6   Subnetwork Dependent Convergence Protocol

SNDCP maps the external PDN characteristics onto the underlying GPRS network characteristics. The underlying network is from the SGSN to the MS. The following are the main functions of SNDCP:

- Multiplexing of several PDPs from one or more different network layers onto the appropriate LLC connections

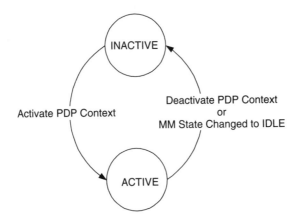

| Figure 8–7 | *PDP context state diagram. Source: © ETSI 2002. Further use, modification, and redistribution is strictly prohibited. ETSI standards are available from http://pda.etsi.org/pda/ and http://www.ets.org/eds/.* |

- Compression/decompression of redundant protocol control information (e.g., TCP/IP header)
- Compression/decompression of redundant user data
- Segmentation of a network PDU into LLC PDUs and reassembly of LLC-PDUs into a network PDU

In Figure 8–8 the terms *NSAPI* and *SAPI* are used and need explanation. The network service access point identifier (NSAPI) identifies the PDP using the services provided by the SNDCP. On the other hand, the SAPI identifies the point at which LLC services are provided to the upper layer. Several NSAPIs can be associated with the same SAPI, and that's how the multiplexing is provided.

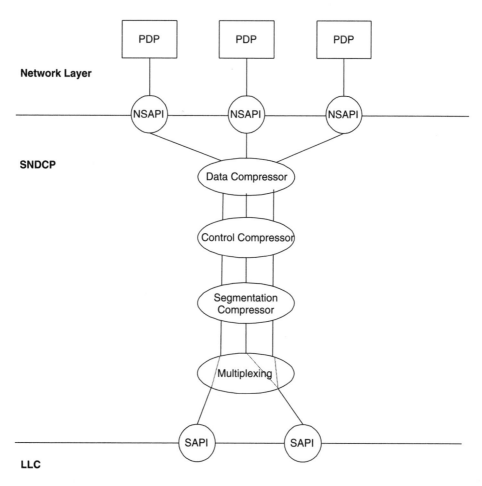

Figure 8–8   *SNDCP functions.*

The SNDCP layer depends on the LLC and the SM layers for some services. The SM layer/function needs to inform the SNDCP about activation, deactivation, and modification of the PDP contexts. During inter-SGSN RA update, the SM needs to inform the SNDCP when the N-PDUs shall be tunneled to the new SGSN. LLC needs to provide in-sequence packet delivery to SNDCP so the segmentation and reassembly can be carried out correctly. It also conveys a QoS profile from the SM to the LLC for the QoS profile-based transfer of PDUs.

8.3.7   Gb Interface

The Gb interface connects the PCU to SGSN. It is composed of frame relay (FR), network service control (NSC), and BSSGP layers. FR provides permanent virtual connections for carrying signaling and user data. The NSC is in charge of the administration of the virtual connections and links between the SGSN and the PCUs. FR and NS transport BSSGP PDUs between a BSS and an SGSN. In R4 release, IP is also defined to carry BSSGP PDUs instead of FR.

BSSGP transmits the radio-related control information between the PCU and the SGSN. This is comparable to the BSSAP function on the A interface. However, unlike BSSAP it is not limited to the transfer of control information. It also transfers user application data. BSSGP provides flow control according to the negotiated QoS level and the load situation on the Gb and the air interface. It manages virtual connections, which are called BVCs. When a user changes a cell, the SGSN informs the BSSGP in PCU. The PCU then either redirects or deletes the buffered LLC frames depending on the transmission mode.

8.3.8   LLC

The LLC layer provides the logical link for transfer of data between an MS and its SGSN. This layer contains all the radio-specific functions. It was designed for an RF-independent purpose, thus making the upper layers of GPRS independent of the radio interface. The LLC layer provides services to the layer 3 protocols, such as GMM and SM, using service access points (SAPs). An LLC layer connection is identified by the DLCI, which consists of the SAPI and the MS's TLLI. The TLLI is given to the LLC by the GMM. Each LLC frame consists of the header, trailer, and information field. The header and trailer fields contain control information such as SAPI, frame number, and checksum. The control information is used to identify the frame and to provide reliable transmission.

LLC can provide more than one logical link connection per user. It also provides ciphering and deciphering of the information fields. LLC supports unacknowledged and acknowledged modes of operation. In the unacknowledged mode, it does not guarantee in-order delivery. It also does not provide error recovery procedures for a received erroneous frame. The unacknowledged mode is known as asynchronous disconnected mode (ADM). The GMM, SM, and SMS applications use the ADM. Some user data transfer can also use ADM.

In the acknowledged mode, peer entities of LLC provide a balanced data link. Each entity assumes responsibility for the organization and error recovery of the data flow it originates. This mode of operation is known as asynchronous balanced mode (ABM) and provides a reliable service with in-order delivery. The acknowledged mode is only allowed for the transfer of user data.

8.4 Radio Functions

This section describes the logical channel structure, coding scheme, RLC/MAC, and procedures for GPRS. The description is intended to give an overview of the enhancements made in the radio functions for data, without going into detail.

8.4.1 Physical and Logical Radio Channels

The physical channel dedicated to the packet data traffic is called the packet data channel (PDCH). The packet data logical channels are mapped onto PDCH. The logical channels consist of different types based on the functions they perform. Figure 8–9 shows the various PDCHs.

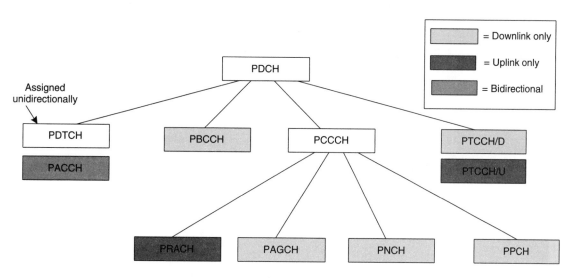

Figure 8–9 Radio channel structure.

PACKET COMMON CONTROL CHANNEL (PCCCH)

The logical channels for common control signaling are called PCCCH. The channels under this category are the packet random access channel (PRACH), packet access grant channel (PAGCH), packet notification channel (PNCH), and packet paging channel (PPCH). The PRACH is used by MS to initiate up-link transfer for sending data or signaling information. It carries an initial network access message from the MS. The PAGCH is used to convey the assignment of dedicated uplink or downlink resources to an MS. The PNCH is used for point-to-multi-point multicast (PTM-M) service. It is used to send a PTM-M notification to a group of MSs prior to a PTM-M packet transfer. The PPCH is used to page an MS prior to downlink packet transfer.

The CCCH for normal GSM can be used instead of PCCCH. Usually PCCCH is provided in a system that has significant packet data traffic. It can also be provided if there is enough bandwidth in the system to dedicate a spectrum for a set of channels just for packet traffic. This also reflects that the GPRS system can be gradually introduced to an existing GSM system.

PACKET BROADCAST CONTROL CHANNEL (PBCCH)

The PBCCH is used to broadcast GPRS-related system information about a cell to all the GPRS-enabled MSs that are currently camping on that cell. This information is used by the MS to access the network for packet transmission operation. In addition to the packet mode parameters, the PBCCH reproduces the circuit mode parameters from the BCCH. This allows circuit switched mode operation by an MS that is only monitoring the PBCCH. The MS after power on always reads BCCH; the BCCH conveys information about the PBCCH (i.e., whether it exists or not).

PACKET DATA TRAFFIC CHANNEL (PDTCH)

PDTCH is the bearer channel allocated for packet data transfer. It is unidirectional and is assigned separately for uplink and downlink directions. It is temporarily dedicated to one MS or to a group of MSs in the PTM-M case. In the multislot operation, one MS may use multiple PDTCHs in parallel for individual packet transfer. The multislot PDTCH can only be assigned on the same carrier. The PDTCH can be released after the guard timer expires due to inactivity, or after the Ack/Nack of all the sent radio blocks.

PACKET DEDICATED CONTROL CHANNEL (PDCCH)

The PDCCH is a control channel allocated to an MS. There are two types of channels under PDCCH: packet associated control channel (PACCH) and packet timing advance control channel uplink/downlink (PTCCH/U and PTCCH/D). The PACCH conveys signaling information related to a given MS. The signaling information includes acknowledgments and power control information. PACCH also carries resource assignment and reassignment messages, comprising the assignment of a capacity for PDTCH(s) and for further occurrences of PACCH. PACCH shares resources with PDTCHs that are currently assigned to one MS. Additionally, an MS that is currently involved in packet transfer can be paged for circuit switched services on PACCH.

The PTCCH is used to derive the correct value for timing advance that the MS has to use for the uplink transmission of radio blocks. The PTCCH/U is used to transmit a random access burst to allow estimation of the timing advance for one MS in packet transfer mode. PTCCH/D is used to transmit timing advance information updates to several MSs. One PTCCH/D is paired with several PTCCH/Us.

8.4.2   Channel Coding Scheme

For offering higher throughput than the traditional GSM, GPRS introduces three new coding schemes (CS-2 to CS-4). These coding schemes trade off transmission errors for throughput. All the coding schemes (CS-1 to CS-4) are mandatory for GPRS MS. Only CS-1 is mandatory for the network. The network chooses the coding scheme for an MS.

The coding procedure adds a block check sequence (BCS) for error detection. It also adds precoding USF (except for CS-1), four tail bits, and a half-rate convolutional coding for error correction. The error correction is not done for CS-4. The data rates, including RLC header and information, for CS-1, CS-2, CS-3, and CS-4 are 9.05, 13.4, 15.6, and 21.4 Kbps, respectively. On the other hand, for EGPRS nine modulation and coding schemes, MCS-1 to MCS-9, are defined for PDTCH. For all EGPRS packet control channels the corresponding GPRS control channel coding is used.

A link adaptation mechanism is provided that selects the best coding scheme based on the channel conditions. The mechanism performs the measurement on the channel quality. If the channel quality is good, a high-rate CS is used because less amount of coding is needed for error correction and detection. On the other hand, if the channel quality is bad, a low-rate CS is used.

8.4.3   RLC/MAC

The RLC and MAC layer operates above the radio physical layer. Let's briefly look into the radio physical interface for GPRS. For details, please refer to GSM TS 03.64. GPRS uses TDMA technology, where one carrier frequency is divided into eight time slots. A TDMA frame is a radio frame containing bursts for the eight time slots. GPRS uses a 52-multiframe structure, where each frame is a TDMA frame. The GRPS resource allocation is done on the block level. The four consecutive appearances of the same time slot within four consecutive TDMA frames is termed as one radio block. Therefore, the 52-multiframe offers 12 radio blocks, leaving 4 TDMA frames for the control information. The RLC/MAC procedures define how to utilize these radio blocks. The RLC/MAC layer messages and signaling procedures are defined in GSM TS 04.60.

The GPRS radio interface uses temporary block flow (TBF) as a notion for RR allocation. TBF is a physical connection used by the two RR entities. It is used to support the unidirectional transfer of LLC PDUs on packet data physical channels. TBF is similar to a channel number in CS transactions. A TBF is identified by a 5-bit temporary flow identity (TFI). The TFI is assigned in a resource assignment message that precedes the transfer of LLC frames belonging to one TBF to/from the MS. In GPRS, the packet data transactions are unidirectional. Therefore, the assigned TFI is unique in each direction. The same TFI value may be used concurrently for TBFs in opposite directions but on different PDCHs. The lifetime of a TBF is limited to the lifetime of the related packet data transaction.

The RLC function provides the procedures for a bitmap selective re-transmission of unsuccessfully delivered RLC data blocks. The RLC/MAC function provides two modes of operation: unacknowledged and acknowledged. The RLC function provides segmentation and reassembly of LLC-PDUs into RLC data blocks. It also provides link adaptation according to the channel conditions.

The MAC layer defines the procedures that enable multiple MSs to share a common transmission medium over the air interface. This medium may consist of several physical channels. For mobile-originated channel access, the MAC function provides arbitration between multiple MSs attempting to transmit simultaneously and provides collision avoidance, detection, and re-covery procedures. The arbitration is provided in the uplink direction with the help of the uplink state flag (USF) bits sent in each downlink RLC block. The USF field identifies the user of the next uplink block on the same time slot. For mobile-terminated channel access, MAC provides scheduling of ac-cess attempts, including queuing of packet access. MAC also provides effi-cient multiplexing of data and control signaling in both uplink and downlink directions. The control of multiplexing resides on the PCU. On the downlink, multiplexing is controlled by a scheduling mechanism. On the uplink, multi-plexing is controlled by the resource allocation mechanism. The MAC also handles priority of different transaction in its functions.

RLC/MAC offers a variety of procedures for different functions. In the following sub-sections we look into RLC/MAC functions only in conjunction with mobile-originated and mobile-terminated packet transfer.

MOBILE-ORIGINATED PACKET TRANSFER

The initial access by an MS is performed by sending a packet channel request message on PRACH. PRACH is used when a PCCCH is provided in a cell. If only CCCH is available, the MS could send a regular GSM channel request message on the RACH to initiate packet access. The GPRS offers two different network access methods (Figure 8–10):

- One-phase packet access
- Two-phase packet access

In one-phase access, the packet channel request is responded to by the network, with the packet uplink assignment reserving the resources on PDCH(s) for uplink transfer of a number of RLC/MAC data blocks. One-phase access needs a contention resolution mechanism because the packet channel request message cannot uniquely identify the sending MS. Another MS may consider the same resource allocation to be destined to itself and start using it. For contention resolution, the first thing the network does is include the TLLI in the RLC header while the contention is being resolved. In this way the MS that sent the request can identify its radio blocks. The second thing the network does is declare who owns the allocation. This is done by inclusion of the TLLI in the packet uplink ack/nack message. If there is a second mobile station using the same uplink resource, it needs to stop its transmission immediately.

In the two-phase access, the packet uplink assignment is sent by the network, granting only a single block on the uplink path to specify its resource requirements and to identify itself. Two-phase access is always used when the access is performed on RACH. This is because on RACH there are only two cause values available for denoting GPRS request. These cause values are not sufficient to specify completely the requested resource. On PRACH, the MS can specify more information about the requested resources. The MS sends a packet resource request message, specifying itself by TLLI and its resource requirement. The network also has the authority to deny

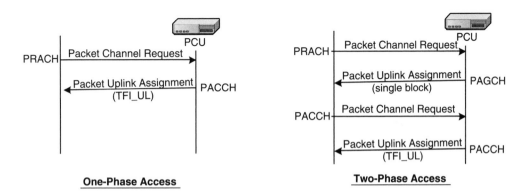

One-Phase Access   **Two-Phase Access**

Figure 8–10   *Access methods using packet channel only. Source: © ETSI 2002. Further use, modification, and redistribution is strictly prohibited. ETSI standards are available from http://pda.etsi.org/pda/ and http://www.ets.org/eds/.*

one-phase access and enforce two-phase access by allocating only a single block, irrespective of the RACH access.

If the network has received more packet channel requests than it can serve, it can send a packet queuing notification to the sender of the packet channel request. The notification provides a mechanism for queuing the request for a short time.

GPRS provides four types of resource allocation:

- Fixed allocation of uplink resources
- Dynamic allocation of uplink resources
- Extended dynamic allocation
- Exclusive allocation

FIXED ALLOCATION • In fixed allocation, the PCU sends a fixed time slot assignment and a block assignment bitmap per time slot to the MS. The bitmap represents the assigned blocks within several consecutive 52-multiframes where the MS may transmit. The network also conveys a start frame to the MS indicating when to start the transmission. If the current allocation is not sufficient, the MS may request additional resources in one of the assigned uplink blocks.

DYNAMIC ALLOCATION • The dynamic method can serve packet transmission more efficiently by allocating radio blocks to different MSs based on priority. This method is based on the use of the USF. The USF is a 3-bit field and is part of the MAC header of each downlink RLC data block that is sent. The USF of a downlink block identifies who is going to use the next uplink block on the same time slot. An MS involved in a multislot assignment could have different USFs assigned, one for each time slot. The MS shall monitor the USF on each PDCH in the list of assigned PDCHs, up to and including the first PDCH currently used for transmission. This monitoring is one of the disadvantages of the method because an MS has to decode all the downlink data blocks to find their USF.

EXTENDED DYNAMIC ALLOCATION • This method is helpful in multislot assignment. It relieves the multislot MS from listening to all downlink blocks on all the assigned time slots to find its USF. This is achieved by setting specific rules for the allocation. The descriptions for the rules are available in GSM TS 03.64. The MS follows the rules in order to understand its uplink allocation.

EXCLUSIVE ALLOCATION • Exclusive allocation does not use the USF and the block assignment bitmap. The MS is free to transmit on the uplink without monitoring the downlink for the USF. In exclusive allocation, the network conveys a start frame and a slot assignment in the assignment message. The MS waits until the start frame and then starts transmitting the radio blocks on the assigned slots. Unused USF values may be used to prevent other mobiles from transmitting on those frames.

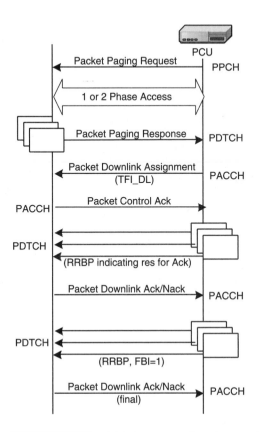

Figure 8–11   *Mobile-terminated packet transfer.*

The uplink TBF is released by using the countdown procedure. The same procedure is used for all types of resource allocation. The mobile initiates the countdown procedure, but the TBF release is confirmed by the network. The procedure uses a 4-bit parameter, called countdown value (CV), in the uplink RLC/MAC radio blocks. CV indicates how many RLC/MAC data blocks are remaining to be transmitted by the MS. When the network sees CV=0, it sends a packet uplink ack message with the final ack indicator bit set to 1. It also allocates an uplink radio block, using the RRBP field, for the final control message from the MS.

MOBILE TERMINATED PACKET TRANSFER

A mobile in MM-STANDBY state is paged by sending a packet paging request message from the PCU to the MS (Figure 8–11). The packet paging request is sent on PPCH or PCH. The MS responds to one packet paging request message by initiating a mobile-originated packet transfer request. This mobile-originated packet transfer allows the MS to send a packet paging response to the network. The network then assigns radio resources to the MS and performs the downlink data transfer.

The PCU allocates PDCH(s) and informs the MS by sending a packet downlink assignment message. If the MS is engaged in an uplink packet transfer, the message is transmitted on PACCH. Otherwise the packet is transferred on PCCCH. If the PCCCH is not allocated in the cell, the message is transmitted on CCCH.

The RLC/MAC blocks destined for different MSs can be multiplexed on the same PDCH. The MSs recognize their blocks by identifying TFI. The MS may need to issue control messages, either packet downlink ack or packet control ack, in the uplink direction. The downlink TBF doesn't provide uplink resources to the MS. The solution is that the network needs to allocate a single uplink block to a given MS dynamically. This is done by using a 2-bit-long parameter, relative reserved block period (RRBP), to identify the uplink block. RRBP is part of each RLC/MAC data and control block in downlink direction and allocates a single radio block in uplink direction to the addressed MS.

For releasing the downlink TBF, the network sets the final block indicator (FBI) bit to 1 in the RLC header, indicating that this block is the last to be sent. Within the same block, the network allocates a single uplink block by using RRBP to the MS to confirm proper reception or to require retransmission in acknowledged mode. The MS sends a packet downlink ack message. In unacknowledged RLC mode, the mobile confirms the TBF release by issuing a packet control ack.

8.5   IP Transport Example

As stated previously, the GPRS network provides underlying mobility-aware transport for packet data between the MS and GGSN. IP is supported as a PDP type by the network. In this section we look into the details of the procedures that occur in the GPRS network to service an IP application. The following assumptions are made for this scenario:

- The MS has a subscription for IP as a PDP type in the HLR.
- The MS has already performed an attach procedure.
- The MS uses a static IP address.

In our application scenario, the SMTP application is considered for sending an e-mail message from a GPRS MS (Figure 8–12). When the user executes an SMTP command to send an e-mail, the application layer in the MS triggers the SM layer to start PDP context activation. For carrying any SM layer message, the MS first needs to establish a packet channel over the radio

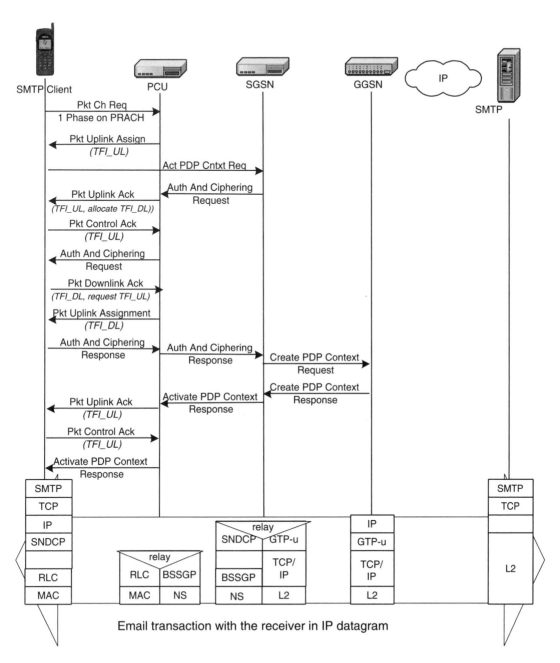

Figure 8–12   *E-mail transaction over GPRS network.*

interface. The MS sends a packet channel request on PRACH and the PCU assigns the resources and sends a packet uplink assignment message. The PCU allocates a TFI for UL (TFI_UL) and sets up a TBF for carrying the SM message in the UL direction.

The activate PDP context request message is converted into radio blocks by RLC/MAC and transported over the air to the PCU using TFI_UL on a PDTCH. The MS includes a set of parameters to specify completely its request in the SM message. It uses its static IP address as a PDP address in the message. For a dynamic PDP address, the MS needs to send the message with an empty PDP address field. The MS includes the desired QoS profile. It also includes the access point name (APN) in the PDP context setup request. The APN is used to determine the serving GGSN for the MS by the SGSN.

After receiving the PDP context request, the SGSN carries out a user authentication procedure to verify the user access. It also sets up ciphering with the mobile for encrypting data over the air interface. Before sending the authentication and ciphering request message to the MS, the PCU needs to establish a DL TBF. In Figure 8–12, DL TBF establishment is combined with the UL ack that is sent for the UL radio blocks carrying the activate PDP context request message. In the packet uplink ack, the PCU allocates TFI_DL. Similarly, for sending an authentication and ciphering response, the MS sends a UL resource request in the packet downlink ack message.

At the time of attach procedure, the SGSN has already established an MM context for the MS and has downloaded its subscription information. This subscription information is used by the SGSN to validate the activate PDP context request. It verifies that the user is allowed to use IP as PDP type and has the associated IP address. It also validates the APN and maps the APN to a GGSN, which serves the desired external data network. If no GGSN address can be derived, the SGSN rejects the PDP context activation request message.

The GGSN creates a GTP tunnel ID for the requested PDP context by combining the IMSI stored in the MM context with the NSAPI received from the MS. The SGSN may restrict the requested QoS attributes given its capabilities, the current load, and the subscribed QoS profile. The SGSN sends a create PDP context request to the GGSN, including the negotiated QoS. The GGSN uses the APN to find the IP network, if it is connected to multiple networks. The GGSN creates a new entry in its PDP context table and generates a charging ID for charging. The GGSN may further restrict the negotiated QoS given its capabilities and the current load. The GGSN then returns a create PDP context response message to the SGSN. In case of a dynamic address, the GGSN sends the PDP address.

The SGSN inserts the NSAPI along with the GGSN address in its PDP context. If the MS has requested a dynamic address, the PDP address received from the GGSN is inserted in the PDP context. The SGSN selects radio priority based on the QoS accepted by the GGSN and returns an activate PDP context accept message to the MS. The SGSN is now able to route PDP PDUs between the GGSN and the MS.

After the signaling has established the radio connection and the GTP tunnel, the MS starts sending user plane data to the target. SMTP uses TCP for reliable transportation. The sender SMTP client processes the IP packets using SNDCP (header and payload compression). SNDCP also segments the IP packet into LLC PDUs. The LLC layer provides ciphering and reliable transmission over the radio link. Using the established uplink TBF, the packets are transferred to the BSS on a PDTCH. The data received by the SGSN are tunneled via the GTP tunnel to the GGSN. The GGSN from the PDP context determines the IP network. In this way, the SMTP mail send command eventually arrives at the SMTP server.

We can see from the flow diagram of Figure 8–12 that a lot of messages are exchanged over the air interface. There are multiple reasons for this. One reason is that a reliable transmission is needed to make sure that all the radio blocks are transferred correctly. Another reason is that TBFs are only established in one direction. Also, a TBF is active only while there are some queued LLC frames or a corresponding guard timer has not expired. The radio interface requires segmentation and ciphering of the IP packet. The GPRS attach procedure helps reduce the layer 3 messages needed to establish a session. The attach procedure downloads the user profile from the home network to the visiting SGSN. This helps in reducing the signaling for authenticating user and verifying access. Another point to note is that although the QoS is set up in the GPRS network, there is no QoS between PCU and the MS. This is solved later in UMTS by provisioning QoS in the radio bearers.

8.6   GPRS Roaming

This section describes how roaming of GPRS users between different networks is supported, and in particular how practical aspects of roaming impact the network model and what type of technical solutions are adopted.

8.6.1   GPRS Roaming Architecture

GPRS roaming enables subscribers to access their GPRS services while connected to a visited network. Roaming requires the ability to connect GPRS operators so that subscribers can move from one network to another and still access the GPRS service they have subscribed to.

According to the specification, the GPRS network architecture does not specify the location of the GGSN (i.e., the GGSN can be located either in the visited network or in the home network). Figure 8–13 describes the two possible models: in model 1, the GGSN for a visited MS is in the visited network,

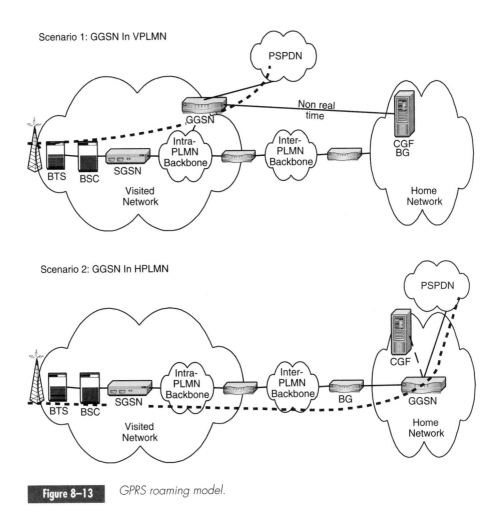

Figure 8-13   *GPRS roaming model.*

and in model 2, the GGSN is in the home network. In model 1, routing is efficient since IP packets can be routed directly from the GGSN to the Internet. However, in such case the home network has no control over the service being provided in terms of the following:

- *Billing:* Among other functions, the GGSN collects the charging information coming from the SGSN and generates additional charging information (e.g., based on packet volume). However, currently there isn't a fast solution to carry such charging information to the home network; therefore, service such as prepaid cannot be supported.
- *QoS:* It is not possible to guarantee end-to-end QoS since the visited network may not have the ability to support the QoS requirements of the user beyond the GGSN.

- *Access to services:* DNS queries, HTML searches, and other services will be provided by the visited network or by the public Internet.

In model 2, routing of IP packets may not be optimal. For example, if the MS is accessing a Web site local to the country of the visited network, packets will be routed from the Web server to the GGSN in the home network, then tunneled backward to the MS in the visited network through GTP. However, in such a scenario the home network has full control on the service provisioning, prepaid access, and end-to-end QoS.

For these reasons, GPRS operators have come to the realization that in order to provide services to roaming users and at the same time maintain control of service provisioning, the GGSN needs to be located in the subscriber home network. The GSM Association has therefore recommended GPRS operators to provide roaming services by locating the GGSN in the home network.

8.6.2   GRX: GPRS Roaming eXchange

The GSM Association (GSMA) has came to the realization that GPRS roaming based on bilateral relationships between individual GPRS operators is incredibly complex and expensive to maintain, in particular if the number of roaming partners is high. In fact, each operator will have to have $N(N - 1)$ dedicated links to other operators (given that N is the global numbers of operators for which roaming should be supported). The GSMA has therefore recommended the use of a GPRS Roaming eXchange (GRX) for the Inter-PLMN GPRS roaming scenario.

The GRX is built on a private or public IP backbone and transports GPRS roaming traffic via the GTP between the visited and the home PLMN (Figure 8–14). A GRX service provider has a network consisting of a set of routers and the links connecting to the GPRS networks. Moreover, the GRX network will have links connecting to other GRX nodes to support GRX peering between networks.

The GRX service provider acts as a hub, therefore allowing a GPRS operator to interconnect with each roaming partner without the need for any dedicated connections. This allows faster implementation of new roaming relations, faster time to market for new operators, and better scalability since an operator can start with low-capacity connections to the GRX and upgrade them depending on the bandwidth and quality requirements of the traffic. Other benefits of GRX are as follows:

- *Support of QoS:* This aspect that will be very important for the GPRS services and, in particular, for the transition to 3G systems.
- *Security:* The interconnection between the home operator and the visited operator uses the private GRX networks, hence does not re-

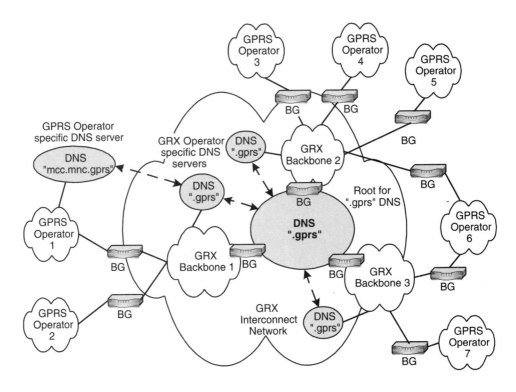

Figure 8-14   *GRX roaming architecture.*

quire the overhead of maintaining expensive IPSEC tunnels over the public Internet.

*   *DNS support:* Through GRX it is possible to support a worldwide ".gprs" DNS root, where the various GRX operators will collaborate in managing the root and each operator's DNS servers will be connected to such roots to provide translation of DNS names specific to one operator.

In conclusion, GRX is introduced for GPRS roaming to facilitate the network operators for the interconnection between networks to support roaming and will play a very important role for the transition to third-generation systems.

8.7   Summary

This chapter provides an overview of the GPRS network. It discusses major advantages of the GPRS network compared to the GSM CS network for data applications. It explains network architecture and the protocol stack. The chapter describes major functions of the GPRS network. It gives an example of how IP is transported over the GPRS network. The chapter also describes GRX to enable roaming between different GPRS operators.

References

TS 123 060 Ver. 4.3.0 Digital Cellular Telecommunication System (Phase 2+) (GSM); Universal Mobile Telecommunication System (UMTS); General Packet Radio Service (GPRS); Service description; Stage 2 (3GPP TS 23.060 version 4.3.0 Release 4)

TS 101 350 Ver. 8.7.0 Digital Cellular Telecommunication System (Phase 2+) (GSM); General Packet Radio Service (GPRS); Service description; Stage 2 (3GPP TS 23.060 version 4.3.0 Release 4) Overall description of GPRS radio Interface; Stage 2 (GSM 03.64 version 8.7.0 Release 1999)

TS 101 344 Ver. 7.7.0 Digital Cellular Telecommunication System (Phase 2+); General Packet Radio Service (GPRS); Service description; Stage 2 (3GPP TS 03.60 version 7.7.0 Release 1998)

3GPP TS 04.60: "Digital cellular telecommunications system (Phase 2+); General Packet Radio Service (GPRS); Mobile Station (MS)—Base Station System (BSS) Interface; RLC/MAC Protocol"

3GPP TS 04.64: "Digital cellular telecommunications system (Phase 2+); General Packet Radio Service (GPRS); Logical Link Control (LLC)"

3GPP TS 04.65: "Digital cellular telecommunications system (Phase 2+); General Packet Radio Service (GPRS); Mobile Station (MS)—Serving GPRS Support Node (SGSN); Subnetwork Dependent Convergence Protocol (SNDCP)"

3GPP TS 05.02: "Digital cellular telecommunications system (Phase 2+); Multiplexing and multiple access on the radio path"

3GPP TS 08.18: "Digital cellular telecommunications system (Phase 2+); General Packet Radio Service (GPRS); Base Station System (BSS)—Serving GPRS Support Node (SGSN) interface; BSS GPRS Protocol (BSSGP)"

3GPP TS 09.60: "Digital cellular telecommunications system (Phase 2+); General Packet Radio Service (GPRS); GPRS Tunneling Protocol (GTP) across the Gn and Gp Interface"

IP in UMTS Networks

Second-generation wireless digital networks have been around for the last decade and more. These networks have provided voice as the primary service. Data services were essentially an add-on to these networks. Typical data rates ranged from 9.6 to 14.4 Kbps. With the explosion of the Internet and the vast array of services and applications that the Internet enabled, users felt the need to access these services via wireless terminals. One of the impediments to providing data services in 2G networks was the limitation of low data rates, which are a result of the radio interface being designed to handle primarily voice. Second-generation radio networks were spectrally inefficient for handling packet data services.

Market trends in the mid-1990s drove networks toward convergence. So the telecom, datacom, and IT networks started network evolution toward a unification path. Wireless networks needed to capitalize on the Internet potential by creating an extension to the Internet via the wireless medium. This has been refered to in various publications as the wireless Internet. The wireless Internet is not a new network in itself but rather an extension of the existing Internet over wireless networks. However, in order to create this wireless Internet, next-generation networks had to provide higher data rates, enhanced air interfaces for supporting packet data, and quality of service for a rich variety of applications. In addition, the rapid increase in the number of wireless subscribers has fueled the need for improving the spectral efficiency and capacity of current networks for voice services as well. The ITU formed the IMT-2000 forum to address the needs of the mobile telecommunication industry, and this resulted in the creation of the driver for third-generation networks.

Requirements for 3G networks with respect to radio access networks, core networks, and data rates were specified by IMT-2000. The Universal Mobile Telecommunication System (UMTS) is an architecture that was developed to meet these 3G requirements.

This chapter introduces UMTS, which was introduced to provide 3G services and the introduction of a new radio access network to meet the 3G goals, referred to as UMTS terrestrial radio access networks (UTRAN). This chapter discusses the UMTS system architecture, radio network, and core network functionalities. It also explains how a UMTS network can be used to transport IP datagrams and enable applications based on IP to be available to the mobile/wireless user.

9.1   Vision of UMTS

The vision of UMTS is to build a mobile wireless system that is access independent and provides personalized services that are accessible from anywhere at any time via different devices. The network architecture allowed for a clear separation of the access network from the core. This enables different types of radio access networks to be developed independently of the core network. At present two types of access networks have been standardized for UMTS networks: UTRAN, which is based on wideband code division multiple access (WCDMA), and GERAN (GSM/EDGE radio access network), which is based on TDMA and is an evolution of GSM. Other access networks in the future could include satellite, wireless LAN, and many others accessing a common core. UMTS packet core improvements make the core network and the operator service machinery totally access independent. The change is invisible to the end user, but it enables the operator to use a common packet core with any access technology.

The operator benefit comes from the fact that the single core investment is shared with many clients and its operation is easier. A common end-user wish is to receive calls on the mobile terminal when moving and on a higher-bandwidth device or terminal when at home or plugged into the wired network. Core and service network access independence is clearly an essential enabling feature to make such a session handover possible in addition to the radio access handover we have today.

UMTS also takes the first step in emphasizing services. The wireless network is intended to be only an enabler that allows subscribers to access many different types of services. 3G networks are expected to fill society's needs for access to information and entertainment in an increasingly mobile world.

The third-generation partnership project (3GPP), which is responsible for UMTS standardization, also has a vision of moving to all IP networks. This means that the access network as well as the core will be essentially packet switched networks. Services that fall in both the real-time as well as the non-real-time realms will be run over packet switched networks.

9.2   UMTS History

As GSM deployments were occuring in Europe and elsewhere in the early 1990s, ETSI in the mid-1990s was investigating several technologies that would meet the requirements specified by ITU as part of IMT-2000. One of the critical roles was the evaluation of the radio access system to be used for UMTS. Among the several proposals that were being evaluated for the air interface, WCDMA was selected by ETSI as the technology of choice. This was also partly influenced by other countries (including Japan and Korea) selecting WCDMA as the preferred radio technology for 3G networks.

At the same time, other standards bodies were working on specifications for meeting the IMT-2000 requirements. In order to coordinate the standardization of WCDMA and the specification of a common technology on a global basis, several standards organizations and companies (including vendors and operators) created a partnership in 1998 called third-generation partnership project (3GPP). The scope of 3GPP was to produce a globally applicable standard for a 3G mobile system based on the evolution of GSM networks and the radio access technologies that they support. The scope was subsequently amended to include the maintenance and development of the Global System for Mobile communication (GSM). Standardization efforts also include evolved radio access technologies such as GPRS and EDGE.

3GPP released its first version of the specifications for UMTS in 1999, referred to as Release 99. The access networks in Release 99 include GPRS, EDGE, and WCDMA-based UTRAN. Further releases include Release 4, which included minor enhancements and corrections and was completed in 2001, and Release 5, which concluded in 2002. Release 5 includes a new subsystem called the IP multimedia subsystem (IMS), which is based on IPv6 and supports new services and support for the IETF's Session Initiation Protocol (SIP). Release 5 also enhances WCDMA radio technology with high-speed downlink packet access. With this enhancement, data rates up to 10 Mbps can be achieved on the downlink. Work on Release 6 is ongoing and aspects of this are discussed in Chapter 15.

9.3   UMTS Spectrum

The World Administrative Radio Conference (WARC) in 1992 identified two frequency bands in the 2-GHz range for a sum total of 230 MHz for IMT-2000 applications. These bands were from 1885 to 2025 MHz and from 2110 to 2200 MHz. The band is further split up to support several different types of 3G services. One of the most important spectrum allocations is called the terrestrial paired band. This spectrum will be used by operators employing ground-based (as opposed to satellite-based) base stations and will use frequency division duplexing (FDD) to separate the bidirectional communications between mobile station and base station. The paired bands that have been allocated in Europe and Asia for terrestrial 3G UMTS service are from 1920 to 1980 MHz and from 2110 to 2170 MHz; thus there is 60 MHz of spectrum for communication in each direction.

Another type of UMTS service is envisioned that will use a different radio technique known as time division duplexing (TDD). For TDD systems, the same frequency band can be used for communicating in both directions. The terrestrial unpaired bands are expected to be used by systems using TDD ground-based networks. The frequency allocated for TDD systems is in the range of 1900 to 1920 MHz and from 2010 to 2025 MHz.

Most of the UMTS spectrum in the IMT-2000 range for FDD is available in Europe and many countries in Asia (Japan and Korea). In China this spectrum will be available after existing services within the spectrum are cleared. In the United States the situation is slightly different. The IMT-2000 spectrum is unavailable as it is used by 2G PCS systems. Hence there are two options: a new spectrum is allocated for 3G or existing spectrum has to be reallocated for UMTS deployment. Figure 9–1 shows the IMT-2000 and UMTS spectrum.

The spectrum for UMTS lies between 1900 and 2025 MHz and 2110 to 2200 MHz. Licensing for the spectrum in many countries has been completed. The licensing process has been either via auctions or "beauty contests"—the process of inviting the existing 2G cellular operators to put forth a proposal

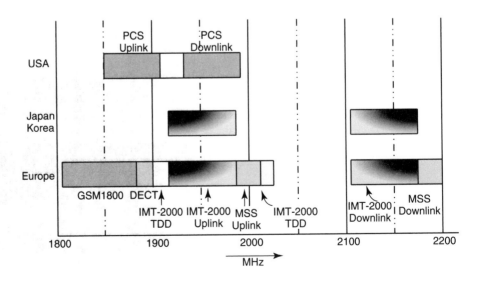

Figure 9–1   *IMT-2000 spectrum.*

and then selecting the best among them. There is no bidding process as is involved in spectrum auctions. Widespread deployment of UMTS networks is expected in 2003 and beyond. NTT DoCoMo's Freedom of Multimedia Access (FOMA) network in Japan is one of the first pre–Release 99 WCDMA networks that is operational today.

9.4   UMTS Requirements and Features

UMTS requirements are driven by market needs and anticipation of new services that make it possible to create a mobile information society. The requirements can be categorized into the following primary drivers:

- *Access to information and content on the Internet:* As the Internet has grown, so has the dependence of its users for information, entertainment, and business. The Internet has become an integral aspect of many people's lives. Since packet data access in 2G wireless networks is limited by slow speeds and inefficient spectral use, 3G networks are expected to alleviate this problem by addressing the shortcomings and thereby enabling the creation of the wireless Internet.
- *Global roaming:* With the wide disparity in types of networks deployed globally, roaming across networks has become an issue. UMTS requires that a common core network be able to support different types of access networks. With this, roaming across heterogeneous access types becomes easier since the core and the protocols to access the network and services remain the same.
- *New services:* UMTS networks are also intended to provide new types of services in addition to traditional voice. Multimedia services such as audio and video streaming, video telephony, and integration of voice and data to provide a rich user experience are expected to be possible with these networks.
- *Convergence of datacom and telecom:* With wired networks moving in the direction of convergence, wireless networks are set to follow suit, and hence a network that is essentially moving in the direction of being a packet based network is another trend.

The 3G networks are feature rich. UMTS networks increase data rates in the radio interface, improve subscriber security, and clarify the functional split between the access and core networks. The achievable data rates with the new WCDMA interface can be as high as 2 Mbps in the hotspots (at pedestrian speeds) and up to 10 Mbps with HSDPA. The WCDMA technology provides flexibility in radio resource allocation. High-bit-rate users consume capacity and leave lower speeds for other users. The radio resource optimization is a complex issue, whose goal is to optimize the number of users, their access speed, and access network coverage in the best possible way. The UMTS packet core inherits many of the GPRS architectural decisions and features but moves all radio-related functionality into the access network.

From the IP networking perspective, the high access data rate alone is a huge improvement over GPRS. How the improvements are achieved—the radio protocols and so on—is irrelevant to IP. The bandwidth increase enables new IP services in addition to the "basic" ones GPRS can provide; real-time services like voice over IP (VoIP) and streaming video will be among the driving applications for UMTS. In order to support such real-time services, the networks will have to support quality of service (QoS).

Subscriber security improvement comes from the stronger cryptography and the two-way authentication UMTS deploys. In GSM and GPRS only the subscriber authenticates himself or herself to the network; in UMTS the network also authenticates toward the user. With the basic GSM voice service the difference is not that significant, but with monetary transactions in UMTS the subscriber really wants to be sure whose network he or she is using.

Core and service network access independence is clearly an essential enabling feature to make a session handover possible, in addition to the radio access handover in place today.

9.5   UMTS Architecture Description

A UMTS network consists of a radio access network (RAN) that is attached to circuit switched (CS) and packet switched (PS) core networks. In principle, either the CS or PS core network is capable of carrying the subscriber IP traffic. A packet switched core is better suited for the task since it does not reserve transport capacity during the idle periods of the bursty data traffic. The service description of the packet switched core network is specified in 3GPP TS 23.060.

The UMTS packet core network adopted many of the GPRS features. The GPRS architecture is described in more detail in Chapter 8, "Data in GPRS Networks." This chapter concentrates on the main differences and the new IP services that the high-capacity WCDMA radio access (UTRAN) enables. The network architecture subchapters describe the PS core, several network access technologies, and IP service networks. The CS domain has been left out from the description since the packet switched core is primarily designed for IP networking.

The UMTS network architecture is shown in Figure 9–2. The network architecture in Figure 9–2 depicts the network elements according to the 3GPP Release 99 standard. WCDMA radio interface was the main new item in Release 99. The packet core network elements are the same as in GPRS, but

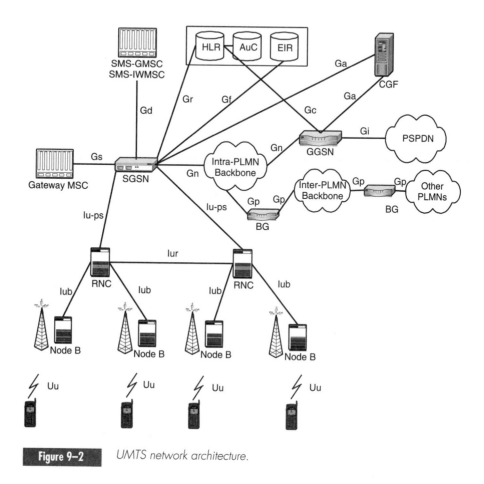

Figure 9–2   *UMTS network architecture.*

the interfaces differ somewhat. From an IP traffic point of view, the main change is that Iu-ps interface replaces Gb between the core and access networks. *IP header compression* is required to improve the bandwidth usage over the air interface. In GPRS the compression resides in the SGSN, whereas UMTS moves it into the radio network controller (RNC). Thus the 3G SGSN in the UMTS network does not know anything about the compression or other access-specific low-bandwidth optimizations. The drawback is slightly larger transmission capacity requirement between the 3G SGSN and RNC due to the full IP headers in the packets.

3GPP Release 5 and later standards define a new IP multimedia subsystem, IMS. The session initiation protocol that has been specified by the IETF will be used for both subscriber and network internal signaling. The radio network transport will move toward IP from the current ATM infrastructure. The trend toward IP transport is again invisible to the subscriber although it is an important network internal property. Since IP traffic can be carried over any physical transmission medium, the operator has much more freedom in the network implementation.

UMTS standards define four different traffic classes: conversational, streaming, interactive, and background. The network implementations map these classes to actual user plane bearers in the radio interface and the transport domain. The standard does not dictate any specific mapping to avoid binding to specific transport technologies. The standard defines a "language" with which the subscribers can request the needed service level, and the network must implement the QoS support consistently over the whole end-to-end user plane path. Thus conversational class traffic makes use of certain queuing priorities in the radio and transport protocols while the other classes utilize some other combination. The radio link setup and PDP context activation specify the exact quality requirements in terms of bit rate, delay, delay variation, and packet loss probability. The admission control in the network may also indicate that the requirements cannot be reached due to network congestion.

3G security architecture follows the GSM architecture in many respects. The trust between the user and home network is based on the subscription and roaming agreement between the home and visited network. A shared secret key between the UMTS subscriber identification module (USIM) and home network is the incarnation of the trust, and the subscriber authentication is based on proving knowledge of this secret key. The authentication procedure also delivers random session keys to cipher and integrity check the traffic between the mobile terminal and radio access network.

Roaming and paging in 3G networks are very similar to their GSM counterparts. Handover is more complex due to the soft handover mechanism used. Link-layer protocols in the RNC receive the mobile station's signal from several directions, combine the signals, and forward the result to higher protocol layers. Radio efficiency is significantly improved over the GSM technology, but the RNC has more work in deciding which signals to combine and when to change the active set.

9.5.1   User Equipment

The user equipment (UE) is the mobile terminal. The UE consists of two parts, the mobile device and the USIM.

The mobile device consists of the radio terminal and interfaces (connects) to the network via the Uu interface. Initial mobile terminals will be at least dual mode and able to support both WCDMA/EDGE as well as GSM/GPRS. This is in view of the limited deployment and coverage of WCDMA in the initial phases.

The USIM is essentially a smartcard that contains the subscriber's identity, keys used for authentication and encryption, and other subscription information. The USIM also assists in the execution of the authentication algorithm.

9.5.2 UTRAN and GERAN

As of Release 5 of UMTS, two types of radio networks now qualify as being UMTS access networks. These are the WCDMA-based UTRAN and the TDMA-based GERAN. UTRAN and GERAN radio network architectures as well as the interfaces are identical.

The UTRAN and GERAN networks consist of two distinct elements: Node B, also referred to as the BTS, and the RNC.

Node B terminates the physical and link-layer connectivity viewed from the mobile station. It bridges the Iub and Uu interfaces. Node B communicates with the RNC for radio resource management.

The RNC is the controlling element of the UTRAN. It manages radio resources associated with multiple Node Bs that are connected to it. The RNC also interfaces the UTRAN or GERAN with the core network via IuPs and IuCs interfaces.

Figure 9–3 shows the UTRAN architecture.

Multiple Node Bs are connected to a single RNC via the Iub interface. The UTRAN can consist of more than one RNC. Inter-RNC communication to enable soft handoffs is accomplished via the Iur interface. RNCs are classified as Serving RNC or Drifting RNC depending on the role played during a mobile-UTRAN connection. An RNC is deemed a RNC (SRNC) if that RNC terminates both the Iu link for the transport of user data as well as the

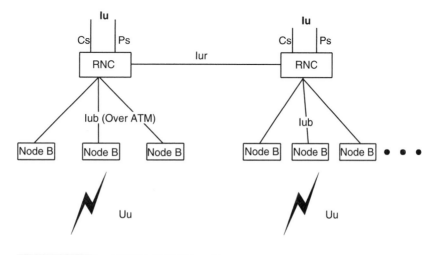

Figure 9–3 *UTRAN/GERAN architecture.*

corresponding control signaling to and from the core network. The SRNC is also the one that terminates the radio resource control (RRC) signaling (UE-UTRAN). A mobile station has a maximum of one SRNC at any time. A Drifting RNC (DRNC) is any other RNC in the UTRAN. The DRNC may be involved in performing macro-diversity combining and splitting. The DRNC simply routes the data transparently between the Iub and Iur interfaces. A mobile station may have zero, one, or more DRNCs at any given time.

The primary role of Node B is to perform the air interface layer 1 processing functions such as channel coding and interleaving, rate adapatation, spreading, modulation/demodulation, and power control. The node B is the layer 2 bridge when viewed from an IP networking perspective.

9.5.3   Packet Switched Core Network

UMTS inherits many of the GPRS packet core features and protocols. Chapter 8 describes the baseline GPRS functionality, and this chapter concentrates on the differences in the protocols.

The first major difference to GPRS is the air interface capacity allocation. WCDMA allows much higher data rates, up to 2 Mbps. Capacity allocation is also much more flexible than in GSM. The terminal classification to combine PS/CS-capable class A phones and PS only class C phones is similar to GPRS. UMTS implements two-way authentication, which means improved security to the users. Active mobiles perform handovers or cell updates, whereas idle ones without RRC connection only update the registration area (RA).

Packet core network functions in the high level are as follows (3GPP TS 23.060—GPRS service description):

- Network access control functions
- Packet routing and transfer functions
- Mobility management functions
- Logical link management functions (GSM only)
- Radio resource management functions
- Network management functions

The network elements that make up the packet switched core are the GGSN, SGSN, and border gateway.

UMTS packet data access also supports four different levels of QoS: conversational class, streaming class, interactive class, and background class. Real-time services such as voice, which are sensitive to delay, are assigned conversational class QoS. Audio and video streaming applications are generally assigned streaming class. Conversational and streaming classes are generally treated as real-time connections over the air interface. The interactive class is for applications such as Web browsing and/or gaming. Background class can be assigned to services such as e-mail and file transfer, which can be run in the background while the user is involved in some other active session. The nature of the service and application determines the type of QoS assigned to it.

GGSN

The GGSN is the anchor point for a mobile station and can be considered as the default router. The GGSN is selected based on the access point name (APN). When mobile stations request a PDP context to be set up, an APN is included as part of the request. Based on the APN request, the SGSN queries the DNS to determine the GGSN to forward the request to. The DNS response determines the GGSN, and the PDP context is established with that GGSN. The GGSN in UMTS is very much the same as in GPRS networks. A few differences include the existence of an interface called Go between the GGSN and the policy control function (PCF), which is in the IP multimedia subsystem (IMS). The Go interface is a COPS protocol-based interface and is used to specify QoS characteristics for PDP contexts that utilize the IMS. The GGSN in UMTS also supports multiple PDP contexts for a single user as opposed to GPRS, where generally the user has a single PDP context. The GGSN in UMTS is also capable of assigning multiple PDP contexts with a single IP address for the mobile station. This was not possible in GPRS.

SGSN

The SGSN in UMTS differs from the SGSN in GPRS networks in terms of the interface that is used to connect to the RNC. The IuPs interface is introduced in UMTS networks, and this is an enhancement over Gb, which is the interface that connects the BSS to the SGSN in GPRS. The IuPs interface is capable of supporting real-time services.

Another difference between 2G and 3G SGSN is the compression and ciphering function. 2G SGSN optimizes the radio link usage with TCP/IP header compression. It is also involved in logical link and radio resource management, whereas 3G SGSN is completely free from these radio-related functions. Another difference to note is that two GTP tunnels for carrying user datagrams now exist instead of only one, as was the case with 2.5G GPRS networks. A GTP-U tunnel between the GGSN and the SGSN and another one between the SGSN and the RNC are established for user plane traffic.

BORDER GATEWAY

The border gateway is essentially a firewall that protects the packet core from security threats. The GGSN connects to packet data networks such as the Internet via the border gateway. The border gateway network element is the same for both GPRS and UMTS networks.

9.6   UMTS Interfaces

The UMTS open interfaces that are important to understand from an IP networking and services perspective are Iu (Cs and Ps), Iub, and Iur.

9.6.1   Iu Interface

The Iu interface connects the UTRAN/GERAN radio network to the core network. Iu is further subdivided as follows:

- *IuC:* This is the Iu interface that connects the radio network to the
  circuit switched core network. The CS core network essentially consists of the MSCs, HLR, VLR, AuC, and EIR functions.
- *IuP:* This interface connectes the radio network to the packet core
  network that comprises the SGSN and GGSN.

The Iu interface has a control plane and a user plane component associated with it. ATM is the link-layer protocol that Iu is currently specified over.
However, the Iu interface could be run over IP in the near future.

The IuCs and IuPs control plane consists of radio access network application protocol (RANAP), which is run on top of SS7. AAL5 is the adaptation
layer used in the control plane. The IuCs user plane resides directly over
AAL2. Since voice is the primary service provided over the IuCs interface,
AAL2 has been selected as the adaptation layer for IuCs. GTP-U (GPRS Tunneling Protocol—User Plane) over UDP/IP/AAL5 is the user plane for IuPs.
The protocol stacks for Iu are shown in Figure 9–4.

RANAP is the signaling protocol whose functionality includes the following:

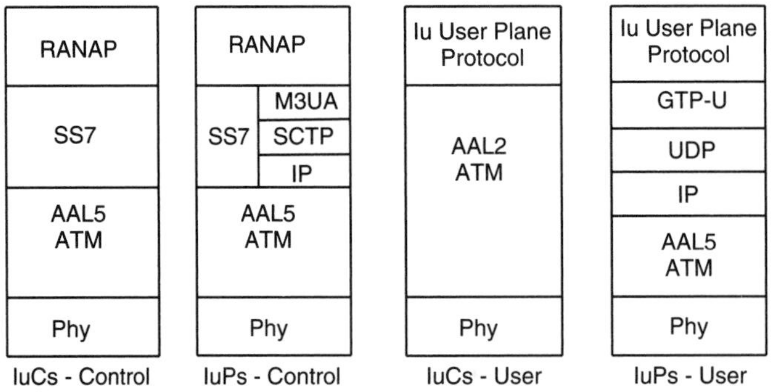

Figure 9–4   *Control and user plane stacks for Iu.*

- *Radio access bearer (RAB) management:* Includes setup, teardown, and modification.
- *Relocation:* This deals with SRNS relocation and hard handoffs.
- *Paging:* Used to page an idle mobile for a mobile-terminated session.
- *Information broadcast:* Used to broadcast system information over a specified area in a repetitive manner.

The user plane protocol in the case of IuCs is the frame protocol. For IuPs, if the payload is of type IP, it is carried via GTP-U.

9.6.2   Iub

The Iub interface connects the Node Bs to the RNC. The Iub interface consists of a control plane and a user plane. Again ATM is used as the underlying protocol for the Iub interaface. The control plane of the Iub interface is called NBAP (Node B application part). NBAP is further divided into common NBAP and dedicated NBAP depending on the signaling link used. The user plane Iub protocol is defined via the frame protocol. It defines the structures of the frames and inband control procedures for every type of transport channel.

9.6.3   Iur

The Iur interface is defined for inter-RNC communication. The control plane protocol is refered to as RNSAP (radio network system application part). RNSAP operates over SS7, which is carried over an AAL5-based ATM interface. The user plane consists of the the frame protocol. Two user plane protocols are defined, namely the dedicated channel (DCH) frame protocol and the common channel (CCH) frame protocol. The user plane is carried directly over AAL2. The interface was originally intended to support inter-RNC soft handovers. However, with the development of this interface, new functionality has been added, including support for basic inter-RNC mobility, support for dedicated and common channel traffic, and support for global resource management.

9.7   Protocol Architecture

The UMTS architecture splits the protocols across the user plane and the control plane for both the UTRAN/GERAN and the CN. The protocol model can be viewed as a multi-layered architecture. Three layers that can be differentiated are:

- Transport Network Layer
- Radio Network Layer
- System Network Layer

The transport network is responsible for providing a general purpose transport for all UMTS network elements. The radio network protocols allow interworking between the Mobile station and core network on all aspects related to the radio access bearer. The system network layer enables the setup of tunnels/PDP contexts and performs mobility management-related functions, authentication, and data delivery.

9.7.1   User Plane

The user plane of 3G GPRS features few changes from the user plane of the Release 97 GPRS (2.5G GPRS) (Figure 9–5). The 2.5G GPRS protocols in SGSN and BSS are designed by considering the reuse of GSM infrastructure. Therefore, the packet controller unit (PCU) was introduced as a logical element between SGSN and BSS. Because of PCU, 2.5G SGSN performs the link-layer functions of SNDCP and LLC. The user plane for 3G GPRS is designed without this consideration. It consists of carefully designed layered structure providing user plane transfer along with the necessary control procedures, such as flow control and error recovery. Thus, the SGSN doesn't have radio protocol layers (i.e., LLC and SNDCP).

The PDCP in the RAN provides protocol transparency to the application protocols over the radio interface. So the new protocols can be supported in the future without changing radio interface. This is unlike SNDCP, which also provides IP payload compression. The 3G GPRS provides only IP header compression. The ciphering function of LLC is moved into RLC and MAC. There is

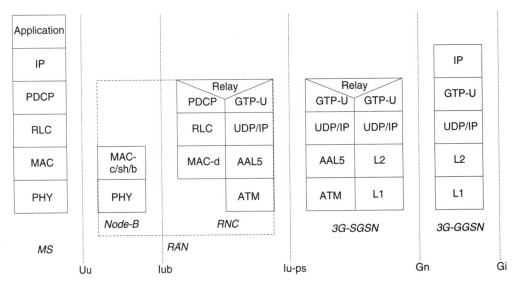

Figure 9–5   *User plane protocol architecture.*

one more GTP tunnel between the RAN and SGSN. The SGSN is connected to the RAN using ATM. AAL5 is used for segmenting the IP packet into ATM cells.

The split of radio protocols between RNC and Node B is mentioned for the WCDMA radio interface. There are four types of radio channels: broadcast, control, shared, and dedicated. Node B has radio physical layer and MAC for the broadcast, control, and shared channels. The RNC has PDCP, RLC, and MAC for the dedicated channels.

An IP packet going in the downlink direction is tunneled from the GGSN to the RNC via SGSN using two GTP tunnels. The PDCP in the RNC performs IP header compression and passes the data packet to RLC. The RLC does segmentation of the packet into radio blocks. The RLC in the nontransparent mode may also cipher the data packet. It may also provide an acknowledgment mode for transferring the packet over the air interface. The MAC provides physical channel mapping and priority handling for a data packet.

9.7.2   Signaling Plane

The signaling plane consists of protocols for control and support of the user plane functions. It provides session management (SM) and GPRS mobility management (GMM) for a user along with the short message service (SMS). The SM consists of PDP context activation, modification, and deactivation procedures. The GMM consists of attach, detach, routing area update, and security procedures.

The RANAP layer provides access control and manages GTP connections. It encapsulates and carries SM, GMM, and SMS protocol messages. It also provides mobility management functions such as SRNC relocation. RANAP is carried between RAN and SGSN using SCCP over ATM using signaling bearers. There are two alternatives for the signaling bearer layer. One option is to use a broadband SS7-based signaling bearer. This is realized by using MTP3-B (Message Transfer Part for Layer 3)/SSCF-NNI (Service-Specific Coordination Function—Network-to-Network Interface)/SSCOP (Service-Specific Connection-Oriented Protocol). The other alternative is to use an IP-based signaling bearer. This is realized by using M3UA (MTP3—User Adaptation)/ SCTP (Simple Control Transmission Protocol/IP.

The RRC protocol between MS and the RAN provides setup, modification, and release of radio resources. It also provides mobility management functions such as radio link measurements, handovers, and cell updates. The RLC protocol provides radio link management for the transmission of higher-layer signaling. The MAC provides access control to the MS. The signaling plane across the UMTS network (UTRAN) is shown in Figure 9–6.

9.7.3   GPRS Tunneling Protocol

GTP is used for both signaling (GTP-c) and data transfer (GTP-u) procedures between the GSNs. It provides a header, which together with the UDP/TCP

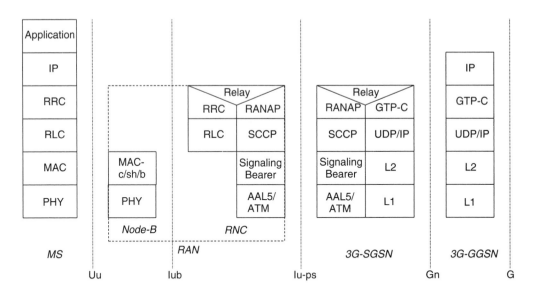

Figure 9–6   *Signaling plane protocol architecture.*

and IP header identifies the destination GSN and handling of the packet at the destination. A variant of GTP, GTP′, is used for transporting charging information to the charging gateway function (CGF) from GSNs.

The header has been changed from 2.5G GPRS. Instead of flow label, 3G uses TEID to identify a GTP flow. Also, instead of LLC frame number, 3G uses N-PDU number to coordinate the data transmission after the inter-SGSN RA update procedure. A new field, called extension header type, is used to carry extension headers. 3G also has some new flags, as discussed next.

The GTP header is depicted in Figure 9–7. The first 8 bytes are the mandatory part of the GTP header. The rest of the bytes are considered as part of the payload.

The GTP header contains the following fields:

- Version indicates different GTP versions; 2.5 G has 0 value and 3G has 1.
- PT (protocol type) differentiates between a GTP and a GTP′ message.
- Extension header flag (E) indicates the presence of the next extension header field when it is set to '1'.
- Sequence number flag (S) indicates the presence of the sequence number field when it is set to '1'.
- N-PDU number flag (PN) indicates the presence of the N-PDU number field when it is set to '1'. This flag is present only for GTP-U.
- Message type indicates the type of GTP message. For GTP-c, this contains the unique message type for a signaling message.

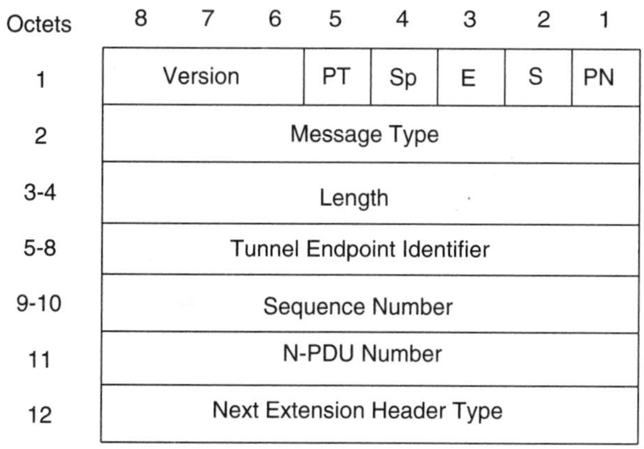

Octets	8	7	6	5	4	3	2	1
1	Version			PT	Sp	E	S	PN
2	Message Type							
3-4	Length							
5-8	Tunnel Endpoint Identifier							
9-10	Sequence Number							
11	N-PDU Number							
12	Next Extension Header Type							

Figure 9–7   *GTP header fields.*

- Length indicates the length in octets of the payload, excluding the mandatory GTP header (first 8 bytes).
- Tunnel endpoint identifier (TEID) uniquely identifies a tunnel endpoint in the receiving GTP-U or GTP-C protocol entity.
- Sequence number is used as a transaction identity in GTP-c; in other words, the value is copied from the request message to the response message. In GTP-u, it is used as a sequence number for the PDUs and is only used when the sequence order must be preserved.
- N-PDU number is used at the inter-SGSN RA update procedure and some intersystem handover procedures (e.g., between 2G and 3G RAN). This field is used to coordinate the data transmission for acknowledged mode of transmission.

Next extension header type indicates the type of extension header that follows this field in the GTP-PDU. There are three types of extension header: PDCP PDU number, suspend request, and suspend response. The PDCP PDU number is used for the SRNC relocation procedure to provide not yet acknowledged sequence numbers of the PDCP PDUs. The suspend request and response headers are used during inter-SGSN handovers for a type of circuit call.

9.7.4   UMTS Mobility Management

Iu mode mobility management (MM) handles the terminal mobility for packet communication just like GMM does for GPRS (see Chapter 8). The mobility management state machines are in the terminal and 3G-SGSN. The states are PMM-DETACHED, PMM-IDLE, and PMM-CONNECTED (3GPP TS 23.060). The main difference from GMM is that PDU transmission and reception are not

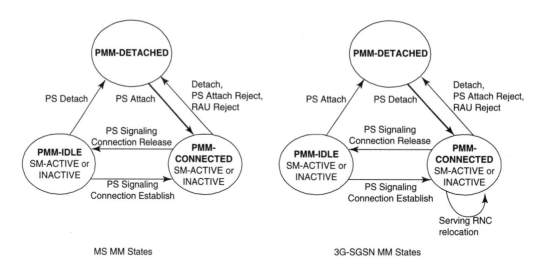

Figure 9–8   *UMTS packet session mobility management.*

visible in the state machine. Only signaling events cause transitions in the Iu mode MM. The state machines are depicted in Figure 9–8.

The states relate to terminal mobility management only. They are independent of the PDP contexts and the number of IP addresses allocated to the mobile terminal. In the PMM-DETACHED state the 3G-SGSN does not know the mobile terminal, and incoming IP packets will not reach it. The mobile terminal initiates communication with the GPRS attach procedure and transition to the PMM-CONNECTED state. The serving RNC tracks the mobile location when connected. PS signaling connection release moves the state to PMM-IDLE, where only the routing area of the terminal is known (i.e., less accurate information than in the connected state is available in the 3G-SGSN). The signaling connection can be reestablished after paging the mobile. Transition to the connected state enables packet data transfer again.

UMTS attach and detach procedures are the same as in GPRS and were discussed in Chapter 8. The key differences and improvements are described below.

UMTS ATTACH AND DETACH PROCEDURES

The UMTS attach procedure moves the MM state to PMM-CONNECTED. In the connected state the mobile station (MS) can activate the PDP contexts. During the attach, MS and the visited network authenticate each other. The network authentication toward MS is an UMTS addition to the GSM authentication. A second improvement over the GPRS procedure is that air interface ciphering takes place in RNC instead of the base station. The third improvement is the signaling integrity protection possibility, which prevents forged control messages between the base station and MS.

LOCATION MANAGEMENT

Core network mobility is different from radio network mobility. CN mobility is only handled when the mobile is attached and is not RRC connected.
Location areas (LAs) are the CS domain mobility management concept inherited from the GSM networks. Routing areas (RAs) are the corresponding PS domain entities. The core network (CN) uses RA in paging. The temporary P-TMSI subscriber identifiers are unique within RA.

Within the radio access network RA is further divided into UTRAN registration areas (URAs). UTRAN initiated paging uses the URA when the terminal signaling channel has been set up (i.e., the terminal is in the RRC-CONNECTED mode). URA is not visible outside UTRAN.

The relationship between the areas is strictly hierarchical, as Figure 9–9 shows (cells are not shown). An LA belongs to one 3G MSC and RA belongs to one 3G SGSN. URA belongs to the RNC. URA and cell-level tracking within UTRAN is done whenever the RRC connection is up. Otherwise, the 3G SGSN is responsible for paging and updating the location information in the RA level.

SECURITY FUNCTIONS

The radio access security architecture of the 3GPP release 99 standard is largely based on the 2G GSM air interface. Advanced encryption algorithms with longer cipher keys, mutual authentication, and signaling integrity protec-

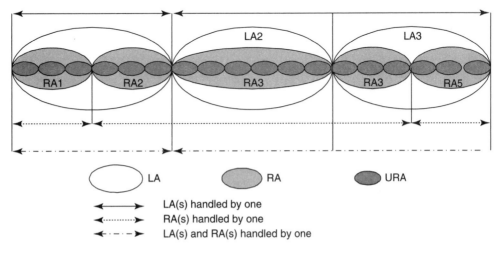

Figure 9–9   *UMTS area concepts (3GPP TS 23.121).*

tion are the main improvements over GSM. GSM-EDGE radio access network (GERAN) will adopt the 3GPP security features in later standards.

The 3GPP Security Threats and Requirements technical specification (3GPP 21.133) lists the main 3G security concerns, prioritizes the associated risks, and sets the goals for the countermeasures. The following examples present only a minor subset of the identified risks. From a security perspective, there are several other reasons to update GSM/EDGE to the UMTS security architecture (both MAJOR and medium risks of 21.133).

Threats

- ***Eavesdropping user traffic:*** *Intruders may eavesdrop user traffic on the radio interface. (MAJOR).* The GSM air interface confidentiality algorithm has been criticized for not being evaluated widely enough. Its 64-bit cipher key is sometimes considered too short and vulnerable to brute force attacks against recorded traffic offline.
- ***Masquerading as a communications participant:*** *Intruders may masquerade as a network element to intercept user traffic, signaling data or control data on the radio interface. (MAJOR).* In GSM the subscriber authenticates toward the network. A GSM subscriber cannot verify the authenticity of the network elements, e.g. base stations, or the origin of the authentication vectors.

Countermeasures

- *It shall be possible to protect the confidentiality of user traffic, particularly on radio interfaces. (T1a, T5a).* A strong WCDMA air interface confidentiality algorithm (f8) with a 128-bit confidentiality key (CK) has been publicly evaluated. Doubling the key length makes brute force attacks practically impossible. The public evaluation of the algorithm ensures that any loopholes have been detected before going to commercial releases.
- *It shall be possible for users to be able to verify that serving networks are authorized to offer 3G services on behalf of the user's home environment at the start of, and during, service delivery.* 3G networks improve the GSM authentication so that also the visited network authenticates toward the subscriber, preventing masquerading as a network element. The subscriber is able to verify that the authentication challenge originated from the home network (i.e., the HLR); thus the visited network must have a roaming agreement with the home.

9.7.5   Session Management

The mobile node is assigned an IP address that corresponds to the GGSN where the PDP context terminates. The UE is anchored to the GGSN for the duration of a session or more. However, the UE tends to move across Node

Bs, RNCs, and SGSNs. Hence delivering packets destined to a UE to the appropriate GGSN is only part of the overall solution of supporting IP mobility. Tunneling technology is used to manage the mobility of the UE. A logical connection for forwarding packets from the GGSN to the RNC via the SGSN is established in advance via the PDP context setup procedure. As the UE moves from one area to another and as a result changes the serving RNC or the SGSN, a new logical connection is created between the GGSN and SGSN and/or between the SGSN and RNC.

UMTS session management (SM) is based on GPRS session management but has been enhanced in many areas. GTP is used as the protocol for managing the mobility within the packet core network. QoS control and logical connection setup methods of 3G GTP are enhanced when compared to the GPRS-based GTP mechanisms. Session management allows a UE to establish a session and terminate a session and also deals with relocation procedures, including tunnel setup and movement.

9.8   Multimedia Session in UMTS

The UMTS network is architected to enable new types of services to be developed and deployed in addition to enhancing capacity, supporting legacy services, and making packet data access spectrally more efficient. While the new air interfaces and technology provide higher bit rates, that in itself is not a driver for widespread adoption of UMTS. New services must be created in order to utilize fully the features of 3G networks. One of the things that 3G UMTS networks enable is multiple applications run at the same time or services that intertwine multiple applications. For example, an instant messaging session is enhanced to include a voice session as well as Web browsing. Such capabilities and services will be the differentiator between second-generation and third-generation networks. Figure 9–10 shows an example of a multimedia session.

Figure 9–10 illustrates the capability of the UMTS network wherein multiple sessions with different QoS characteristics are set up as part of a multimedia call. Such types of applications can only be enabled by 3G networks due to the availability of more bandwidth and improved provisioning of QoS. Figure 9–10 shows the establishment procedures for different multimedia sessions using primary and secondary PDP context activation. The details of PDP context activation procedures are omitted for brevity. The primary PDP context (PDP1) is activated first as the base PDP context. It selects certain parameters such as PDP (MS IP) address and APN that are not modified by the secondary PDP contexts. It is mainly used for exchanging application signalling. In our example, SIP is the application level signalling. INVITE and 200 OK messages are exchanged on PDP1 with the terminating node to es-

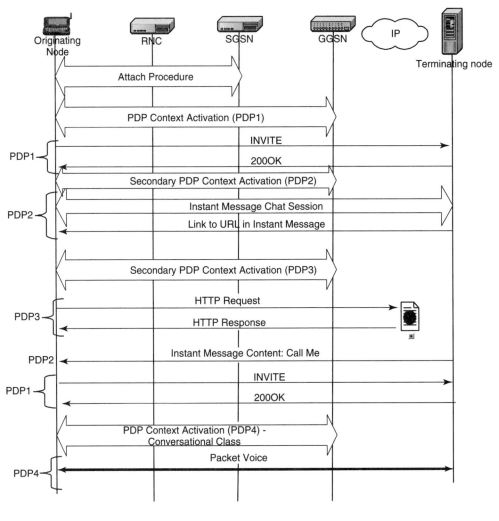

Originating
Node
RNC
SGSN
GGSN
IP
Terminating node

Attach Procedure

PDP Context Activation (PDP1)

INVITE

PDP1 — 200OK

Secondary PDP Context Activation (PDP2)

Instant Message Chat Session

PDP2 — Link to URL in Instant Message

Secondary PDP Context Activation (PDP3)

HTTP Request

PDP3 — HTTP Response

Instant Message Content: Call Me

PDP2 —

INVITE

PDP1 — 200OK

PDP Context Activation (PDP4) -
Conversational Class

Packet Voice

PDP4 —

Figure 9–10   *Multiple session example.*

tablish a data connection. The secondary PDP contexts (PDP2, PDP3, and PDP4) are activated for different data sessions. They reuse PDP address and other information from the primary context, but may change QoS for different sessions depending on the need. PDP2 is activated for an instant message chat session. During the chat session, the MS is sent a URL for downloading a Web page. Assuming that the same APN is used for connecting to the Web server, the MS initiates another secondary PDP context, PDP3, for the Web page. It transfers HTTP messages with the Web server on PDP3. After the download, the MS may terminate PDP3 without terminating PDP1 and PDP2.

After Web page download, the MS is asked on the instant message chat session (PDP2) for voice call. The MS first establishes a new SIP connection for the voice call with terminating node on PDP1. After that it establishes the PDP4 for the voice call using conversational class QoS.

9.9 Summary

This chapter has described the UMTS network architecture and the key features of UMTS that make it possible to support packet data and multimedia applications. UMTS networks will be deployed starting in 2003. At this time a pre–Release 99 network called as FOMA has been deployed by NTT DoComo in Japan.

References

3GPP Technical Specification 25.401, *UTRAN Overall Description*.

3GPP Technical Specification 25.410, *UTRAN Iu Interface: General Aspects and Principles*.

H. Holma and A. Toskala, *WCDMA for UMTS*, John Wiley, 2000.

H. Kaaranen, A. Ahtiainen, L. Laitinen, S. Naghian, and V. Niemi, *UMTS Networks, Architecture, Mobility, and Services*, John Wiley, 2001.

Data in cdma2000 Packet Networks

A *packet switched network has been developed for cdma2000 radio access technology, which utilizes protocols developed by the IETF (Internet Engineering Task Force) to provide packet data services. The network functionalities of the packet network are specified in TIA/EIA/IS-835 and 3GPP2 P.50001-A.[1] The radio functionalities are specified in TIA/EIA/IS.2000. The packet network supports only IP data. In comparison, the GPRS (general packet radio services) network is designed to provide access not only to IP but also other packet data networks (e.g., X.25). Another design approach that is different from GPRS is that the cdma2000 IP network uses the existing circuit switched (CS) radio network (RN composed of BSS, MSC/VLR, and HLR) for mobility functions, such as paging and hard handover. This implies that the packet network for cdma2000 cannot be deployed as a standalone packet network like GPRS. On the other hand, the packet network for cdma2000 is built on already available and well-understood IP protocols.*

The network is based on IP version 4. IP version 6 is being incorporated as a future enhancement. The network also supports high-speed circuit switched data (HSCSD) service, but in this chapter the focus is on the IP services. The HSCSD service is similar to the HSCSD offered by IS-95 and is described in Chapter 6.

---

[1]For further information on how to obtain 3GPP2 technical specifications and technical reports, please visit http:/www.3gpp2.org or contact its publication coordinator at 703-907-7088.

The cdma2000 air interface development effort was initially planned into two phases. Phase 1 was called 1xRTT; it employs 1.25 MHz of bandwidth and can deliver a peak date rate of 1.03 Mbps. Phase 2 was called 3xRTT; it was supposed to use 5 MHz and was promised to deliver up to 2 Mbps. Only 1xRTT is deployed by cellular operators, and 3xRTT was not deployed. The focus of the industry is on the evolution of 1xRTT for higher data throughput by using technologies such as 1X-EV-DO (1x evolution for data only) and 1X-EV-DV (1x evolution for data and voice).

10.1   Architecture Description

The packet network for cdma2000 is an adjunct to the IS-41 based cdma2000 CS network. The IP network is composed of PCF, PDSN, mobile IP home agent, and AAA servers. The packet network for cdma2000 offers mobility as an option. It provides two types of access: simple IP and mobile IP. Simple IP provides nomadic access, meaning the user cannot carry its IP sessions from one point of network attachment to another. Mobile IP provides complete IP mobility based on a set of IETF specifications, including RFC2002. It is possible for a cdma2000 MS to have simultaneous mobile IP and simple IP services for different IP sessions. The network architecture for both simple IP and mobile IP is illustrated in Figure 10–1.

10.1.1   AAA Home, Visited, and Broker Server

The authentication, authorization, and accounting (AAA) services can be provided by either the RADIUS (remote authentication dial-in user service) or Diameter protocol. The cdma2000 network first selected the RADIUS protocol and therefore RADIUS is widely used. The TIA/EIA/IS-835 specification mentions that the Diameter protocol will be supported also. In this chapter, AAA services are explained using RADIUS.

The AAA servers provide roaming. The AAA server that resides in the home IP network is called the AAA home server. The server that resides in the visited access provider network is called the AAA visited server. The AAA home server contains the subscriber profile for a user, whereas the AAA visited server contains only temporary information regarding the sessions in use by a given user. The profile may contain information such as QoS subscription and is transferred to the PDSN. The PDSN may utilize this information for authorizing access to certain services or allocating resources based on QoS requests. The AAA broker server is an intermediate server that has security relationships with the visited and the home AAA server. It is used to transfer AAA messages securely between the visited access provider network and the home IP network. A network may or may not involve any AAA broker server.

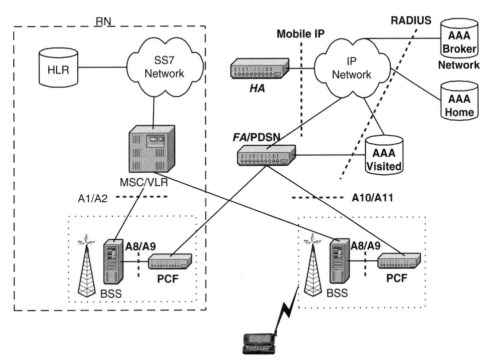

NEs and Interfaces in bold are introduced for Simple IP network
NEs and Interfaces in bold italics are introduced for Mobile IP network

Figure 10–1   *Simple IP and mobile IP network architecture.*

10.1.2   Packet Data Serving Node

The PDSN acts as an anchor network element (NE) inside the visited network and performs multiple functions in this role. For the mobile IP service, it provides foreign agent (FA) functionality as specified in RFC 2002. The FA is a router and provides routing services to an MS in a visited network. For both mobile and simple IP, the PDSN provides the data link layer connection to the MS by using point-to-point protocol (PPP). It is connected to the PCF using A10/A11 interface (R-P interface). It provides an association between the cellular link layer address and the IP address of a MS. The link layer address is composed of MS identifier (e.g., IMSI) and MS connection identifier (a parameter to distinguish multiple sessions per MS). The PDSN also acts as a RADIUS client and communicates user authentication information to the visited AAA server. It also collects accounting data from the PCF, correlates the data, generates accounting information, and relays it to the visited AAA server.

10.1.3 Packet Control Function

The PCF maintains a state of reachability between the RN and the MS. When packets arrive for an MS that is not reachable, the PCF buffers the packets and requests the RN to page the MS. It also collects and sends accounting information to the PDSN. The PCF interworks with the BSC and the PDSN to perform handover. In the Inter-Operability Standards (IOS) specifications, 3GPP2 A.S00001, PCF is connected to BSC by using an open A8/A9 interface. Usually in commercial products PCF is implemented as part of the BSC with a proprietary interface.

10.1.4 Radio Network

The RN is used for all the NEs used in the CS network, such as MSC/VLR, HLR, and BS. These NEs and the corresponding interfaces are enhanced to support the IP services. The MSC implements IS-41 MSC and is connected to the BSC using the A1 (control plane) and A2 (user plane) interface protocols. It performs the telephony switching functions and the mobility functions of the system. The HLR/VLR contains the subscriber information, which is needed in servicing a roaming MS. The cdma2000 BSC has radio resource management (RRM), mobility management (MM), and interconnections to the MSC. It provides bypass of voice codecs for the data packets.

10.1.5 Home Agent

The Mobile IP HA is a router on an MS's home link, which has the serving FA/PDSN registered for an MS. The serving PDSN for an MS is registered using the notion of care-of address (CoA), which is an IP address of the serving PDSN. While the MS is away from home network, the HA intercepts packets on the home link destined to the MS's home address, encapsulates them in another IP header, and tunnels them toward the PDSN.

10.2 Packet Data Services Description

10.2.1 Simple IP

The main characteristic of simple IP is that it does not provide mobility beyond the serving PDSN. The network only provides IP routing service to the current point of attachment in the network (i.e., PDSN). This is equivalent to the dial-up Internet service provider (ISP) service. An MS can roam from one RN to another using the location update procedure, but once a session is established with a PDSN, the MS can't hand over the session to another PDSN. PPP is used to provide the data link protocol between a user and the PDSN. The PDSN assigns an MS a dynamic IP address during the IPCP (IP Control

Protocol) phase of PPP. The A10/A11 interface is used to provide the user plane tunneling and intra-PDSN handovers. The user retains its IP address and uses IP connectivity as long as it is served by the same serving PDSN. The network can also provide virtual private network (VPN) service with the addition of VPN software on the MS.

The user authentication is provided by the Password Authentication Protocol (PAP) and the Challenge Handshake Authentication Protocol (CHAP) procedures. The PDSN, acting as an AAA (RADIUS) client, communicates user CHAP or PAP authentication information to the AAA server. PAP is the most basic form of authentication, in which a user's name and password are sent by the user and compared to a table of name-password pairs by the network. The main weakness of PAP is that both the username and password are transmitted in an unencrypted form. CHAP removes this weakness by sending the MS a key for encrypting the username and password. In CHAP, first the network sends a challenge message to the MS, which responds with a value obtained by using the key. If the values match, the user is authenticated. The user authentication is optional in simple IP. A PDSN can also be configured to allow an MS to receive simple IP service without CHAP or PAP.

Simple IP supports header and payload compression as defined in the TIA/EIA/IS-835 specification. The Van Jacobson's TCP/IP header compression is supported as specified in RFC 1144. The PPP Compression Control Protocol is also optionally supported, which is used to negotiate a PPP payload compression algorithm from the following list:

- Stac-LZS (RFC 1974)
- Microsoft Point-to-Point Compression Protocol (RFC 2118)
- Deflate (RFC 2394)

10.2.2   Mobile IP

The mobile IP service (RFC 2002)[2] provides complete mobility to a user. The PDSN has the functionality of an FA. A user is assigned an HA in its home IP network. The MS is assigned an IP address, called home address, which is in the same subnet as the HA. The MS uses CoA (IP address of the FA) to register with the HA. Registration causes the HA to perform proxy ARP on the home subnet and begins intercepting all packets destined to the MN's home address. The HA also creates a binding between the home address of the MN and the care-of address specified in the Registration request. When the HA receives data for an MS, it forwards the data to the FA using CoA and the FA forwards the data to the MS. Packets destined for the MN are tunnelled using IP-in-IP tunnelling to the care-of address. IP-in-IP tunnelling is specified in RFC 2003. Mobile IP allows an MS to be reachable regardless of whether it is

---

[2]As this book was going to press, RFC 2002 was made obsolete by RFC 3344.

roaming in a public or private network. The only criteria is that the care-of address and the home agent have public IP addresses that are globally routable. In case of private network access, the MS uses reverse tunneling via the FA to send the data through the private network.

As in simple IP, the data link protocol between MS and PDSN is provided by PPP. If the PDSN receives a packet for an MS with no established PPP session, the PDSN discards the packet and sends an ICMP destination unreachable packet to the source. A single PPP session can support multiple IP home addresses, thus allowing different applications per MS.

Mobile IP signaling is exchanged on the traffic channels over the air interface, which is an inefficient usage of the expensive radio resource. There are some improvements with respect to the base mobile IP protocol to make the signaling more RR efficient. One such improvement is that the agent advertisement messages are not broadcast continuously and periodically by the PDSN to all the MS. Instead, they are sent to an MS after establishing PPP connection. Another improvement is that the PDSN can only repeat the advertisements a configurable number of times for an MS. Also, the PDSN stops sending the advertisements to an MS once it receives a registration request from the same MS. As mobile IP runs over the PPP connection, the mobile IP registration lifetime should be smaller than the PPP inactivity timer.

Mobile IP provides its own set of security procedures between mobile client (MS) and mobile agents, and also between the mobile agents. It only mandates a strong security association for authentication between the MS and HA for the registration messages. This security association can be established simply by static provisioning (e.g., at subscription time) of the keys in the MS and HA. Mobile IP does not mandate an authentication mechanism between the HA and FA (PDSN). However, in a commercial environment such as cellular, it is important to authenticate all the messages between the FA and the HA to stop any encroachment of services and establish reliable billing between home and visited network. The standard (TIA/EIA/IS-835) supports the following options for the key distribution between FA and HA:

- IKE and public certificates (X.509)
- Dynamic pre-shared IKE secret distributed by the home AAA server
- Statically configured IKE pre-shared secret

The MS-FA security procedure is provided by using MS-FA challenge/response mechanism as described in RFC 3012. It is initiated by the PDSN to authenticate a user in a visited domain upon user registration. The PDSN includes an MS-FA challenge extension in the agent advertisement. Since the advertisements are rarely sent, the PDSN includes the next challenge in the registration reply. The MS uses this next challenge in the next re-registration with this PDSN. The PDSN communicates the FA challenge response, received from the MS, to the home AAA server through the visited AAA server.

10.3 Protocol Architecture

This section illustrates the end-to-end protocol architecture for the mobile IP and simple IP services. There are some enhancements in the protocol messages between MSC and BSC for IP services, but the protocol stack between them is the same as in the CS network (i.e., A1/A2 over SS7), and is not shown for simplicity. All the control messages at PPP and above layers are user plane data for the radio link layers.

10.3.1 Simple IP

The control plane for simple IP is illustrated in the Figure 10–2. PPP is used for establishing link layer connection between MS and PDSN. A11 is a modified version of simple IPv4 and is used for providing mobility management, charging data collection, and GRE tunnel management between PDSN and PCF. A11 is transported over UDP as specified for simple IPv4. A9 is defined to provide mobility management and GRE tunnel management between PCF and BS. Link access control (LAC) is used between BS and MS for processing cdma2000 layer 3 signaling messages.

Figure 10–3 shows the user plane for simple IP protocol architecture. The PPP layer encapsulates and transfers IP packets between MS and PDSN. A10 and A8 use GRE tunnels to transfer packets.

10.3.2 Mobile IP

The control plane for mobile IP is shown in Figure 10–4. In the stack shown, IKE is assumed as a key distribution mechanism between PDSN/FA and HA. Also, IPsec is assumed for both control and user plane between PDSN/FA and

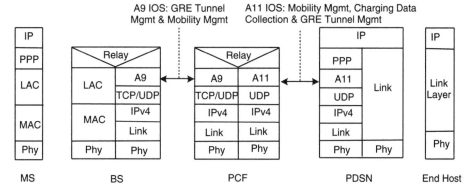

Figure 10–2   *Simple IP protocol architecture control plane.*

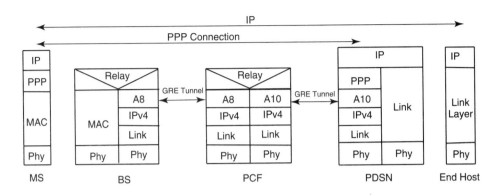

Figure 10–3   *Simple IP protocol architecture user plane.*

HA. All the protocol layers underneath the PPP layer stay the same as in simple IP. The main difference from simple IP is a layer of mobile IP signaling, which is transported over UDP. The mobile IP layer provides mobility across PDSNs.

The user plane protocol for mobile IP is illustrated in Figure 10–5. The end host (or correspondent node) sends packets to the MS. The packets arrive at HA and are tunneled to the PDSN/FA using IP tunnels. The stack under PPP is similar to simple IP, where packets are carried using GRE tunnels from PDSN to BS.

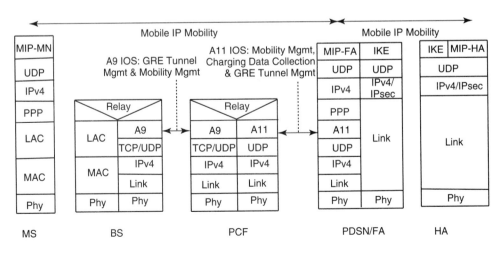

Figure 10–4   *Mobile IP protocol architecture (control plane).*

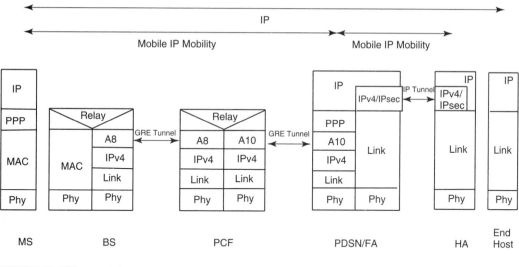

Figure 10–5 *Mobile IP protocol architecture (user plane).*

10.4 Core Network Procedures

The packet network for cdma2000 uses IETF-defined procedures for mobility, security, and session management. Some of these procedures are enhanced for the packet network. This section describes these procedures, along with the enhancements.

10.4.1 R-P Interface (A10/A11 Interface)

The R-P interface is an extension of the mobile IP version 4 to allow MM between the RN and the PDSN. More specifically, it is the interface between the PCF and the PDSN. The R-P interface is standardized by ITU documentation in the IOS specifications. The R-P interface is also referred to as A10/A11 interface in the specifications.

MOBILE IP ENHANCEMENTS FOR A10/A11 (R-P)

For the A11 interface, base mobile IP is extended to accommodate specific changes for the cellular access. A mechanism is added to enable the generic routing encapsulation (GRE) and reverse tunneling during A11 registration. GRE and reverse tunneling are used to tunnel user plane packets for an MS between the PCF and PDSN.

Two new messages, registration update and registration acknowledge, are added to support the R-P session disconnection during handover. The base mobile IP depends on lifetime timer expiry for releasing a registered session. For cellular, this would increase the blocking time for the radio resource allocated at the source RN. Therefore, explicit messages are defined to expedite the release of the resources at the source RN.

Addressing is also handled differently in the A11 messages compared to the base mobile IP. In the A11-registration request message, the IP source address in the IP header and the CoA field are set to the IP address of the PCF. The IP destination address and the HA address field are set to the address of the PDSN designated for the call. The home address field is set to zeros. Instead of home address, the PCF sets a session-specific extension to identify a session. This extension uniquely identifies a session between an MS and its serving PDSN. This extension is mandatory in all the A11 messages and is shown in Figure 10–6.

The following are the fields in the SSE:

- Type is the extension type and equals 39 for SSE.
- Length indicates the rest of the length (in bytes) of the extension.
- Protocol type indicates the type of the protocol to be tunneled across the RP interface. It is the same as the protocol type field in the GRE header.
- Key is the packet session identifier (PSI) used for identifying bearer connection.
- MS connection ID differentiates the multiple sessions from the same MN.
- MS ID type indicates the type of the MS ID (e.g., value 1 indicates IMSI encoded in ASCII format).
- MS ID length indicates the length (in bytes) of the following MS ID field.
- MS ID is the unique global ID value for an MS (e.g., IMSI).

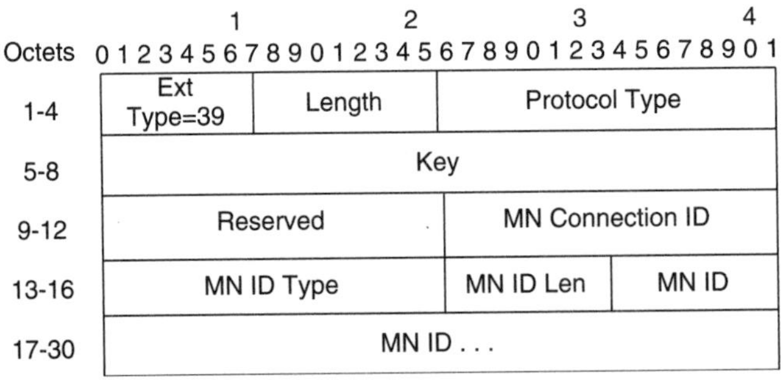

Octets	Ext Type=39	Length	Protocol Type	
1-4	Ext Type=39	Length	Protocol Type	
5-8	Key			
9-12	Reserved		MN Connection ID	
13-16	MN ID Type		MN ID Len	MN ID
17-30	MN ID . . .			

Figure 10–6 *Session-specific extension.*

GENERIC ROUTING ENCAPSULATION (GRE) FOR A10

GRE framing is used for tunneling the user plane between the PCF and PDSN. GRE is a simple tunneling protocol and is carried over IP, which in turn is carried over the A10 bearer connections. The PCF and the PDSN IP addresses are used in the source and destination address fields of the IP header used with a GRE packet. For identifying an A10 bearer connection, the PSI (packet session ID) is used and is inserted as the key field in the GRE header. The PCF informs the PDSN about the PSI by inserting it in the A11-registration request message. The PSI is only unique in a PCF; therefore, the MN session reference ID (MN-SRID) is used together with the mobile identifier (IMSI) over the A10/A11 connection to identify a packet session for a specific mobile across PCFs and PDSNs.

10.4.2   A8/A9 Interface and A1 Interface Interactions

The A8/A9 interface links the packet session management on PCF/PDSN with the MSC call control (CC) procedures and the BSC RRM. The standards have specified an open interface between the BSC and PCF called A8/A9 interface. However, the vendors have not implemented PCF as a separate NE. The implementation of the A8/A9 interface varies from one vendor to another. In this section the standardized A8/A9 interface is assumed.

An interaction between A8/A9 interface and the CC messages occurs during the setup for a packet data session. The MS initiates a packet data session by exchanging the same set of CC messages toward MSC as it would exchange for a voice call, but with the data service request. During the session establishment, the MSC recognizes that the service request is for data and sends an assignment request for data service to BSS without allocating a circuit. The BSC at this point initiates A8/A9 connection setup.

Another interaction between A8/A9 and CC messages occurs for the dormant state. An MS goes into the dormant state when it is not exchanging data with the network for a certain time. In the dormant state, only RR and CC connections are released at the BSC and MSC to conserve the most needed radio resources. The A10/A11 and PPP connections are maintained for the MS. The BSC uses A9 signaling to notify the PCF, which keeps the A10/A11 connection and releases the A8/A9 connection. At the same time the BSC also notifies the MSC to release the call connections. An MS can reactivate the dormant state by performing a call establishment procedure with the BSC and MSC. The resulting A8/A9 connection reconnects to the existing A10/A11 connection. The dormant state can also be reactivated by the network when the data packets arrive for a dormant MS at the PCF. The PCF starts buffering the packets and initiates a service request toward the BSC containing the identity of the MS that needs to be paged. The BSC forwards the request toward the MSC. The MSC pages the MS and proceeds with the rest of the CC procedure as in a mobile-terminated call. Once the call connection is established, the PCF starts delivering buffered and oncoming packets to the MS.

10.4.3   Mobility Management (MM)

The IP services use both the PS network MM procedures as well as the CS network MM procedures. The PS network MM procedures are A11 registration, mobile IP registration, handovers, and security. The CS network MM procedures are location update, handovers, and security. Some PS network MM procedures need CS network MM procedures for complete execution. For example, the PS hard handover signaling interacts with the CS hard handover for complete execution. Other PS network MM procedures execute independent of the CS network MM procedures. For example, the PS user authentication procedure (CHAP/PAP) is executed independent of the CS user authentication procedure.

In this section, only the different types of the PS network handovers are described. The PS network registrations and security were explained in Sections 10.2.2 and 10.4.1.

DORMANT HANDOVER

An MS stays dormant by releasing the radio resources but keeping the A10 and PPP connections. When the MS moves under a different BSC, which is attached to a new PCF, the dormant handover takes place to move the A10 connection to the new PCF.

An MS in the dormant state monitors the packet zone identifier (PZID), system identifier (SID), and network identifier (NID). When any of these identifiers changes, the MS sends a request for the dormant handover. The MS sends the old PZID, SID, or NID to the target PCF via BSC. The target PCF establishes an A10 connection with the PDSN. The target PCF sends the source and the target PCF information to the serving PDSN. The serving PDSN uses this information to determine whether the PDSN is changed or not. If the PDSN is changed, it performs mobile IP registration. If the new PCF is attached to a different PDSN, the target PDSN sends registration update to the source PCF to release the resources at the source PCF.

HARD HANDOVER

Hard handover is initiated by the source BSC during the active state of a data session. The packet data hard handover involves both CS and PS network handover. The handover request is first communicated to the target BSC through the MSC as in the CS network handover. The target BSC after realizing that the request is for a data session initiates A8/A9 connection setup with the target PCF. After the setup of A8/A9 connection, it acknowledges the handover request to the source BSC as in the CS network handover. When the

MS acquires the target BSC, it sends a notification to the target PCF. This notification triggers PCF to establish an A10 connection with the PDSN.

PDSN functions differently for intra-PDSN and inter-PDSN hard handovers. In case of intra-PDSN hard handover, PDSN only releases the A10 connection with the source PCF. In case of inter-PDSN hard handover, the source PDSN has to wait for the expiry of the registration timer before it can release the A10 connection. This is because of the absence of any inter-PDSN interface. Inter-PDSN hard handover also requires establishment of the PPP link between the target PDSN and the MS, and the mobile IP registration of the new PDSN with the HA. The MS does not start getting data from the network until the completion of the mobile IP registration and the establishment of the PPP link. This makes the overall procedure very slow and may result in considerable loss of data packets. The hard handover mechanism by itself can't recover the loss of data packets. It is up to the application (e.g., TCP) to recover from this loss.

FAST HANDOVER

Hard handover is slow and results in packet loss; this makes it unsuitable for delay sensitive or real-time traffic. To solve these problems of hard handover, a fast handover procedure was developed by 3GPP2. This fast handover procedure is different from the fast handover process developed by the Mobile IPWG in the IETF. The fast handover is achieved by anchoring the call to the serving PDSN. Layer 2 sideways tunnels, called the PP interface, are created between the PDSNs for the bidirectional transport of bearer data (PPP frames) between the target PDSN and the serving PDSN. Effectively, the MS remains connected to the serving PDSN during the active state of the session. PPP establishment at the target PDSN and mobile IP registration are performed only when the MS moves to the dormant state of the call.

The PP interface supports both the signaling and bearer channels. The PP signaling channel provides capabilities for the bearer channel control. The sideways tunnel is terminated when the MS registers at the target PDSN during the dormant state. The target PDSN now becomes the serving PDSN for subsequent activations of the packet session. The future enhancements of fast handover procedures are planned to enable mobile IP registrations to occur during the active state of the call.

10.4.4   QoS in the CN

The standards have specified QoS in the core network based on differentiated services. But the reality is that QoS is not supported in the core network. This section gives an overview of QoS from the specifications.

QoS is provisioned in the home AAA server as a user profile parameter and is called 3GPP2 differentiated service class options. It is sent to the PDSN in the RADIUS access accept message. The MS can optionally support differentiated services or may rely on the network to perform packet marking. The network may overwrite the marking of the packet by the MS.

The 3GPP2 differentiated service class options specify groupings of differentiated service classes. The exact grouping is not specified in the specifications. Classification rules and policing parameters for use of the differentiated services classes are configured by the visited access provider in the PDSN and are not sent in the RADIUS profile parameter. The method by which service providers agree to the same PDSN configuration definitions for each class is also needed but not specified.

The differentiated services class, from a downlink packet, is copied to the differentiated service field of the mobile IP tunnel (RFC 2002). This is done by HA for every downlink packet. In the uplink direction, the PDSN determines the differentiated services field of each tunneled packet to the HA if reverse tunneling is enabled.

10.5   Radio Layer Functions

The radio link layer is composed of different sublayers. The sublayers of interest for IP services are link access control (LAC) and media access control (MAC). This section describes some of the important functions of LAC and MAC.

10.5.1   Link Access Control

The purpose of the LAC sublayer is to process cdma2000 layer 3 signaling according to the radio characteristics of the physical channel without the need for the upper layers to be aware of them. LAC does not process IP-level signaling (e.g., MIP registration request). The IP level signaling is processed as a user data packet by the MAC sublayer.

The processing within LAC is done sequentially, with processing entities passing the partially formed LAC protocol data unit (PDU) to each other in an established order. The following are the functions performed by the LAC sublayer (Figure 10–7):

- Access control through "global challenge" authentication (refer to TIA/EIA/41). If a message fails authentication, then it is not delivered to the upper layers.
- Reliable delivery to the peer entity, on the other side of the air interface, using ARQ techniques.
- Addressing to ensure delivery based on the addresses, which identify particular mobile stations.
- Utility functions for assembling and validating the PDUs.

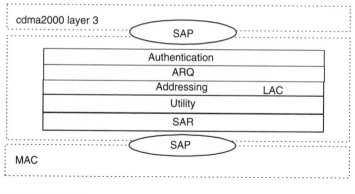

Figure 10–7 *LAC sublayer functions. Reproduced under written per-mission from Telecommunications Industry Association.*

* Segmentation/reassembly of encapsulated PDUs into fragments of sizes suitable for transfer by the MAC sublayer.

10.5.2   MAC

MAC provides access control by managing physical layer resources. It is also responsible for providing the QoS level requested by a user data service. Data services use two important MAC functions: radio link protocol (RLP) and multiplex/QoS.

RADIO LINK PROTOCOL

The RLP sublayer divides the PPP packets into radio frames for transmission. RLP provides ARQ, FEC, and flow control functions. These functions improve performance in the radio segment of the data connection. RLP was already present in IS-95 and it is enhanced in cdma2000 to accommodate higher data rates.

MULTIPLEX AND QOS SUBLAYER

The multiplex sublayer multiplexes signaling, voice, and data blocks received through LAC, voice services, and RLP (Figure 10–8). It forms physical layer service data unit (SDUs) for transmission. There are two types of physical layer channels available for transferring IP traffic: fundamental channel (FCH) and supplemental channel (SCH). On the SCH only data blocks can be multiplexed and CRC is added for protection against errors. This combination of data and CRC is called the link transmission unit (LTU). In the reverse direction, the multiplex sublayer de-multiplexes the information contained in the

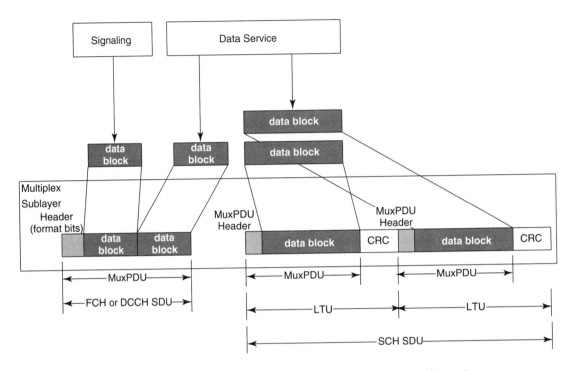

Figure 10–8   *Multiplex sublayer function. Reproduced under written permission from Telecommunications Industry Association.*

physical layer SDUs and directs the information to the correct entity (i.e., upper-layer signaling, data, or voice service).

QoS for over-the-air transmission is specified in terms of these parameters: assured/nonassured, user priority, minimum data rate, maximum data loss rate, and maximum delay. The multiplex sublayer may use QoS in delivering data over the air. The exact manner for using the QoS to deliver data over the air interface is not specified in the standard and is left for implementers to decide.

10.6   IP Application

Let's look at a complete picture of an IP application running over the network. The overall message flow is split up into two figures for clarity. Figure 10–9 illustrates the message flow with RN as a black box. Figure 10–10 gives the inside view of RN and shows the message flow between the different components of RN.

It is assumed that an MS is sending an e-mail message using SMTP. When the MS executes command to send an e-mail message, it invokes the

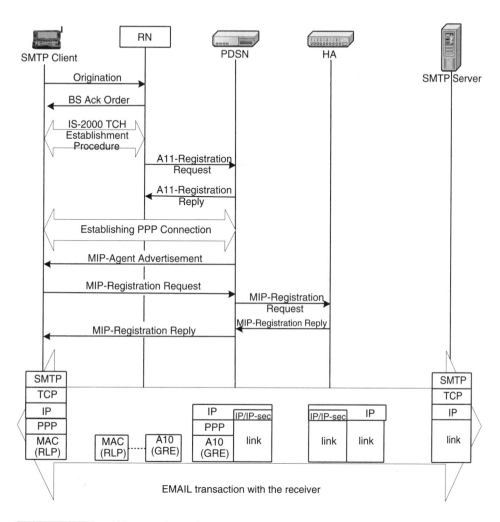

Figure 10–9 *MS-initiated e-mail transaction.*

underlying TCP layer. The TCP invocation causes the cdma2000 layer 3 functions to send an origination message with the data service option to the BSC. The message is sent over the access channel of the air interface with layer 2 acknowledgment required. The BSC acknowledges the receipt of the message with a BSC acknowledgment order message.

The BSC constructs the CM service request message, sends the message to the MSC, and starts timer T303. The MSC, after recognizing that the request is for data service, sends an assignment request message, without allocating any terrestrial circuit to the BSC, to request assignment of radio resources and

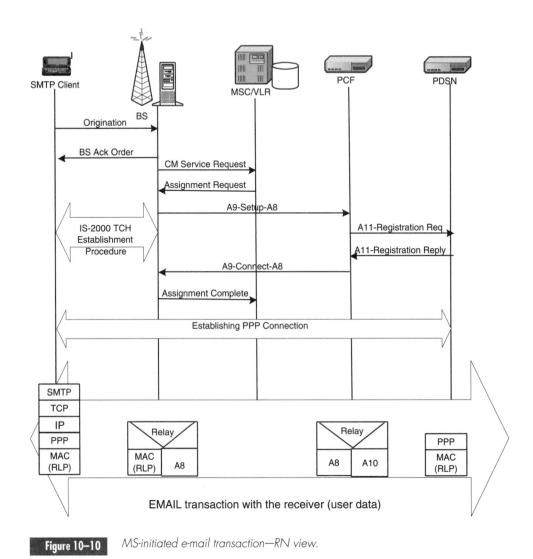

Figure 10–10   *MS-initiated e-mail transaction—RN view.*

starts timer T10. The BSC and the MS initiate the establishment for a radio traffic channel.

Now that the CC connection through the BSC and MSC is completed, the BSC initiates the data session connection through the PCF and PDSN. For this, the BSC sends an A9-setup-A8 message to the PCF to establish an A8 connection and starts timer TA8 setup. The PCF recognizes that no A10/A11 connection associated with the MS is available and selects a PDSN for the call. The PCF sends an A11 registration request message to the selected PDSN and starts timer T-regreq.

The PDSN validates the A11 registration request message and accepts the connection by returning an A11 registration reply message with an accept indication and the lifetime set to a preconfigured value. The A10/A11 connection, once established, will be periodically refreshed after every expiry of the lifetime timer. Upon establishment of the A10/A11 connection, the PCF completes A8 connection by transmitting an A9-connect-A8 message to the BSC. The BSC sends an assignment complete message to the MSC, thus completing CC connection through the MSC. In this way a bearer path is established to transport user plane data between the MS and the PDSN through the PCF/BSC.

The PPP connection establishment procedure is initiated at this point. The network may ask for the CHAP/PAP user authentication as part of this procedure, which involves AAA agents for the verification of the authentication information.

The PDSN sends an agent advertisement to the MS over the PPP link. The MS sends a registration request to the PDSN along with its CoA. The PDSN forwards the registration request to the HA. The HA verifies the mandatory MS-HA authentication extension and sends the registration reply back to the MS through the PDSN. The other security associations (refer to Section 10.2.2) may also be verified as part of registration.

At this point all the necessary signaling has been performed and the HA knows where it needs to send data for the MS. In the user plane path the IP packets sent by the e-mail application in the MS take different forms. The PPP layer encapsulates the IP packets into PPP frames. The RLP layer converts the PPP frames into radio frames. The radio frames go through the multiplex sublayer, which converts them into physical layer SDUs. On the network side the reverse operation takes place in the BSS and PDSN. The PCF tunnels the PPP frames using GRE tunnel to the PDSN. The PDSN recovers the IP packets from the PPP frames and sends them over the reverse tunnels to the HA. The HA forwards them to the SMTP server.

10.7 Summary

This chapter gives an overview of the cdma2000 packet network. The network basically provides two different services, simple IP and mobile IP. This chapter describes the packet network architecture for both services. It describes interfaces of the core network along with the mobility management and QoS functions. It describes some of the main radio functions used for packet data transfer, such as LAC, MAC, and RLP. The chapter describes an e-mail transfer to a mobile client, which is accessing e-mail through a cdma2000 network.

References

C. Perkins, "IPv4 Mobility," *RFC2002*, IETF, May 1995.

G. Montenegro, "Reverse Tunneling for simple IP," *RFC2344*, May 1998.

P. Calhoun, C. Perkins, "simple IPv4 Challenge/Response Extensions," *RFC3012*, November 2000.

W. Simpson, "The Point to Point Protocol (PPP)," *RFC1661*, July 1994.

W. Simpson, "Mobile-IPv4 Configuration Option for PPP IPCP," *RFC2290*, February 1998.

D. Rand, "The PPP Compression Control Protocol (CCP)," *RFC1962*, June 1996.

R. Friend, W. Simpson, "PPP Stac LZS Compression Protocol," *RFC1974*, August 1996.

W. Simpson, "PPP Challenge Handshake Authentication Protocol (CHAP)," *RFC1994*, August 1996.

G. McGregor, "The PPP Internet Protocol Control Protocol (IPCP)," *RFC1332*, May 1992.

K. Nichols, S. Blake, F. Baker, D. Black, "Definition of the Differentiated Services Field (DS Field) in the IPv4 and IPv6 Headers," *RFC2474*, December 1998.

S. Blake, D. Black, M. Carlson, E. Davies, Z. Wang, W. Weiss, "An Architecture for Differentiated Services," *RFC2475*, December 1998.

C. Rigney, "RADIUS Accounting," *RFC2139*, April 1997.

C. Rigney et al., "Remote Authentication Dial In User Service (RADIUS)," *RFC2138*, August 1997.

V. Jacobson, "Compressing TCP/IP Headers for Low Speed Serial Links," *RFC1144*, February 1990.

D. Harkins, D. Carrel, "The Internet Key Exchange (IKE)," *RFC2409*, November 1998.

TIA/EIA/IS-2001-A, "Interoperability Specification (IOS) for cdma2000 Access Network Interfaces," April 2001.

TIA/EIA/IS-707-A-2.12, "cdma2000 High Speed Packet Data Service Option 33," March 2001.

TIA/EIA/IS-2000.1-A: "Introduction to cdma2000 Standards for Spread Spectrum Systems," March 2000.

TIA/EIA/IS-2000.2-A: "Physical Layer Standard for cdma2000 Spread Spectrum Systems," March 2000.

TIA/EIA/IS-2000.3-A: "Medium Access Control (MAC) Standard for cdma2000 Spread Spectrum Systems," March 2000.

TIA/EIA/IS-2000.4-A: "Signaling Link Access Control (LAC) Standard for cdma2000 Spread Spectrum Systems," March 2000.

TIA/EIA/IS-2000.5-A: "Upper Layer (Layer 3) Signaling Standard for cdma2000 Spread Spectrum Systems," March 2000.

ITU-T Recommendation X.509, "Public-key and Attribute Certificate Frameworks."

3GPP2 A.S00001, "3GPP2 Access Network Interfaces Interoperability Specifications, version 4.1," December 2001.

3GPP2-P00-20010212-007, "Fast Handoff in cdma2000 Wireless IP Networks — PP Interface Stage-2 and Stage-3 Descriptions."

TIA/EIA/IS-835-1, "cdma2000 Wireless IP Network Standards—Draft," April 2001.

TIA/EIA/41-D, "Cellular Radio Telecommunications Inter-System Operations," November 1997.

3GPP2 S0001-B, Version 1.0.0, "Wireless IP Network Standard," September 2001.

Vijay K. Garg, "IS-95 CDMA and cdma2000."

IP in 802.11 Networks

In today's world, local area networks (LANs) are almost ubiquitous in their existence as the uniform method of data communication across various devices, including computers. Although they were initially defined to be smaller in size (typically the size of an office building or campus), LANs now may span several cities or even continents.

LANs consist of computers, servers, printers, and other devices connected through wires or physical cables that run through the premises. LANs are typically extended to new locations by drawing physical cables and creating ports for computers to access the LAN.

The addition of wireless capabilities allows LANs to be extended without the use of wires or cables, thus enabling untethered communications. This is especially useful when reconstruction may be required to lay new cables in older buildings or in hazardous areas. Thus, in one point of view, wireless versions of LANs allow current "wired" LANs to be extended to new places, and thus augment the capabilities of a LAN.

The other advantage of wireless LANs (WLANs) is their inherent mobility, as computers do not have to be attached to LAN ports using cables. The advantage adds a new dimension that allows new configurations such as wireless-only LANs. It also allows for a new set of applications and services (for example, doctors can access patient databases on site at the patient's bedside to quickly determine a course of action).

11.1 IEEE 802 Family, LAN Standards, and IP

The 802 family of standards from the Institute of Electrical and Electronics Engineers (IEEE) defines various types of LANs. Of these, 802.3 (which is commonly known as the Ethernet) is the most popular LAN technology and is deployed widely throughout the world. Other LAN standards from IEEE include 802.4 (token bus), 802.5 (token ring), and 802.6 (FDDI) (Figure 11–1).

The IEEE 802.1 standard provides an introduction to the set of 802 series of standards and defines interface primitives. The IEEE 802 series of standards operate in the layer 1 and layer 2 (i.e., the physical and data link layers), of the seven-layer OSI or the TCP/IP protocol models.

The logical link control (LLC) is the upper part of the data link layer and helps establish peer-to-peer logical links between two 802 LAN protocol entities. The LLC layer is common to all 802 LAN protocols, creating a layer of transparency between data link and network layer protocols. This allows several 802 LAN protocols to be defined beneath the LLC layer that differ in their physical layer and media access control (MAC) layer characteristics.

The MAC layer is the lower part of the data link layer. The MAC layer defines different addressing formats and specific protocols used to arbitrate access to the 802 LAN system, for the various 802 LAN standards. The MAC address is 48 bits in length and is a layer 2 address, used only in the data link layer. Of the 48 bits, the first two bits are for control and administrative purposes. The next field is the vendor ID, which is generally assigned by the IEEE to any organization that needs it for use on devices such as personal computers, servers, and printers.

The second part of the MAC address is "locally assigned" by the organization that owns the vendor ID. When the IEEE assigns these addresses, they are truly global addresses and ensure that no two stations in the world have the same MAC address.

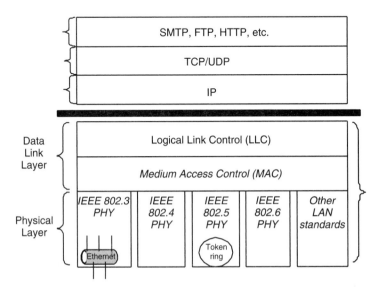

Figure 11–1   *IP and the IEEE 802 family.*

The physical layer defines signaling mechanisms and transmission characteristics for the different LAN standards. For example, in the 802.3 protocol, the physical layer defines data over media such as coaxial cable, copper, and fiber-optic cable.

11.1.1   IP over LANs

IP is a network layer protocol, and the power of internetworking is that the IP layer does not depend on any specific layer 2 protocol. The existence of the IEEE 802.2 LLC layer beneath the IP layer was designed to allow e-mail, business applications, or network management software to work on different types of 802 LANs, creating transparency at the LLC layer. The LLC layer also allows other protocols, such as AppleTalk, to run over 802 LANs as well.

The most common LAN in the 802 family is the 802.3 Ethernet LAN. Mechanisms are clearly defined to map IP addresses to 48-bit MAC layer addresses. For example, this may be provided as part of the driver software when installing a LAN card in a computer. This driver software creates a mapping of the IP address to a specific MAC address of the computer.

Other mechanisms to help associate IP addresses to MAC addresses include the Address Resolution Protocol (ARP). In addition, the IEEE 802 standards define mechanisms to map unicast, multicast, and broadcast IP addresses to MAC layer addresses, allowing various types of applications to run over Ethernet LANs.

11.2   Brief History of Wireless LAN

This section provides a brief history of wireless LAN and its relationship with other IEEE LAN standards. Similar to LANs, many of the initial WLANs were proprietary. Prior to 1998, many of these wireless applications were characterized by low data rates, high cost, and a lack of a worldwide standard that limited widespread deployment. These WLANs were used in many areas, such as manufacturing, retail, and warehousing. It was at this juncture that IEEE stepped in and created the standards for WLANs.

11.2.1   IEEE 802.11 Family

IEEE initiated the standardization efforts in the area of WLANs, similar to the LAN technology it had standardized earlier. In May 1991, a project authorization request (PAR) was initiated to create a new working group called IEEE 802.11 for WLANs. This effort resulted in the IEEE adopting a new standard for WLAN, IEEE 802.11-1997, released in 1997.

There have been enhancements made to this initial release (referred to as IEEE 802.11-1999) that resulted in other standards being developed that in-

crease the peak data rates. A brief description of the basic IEEE 802.11 protocol model is provided next. This framework is used by the initial and subsequent releases of the IEEE 802.11 standards.

11.3   IEEE 802.11 Protocol Model

The IEEE 802.11 standards were developed with the primary goal of being
very similar to the makeup of the 802 LAN family that we introduced earlier.
This means that all the applications, protocols, and management mechanisms
need to execute seamlessly in the IEEE 802.11 environment as well. Users ac-
customed to the mode of operation in a LAN environment (for example, the
IEEE 802.3 LAN), should not notice any significant difference while operating
in a IEEE 802.11 environment.

   One of the key protocol layers that was discussed in the IEEE 802 LAN
family is the logical link control (LLC) layer. This layer creates the transparency between the network layer protocols like IP and the data link and
physical layer mechanisms. The IEEE 802.11 protocol is designed to operate
as a peer protocol to the IEEE 802.3 LAN, as another data link and physical
layer mechanism. This means that the LLC layer is the same across multiple
LAN technologies, including the IEEE 802.11 family, as shown in Figure 11–2.

   The LLC layer in the IEEE 802.11 protocol model isolates the various
LAN and WLAN protocols from the network layers like IP. This allows seamless execution of applications, upper layer protocols, and management mech-

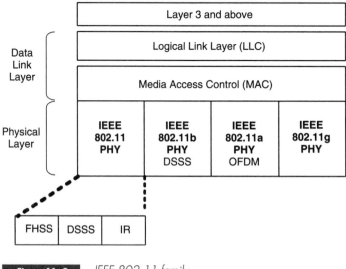

Figure 11–2   *IEEE 802.11 family.*

anisms over IEEE 802.11. The 802.2 LLC layer makes the IEEE 802.11 WLAN protocol indistinguishable from the other IEEE 802 protocols.

The IEEE 802.11 WLAN protocol model includes two layers below the LLC layer, the MAC layer and the PHY layer. The PHY layer is the layer responsible for transmission over the air. There are many mechanisms used to transmit over the air, and they all work with the same MAC layer above.

The MAC layer in 802.3 LANs provides a reliable communication mechanism that allows multiple users fair and consistent access to the shared medium. These same functions are needed in IEEE 802.11 LANs as well, along with additional functions needed due to the wireless nature. There are differences brought about due to the wireless nature that create new functions of the MAC and PHY layer.

802.3 LAN users are used to the privacy afforded by the use of wires and the security of all information transmitted over wires. Going wireless with IEEE 802.11 WLANs raises the level of awareness regarding security and privacy. These issues need to be addressed when creating the standards for the IEEE 802.11 family.

Another implication of going wireless is that the medium is no longer as predictable as when using cables in a LAN environment. Wireless interface creates additional issues such as reliability of the wireless medium and power used to transmit. These issues need to be addressed in IEEE 802.11 to create a viable WLAN mechanism.

Mobility is one of the fundamental results of going wireless. Wireless communication allows users to access the network in any location, if appropriately configured. Mobility allows users to roam around campus with no need to look for ports of access and may allow large-scale deployments in public areas as well.

Going wireless allows a new set of applications that were not possible with wired 802.3 LANs. However, the fundamental premise of 802.3 LANs, such as secure, reliable, high-speed communication that allows multiple users fair and consistent access to the medium, needs to be realized in the 802.11 WLAN family as well.

11.3.1   IEEE 802.11 and Its Features

The initial IEEE 802.11 protocol introduced the IEEE's standard to a wide audience and was standardized in 1997. It introduced the use of new MAC and PHY layers. It also introduced a logical architecture that allowed devices with IEEE 802.11 capability to communicate with each other. It introduced the notion of devices communicating with an access point, which in turn connects to the wired LAN network.

The data rates of the initial IEEE 802.11 went from 1 Mbps to a peak rate of 2 Mbps. The data rate of 1 Mbps is mandatory, and the 2 Mbps is an optional data rate depending on the type of physical layer mechanism used. There are three different types of PHY layer transmission technologies that have been standardized in IEEE 802.11. Two of these methods are based on radio frequency (RF) technologies, and the third is an infrared mechanism.

One of the key requirements of IEEE 802.11 Project Authorization Request (PAR) is the need for global availability. This prompted the use of the unlicensed 2.4-GHz spectrum that is available in most parts of the world known as the industrial, scientific, and medical (ISM) band. The amount of bandwidth available in the 2.4-GHz range depends on the country. In the United States, 79 MHz of spectrum is available in the 2.4-GHz range.

Countries also regulate the different types of technologies and the amount of power used, as there are other technologies that operate in this band, including Bluetooth, HomeRF, and even garage door openers and baby monitors. By using the ISM band consistent with the appropriate amount of power allowed in each country, IEEE 802.11 can be deployed throughout the world. This ISM band is used for the two modes of the PHY layer that operate in the RF layer. The infrared option operates in the nearly visible 850 to 900 nanometers range at a maximum transmit power level of 2 watts peak optical power.

The data rates of 1 and 2 Mbps, although not very fast when compared with today's data rates available in IEEE 802.3 LANs, provides enough data rates to allow a vast array of applications. The IEEE 802.11 WLAN also provides a very viable alternative to mobile users and compares favorably with other 2.5G and 3G cellular technologies, which also provide wireless Internet access, albeit at much lower data rates.

Realistically, the actual transmission rate will be lower than the peak of 2 Mbps, given the wireless media and the need for reliability, which requires retransmissions. It should still allow for devices to use IEEE 802.11 in residential, manufacturing, retail, warehousing, remote monitoring, hospitals, and other areas where high data rates are not a requirement. An example of this is bar code applications, which should work well with the 2 Mbps data rates offered by IEEE 802.11.

11.3.2   IEEE 802.11b and Its Features

One of the concerns with the initial IEEE 802.11-1997 standard was the data rate that can be achieved. The upper limit of 2 Mbps was slow for situations where large data blocks needed to be transmitted (increasing transmission delay in the network) and multimedia applications, resulting in the arrival of IEEE 802.11b. The introduction of newer standards was also facilitated by advancements in digital signal processors and chipsets.

In October 1997, the IEEE 802 executive committee allowed the creation of two new projects to increase data rates beyond the initial IEEE 802.11 standard. This led to the development of IEEE 802.11a and an IEEE 802.11b

IEEE 802.11b, Wi-Fi, and WECA

The IEEE 802.11b standard is also referred to popularly as Wi-Fi (wireless fidelity). In order to certify the interoperability of various 802.11b products, a Wireless Ethernet Compatibility Alliance (WECA) has been formed with several companies. Products purchased with the Wi-Fi logo are interoperable and this provides additional flexibility when deploying WLANs.

WECA also serves as a marketing arm for Wi-Fi as the global standard. Members include WLAN semiconductor manufacturers, WLAN providers, computer system vendors, and software makers—such as 3Com, Cisco, Intel, Texas Instruments, Apple, Breezecom, Cabletron, Compaq, Dell, Fujitsu, IBM, Intersil, Lucent Technologies, Nokia, Samsung, Symbol Technologies, Wayport, and Zoom.

standard, which only modifies the PHY layer with the same MAC layer defined for IEEE 802.11 standard. Both standards were approved by the IEEE in September 1999.

The maximum data rate supported by the IEEE 802.11b standard is 11 Mbps. It also supports additional data rates of 1, 2, and 5.5 Mbps besides the 11 Mbps. The standards also provide a sliding mechanism to traverse among these different data rates. The lower rates of 1 and 2 Mbps are backward compatible with the same 1 and 2 Mbps in the IEEE 802.11 standard, when using the same RF mechanism.

Unlike the IEEE 802.11 standard, which supports multiple RF and infrared mechanisms, the IEEE 802.11b standard only supports one RF PHY layer mechanism. The IEEE 802.11b standard operates in the same 2.4-GHz ISM band that the IEEE 802.11 standard operates in as only the RF mechanism is employed.

With higher data rates, several applications are possible with the IEEE 802.11b standard. This includes applications that the IEEE 802.11 standard is used for as well as newer applications, such as streaming applications and transmission of large data blocks without adversely affecting the transmission delay in the system.

As the IEEE 802.11b standard is backward compatible with the IEEE 802.11 standard when using one flavor of the PHY layer, introduction or overlay of the IEEE 802.11b standard devices in an IEEE 802.11 standard system should be possible, where the IEEE 802.11b standard device can operate in 1 or 2 Mbps if desired.

11.3.3   IEEE 802.11a Features

As mentioned earlier, a project was initiated in the IEEE 802 working group to create a new high-speed wireless LAN standard known as IEEE 802.11a. One of the more obvious reasons is the need for higher data rates as compared to the IEEE 802.11 standard and the IEEE 802.11b standard. Another reason for the creation of the IEEE 802.11a standard was the fact that many countries, including the United States, had allocated a new unlicensed band in the 5-GHz range for use, which is not as prone to interference as the 2.4 GHz that the IEEE 802.11 standard and IEEE 802.11b standards were using.

The fact that more bandwidth was available (up to 300 MHz available in the 5-GHz band as opposed to a maximum of 79 MHz available) in the 5-GHz range necessitated a fresh look at technologies that could be used for extending services to include applications such as voice, image, and video services besides the tried and tested packet data services.

The IEEE 802.11a standard was completed in the same time frame as the IEEE 802.11b standard (September 1999), and devices using this technology are coming out at this time.

A new technology is used in IEEE 802.11a standard, which is very different (and incompatible as well) with the other standards. The data rates for the IEEE 802.11a standard can go as high as 54 Mbps achieving the necessary data rates for all types of applications. The IEEE 802.11a standard provides a wireless LAN with data payload communication capabilities of 6, 9, 12, 18, 24, 36, 48, and 54 Mbps. The support of transmitting and receiving at data rates of 6, 12, and 24 Mbps is mandatory.

The spectrum that the IEEE 802.11a standard operates is in the unlicensed 5-GHz range. Several countries around the world created additional spectrum in the 5-GHz range. For example, the U.S. government released 300 MHz of spectrum in the Unlicensed National Information Infrastructure (U-NII) band in the range of 5.15–5.25, 5.25–5.35, and 5.725–5.825 GHz. Many other countries have released up to 200MHz in this band.

An increase in the data rates opens the door for a wide variety of applications, including delay-sensitive (or referred to in the standards as time-bound applications) such as voice and video. IEEE 802.11a standard is not backward compatible with the IEEE 802.11 standard and the IEEE 802.11b standards and, therefore, care should be taken to decide on the technology that best suits the requirements of WLAN deployment.

A comparison of the various IEEE WLAN standards, including those that are being created during the publication of this book, is shown in the following table:

Feature	IEEE 802.11	IEEE 802.11b	IEEE 802.11a	IEEE 802.11g	IEEE 802.11h
Data rate	1–2 Mbps	1–11 Mbps	Up to 54 Mbps	45 Mbps (proposed)	Up to 54 Mbps
Standards	IEEE 802.11–1997	IEEE 802.11b–1999	IEEE 802.11a–1999	Standardization in progress	Standardization in progress
Frequency band	ISM band 2.4 GHz	ISM band 2.4 GHz	5 GHz	ISM band 2.4 GHz	5 GHz

> **Note**
>
> Before the next section, some key definitions that will be used throughout this chapter are provided here. The term *IEEE 802.11 family* or *IEEE 802.11 system* refers to the entire family of IEEE 802.11 systems, and any feature of the IEEE 802.11 family or system means that this is applicable to all variations of PHY layer mechanisms. When referring to a specific PHY layer technology, the term *IEEE 802.11X standard* will be used, where X may be a, b, g, or other flavors of 802.11 PHY layer. The initial IEEE 802.11 PHY layer will simply be referred as the IEEE 802.11 standard.

11.4   802.11 Family Wireless LAN Architecture

This section examines the architecture common to the IEEE 802.11 family. IEEE 802.11 has defined a logical architecture that not only includes devices but other logical entities to create a robust yet flexible architecture. The architecture is distributed in nature and also includes key functions as power savings as part of the architecture. The architecture is flexible to allow transient or ad hoc networks and can also support permanent networks at home and enterprise networks. This section introduces the basic concepts of the architecture, including stations and access points, and then presents the two modes of the IEEE 802.11 family.

11.4.1   IEEE 802.11 Family Entities

The IEEE 802.11 family defines two basic entities in its architecture:

- A *station* is the entity that connects using the wireless medium. This could be a network interface card (NIC) in a PC or a laptop.
- An *access point (AP)*, which is an entity that forms a bridge between the wireless medium and a wired network like the IEEE 802.3 LAN. The access point (referred to as AP throughout this chapter) acts as a base station for the IEEE 802.11 devices and aggregates them on to the wired network like the LAN.

The IEEE 802.11 architecture consists of basic service sets, which is a collection of stations communicating with each other. There are two operating modes for the basic service set defined in the IEEE 802.11 system.

11.4.2   Independent Basic Service Set

The first operating mode defined in IEEE 802.11 architecture is the independent basic service set (IBSS). In the IBSS mode, stations are communicating with each other without an access point (i.e., without any connectivity to the wired network like the LAN). This is an example of an ad hoc network, characterized by a short-term network created for a purpose. All stations may not able to communicate with each other, and no function exists to relay traffic to other stations.

The IEEE 802.11 standard provides information on how these stations can discover each other, synchronize all the timers in an IBSS, and manage battery power. Examples of this may be a few clients at a conference exchanging documents, or a few salespersons exchanging sales information in airports or in situations where no access to wired network exists (such as a consultant in a client's site).

11.4.3   Access Points
and Infrastructure Basic Service Set

The other operating mode defined in the IEEE 802.11 family is the infrastructure BSS, referred to as BSS throughout this chapter. This configuration includes the presence of a single access point (AP) in each BSS, which provides connectivity to the wired network. The AP plays the critical role of a central coordination entity and provides the ability to register stations with the BSS and authenticate them and provides functions to handle roaming or mobility of stations. The AP is identified by a MAC address similar to the other wireless stations. Please refer to Figure 11–3 for a depiction of Independent BSS and Infrastructure BSS.

Even though most of the IEEE 802.11 WLAN operations are common to both operating modes, the infrastructure BSS or BSS is the more common configuration and will be discussed more throughout the rest of this chapter.

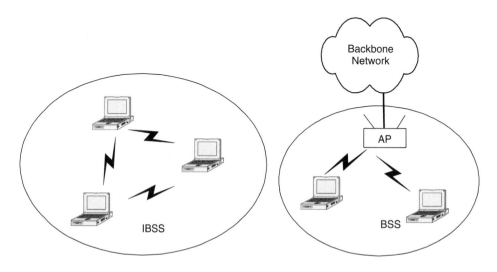

Figure 11–3   *Independent BSS and infrastructure BSS.*

The access point may contain several additional features such as firewalls, network address translators (NATs), Dynamic Host Configuration Protocol (DHCP) server, DCHP client, security, and virtual private network (VPN) software. The features that an AP contains depend on its use in home or enterprise applications.

11.4.4   Distributed System

In the BSS mode, the access point serves as an entry point to the wired network. In a typical home environment, there is only one AP with one or more wireless stations. IEEE 802.11 family allows intra-BSS mobility, where the wireless stations may roam around the coverage of an AP and still obtain service.

The advantage of going wireless is the ability to move around. It would be beneficial for users to move around a collection of BSSs so that they can run the same applications anywhere in a conference center or a campus. This facet of mobility is one of the key advantages of the IEEE 802.11 family.

Several BSSs may be deployed to provide extended coverage connected by a backbone network. This backbone network, referred to as the distributed system (DS), helps interconnects all the access points or BSSs. This allows the wireless stations to move around a collection of BSSs over a coverage area such as a campus. Each BSS is identified by a BSS identifier (BSS ID), which is a 48-bit MAC address similar to 802.3 LAN MAC addresses. This allows multiple BSSs to be collocated with each wireless station using the BSS ID to attach to a specific BSS.

11.4.5   ESS and Roaming in IEEE 802.11 WLAN

As stations roam from one BSS to another, the distributed system allows users to roam freely and still receive packets in their new location. The DS could be any type of network (wired, wireless); it typically is the IEEE 802.3 LAN network.

When two or more BSSs are connected using a distributed system to form a single subnetwork, this is referred to as an extended service set (ESS). Each ESS is identified by an ESS identifier (ESS ID) and, typically, wireless stations lock onto a specific BSS (identified by a BSSID) and a specific ESS (identified by an ESS ID). For example, an ESS may be used to provide campus-wide coverage or even public WLAN coverage.

The IEEE 802.11 family specifies that as wireless stations move from one BSS to another within the same ESS, packets should be routed to the appropriate wireless station. This allows roaming to be realized in the IEEE 802.11 family. The access point contains a distributed system client that is used to route the packets to other wireless stations within the BSS, or to other BSSs in the same ESS. To the LLC sublayer of each station, the ESS has the appearance of one large BSS.

11.5   802.11 Family Physical Layer

This section examines the various PHY layer mechanisms that have been standardized in the IEEE 802.11 family. The architecture described in the previous section is common to all the physical layer technologies. This section begins with the IEEE 802.11 standard and then discusses the IEEE 802.11b standard and the IEEE 802.11a standard. The other evolving standards, such as IEEE 802.11g and IEEE 802.11h, are not discussed as they are still in their formative stages.

The protocol model of the IEEE 802.11 standard shows a new PHY layer that was introduced for wireless transmission. The PHY layer portion of the IEEE 802.11 standard has been partitioned into multiple layers for separate functions. The physical layer is responsible for transmission and reception over the air. However, many physical layer mechanisms are available, such as RF and IR mechanisms. The physical layer also needs to work with the MAC layer to transfer and receive MAC layer protocol data units (MPDUs).

11.5.1   IEEE 802.11 Physical Layer

There are three different types of PHY layer transmission technologies that have been standardized in the initial IEEE 802.11 standard. Two of these methods are based on RF technologies, and the third is an infrared mechanism. The two RF mechanisms employ the spread spectrum technique to achieve the PHY layer transmission.

SPREAD SPECTRUM TECHNIQUES

The wireless spectrum is always a scarce resource, with tight regulations in terms of usage and power radiated along with licenses required to operate. This is true for most of the wireless systems in place. However, the ISM band is one of those bands that does not require a license to operate.

One of the key issues in an unlicensed band is the interference due to various technologies operating in the unlicensed band. The spread spectrum technique is inherently less sensitive to interference. The two types of spread spectrum techniques are frequency hopping spread spectrum (FHSS) and direct sequence spread spectrum (DSSS).

In the case of the IEEE 802.11 physical layer that employs FHSS, every country has designated a fixed number of 1-MHz channels for use, along with details such as the power to be used and the dwell time. In the United States, there are 79 of these 1-MHz channels available for use in the IEEE 802.11 standard. Each country also defines hopping sequences. For example, in North America, there are three sets of hopping sequences, and the hopping sequence to be used is selected when a FH device is configured for wireless LAN operation.

Frequency Hopping Spread Spectrum

Frequency hopping is one of the spread spectrum techniques used in the IEEE 802.11 standard.

The 2.4-GHz frequency spectrum that is available for use is divided into several 1-MHz frequency bands. The transmitter and receiver "hop" from one 1-MHz frequency band to another, in a near-random sequence. The transmitter will send data in each of the 1-MHz frequency bands, and if the receiver is locked onto the appropriate 1-MHz band, it should be able to receive the information from the transmitter.

The amount of time spent by the transmitter or the receiver in a 1-MHz band is referred to as the dwell time. Typically, any narrowband interference is limited to the dwell time in each band.

The wideband used in the IEEE 802.11 DSSS mechanism is 22 MHz. The allocation of DSSS frequencies is dependent on the country of operation. For example, in most of North America and Europe, the available 2.4-GHz spectrum in the ISM band is divided into 14 channels of 22 MHz each that overlap one another (Figure 11–4). Any of these 14 channels may be used, based on the configuration of the WLAN.

If multiple WLAN systems are needed for increased capacity, there are three non-overlapping or distinct 22-MHz channels available. This allows

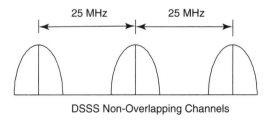

DSSS Non-Overlapping Channels

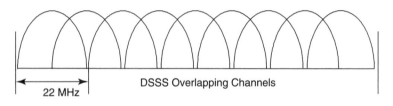

DSSS Overlapping Channels

Figure 11–4   *Direct sequence spread spectrum channel allocation in North America.*

Direct Sequence Spread Spectrum

DSSS is another mechanism used in IEEE 802.11 to provide data rates of 1 and 2 Mbps.
    In the IEEE 802.11 DSSS system, an 11-bit code called a Barker sequence is used to transform the original data bits. The resulting transformed bits are modulated to send over a carrier frequency using one of two modulation techniques: differential binary phase shift keying (DBPSK) or differential quadrature phase shift keying (DQPSK).

three 22-MHz DSSS systems to coexist without causing the WLAN systems to interfere with one another.

INFRARED TECHNIQUE

Infrared is the third mechanism for physical layer transmissions available for use in the IEEE 802.11 standard. This technique uses infrared light in the 850 to 950 nm range. This mechanism typically operates with a range of up to 10 m and does not require a direct line of sight. Operation is possible in a diffused mode, where reflection off walls is allowed. This mechanism is typically used in indoor environments such as classrooms or conference rooms, since infrared light cannot penetrate obstructions and is attenuated easily. This technology is not as popular as FHSS or DSSS since it is not suitable for mobile users.

11.5.2   IEEE 802.11b Physical Layer

The key need for the IEEE 802.11b standard was to provide data rates of 5.5 Mbps and 11 Mbps in addition to the basic 1Mbps and 2 Mbps data rates introduced by the IEEE 802.11 standard. In contrast to the IEEE 802.11 standard, which provides multiple physical layer options for wireless mediums, the IEEE 802.11b standard only allows the DSSS mechanism to achieve the higher data rates of 5.5 Mbps and 11 Mbps. This is because use of the FHSS mechanism at these higher data rates may violate government regulations for operating in the unlicensed band.
    The following table lists the various techniques used in the physical layer of the IEEE 802.11b standard:

Data Rates	Code	Modulation	Symbol Rate	Bits/Symbol
1 Mbps	11 bit Barker	DBPSK	1 Msps	1
2 Mbps	11 bit Barker	DBPSK	1 Msps	2
5.5 Mbps	8 bit CCK or PBCC	DQPSK	1.375 Msps	4
11 Mbps	8 bit CCK or PBCC	DQPSK	1.375 Msps	8

CCK: complementary code keying
PBCC: packet binary convolutional coding

The IEEE 802.11b physical layer uses the same formats for 1 and 2 Mbps. However, if higher throughput and no interworking with legacy is required, the newer format allows 5.5 and 11 Mbps. The IEEE 802.11b standard also allows dynamic rate switching depending on radio conditions. If good transmission conditions exist, then higher data rates of 5.5 and 11 Mbps may be used. If radio conditions are poor, the data rates may drop down to 1 and 2 Mbps.

11.5.3   IEEE 802.11a Physical Layer

The IEEE 802.11a standard uses the 5-GHz range, which is not as interference-prone (compared to the 2.4-GHz band) due to the relatively minimal technologies operating in this domain. According to the IEEE, the role of the IEEE 802.11a standard, which was approved in September 1999, is to "develop a higher speed PHY for use in fixed, moving or portable wireless local area networks."

Several PHY layer technologies were investigated, and the IEEE finally decided on orthogonal frequency division multiplexing (OFDM) as the technology for transmission. This is a new encoding scheme that offers benefits over spread spectrum. In OFDM, each user transmits using 20-MHz, which is in turn divided into 52 subcarriers of 300 KHz each.

The subcarriers are transmitted in parallel, with each subcarrier transmitting at a much lower rate than the total combined data rate. The receiving device processes and combines these individual signals, each one representing a fraction of the total data, to make up the actual signal. The mandatory data rates are 6, 12, and 24 Mbps, and other data rates up to 54 Mbps are optional.

Orthogonal Frequency Division Multiplexing

To achieve high data rates, a divide and conquer approach is chosen. One high-speed channel is split into several low-speed channels when transmitting information. At the receiver, all of these different low-speed channels or carriers are combined to re-create the high-speed channel.

The advantage of these many subcarriers is that high data rates can be achieved easily. Another advantage is that as the subcarriers tend to carry data at lower rates, multipath or reflective signals do not cause undue concern. The IEEE 802.11a standard also adds additional features in the PHY layer, such as forward error correction (FEC) codes, to recover from any errors, especially given the high data rates.

As the technology is complex, the market has not been flooded with new IEEE 802.11a standard devices. Higher-frequency radio technologies have historically required exotic, expensive semiconductor processes, and the technical challenge before the industry is to implement 802.11a functionality economically. This would allow for mass production, bringing about the desired side effect of reduced prices.

11.5.4 Compatibility of 802.11, 802.11b, and 802.11a Technologies

A wireless LAN user may take several paths depending on the throughput needed and the applications employed. One such evolution may be to max out the capacity of the 802.11 system in the 2.4-GHz range by going from 802.11 to 802.11b and 802.11g (in the future).

If bandwidth is an immediate need, then operators may deploy 802.11 or 802.11b for their current users and then jump to another new standard, 802.11a. The issue with this is that these technologies are not backward compatible, and significant costs may be involved in the changeover.

However, 802.11a can be overlaid over an 802.11 or an 802.11b system as they operate in different bands. So the network administrator may deploy 802.11a in hot spots and provide extended coverage using 802.11b or 802.11 systems.

Between 802.11 and 802.11b systems, the network administrators should go for 802.11 DSSS systems if backward compatibility with 802.11b is desired. Otherwise, the option that best suits current requirements and meets future needs should be selected.

11.6 IEEE 802.11 Medium Access Control Layer

The IEEE 802.11 family MAC layer is common to all types of PHY layers mentioned previously and this section discusses features of the MAC layer. Many of the functions have been modeled after the previously introduced IEEE 802.3 LAN with modifications and additional functions needed for wireless capability. The goal of the IEEE 802.11 family of MAC standards is to provide equivalent or better functions as compared with the IEEE 802.3 LAN MAC layer.

As mentioned before, a common LLC layer is used across the other LAN standards and IEEE 802.11 family WLANs that creates an easy bridge between WLANs and LANs. The IEEE 802.3 LANs provide a mechanism for multiple users to share a medium, and this continues, albeit with some changes, in the IEEE 802.11 family. The IEEE 802.3 LANs are very reliable, and this needs to be realized in the IEEE 802.11 family, keeping in mind the issues confronting wireless mediums.

Other features of MAC are more particular to the wireless nature of IEEE 802.11. Mechanisms such as cyclic redundancy checksum (CRC) and packet fragmentation have been added to cope with the wireless media. Security- and mobility-related features have also been added due to the wireless aspect of IEEE 802.11.

11.6.1   Contention Resolution — CSMA/CA

Medium access control, as the name implies, has to provide a fair and consistent method for users to access the shared medium. IEEE 802.3 LANs introduced carrier sense multiple access/collision detection (CSMA/CD) for sharing the physical medium. The IEEE 802.3 Ethernet LAN devices "sense" or listen to the wired medium for any other transmissions from other nodes in the IEEE 802.3 LAN. IEEE 802.3 frames are sent if there is no one sending data.

If there is a collision in the physical medium, the IEEE 802.3 LAN detects this collision and waits a random amount of time before it transmits again. This mechanism works well with wired LANs as the sending device can listen to the transmissions and detect if there are collisions.

PHYSICAL CARRIER SENSE

The IEEE 802.11 physical medium is also shared among all devices. The same CSMA mechanism, where the physical medium or carrier is sensed, can be employed in the IEEE 802.11 family as well. This is because the sending stations can listen for any transmissions before sending frames using the wired medium. However, detection of collisions is not easy in wireless mediums, as typically the transmission overpowers the sending station's ability to detect or hear any collision, and expensive equipment is required for simultaneous reception and transmission.

Therefore, the collision detection used in IEEE 802.3 LANs is not suitable in the IEEE 802.11 family. The change is to use a collision avoidance (CA) mechanism, where the receiving station sends an acknowledgment (ACK) packet to confirm that the packet has arrived uncorrupted.

This is referred to as the *basic access mechanism* and is formally referred to as the distribution coordination function (DCF) in the MAC layer of the IEEE 802.11 family. This explicit ACK mechanism adds some extra overhead as compared to IEEE 802.3 LANs. This method of ACKs for packet transmission adds additional reliability in an otherwise noise-filled and unreliable wireless medium.

One of the problems associated with the basic access mechanism is that it assumes that the sending station can listen to all stations and sense the carrier. However, due to physical obstructions and the fact that not all stations may be within hearing range of each other, all nodes may not be able to listen to each other. This is referred to as the hidden node problem.

HIDDEN NODE PROBLEM

As shown in Figure 11–5, there are three stations with IEEE 802.11 connectivity. Stations A and B are in range with each other, and stations B and C are within range of each other. Therefore, if station A were to transmit to station

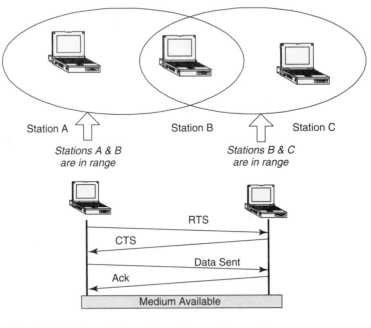

Station A Station B Station C

Stations A & B
are in range

Stations B & C
are in range

RTS

CTS

Data Sent

Ack

Medium Available

Figure 11–5 *Hidden node problem and its resolution.*

B, any transmission by station C at the same time would corrupt packets arriving at station B. Station C is not aware that there are other stations transmitting to station B as well.

To alleviate this problem, on top of the basic access mechanism mentioned earlier, two more frames are exchanged. This requires the sending station, in our example station A, to first send a request to send (RTS) message to station B. Station B, if it receives this correctly, will respond with a clear to send (CTS) message. Station B's CTS is heard by both stations A and C. Only station A will transmit at this time, as it received a clear to send from station B.

These two messages on top of the basic access mechanism of CSMA/CA create a solution for dealing with wireless medium access and the hidden node problem. Stations hearing a CTS will wait until the ACKs are sent for the packet transmission. Once the ACKs are heard, the other stations can contend for resources. The use of the RTS/CTS mechanism is optional and is typically used for large packets.

11.6.2 Addressing

The same MAC address format that is used in the IEEE 802.3 LANs is used in the IEEE 802.11 family as well. This is the same 48-bit address as shown in Figure 11–6.

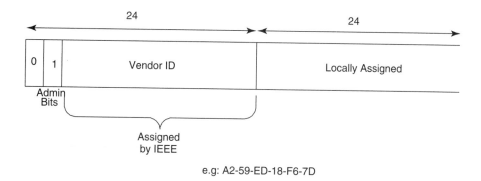

Figure 11–6   *MAC address.*

The use of this address is similar to the IEEE 802.3 LANs, where the source and the destination are identified by a MAC address, referred to in the IEEE 802.11 family standards as source address (SA) and destination address (DA). However, unlike the IEEE 802.3 LANs, additional types of addresses (using the same MAC address format) have been defined in the IEEE 802.11 family. These are the transmitter address (TA), receiver address (RA) and the basic service set identifier (BSS ID). These additional addresses facilitate mobility as well as multicast-related operations.

11.6.3   Reliability and Robustness

The benefit of wired LANs is the inherent reliability that accompanies them. One of the key requirements of the IEEE 802.11 family MAC layer is to be robust against interference in the 2.4-GHz band. The cyclic redundancy checksum (CRC)-32 that was used in IEEE 802.3 LANs is continued here as well. The MAC frames include a frame check sequence (FCS) field that contains the CRC for the packets, and the receiver checks for any errors. Another new mechanism added for robustness is a fragmentation function.

Packet fragmentation allows large packets to be broken into smaller packets. This is useful when transmitting in congested environments or when there is heavy interference. The MAC layer reassembles the fragments, and this prevents the upper layers from having to retransmit. Also, using smaller fragments minimizes the amount of retransmissions, especially as large packets tend to get corrupted.

11.6.4   Security

One of the key additions to the IEEE 802.11 family is new security mechanisms. The wired LAN is inherently secure due to the physical medium used (coaxial cables or wires used). The cable needs to be plugged in to obtain connectivity. Users connect to the wired LAN within the secure confines of a building, and privacy is assured as the information travels within the home or enterprise, where the wired LAN is deployed. Typically the wired LAN must be physically compromised to tap the data.

The concern with wireless is that anyone within proximity of the wireless devices can transmit and listen to the wireless transmission. To prevent this, the IEEE 802.11 standards created wired equivalent privacy (WEP), which includes mechanisms for authentication of the 802.11 users and as well privacy of the packets. WEP is an optional feature of the MAC layer. However, if devices are Wi-Fi certified, then WEP is a requirement for Wi-Fi certification.

Authentication is the mechanism that verifies that you are who you say you are. This is important in the IEEE 802.11 family and employs a shared key mechanism. Using a shared WEP encryption key, which is input into both the sending and receiving stations, both stations independently encrypt the same piece of information. The encrypted result provided by the sending station is compared with the receiving station's result. If the results are exactly the same, then the sending station is authenticated.

Privacy is very important to wireless LANs due to casual eavesdropping. Again, WEP provides an encryption mechanism where the content of the data packets to be sent passes through an encryption algorithm. The receiver needs to have the same shared key to decrypt the encrypted packets. WEP uses a symmetric cipher algorithm, where the same shared key is used for encryption and decryption.

Although WEP is the security mechanism in the IEEE 802.11 family, there are some important considerations when securing wireless LAN. IEEE does not mandate a mechanism to administer or manage these shared keys. Therefore, if the keys are compromised, significant security concerns may result. Also, the authentication mechanism is only in one direction, where the receiver authenticates the sending station. The preference is for bidirectional authentication and for keys to change periodically. Many of these concerns, including the strength of the WEP algorithm, are being considered actively by the IEEE. A new working group was created in 2001, known as IEEE 802.11i, to address the deficiencies of the MAC layer with respect to security.

11.6.5   Power Management

With the advent of the IEEE 802.11 family, clearly one of the requirements of the MAC layer was to support the users going wireless or "untethered" for a significant amount of time. The IEEE 802.11 MAC layer allows the devices to turn off their receiver and transmitter to conserve power.

The MAC layer provides the ability for stations to inform other stations, whether they are continuously listening known as continuous aware mode, or listening intermittently to save battery, known as power save mode (PSM).

The PSM is requested by the station and lets recipients know how frequently they will wake up to check if there are any messages for them. Any incoming packets destined for the device in PSM will have to be queued. The recipient may be informed of waiting packets using broadcast mechanisms.

11.7   Services Provided in the IEEE 802.11 Family

In this section, we shall provide an overview of the various services expected of an IEEE 802.11 system. Some services are required in all stations, including the access point, and a few of them are very specific to the infrastructure mode. There are two categories of services provided in an IEEE 802.11 system. The first category is called station services, and the second category is the distributed station services (DSS).

11.7.1   Station Services

Services that are common to all stations are referred to as station services. All IEEE 802.11 family devices, including the access point, will execute these services, and it does not matter whether it is the infrastructure mode or independent mode. Stations services support establishing basic connectivity to wireless LANs, which helps provide functions similar to that of plugging into a wired LAN port.

There are four station services defined in IEEE 802.11 systems. *Authentication* and *deauthentication* are two station services similar to the function of physically connecting to the wired network like the LAN. These two services allow the IEEE 802.11 user to be authorized to use the WLAN services, and unauthorized users can be deauthenticated to preclude any services.

Two other station services are *privacy* and *data delivery*. Privacy provides the security of using a wired LAN network within a building by encrypting data over the air. Data delivery services ensure that data are transported reliably over the wireless medium.

11.7.2   Distributed Station Services

The other category of services provided in the IEEE 802.11 family has no equivalent in wired LANs. This is known as the distribution system services (DSS). There are five different services, and these services are provided across a distribution system mentioned earlier. This requires the presence of an access point as one of the key elements, which communicates with the distributed system.

The five different DSSs are *association, disassociation, distribution, integration with wired network like LANs,* and *reassociation.* The wireless station uses the association and disassociation services to gain access and remove access to WLAN services. Distribution is the process of using the

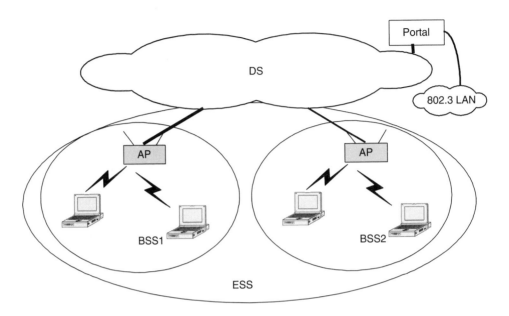

The entire IEEE 802.11 architecture, including connectivity to IEEE 802.3 network.

backbone distributed system to update information about wireless stations and deliver packets to the appropriate destination.

Integration with wired network like LANs is a feature to connect the wireless systems to the wired network. For example, users may be using an IEEE 802.11 family system and may send messages to their colleagues who are connected to the wired LAN like the Ethernet. Special functions called portals may exist as part of the access point. These portals are used to convert between IEEE 802.11 frames and the wired LAN frames and vice versa. A representation of the portals along with the IEEE 802.11 family network is shown in Figure 11–7.

11.8   IEEE 802.11 Family Operations

This section examines the operations of an IEEE 802.11 family device in an infrastructure BSS. Although very similar mechanisms exist for the independent BSS as well, this section focuses on the more ubiquitous infrastructure BSS, or just simply BSS. To obtain service in a WLAN environment, each station has to execute a few functions or services as noted in the IEEE 802.11 standards.

The scenario explored in this section is an IEEE 802.11 family user who wishes to use his or her device to access a Web server in the Internet. In the wired LAN, when properly configured, the user simply plugs into the LAN port and requests the Web page needed. An equivalent process in the IEEE 802.11 WLAN to obtain access to the Internet is examined in Figure 11–8.

11.8.1   The First Step: Synchronization and Scanning

The IEEE 802.11 family station (shortened to 802.11 station) needs to first look for access points within its coverage range and synchronize with a specific BSS. There may be several IEEE 802.11 family systems in the same location, and the 802.11 station needs to lock onto a preferred or preconfigured BSS. To facilitate this, access points send out periodic information that is broadcast within their coverage area.

This periodic information is referred to as a beacon and contains information such as BSS ID (helps identify the BSS), ESS ID (identifies the ESS), PHY layer parameters, and the native clock of the access point. The 802.11 station can passively listen for all the beacons in a neighborhood and synchronize its clock with the access points. Once a list of valid beacons is obtained, the 802.11 station selects an access point based on a selection criterion (PHY layer parameters, ESS ID, and load in the system). This method of selection is known as *passive scanning*.

Another method is known as *active scanning*, where the 802.11 station proactively looks for access points in the neighborhood by sending probe requests. The access points that hear these probe requests respond with a probe response that contains broadcast information similar to the beacon frames mentioned earlier. Again, the 802.11 station selects the best BSS that fits its selection criteria.

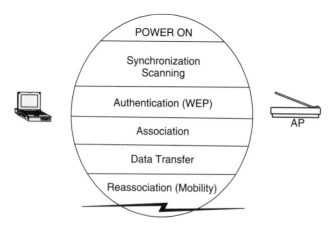

Figure 11–8   *IEEE 802.11 family operations.*

11.8.2   Authentication

The next step is authentication, which is an integral part of the IEEE 802.11 family. However, there are two flavors of authentication. An *open system authentication* mechanism is the default authentication service, which always returns a successful result. It is used in situations where it is not necessary to validate the users positively.

WEP provides the second mechanism of authentication, which uses the shared key mechanism. The access point challenges the 802.11 station, and if the challenge is successful, this results in the 802.11 station being authenticated. The IEEE 802.11 family allows a station to authenticate with multiple BSSs if necessary to facilitate roaming from one BSS to another. If products with Wi-Fi certifications are purchased, shared key authentication is required and the shared keys need to be configured in the 802.11 station and the access point(s).

11.8.3   Association

Until this point, the presence of the 802.11 station is unknown to the 802.11 distributed system. To enable routing of packets to the appropriate destination, once the authentication process is completed, the 802.11 station needs to *associate* with the access point. This creates a logical link between the 802.11 station and the access point. If this association is accepted, the access point forwards the MAC address of the 802.11 station (which was supplied in the association request from the 802.11 station) to the distributed system.

The distributed system makes a note of the association of the 802.11 station in a specific BSS for routing of packets within the ESS. The access point sends an association response with an association identifier (AID) that is used by the 802.11 station for further communication with the access point.

11.8.4   Data Transfer

The data itself may be sent to someone within the same BSS or someone in the same ESS or outside to others as well. The distributed system helps the AP route packets to the appropriate destination. When the AP receives a packet from the 802.11 station, it checks to see if the destination is in the same BSS.

If the packet is in the same BSS, the AP forwards it to the BSS. If the destination is another BSS or the Web server, using the information provided by the distributed system, the AP forwards the data packets to another BSS or a *portal* to send it over the wired network.

11.8.5   Reassociation Process

One of the unique features of the IEEE 802.11 family is the ability to roam from one BSS to another in the infrastructure mode. This is referred to as roaming, where the 802.11 station may move from one BSS to another. The process of registering or establishing a new logical link with another BSS is referred to as *reassociation.*

The reassociation process occurs due to the movement of the 802.11 station from one access point to another. It may also occur due to changes in the radio environment or due to the increased load in the initial access point, known as load balancing. This process of reassociation allows extended coverage needed for enterprise as well as public WLAN operators that provide citywide or even larger coverage.

The reassociation process helps refresh the distributed system with the latest location of 802.11 station. The new access point receives the reassociation request message and, if allowed access, passes this information to the distributed system, which records this information for any further routing of data packets. A station may only be associated with one AP at any time.

The new access point contacts the old access point to remove old associations and obtain any queued packets. Although the mechanisms are not standardized for two access points to communicate with each other, working groups in the IEEE such as the 802.11f are working on the Inter-Access Point Protocol (referred to as IAPP) to enable a communication mechanism across multivendor access points.

11.8.6   Moving Out of Coverage of an ESS

The 802.11 station may eventually move out of coverage of one ESS, which consists of a few BSSs for providing extended coverage. When 802.11 stations move from one ESS to another, the IEEE 802.11 family has not defined any specific mechanisms to facilitate roaming. It is up to the vendors or the IT managers that employ the WLAN solution to roam across ESS.

The IEEE 802.11 family does not provide any standard mechanisms for movement across ESSs. Higher-level protocols like mobile IP may be used to forward packets to the new ESS if required. If mobile IP is not implemented, the 802.11 station may at a minimum acquire a new BSS in the new ESS by starting the whole process of scanning, selection of a new BSS, authentication, and association as described earlier. It may also use DHCP to obtain IP addresses if needed.

11.9   Deployment of IEEE 802.11 WLAN Systems

Let us now explore some of the deployment scenarios with wireless LAN and some deployment considerations. Although the IEEE 802.11 family was seen as an extension of wired LAN, in some cases for new locations, the popularity of the IEEE 802.11 family has extended beyond applications such as conferences. WLAN systems are gaining ground at residential applications to create a wireless LAN without any cabling. Enterprise and industrial applications, including manufacturing, retail, warehousing, hospitality, health care, and education are some of the applications where WLAN finds its niche success.

One of the newer applications of the IEEE 802.11 family is the public WLAN system, due to the attractiveness of the lower cost and operation in the unlicensed band. This would allow subscribers to access their corporate networks or other systems using a high-speed wireless interface. This could be in locations such as airports, coffee shops, and malls around the United States or even international access, as the 2.4-GHz band is available throughout the world.

One of the interesting contrasts with the increasing demand for high-speed access is the WLAN deployments versus public cellular systems such as GSM or CDMA IS-95 and especially the 3G systems.

11.9.1   Deployment Considerations

There are several items to consider when deploying a wireless LAN. We shall highlight some of the key issues. Most of these deployment issues vary based on the deployment scenario (such as home versus enterprise versus public WLAN).

COST

The first deployment issue is simply cost. Although the prices of the access points and the WLAN access cards have been dropping, cost still needs to account for the number of these devices that are needed. As well, connections to the existing wired network, additional software needed in the access points, setting up shared key infrastructure, deploying enough access points for adequate coverage, and so on are factors that indirectly add to the cost of deployment.

THROUGHPUT

Another set of related factors is throughput. The appropriate IEEE 802.11 system should be chosen that best meets the throughput needs. The deployment should choose the various PHY layer options available in the IEEE 802.11 family for throughput, as well as consider future needs for higher data rates. The nature of applications dictates the use of appropriate WLAN technology as well. Retail and warehousing may work well with the IEEE 802.11 standard. Higher-speed data requirements may require the need for IEEE 802.11b standards or even the IEEE 802.11a standard.

RANGE, COVERAGE, AND MOBILITY

Depending on the application scenario such as a home versus enterprise, the range and coverage of the WLAN systems need to be carefully considered. Mobility (mostly applicable in enterprise and public WLAN systems) introduces newer wrinkles such as extended coverage, WEP key management, billing, connectivity to wired networks, and other issues that need to be considered when deploying WLANs.

INTERFERENCE

When deploying the 2.4-GHz IEEE 802.11 systems, a key consideration is the amount of interference starting from microwave ovens to new technologies like Bluetooth. Sufficient testing should be performed to minimize or avoid these interferers and, with respect to Bluetooth, examine the recommendations made by the IEEE 802.15.2 committee on the coexistence of Bluetooth and IEEE WLAN systems in unlicensed spectrums.

SECURITY

Security, management of shared keys, and authentication mechanisms need to be considered as one of the key requirements. Residential applications may use simple authentication management mechanisms. Enterprise and public WLANs may require different levels of security such as MAC address filtering, IP security mechanisms, and application-layer security mechanisms.

Security is one of the primary concerns when using IEEE 802.11WLAN systems. One of the more common methods to eliminate any security risks is to only use virtual private network (VPN) applications that employ some form of IP security. This ensures that the information is carried securely over the wireless medium.

11.10   Summary

The addition of wireless capabilities allows LANs to be extended without the use of wires or cables, thus enabling untethered communications. The other significant advantage is inherent mobility for the users.

The IEEE introduced the standards for local area networks using the 802 standards. The standards were enhanced to also include wireless LAN (WLAN) standards under the 802.11 umbrella. The 802.11 family continues to use the same logical link control (LLC) layer as the other wired LAN systems.

The IEEE introduced the 802.11 standards initially, followed by other standards such as 802.11b and 802.11a that provide higher data throughputs. 802.11 also introduced a common architecture model that includes the independent base station subsystems (IBSSs) or the infrastructure base station subsystems or simply BSS. The BSS includes the wireless stations, which are coordinated by an access point (AP). A distributed system allows mobility and also forms the backbone network to provide extended coverage.

IEEE 802.11 allowed several physical layer mechanisms, such as spread spectrum and infrared techniques. When the higher data rate 802.11b was introduced, only direct sequence spread spectrum (DSSS) was allowed and achieved data rates of up to 11 Mbps. 802.11a uses the OFDM technique in the new 5 Ghz band to achieve peak data rates of up to 54 Mbps.

The MAC layer provides consistent and fair access to the wireless medium. Several wireless-specific features, such as added reliability, security, and contention resolution were added for the IEEE 802.11 family.

The life of an 802.11 station requires operations to scan, select, authenticate, and associate itself with the IEEE 802.11 system. To facilitate roaming, the IEEE 802.11 standards have defined mechanisms such as reassociation to refresh the 802.11 station's location within a WLAN system.

The applications of IEEE 802.11 WLAN, such as home versus enterprise versus public WLANs, may dictate the key factors to be considered and prioritized for deployment. Several factors, such as cost, range, throughput, mobility, and security, need to be considered and the appropriate decisions made based on service affecting features.

References

O'Hara, Bob and Petrick, Al, *IEEE 802.11 Handbook*. New York: The IEEE Press, 1999.

ANSI/IEEE Standard 802.11, 1999.

IEEE Standard 802.11b-1999 (Supplement to ANSI/IEEE Standard 802.11), 1999.

IEEE Standard 802.11a-1999 (Supplement to ANSI/IEEE Standard 802.11), 1999.

Geier, Jim, *Wireless LANs—Interoperable Networks*. McMillan Technical Publishing, 1999.

Santamaría, Asunción and Hernández, Francisco López, *Wireless LAN—Standards and Applications,* Norwood, MA: Artech House Publishing, 2001.

IP in Bluetooth

Bluetooth is a low-power, short-range wireless technology for connecting personal, handheld, and portable electronic devices. The low cost and reasonably high data rates make it an attractive solution for replacing cluttered wired connections within short distances. The Bluetooth technology is a hybrid packet-switched wireless communication system capable of supporting both voice and packet data communication services. It was developed for worldwide use in the unlicensed 2.4-GHz radio spectrum.

The motivation for Bluetooth was governed by seven requirements.

1. Small form factor to enable handheld devices to support the technology
2. Robustness and low complexity
3. Low cost to allow widespread use
4. Low power for extended battery life for small devices
5. Interoperable among different manufacturers and regions
6. Application support for widely used tasks
7. Ad hoc connectivity for automatic link setups without user intervention

Bluetooth will be adopted by manufacturers of PDAs, laptop and desktop computers, and other mobile devices. The main applications for Bluetooth are replacement of cables for keyboard, mouse, and personal communication devices; personal ad hoc connectivity; and mobile routers.

12.1   Bluetooth History

The name Bluetooth was derived from the Danish king Harald Blatand (Bluetooth), who is credited with uniting the people from Scandinavia during the tenth century. The Bluetooth SIG (Special Interest Group) was formed in February 1998. The original founding members of Bluetooth SIG consisted of Ericsson, IBM, Intel, Nokia, and Toshiba.

By June 2001, the member list of participating companies exceeded 2400. The role of the SIG is to develop the specifications for Bluetooth as per the requirements, promote and market the technology and brand name, handle legal and regulatory issues, and certify the Bluetooth products that meet the conformance and interoperability requirements. Any company, by signing a zero-cost agreement, has complete access to the SIG specifications and can qualify for a royalty-free license to build products based on the Bluetooth technology.

The Bluetooth SIG completed the initial specification work and released the first version of the official Bluetooth standard in July 1999.

12.2   Technology Introduction

Table 12–1 provides a summary of the Bluetooth technology. More in-depth details are covered in later sections.

It is estimated that by 2005 there will be over 500 million Bluetooth devices in various forms on the market. The technology will be used in a wide variety of devices like computers, mobile phones, PDA, and other personal devices for a vast number of applications by means of data transfer between these devices.

Table 12–1	*Bluetooth Summary*
Feature	**Details**
Topology	Supports 7 simultaneous links
Flexibility	Works through walls
Data rate	1 Mbps (nominal), 721 Kbps* (user)
Power	0.1 watts of active power
Size/weight	25 mm × 13 mm × 2 mm, few gm
Range	Up to 10m and 100m with amplification
Security	Link layer security, SS security
Communication	Frequency hop spread spectrum

*Bluetooth signaling overhead decreases the effective user data rate.

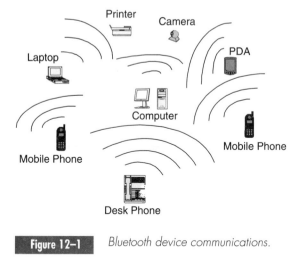

Printer

Camera

PDA

Laptop

Computer

Mobile Phone

Mobile Phone

Desk Phone

Figure 12–1   *Bluetooth device communications.*

Bluetooth will replace the wiring around your desktop computers connecting the monitors, speakers, printers, and even the keyboard and mouse. Bluetooth can replace the wiring around your gaming consoles, and you will be able to synchronize your daily e-mails, phone, calendar, and other personal data in your Bluetooth-enabled PDA without any physical connections to your laptop or desktop. These possibilities are illustrated in Figure 12–1. The user data rates of 721 Kbps will enable digital cameras and MP3 devices to transfer loads of files without any cables. The Bluetooth SIG has specified numerous other usage profiles for other applications.

Other commercial applications involve Bluetooth access points to provide network access at hotspots and kiosks to access e-mail, Web browsing, and other office applications. Another important application is the idea of the wireless personal area network (WPAN), where up to eight different Bluetooth devices can communicate with each other simultaneously within a short range by forming a small network called a *piconet.* A more complex network of piconets, called a *scatternet,* can be formed for wider ad hoc communication applications.

12.3   Technology Overview

Bluetooth is a wireless technology operating in the unlicensed 2.4-GHz ISM (industrial/scientific/medical) spectrum capable of providing radio connectivity up to 10 m between Bluetooth-capable devices. It offers frequency hopping to reduce interference and fading. A shaped, binary FM modulation is applied to minimize the transceiver complexity. A slotted channel is applied with a nominal slot length of 625 μs. For full duplex communication, a time

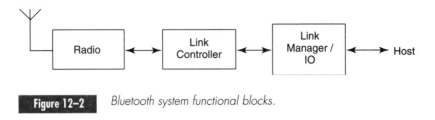

Bluetooth system functional blocks.

division multiplexing (TDM) scheme is used. On each channel, information is exchanged through packets that are transmitted on a different hop frequency.

Bluetooth offers two different link types. The synchronous connection oriented (SCO) link type provides a circuit-switched connection, mainly intended for audio connections between two Bluetooth devices at a data rate of 64 kbps in the full-duplex mode. The asynchronous connectionless (ACL) link provides packet-switched communications at a maximum data rate of 432 Kbps in symmetric or 721 Kpbs in asymmetric modes.

Link-level security mechanisms, which include device-level authentication and ciphering, is specified for the Bluetooth. Robustness in the link level is guaranteed by the use of error correction control mechanisms.

The Bluetooth system mainly consists of a radio unit, a link control unit, and a support unit for link management and host terminal interface functions (Figure 12–2). A more in-depth protocol stack is discussed in the following sections.

12.4   Bluetooth Protocol

The Bluetooth protocol architecture is shown along with the OSI model in Figure 12–3. The radio and baseband functions are mapped to the physical layer on the OSI model. The data link layer of OSI translates to several layers on a Bluetooth stack due to varied capabilities and applications it can support. From an IP stack point of view, the TCP/IP layer in the Bluetooth protocol provides the network, transport, and session layer functions. The following sections describe the functionality of each of those layers.

12.4.1   Bluetooth Radio

The physical layer of the protocol stack defines the radio characteristics of the Bluetooth wireless technology. The Bluetooth radio uses FHSS (frequency hopping spread spectrum), which divides the frequency spectrum into equal number of 1 MHz channels (2.402–2.480 GHz, yielding 79 channels). The radio transceivers hop from one channel to another channel at a rate of 1600 per second in a pseudorandom fashion as determined by a master device.

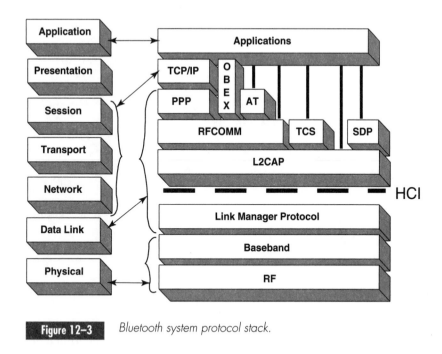

Figure 12–3   *Bluetooth system protocol stack.*

The FHSS technique offers robust communications with less interference and higher security against eavesdropping.

The modulation technique is a binary Gaussian frequency shift keying (GFSK) at a symbol rate of 1 Mbps. Three different power classes are defined depending on the transmit power. Class 1 radios have transmitting power of 20 dBm (100 mW); class 2 radios have transmitting power of 4 dBm (2.5 mW); class 3 radios have transmitting power of less than 1 dBm (1 mW).

12.4.2   Baseband

Each Bluetooth device has two parameters that are involved in practically all aspects of Bluetooth communications. The first one is a unique IEEE 802–type 48-bit address assigned to each Bluetooth device at manufacture time, much like the MAC address for Ethernet devices. The second parameter is a free-running 28-bit clock that ticks once every 312.5 μs, which corresponds to half the residence time on a frequency hop at a nominal rate of 1600 hops per second.

12.4.3   Piconet and Scatternet

A piconet is a collection of devices connected with Bluetooth radio in an ad hoc manner. One of the participating Bluetooth devices that initiates the connection acts as a *master*, and the other devices in the formation act as *slaves* for the duration of the piconet connection. Each master can actively communicate with up to 7 simultaneous slaves or over 200 inactive or *parked* slaves in a piconet. The parked slaves are registered with the master but not currently active in communication, but can become active as necessary. For this reason, the span of piconet is limited to the distance reachable by the master device. Devices within the range of the master that are not part of any piconet are in the *stand-by* mode.

The standard does not specify how the master is determined. Devices in communications can determine who is the master by inquiry/paging messaging. Usually, the master is a paging device in a centralized system like a PC or a laptop. The master controls the communications in the piconet by deciding who transmits and when. Each node can participate in more than one piconet with different behavior, master or slave, in each piconet. The roles of master and slave can be exchanged at any time within a piconet while the piconet is active. Figure 12–4 shows two piconets and the different roles of the Bluetooth devices.

12.4.4   Physical Channels and Links

The channel is represented by a pseudo-random hopping sequence hopping through one of the 79 radio channels. In a piconet, the master device always sets the clock and the hop pattern or a sequence. Each piconet has a unique hopping sequence. The phase in the hopping sequence is determined by the clock of the master. The channel is divided into time slots, where each slot corresponds to an RF hop frequency. Consecutive hops correspond to different RF hop frequencies. All Bluetooth devices in a piconet are time- and hop-synchronized to the channel.

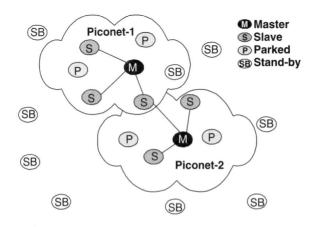

| Figure 12–4 | *Piconet and scatternets.* |

Each time slot in the channel is of 625 µs in length. The slots are numbered as per the clock of the master ranging from 0 to $2^{27}-1$ and is cyclic. In the time slots, the master and slaves can transmit packets. The master shall start transmission in the even-numbered packets only, while the slaves shall transmit in odd-numbered slots only. The packets can be extended up to five time slots.

The master and slave(s) establish one of the SCO or the ACL links between them. SCO links are used for point-to-point connections between master and single slave in a piconet, while the ACL link is used as point-to-multipoint link between master and all the slaves in the piconet. Piconets can form scatternets. A scatternet is the linking of multiple co-located piconets through the sharing of common slave or master devices.

12.4.5 Addressing

The Bluetooth device address (BD_ADDR) is engraved and cannot be modified. It is divided into three fields as shown in Figure 12–5.

- LAP field: Lower address part consisting of 24 bits
- UAP field: Upper address part consisting of 8 bits
- NAP field: Nonsignificant address part consisting of 16 bits

The total address space obtained is 2^{32} corresponding to the LAP and UAP fields.

Bluetooth devices can communicate with each other by acquiring each other's addresses and clocks.

12.4.6 Packet Format

The bit ordering when defining the packets and messages over the Bluetooth air interface follows the Little-Endian format. Each packet consists of three entities—the access code, the header, and the payload. Except for the payload, the other two parts are of fixed sizes, 72 and 54 bits, respectively (Figure 12–6).

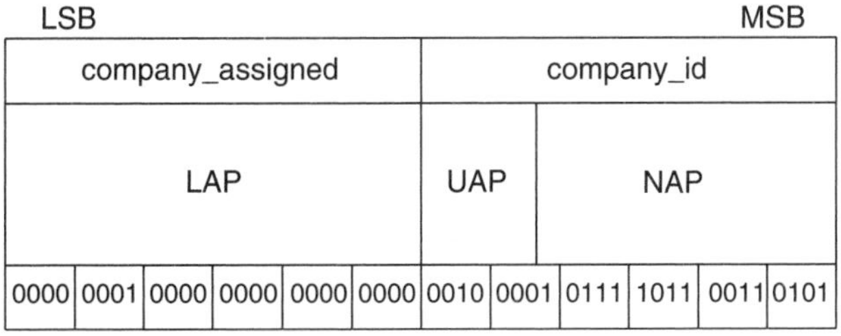

LSB											MSB
company_assigned						company_id					
LAP						UAP	NAP				
0000	0001	0000	0000	0000	0000	0010	0001	0111	1011	0011	0101

Figure 12–5   *Bluetooth device address.*

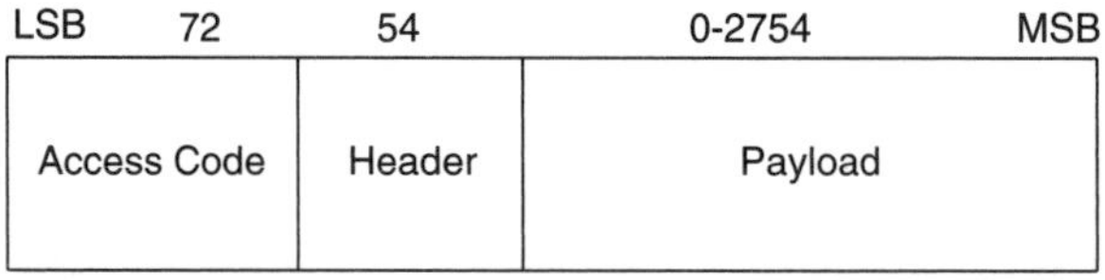

LSB 72	54	0-2754	MSB
Access Code	Header	Payload	

Figure 12–6   *Standard packet format.*

The access code identifies all packets exchanged within a piconet. The access code is also used in paging and inquiry procedures, in which case the header and payload are not required in the message. Accordingly, three different kinds of access codes are defined.

- Channel access code (CAC)— identifies the piconet
- Device access code (DAC)—for paging requests and responses
- Inquiry access code (IAC)—to discover Bluetooth units in range

The packet header contains link control information with six fields that includes member address, type code, flow control, acknowledge indication, sequence number, and header error check.

The total header, including the header error check field, consists of 18 bits and is encoded with a rate 1/3 forward error correction (FEC) resulting in a 54-bit header. The payload formats are distinguished as the (synchronous) voice field and the (asynchronous) data field. The ACL packets only have data fields, while the SCO packets have only the voice field.

12.4.7   Packet Types

Twelve different packet types, indicated by a 4-bit TYPE code, are defined for the two types of links: the SCO link and the ACL link. They are subgrouped into four segments. The first segment is reserved for four control packets and will be common to both the link types, and the TYPE code for these control packets is unique irrespective of the link type. The second segment is reserved for packets occupying the single time slot. The third segment is reserved for packets occupying three time slots, and the fourth segment represents packets that occupy five time slots.

12.4.8   Error Correction

Bluetooth defined three different error correction schemes.

- 1/3 rate FEC: bit-repeat code (repeated 3 times)
- 2/3 rate FEC: shortened Hamming code, corrects double bit errors and can correct single bit errors

- ARQ scheme: 1-bit fast ACK/NACK scheme using a 1-bit sequence number with header piggybacking

The packet headers contain valuable link information and should be able to sustain more bit errors; therefore, they are protected by the 1/3 FEC. However, in a reasonably error-free environment, FEC is optional as it adds unnecessary overhead, reducing throughput.

12.4.9   Logical Channels

Five logical channels are defined in the Bluetooth system:

- LC control channel
- LM control channel
- UA user channel
- UI user channel
- US user channel

The control channels LC and LM are used at the link control level and link manager level, respectively. The user channels UA, UI, and US are used to carry asynchronous, isochronous, and synchronous user information, respectively. Except for LC channels, which are carried in the packet headers, all other types are indicated in a header field and carried in the payload. The US channel is carried by SCO link only; and the UA and UI channels are normally carried by the ACL link with the exception of the DV packet, which can be carried on the SCO link. The LM channel can be carried by either of the link types.

12.4.10   Link Controller State Machine

Figure 12–7 shows the state diagram of the link controller. There are two major states STANDBY and CONNECTION. The other states are sub-states that define device link status whenever a new slave is added to the piconet. State transitions are triggered either due to link manager commands or due to internal event signals.

STANDBY state is the low-power default state in the device. The device initiates or responds to other devices' page and inquiry requests. It can transition to the CONNECTION mode if a suitable link is determined. The device acts as a master when it initiates a page scan request to other devices.

12.4.11   Link Manager Protocol

Link Manager Protocol (LMP) messages are exchanged at the link manager level and used for link setup between Bluetooth devices. They provide control and negotiation of packet size when transmitting data. LMP also provides

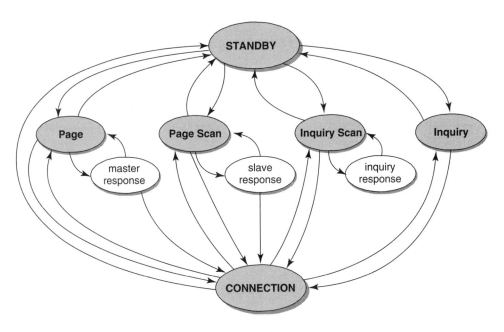

Figure 12–7   *Bluetooth link controller state machine.*

power control and management, addressing, connection mode handling, and master-slave switching of link configuration and link states in a piconet. It also offers security functions, including exchange of encryption keys between devices for authentication and encryption. The LMP messages have higher priority than the user data. The link controller in the baseband offers a reliable link and, therefore, the LMP protocol can work without explicit acknowledgments.

12.4.12   Host Control Interface

The host control interface (HCI) is not part of the protocol stack, but it provides a uniform interface method of accessing the Bluetooth hardware capabilities. The HCI firmware implements the HCI commands for the Bluetooth hardware by accessing Baseband commands, link manager commands, hardware status registers, control registers, and event registers.

12.4.13   Logical Link Control and Adaptation Protocol

The logical link control and adaptation protocol, L2CAP, is one of the two link-level protocols layered over the baseband protocol. It provides connection-oriented and connectionless data services to the upper protocol layers with protocol multiplexing capability, segmentation, and reassembly operation, conveying quality of service information and group abstractions.

Defining channels where one or more channels are bound to a single protocol in a many-to-one fashion supports protocol multiplexing. But one channel cannot be bound to multiple protocols. The channel number is used to identify the appropriate higher-level protocol and all L2CAP packets are delivered accordingly. L2CAP supports large packets up to 64 kB by the use of segmentation and reassembly operations. This function reduces overhead and improves efficiency by supporting MTU sizes larger than the largest base-band packet.

Group abstraction management allows efficient management between groups and members of the Bluetooth piconet. L2CAP exchanges QoS information across channels and performs some admission control to prevent additional channels from violating the existing QoS contracts.

12.4.14   Service Discovery Protocol

The Service Discovery Protocol (SDP) is a client/server protocol that addresses service discovery specifically for the Bluetooth environment. It provides a means for client applications to discover the available server services and also the characteristics of those services within the Bluetooth range. Each Bluetooth device can at most run one SDP server to manage services information and handle client requests. An SDP entity can act as both a server and a client. The characteristics or the attributes of the service are stored as a service record for each service that includes the service name, description, class of service or identifier, and protocol information to utilize the service. The service records are populated based on a standardized hierarchy for easy browsing.

The availability of the services is dependent on the RF proximity of the devices offering the services. For client devices seeking specific services, SDP provides search and browse functions based on some desired characteristics of the services. The protocol is designed to have a simple flow control by limiting not more than one unacknowledged request at any time.

12.4.15   RFCOMM

RFCOMM is a simple transport protocol that provides emulation of COM ports to support RS232 serial communications over the L2CAP protocol. The RFCOMM protocol is mostly based on the ETSI standard TS 07.10, but the Bluetooth SIG further specified some adaptations and specific extensions. Some of these adaptations include media adaptations, multiplexer start-up and close-down procedures, multiplexer control commands and system parameters, and flow control. RFCOMM supports up to 60 simultaneous connections between two Bluetooth devices. It is intended to cover applications that make use of serial ports of the devices in which they reside.

12.4.16   Telephony Control Protocol Specification

The Bluetooth Telephony Control protocol Specification (TCS) is based on ITU-T Recommendation Q.931. The TCS contains the following functionality:

- Call control (CC)—signaling for the establishment and release of speech and data calls between Bluetooth devices
- Group management—signaling to ease the handling of groups of Bluetooth devices
- Connectionless TCS (CL)—provisions to exchange signaling information not related to an ongoing call

TCS may use either point-to-point signaling or point-to-multipoint signaling. Point-to-point signaling is mapped toward a connection-oriented L2CAP channel, whereas point-to-multipoint signaling is mapped toward the connectionless L2CAP channel, which in turn is sent as broadcast information on the piconet broadcast channel.

In addition to the aforementioned basic functionality, TCS also provides support for supplementary services like calling line identity, DTMF tones (if carried by the external network), and register recall.

12.4.17   OBEX

OBEX is an optional application-layer protocol designed to enable devices to exchange data and commands in a resource-sensitive standardized fashion. OBEX uses the client/server model and user RFCOMM as the main transport layer.

12.5   Bluetooth Security

Bluetooth offers three different modes of security.

- Security Mode 1: There is no security in this mode.
- Security Mode 2: Security is provided at the service level.
- Security Mode 3: Security is provided at the link level.

Security Mode 1 is a nonsecure mode. Security Mode 2 is handled by higher layers based on the access policies and procedures defined at the service levels. No security procedures are initiated before channel establishment on the L2CAP level. Security Mode 3 involves link-level security procedures before the link is set up and before the channels are established. Figure 12–8 shows the security architecture. The security manager is the key functionality

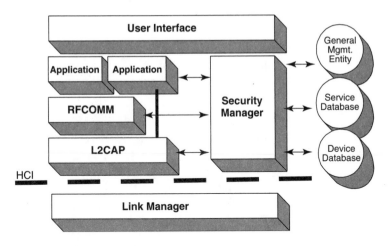

Figure 12–8   *Bluetooth security architecture.*

that manages the security keys and performs security procedures for different protocol layers. The rest of the security discussion is limited to Mode 3.

Table 12–2 shows the four different entities that are used for maintaining security at the link layer: a public address that is unique for each Bluetooth device, two secret keys, and a random number that is different for each new transaction. The secret keys are derived during initialization and are further never disclosed.

Normally, the encryption key is derived from the authentication key during the authentication process; however, the encryption key can also be regenerated when needed. The authentication algorithms are based on 128 bits. For encryption algorithms, the key size can vary between 1 and 16 octets (8–128 bits) to accommodate different cryptographic algorithms in different countries, but the size is fixed for a specific device unit. The encryption key length is negotiated between the master and the slave devices to an acceptable size in octets as determined by the each application. The RAND is a random number generated by a pseudorandom generator in the Bluetooth unit.

Table 12–2   *Entities Used to Maintain Security at the Link Layer*

Entity	Size
BD_ADDR	48 bits
Private user key, authentication	128 bits
Private user key, encryption configurable length (byte-wise)	8–128 bits
RAND	128 bits

Bluetooth security is not foolproof and has some limitations. For instance, it performs only device authentication but does not support user-level authentication; however, it can be implemented at higher layers. Another aspect relates to lack of support for unidirectional traffic, although the access control checks can be performed asymmetrically at connection setup.

12.5.1   Authentication

The entity authentication in Bluetooth uses a challenge-response scheme in which the claimant's knowledge of a secret key is checked through a two-move protocol using symmetric keys, as shown in Figure 12–9. The verifier, either the master or slave, challenges the claimant to authenticate a random input, AU_RAND_A, with an authentication code, E_1, and return the result SRES to the verifier. This value is verified against the one, SRES', generated by the verifier itself.

The link key is the current link key shared by the A and B Bluetooth units. The use of BD_ADDR_B is to prevent a simple reflection attack. For a successful authentication, the value of ACO (authenticated ciphering offset) is retained. This authentication mechanism is only one way. Certain applications need only one-way authentication. For peer-to-peer communications, both devices perform the authentication in each way to authenticate the other.

12.5.2   Encryption

Encryption is used to protect the user packet payload and is carried out with a stream cipher called E_0 that is resynchronized for every payload. But the access code and the packet header are never encrypted. Figure 12–10 shows the encryption procedure.

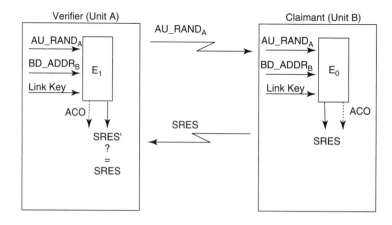

Figure 12–9   *Challenge response authentication.*

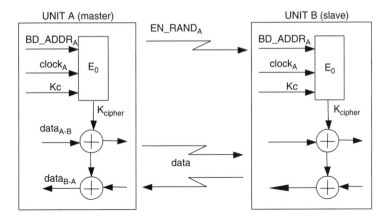

Figure 12–10   *Encryption with E_0.*

The stream cipher system E_0 consists of three parts: generation of payload key, generation of key stream bits, and encryption and decryption. The payload key generator simply combines the input bits in an appropriate order and shifts them into the four linear feedback shift registers (LFSRs) used in the key stream generator. In the second part of the cipher system, the key stream bits are generated by a method derived from the summation stream cipher generator attributable to Massey and Rueppel.

The cipher algorithm E_0 uses the master Bluetooth address, 26 bits of master real-time clock, and the encryption key K_c as input. The random number, EN_RAND, is issued by the master as plaintext over the air. The encryption algorithm E_0 generates a binary keystream, K cipher, which is modulo 2 added to the data to be encrypted. The cipher is symmetric; decryption is performed exactly the same way using the same key as the encryption.

12.6   Bluetooth Profiles

The purpose of the Bluetooth profiles is to describe the application-level usage models and their implementation. The usage models describe the usage scenarios utilizing the Bluetooth radio for specific applications. A profile describes the behaviors vertically down the protocol stack and defines the parameter ranges for each protocol. The Bluetooth profiles are needed for interoperability reasons, which is quite important considering the different types of devices that may be available and different vendors that will be developing Bluetooth devices. Definitions of profiles will enable interoperability not only at the radio level but also at the application level. Figure 12–11 shows different profiles that are currently defined for Bluetooth.

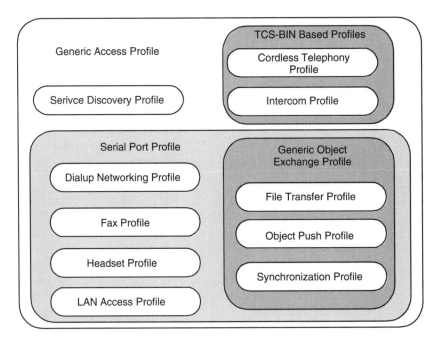

Bluetooth profiles.

The following sections briefly describe the significance of some widely used Bluetooth profiles. In addition to these profiles that are defined as part of Bluetooth specifications v1.1, new profiles for various other applications are currently being defined. Among them, imaging, printing, hands-free, ISDN access, and SIM access are noteworthy. Importantly for the purposes of IP connectivity, a new profile for personal area networking (PAN) is being defined and is discussed in this section for relevance.

12.6.1   Generic Access Profile

Bluetooth devices are required to connect to other Bluetooth devices irrespective of the manufacturer and common applications supported in those devices. Therefore, a set of basic device discovery, connection management, and security capabilities are provided as the basic Bluetooth capabilities under this profile. For the reason of basic interoperability and compatibility of all Bluetooth devices, this profile is a mandatory requirement for all Bluetooth devices.

The main objective of this profile is to describe the use of lower layers of the Bluetooth stack (LC and LMP). For security-related alternatives, higher-layer protocols (L2CAP, RFCOMM, and OBEX) are also used.

12.6.2   Service Discovery Profile

The service discovery profile (SDP) does not provide serve a specific user application, but it defines usage to discover the services offered by the Bluetooth devices in the vicinity. These services discovered are usually the other profiles (e.g., file transfer, cordless telephony). This profile is used by user-initiated requests and makes use of the SDP in the lower layers of the Bluetooth protocol stack.

12.6.3   Cordless Telephony Profile

The cordless telephony profile (CTP) defines the features and connection procedures so that a Bluetooth device can function as a cordless phone. The profile describes the interoperability aspects with a Bluetooth base station that is connected to a fixed telephony network. This profile completely defines the call setup and connection scenarios, DTMF signaling, call line identification features supported in the fixed network, and the audio over Bluetooth. This feature enables Bluetooth-capable cellular phones to be able to use fixed telephony networks by the use of some phone based on the user location. Two roles are defined for this profile:

> *Gateway (GW)*—GW acts as a Bluetooth base station that could serve several (up to seven) Bluetooth terminals supporting CTP. It has other capabilities to connect to the fixed network for telephony call establishments.
>
> *Terminal (TL)*—TL is the Bluetooth terminal, or simply a cordless phone with Bluetooth radio, or an integrated cellular/Bluetooth device with CTP support.

12.6.4   Headset Profile

Headset profile (HSP) was one of the first profiles developed by the SIG because of the importance of the wireless headset usage scenario. HSP is not related to telephony-oriented TCS-BIN but is related to SPP. HSP provides simple audio communications by utilizing AT telephony control over RFCOMM.

12.6.5   Serial Port Profile

The serial port profile (SPP) utilizes the RFCOMM protocol to enable many cable replacement scenarios. There is no need for master/slave roles in SPP, but instead SPP defines peer device roles for general serial communications. SPP defines the steps required to establish an RFCOMM serial port connection. SPP acts as the base or as an abstract profile for several other profiles. Dialup networking, fax, and LAN access profiles are derived from the SPP.

12.6.6   Dialup Networking Profile

The dialup networking profile (DUNP) utilizes RFCOMM to establish modem connections using the AT command set to support data calls. DUNP defines the GW and TL roles similar to the CTP scenario. The GW provides the modem service, and TL is another Bluetooth device requesting modem service to access a data network. Once the DUNP connection is established, higher-layer protocols like TCP/IP and above can be run. DUNP has capabilities similar to the LAN access profile with minor differences in the link connection establishments.

12.6.7   Fax Profile

The fax profile is also based on SPP and is similar to the DUNP profile in defining device roles and in utilizing the RFCOMM to establish modem connections using the AT command to set up fax connections. The AT command set depends on the fax classes supported. Three different classes are supported, of which at least one class is mandatory.

- Fax Class 1 is specified by TIA-578-A and ITU T.31.
- Fax Class 2.0 is specified by TIA-592 and ITU T.32.
- Fax Service Class 2 is manufacturer defined without any standards.

12.6.8   LAN Access Profile

The LAN access profile (LAP) describes how PPP connections can be set up over RFCOMM for Bluetooth devices to get connected and access LAN services. It also defines how connected devices in a piconet can form an independent LAN by using the same PPP connection mechanisms. There are two roles defined for the Bluetooth devices supporting LAP.

LAN access point—This Bluetooth device provides service access to LANs supporting various link-layer protocols.

LAN data terminal—This is a PPP client device that requests for access to the LAN through the LAN access point.

12.6.9   Generic Object Exchange Profile

The generic object exchange profile (GOEP) is similar to SPP in acting as an abstract profile for other profiles. It defines common aspects, including device roles, connection establishments, and security considerations. It utilizes the OBEX protocol to enable common data exchange operations supported by object push, file transfer, and synchronization profiles.

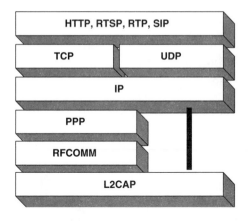

Figure 12–12   *IP protocol stack in Bluetooth.*

12.6.10   Synchronization Profile

The synchronization profile defines the requirements, protocol behavior, and procedures that shall be used by Bluetooth devices providing synchronization applications. It makes use of the GOEP to define the interoperability requirements for the synchronization profile protocol. The most common devices using the synchronization profile might be notebook PCs, PDAs, and mobile phones exchanging various kinds of data like PIM (personal information management) data, phone numbers, calendar, and personal information among Bluetooth devices. The synchronization features can either be user driven or automatically handled by the devices when in proximity based on some preconfigured behavior.

12.7   IP Applications in Bluetooth

The LAN access profile in Bluetooth supports several different types of LAN networks. With the LAN connection, devices essentially have the IP or the Internet connectivity and all applications supported in that network. Figure 12–12 shows how the TCP/IP protocols can be run over the Bluetooth radio by setting up a generic PPP connection. Current data rates supported in Bluetooth allow broadband access to a gateway device from computers or PDAs. Higher-level protocols like HTTP, RTSP, and RTP can be run transparently over the PPP connection.

   The PAN profile provides IPv4 and IPv6 connectivity without setting up a PPP connection through the use of BNEP and utilizing L2CAP to carry the ethernet payload. All IP applications can be run transparently using the PAN profile.

12.8   Competing Technologies

12.8.1   Bluetooth and the Infrared Data Association

The Infrared Data Association (IrDA) specified three infrared communication standards:

- IrDA-Data
- IrDA-Control
- A new standard Alr

IrDA-Data is a similar technology to Bluetooth used as a short-range wireless connectivity technology. It is a point-to-point, narrow angle (30° clone) data communications standard specified to provide wireless communication capabilities at distance of up to 1 meter and at data rates of 9600 bps to 16 Mbps. It is currently used in several million devices, primarily for cable replacement to exchange data using line-of-sight wireless communications. It is incorporated in notebook computers, printers, mobile phones, watches, medical equipment, and so on.

Bluetooth and IrDA may have overlapping functionalities, but Bluetooth supports a wider set of applications than what is supported by the IrDA. Both of the technologies use the same upper-layer protocol (OBEX) to implement the common set of applications. In this way, Bluetooth ensured interoperability with IrDA. IrDA has no security mechanisms defined, anyone can snoop into data being exchanged between two devices. Line-of-sight communications minimize such problems. In contrast, Bluetooth provides better security by needing to perform authentication and then encrypt data exchanges. Bluetooth, because of the use of spread spectrum radio frequency that enables omni-directional multiple connections, overcomes the line-of-sight problem. Further, Bluetooth has gained wider acceptance for use in numerous devices to be built by many manufacturers.

12.8.2   Bluetooth and IEEE 802.11b

IEEE 802.11 specified related technology intended for high-bandwidth wireless LAN applications. Because of the low-cost, low-power, short-range operation at smaller data rates of 1 Mbps, Bluetooth does not compete with the IEEE 802.11 WLAN technology. Bluetooth technology is intended as WPAN usage and is intended to solve entirely different set of problems. However, the operating spectrum for both technologies is in the same 2.4-GHz ISM frequency band.

Due to this, although Bluetooth and 802.11b have completely different technologies and distinct applications, they will have mutual interference. The

IEEE 802.11 charter had undertaken to study the coexistence model and quantify the interference effects. The model results indicated a reduction of network throughput and increase in network latency in both Bluetooth and IEEE 802.11b. The coexistence mechanism currently under study includes both the collaborative and noncollaborative mechanisms in sharing the medium between the radios.

12.8.3   Bluetooth and IEEE 802.15

IEEE also initiated a similar technology interest and in early 1999 formed WG15 within 802 standards committee. The newly formed IEEE 802.15 group formed a charter for personal area networks (PANs) and solicited for proposals. But Bluetooth SIG was the only respondent. Even though the Bluetooth specifications do not meet the complete requirements of the IEEE 802.15 charter, Bluetooth was accepted with some arrangements on the use of the specifications. This adoption into IEEE validates the technology merits and ensures future growth and development of Bluetooth.

12.9   Summary

Bluetooth technological merits are quickly catching up in the industry and the marketplace. It is estimated that over 100 million units with Bluetooth radio will be shipped in 2003 by various device manufacturers (and about 1 billion by 2006). As of this writing, there are numerous Bluetooth-enabled devices that are already available on the market. Ericsson, one of the founders of the technology, showed its commitment by integrating this technology with some mobile phones and headsets and by developing PC cards for the laptops. Desktop, laptop, and PDA manufacturers have integrated the Bluetooth radio into their product lines.

As more and more applications are supported by the technology, Bluetooth will be integrated into more and more devices. Hence, the Bluetooth SIG focuses on developing as many application profiles as possible and ensuring the interoperability between them.

References

"Specification of the Bluetooth System—Core," *Bluetooth SIG* Version 1.1, February, 2001.

"Specification of the Bluetooth System—Profiles," *Bluetooth SIG* Version 1.1, February, 2001.

The Official Bluetooth Homepage—*http://www.bluetooth.com.*

Wireless Application Protocol and I-Mode

T he primary objective of the Wireless Application Protocol (WAP) is to bring Internet content and Web services to mobile devices and cellular phones. WAP is an open, global specification to enable communications between mobile wireless users to access and interact with Web information and services. One of the fundamental aspects of WAP is the customization of Web content for data transfer over the wireless medium.

The success and ubiquity of the World Wide Web (WWW) and mobile phone technologies have created a great demand for convergence and data transfer across domains. A wide variety of Web applications and services that are suited for wired networks could not readily work over wireless links and on resource-constrained mobile phones. The limitations of wireless networks have been discussed in Chapter 7. Hence, customization of Web data over wireless links was necessary. Initial proposals for WAP came from Ericsson, Nokia, and Phone.com. With increased interest from other companies, a WAP forum was created to handle the task of designing and developing an open wireless communications protocol that can work over several wireless technologies (e.g., CDPD, CDMA, GPRS, iDEN, TDMA, PHS, FLEX, TETRA, DECT). The WAP Forum is open to all, and several network operators and manufacturers have joined hands to develop WAP specifications. The WAP stack can operate on a wide variety of mobile devices supporting various operating systems like PalmOS, EPOC, Windows CE, and JAVA OS. The first draft of WAP architecture was published September 1997, and a complete WAP 1.0 specification was ready by April 1998 for product development.

There are about 50 million WAP mobile phones in circulation world-wide. There are several million pages of WAP content and about 10,000 sites that support WAP users. WAP-related content and services are increasing on a daily basis as the demand is increasing. Currently, commerce, finance, entertainment, and messaging applications are the most widely used services within WAP.

The rest of the chapter provides WAP architecture details and discusses its role in providing wireless IP services. The second part of the chapter includes a discussion of I-mode and how it is related to WAP. The WAP technology presentation is not specifically related to a specification release, but the latest specification has been used to provide up-to-date information. At the end of this chapter, the most recent changes are noted in the discussion of WAP 2.0.

13.1   Architecture Overview

The WAP architectural model is similar to the Internet WWW model with a few enhancements. Figure 13–1(a) shows the communication model for WWW and WAP. The WWW model in a wired network is a client/server

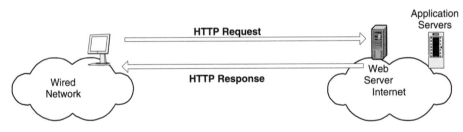

a. WWW Communications Model

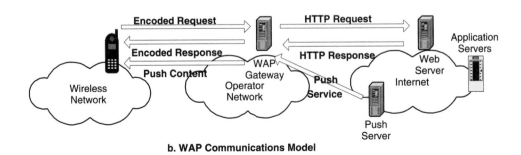

b. WAP Communications Model

Figure 13–1   *Communication models.*

model, with HTTP requests being generated from the browser on the user terminal. Figure 13–1(b) shows the WAP communication model involving a proxy between user terminals and the content servers. The WAP proxy provides the WAP protocol interfaces to the user terminal over the radio with encoded communications. This model also includes a push server to push services toward the user through the proxy. Another enhancement from the WWW model not shown in Figure 13–1 is the support for telephony applications in the WAP model.

The use of proxy server in the WAP communication model is to optimize and enhance the communications between wireless devices and the Internet. Specifically, the WAP proxy provides the following functions:

- *Protocol gateway:* The proxy translates the WAP protocols to the protocols understood in the Web, like HTTP and TCP/IP. Another function of the gateway is to perform DNS lookups of the servers named by the WAP clients in the URL requests.
- *Content encoders and decoders:* The use of content encoders is to translate WAP content into a compact format for transfer over the radio.
- *User agent profile management:* User agent profiles that define the client capabilities and user preferences are composed and presented to application servers for personalized services.
- *Caching proxy:* Frequently, request pages can be cached for improvement in performance and network utilization.

Figure 13–2 shows the WAP protocol architecture and the corresponding protocols in the Internet Protocol stack. Different layers within the WAP protocol stack provide different features. Applications and services, based on need, can use any layer of the protocol directly. The following sections define requirements and deployment details of individual layers.

13.1.1   Wireless Datagram Protocol

The main goal of WDP is to allow application services to be designed independent of the specific transports. Hence, WDP provides a common interface to various physical transport mechanisms, called bearers. WDP is designed for narrow to medium bandwidth channels and also to be extensible to a wide variety of cellular protocols with scope for future transport definitions. It provides an abstraction to the upper-layer protocols by providing a port-based interface.

The basic capability of WDP is to provide a connectionless, unreliable datagram communication service. It provides similar functions as the UDP in the Internet stack of protocols. It allows peer-to-peer, client/server, and one-to-many applications while ensuring multivendor and multidevice interoper-

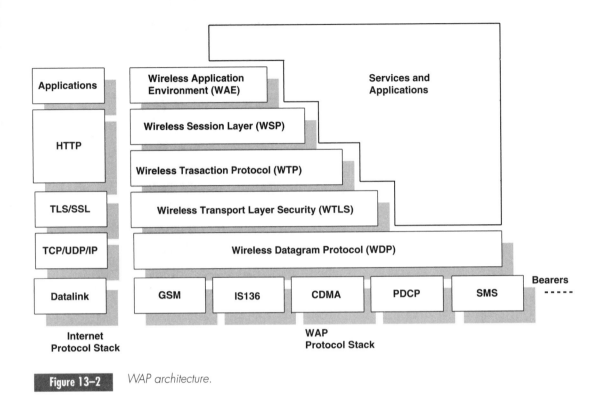

Figure 13-2   *WAP architecture.*

ability at the WDP layer. WDP provides implementation capability for standard or resource-constrained devices.

13.1.2   Wireless Transport Layer Security

The WTLS layer is responsible for security features between the terminal and the counterpart application server. It must support security features like privacy, integrity, authentication, and end-to-end security between protocol endpoints. WTLS is based on transport layer security (TLS) 1.0 and is very efficient in bandwidth usage. It implements optimized handshaking and supports datagram-oriented bearers and lightweight public key certificate format. WTLS can enable long-living secure sessions and provides a choice of different algorithms.

13.1.3   Wireless Transaction Protocol

The WTP layer provides both reliable connection-oriented and transaction-oriented services for certain application services that require these features. WTP also supports the selection of underlying bearers to the upper layers of the protocol stack. WTP allows packet concatenation and supports transaction ID negotiation.

The primary characteristics of the connection-oriented WTP (WTP/C) layer is to allow negotiation of connection setup parameters. It provides a deterministic flow control appropriate for radio transmissions, retransmission of lost packets, selective retransmission, segmentation/reassembly, and port number addressing.

One of the important requirements of both WDP and WTP is to be efficient with respect to communications and, hence, provide the support for header compression with low transmission overhead with optimum handshakes. Other requirements are with respect to scalability to operate over a range of wireless networks and devices and to be modular to allow various security solutions.

The following classes of service are supported in the WTP layer.

- Class 0 provides an unconfirmed *Invoke* message with no result message.
- Class 1 provides a confirmed *Invoke* message with no result message. This service class is used for push data operations, where no response from the destination is expected.
- Class 2 provides a confirmed *Invoke* message with one confirmed result message. In this mode, a single request produces a single reply.

13.1.4 Wireless Session Protocol

The main requirements of the Wireless Session Protocol (WSP) are to provide HTTP 1.1 functionality, interrupt ongoing transactions if needed, provide application acknowledgment, push content from the server to client asynchronously, and exchange static client and server state during session creation. Some of the ongoing work items in the WSP group are to support QoS parameters, multicast data, ordered pipelining, chunked data transfer, and WSP management entity.

13.1.5 Wireless Application Environment

The wireless application environment (WAE) provides application-level services, tools, and languages required for authoring content and for transferring content in WAP-enabled wireless networks. One of the objectives is to leverage the existing technology and provide a universal applications platform for Web browsing and telephony services. The WAE work group within the WAP Forum focuses on the core areas of application architecture, markup languages, scripting languages, and telephony integration.

The wireless network and mobile device characteristics have a great influence on the design of markup and scripting languages. Figure 13–3 shows the client-side WAE architecture. The WAE framework involves the user agents and services and formats to support the user agents.

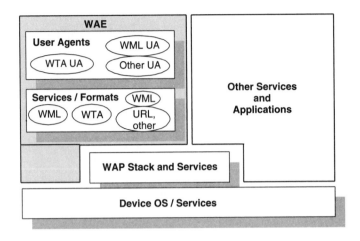

Figure 13–3   *WAE client architecture.*

13.2   WAP Network Elements

Network elements in a typical WAP network are shown in Figure 13–4. WAP clients in the mobile devices communicate with application servers through a number of different proxies or directly. There may be several proxies sup-

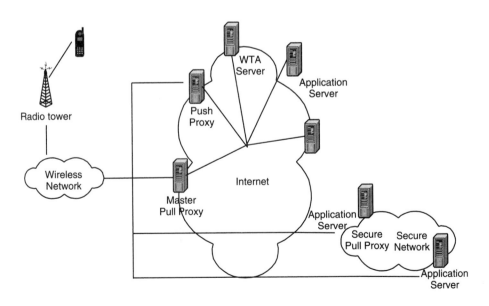

Figure 13–4   *Example WAP network.*

porting proxy functions for one or more application services. WAP clients support a mechanism for proxy or application server selection so that they can utilize the most appropriate proxy for a given service or application server discovery. Proxies can be located either in wireless carriers network or independent service providers in order to provide feature enhancements integrated with the wireless network. Proxies may also be located in a secure network to provide a secure communication channel between the WAP client in a wireless device and the secure network.

13.3   Sample WAP Configurations

The architecture and protocol stack discussions in the previous sections show that there are several possible stack configurations using the WAP technology. WAP proxy capabilities can be tuned to specific service requirements. Figure 13–5 shows a complete protocol stack from the original WAP architecture. The WAP proxy translates HTTP traffic between datagram-based protocols (ESP, ETP, WTLS, WDP) and the connection-oriented protocol commonly used on the Internet (HTTP, SSL, TCP).

Figure 13–6 shows a WAP client device directly accessing a Web server via the Internet. The wireless IP router represents a standard part of IP network with specific wireless technology support. In this direct access scenario, the client will not be able to use wireless optimizations defined for TCP and HTTP.

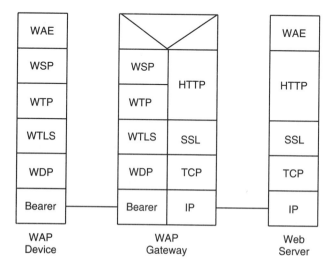

| Figure 13–5 | *Sample WAP 1.0 gateway* |

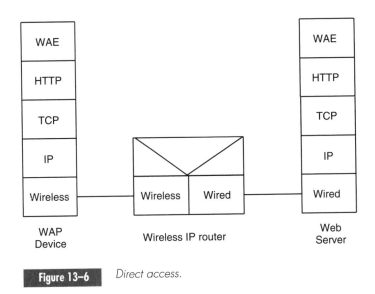

Figure 13–6   *Direct access.*

13.4   Wireless Markup Language

This section provides a brief overview of the Wireless Markup Language (WML) used in WAP architectures. WML is the official WAP markup language for exchange of content between wireless terminals and the WAP-enabled network. The most important design elements of WML are due to the nature of mobile personal devices with the following characteristics:

- Small display screens
- Limited computing power
- Limited memory resources
- Low bandwidth network connections
- Limited and simple browsing abilities

While meeting these constraints, WML shares common characteristics with HTML, which is widely used on the Internet; HDML (Handheld Device Markup Language), an earlier markup language; and XML (eXtensible Markup Language). Utilizing features from these different sources, WML is defined with four major functional areas:

- Text presentation and layout
- Deck/card organization in WML makes all information organized as *decks* and *cards*
- Intercard navigation and linking is used when navigating between cards and decks

- String parameterization and state management are possible in WLM decks.

Naming within WML is implemented with uniform resource locator (URL) to be compatible with WWW naming. The WML character set is derived from the XML document character set. WML also inherits the syntax information from XML. WML content can include scripts, and these scripts can be invoked from WML. The scripting language used here is WMLScript, which is similar to Javascript but optimized for high-latency, low-bandwidth communications.

WMLScript supports most standard programming constructs and it can be compiled on the server to yield a byte code executable format, which is smaller than the text format, so that it is suitable for the radio. WMLScript matches the WAE requirements for a lightweight language that can be easily parsed and interpreted, is easy to program, integrates with WML, and is a well-known language.

13.5   Applications in WAP

13.5.1   Multimedia Messaging Service

Multimedia messaging service (MMS), as the name implies, provides multimedia content between communication endpoints in a messaging context. For example, the user may receive a greeting card with a nice picture and a recorded voice messages wishing him well. Multimedia messaging service is viewed as a non-real-time service, and it seems like an extension of the SMS service in that SMS handles only limited text, while MMS is expandable to a wide variety of services from traditional e-mail to content-rich chat services. However, future versions of MMS may support real-time messaging like Instant Messaging and chat services.

Addressing in MMS can be done in the form an Internet e-mail address like user@domain-a.com. Additionally, MMS can support addressing with the MSISDN (id@domain-a.com), which is used in cellular networks for backward compatibility.

13.5.2   Wireless Telephony Applications

Wireless telephony applications (WTAs) are defined as part of WAP specifications to allow access to telephony functionality. WTA provides tools for value-added telephony applications and provides a bridge between wireless telephony and data. WTA applications are developed using WML and WMLScript and are defined as a WAE user agent. WTA is covered in details in the WAP specifications.

13.5.3   Push Services

Wireless users can subscribe to push services which can be delivered to the user asynchronously when a preferred event happens. Normal uses of push services are calendar reminder services, voice mail or message indicators, and other information reporting services.

WAP specifies push architecture for the support of push services in the WAP network. Push architecture involves a push application server called the push initiator (PI) and a push proxy gateway (PPG) and the wireless devices. Over the air, a special protocol, called Push Over-the-Air Protocol, to communicate between the PPG and mobile device is used. A Push Access Protocol (PAP) is used between the PI and the PPG.

13.6   Relation to I-Mode

Although the problem solved by WAP and I-Mode is the same, the approach taken is different. WAP is a product of industry initiative to develop an open standard for Web data transfers over various radio links. I-Mode solved a problem by use of nonstandard solutions specific to network architectures applicable to NTT DoCoMo. One of the aspects of such differences is in the use of markup language. I-Mode uses compact HTML (cHTML), and WAP uses WML.

Nevertheless, I-Mode has undoubtedly been one of the most successful wireless Web services offered by NTT DoCoMo. The success of I-Mode is evident from the subscription base of 32 million customers in Japan alone in early 2002. It was first offered in February 1999, and provides e-mail, banking, entertainment, and Web browsing services for mobile phones.

13.6.1   I-Mode Network Architecture

Figure 13–7 shows the network architecture for I-Mode. Similarities with WAP architectures are evident in the model with the introduction of the I-Mode proxy server to handle user requests over the radio. Content providers supply I-Mode service directly or through the I-Mode server. The architecture also includes support for corporate customers to access enterprise private data through the I-Mode network with the help of firewall functions.

13.6.2   I-Mode Business Objectives

One of the drivers of the I-Mode is to increase operator revenues for DoCoMo. I-Mode provides architecture for DoCoMo to provide network capabilities for I-Mode services, but the actual content is provided by third-party service providers. Figure 13–8 shows the business model for I-Mode. The subscriber pays the subscription charges and the content charges based on

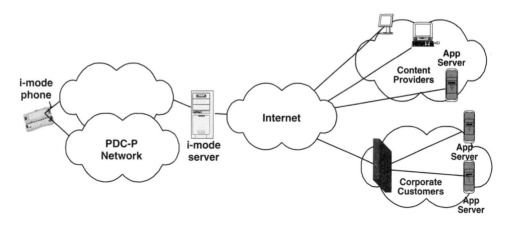

Figure 13–7 *I-Mode architecture.*

the amount of information used. The content provider collects the charges from DoCoMo and at the same time provides commissions for network services and resources used.

13.6.3 I-Mode Protocol Stack

The I-mode protocol stack is shown in Figure 13–9. I-Mode uses the PDC (personal digital cellular) packet bearer for all I-Mode services. Mobile node communications to M-PGW (message packet gateway) module utilize the

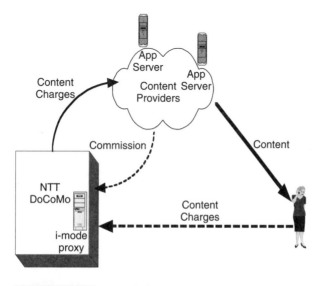

Figure 13–8 *I-Mode business model.*

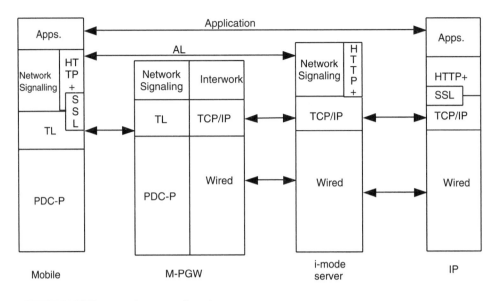

Figure 13–9   *I-Mode protocol stack.*

transport layer (TL) functions. M-PGW translates the TL packets to the TCP packets within the network before forwarding the messages to the I-Mode server. TL packets are more efficient than TCP packets due to smaller overhead and supports basic functions like error detection, response confirmation, and data piggybacking. TL has functions similar to the WTP layer in the WAP network but may be simpler due to simpler HTTP functions.

The AL (application layer) protocol is used between the mobile device and the I-Mode servers or the application servers for sending and receiving the content data. AL has smaller functions than the WAE framework but provides similar functions such as *push* and *pull* mechanisms.

13.6.4   I-Mode Security

Security is an important feature for I-mode users and content providers offering banking, shopping, and other transaction services to ensure the authentication, data validity, and non-repudiation for accounting reasons. Although the underlying radio protocols are secure, providing an end-to-end, common security protocol and algorithms across different I-mode terminals, I-mode servers and the content servers has been a challenging task for DoCoMo. The I-mode terminals and the content servers make use of the Secure Sockets Layer (SSL) to offer the security features.

SSL provides authentication mechanisms by the use of certifications as specified by ITU Recommendation X.509. The public key cryptosystem uses a

A primer on cHTML and XHTML

cHTML, like WML, is a markup language that was designed and developed by Access Company, Ltd. for small handheld devices and mobile phones and submitted to W3CM in 1998 to meet the requirements of devices with limited battery power, display area, computing, and memory resources. It provides a subset or a compact version of standardized Hypertext Markup Language (HTML) 2.0, 3.2, and 4.0 versions as defined by W3C recommendations. The main differences from the full-fledged HTML version are due to lack of support for some image types, backgrounds, tables, frames, a lot of fonts other than basic ones, and style sheets. JPEG image compression is not supported, but GIF images are supported. Features like scrolling and cursor movements are not supported since the cHTML pages are expected to fit within the small display screens. But navigation can be done by use of four buttons: cursor backward, cursor forward, select, and back/stop.

The benefit of backward compatibility with HTML ensures that the devices using cHTML can connect to the WWW while still using the knowledge and authoring tools already available for HTML. The following figure shows an example of a cHTML page. Although cHTML has been popular for I-Mode services, cHTML will probably be replaced by basic versions of Extensible Hypertext Markup Language (XHTML). The figure shows the markup language family tree.

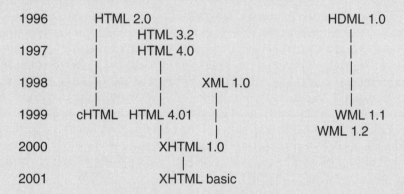

cHTML and WML, developed by OpenWave Systems, have taken separate routes, resulting in a lack of easy content portability. The founders of WML and cHTML have agreed on a common XHTML definition. XHTML is a hybrid between HTML and XML providing a more robust mechanism for universal mobile Internet communications understood by all devices.

public key/private key duo to verify the authenticity by being able to decrypt only by use of the public key. SSL also verifies if the certificate data have been tampered with, by calculating the message digest of the certificate data by use of the one-way hash function and by verifying the results with the decrypted signature part.

13.6.5   I-Mode Evolution — FOMA

Japan was the first nation to experience 3G cellular services with WCDMA. 3G UMTS systems have provided significant improvements from the 2G networks in terms of the supported radio bandwidth capabilities, and Japan was eager to adopt the 3G UMTS standard due to a need for higher-bandwidth applications on the packet data network. DoCoMo uses the term *FOMA* to market the 3G circuit services and packet services. I-Mode services in FOMA are improvised to support video distribution services, music distribution services, and other high-bandwidth applications. Future versions of I-Mode will use WAP 2.0 specifications described in the following section.

13.7   WAP 2.0

WAP 2.0, which was launched in the middle of 2001, is a significant step toward integrating the individual and incompatible technologies of previous WAP releases and the I-Mode technology in Japan. As discussed in previous sections, WAP 1.x uses XML-based WML for queries over the radio. In contrast, I-Mode uses a derivative of HTML called compact HTML. However, both NTT DoCoMo and the WAP Forum have collaborated for the development and support WAP 2.0 and will use them in future networks.

The technical differences from WAP 1.x include a clear division in conceptual components like application environment, protocol framework, security services, and service discovery. The WAP 1.x architecture environment consisted of the user terminal, WAP gateway, and origin server. WAP 2.0 allows application services to be outsourced to capability servers in a WAP network that provide specific application services. There is also incompatibility between the two versions of the protocol, since WAP 2.0 relies more extensively on the Web protocol by adopting XHTML and, hence, is closer to WWW.

WAP 2.0 has been improvised by the support of several aspects of the whole stack, ranging from expansion of supported bearers to a wide range of application services. One of the interesting application-level capabilities and services includes support for color graphics, animations, context-sensitive menus, and data synchronization with desktop personal information management (PIM). WAP 2.0 supports more bearers than the previous WAP release by supporting SMS, FLEX, USSD, and GUTS as well as IP version 4 and IP version 6. Connection-oriented services are enabled by supporting TCP. The service discovery component allows terminals to discover services that are supported in the network. The security services component provides additional security features like end-to-end encryption and PKI support in WAP 2.0 architecture. Security is supported in every layer of the protocol and hence can support extremely secure environments for various Web transactions.

13.8   Summary

This chapter presented the role of WAP technology in delivering the Internet content and more to wireless users. The convergence of these two technologies, I-Mode and WAP, will yield an open and universal standard and enable interoperability and content transfer between the two networks.

References

"Wireless Markup Language," *WAP-191-WML, WAP Forum,* February 2000.

WAP Specifications and Resources—*www.wapforum.org.*

Open Mobile Alliance Technical Specifications—*http://www.openmobilealliance .org/documents.html.*

I-Mode Architecture and Specifications, NTT DoCoMo Technical Reports.

Future Applications in Wireless IP Networks

Applications and services are what the end user eventually sees. The underlying technology is invisible or irrelevant from a user's perspective. What the user really cares about is the usability of a feature. So performance and interaction as well as presentation becomes important. Third-generation networks enable the delivery of feature-rich applications by incorporating support for quality of service, high bit rates, and greater capacity.

Two distinct trends have emerged that are the primary drivers for convergence of packet and circuit based networks. First is the need for access to information. The vast availability of information on the Internet has made the need to access the Internet a vital commodity. The Internet is an example of a packet data network that most people recognize today. Second, people and society in general are more mobile and have the need to be constantly connected. This has fueled the rapid growth of wireless networks. Second-generation wireless networks have been primarily driven by voice services and are essentially circuit switched networks. The wireless Internet is the combining of the features of these two types of networks. Access to information from mobile devices is increasingly felt as one of the key applications for third-generation wireless networks. However, there is a clear difference in the way a user interacts with and experiences the wireless Internet. It is not the same as the traditional Internet experience using desktop and laptop computers. Form factors of the devices as well as the interfaces to the services will make the wireless Internet a new experience. The richness of this experience and applications are still under development, and it will be some time before consumers are able to embrace this concept on a wide basis. The acceptance of the wireless Internet is also based on regional views and cultural differences. Consumers in Japan and elsewhere who have been exposed to a kind of wireless Internet with the I-Mode network are more willing to try the new wireless Internet as opposed to users in the United States, where the traditional Internet, with access via desktop and laptop computers, has primarily flourished. While the Internet has influenced the current design of 3G wireless networks, it is also the case that wireless networks will eventually change the way we view and interact with the Internet today.

The mobile market is changing from an environment dominated by voice to one where mobile Internet and enhanced data services will be equally important. The mobile device, which to some is as essential as the wallet or purse, is evolving toward becoming a life management tool. Functions such as calendars for appointments, web browsers, and e-mail are being incorporated into the devices. In the mobile world the key to success is via delivering targeted, timely, and essential services. It is extremely important that application developers understand consumers, their lifestyles, and their needs when designing and building services for the future. Nokia, which is a frontrunner in mobile wireless communication, has been projecting the vision of a mobile world and mobile information society wherein a major part of all personal communication will be wireless based in various forms such as voice calls, data exchanges, or multimedia sessions.

This chapter takes a look at some of the applications that we can expect to see in the future via the IP-enabled wireless networks.

14.1   Applications and Services

So is there a difference when we speak of applications and services? From an end-user perspective, applications and services can be defined as follows:

> An application is a piece of software that enables a service. For example, Instant Messaging is a service. Application software, which includes the underlying protocols, middleware, and user interface, is combined to deliver a service. The service may require multiple network elements to work together cohesively. Network operators who view the network as a system are more interested in the services that can be offered to end users that generate revenue. The end user sees an application on the mobile terminal or device.

Applications and services can be classified into four main categories, namely:

- *Infotainment:* Information content, which includes news, maps, weather, financial data, local guides, shopping, and entertainment services such as streaming music, video on demand, and games.
- *Personal and group communication:* These include services such as messaging, e-mail, and voice calls.
- *Lifestyle management:* Applications such as calendars and appointments, address books, and information organizers.

- *Business services:* Access to the Intranet and mobile office applications.

Services can also be classified into push and pull services. Push services are those that are delivered to the user without the user actively requesting them. Weather or flight updates, stock quotes, and news could be types of content that can be delivered via push services. Advertisements can also be classified as push services. The network has to be designed to support push services. User profiles would specify the type of services that the user has subscribed to or is capable of accessing. Pull services are typically the ones where the user initiates a request and obtains the content or sets up a session as a result. Web browsing is a typical pull service where the user requests information from some URL.

The types of services and applications that are offered and used by subscribers depend on whether the mobile service is used for business reasons or for personal use. Corporate and enterprise users are generally heavy users of mobile services and hence are normally targeted by the operators when launching new services.

14.2   Networks and Devices

While we have discussed a lot about the networks themselves, which are evolving to support packet data services, it is important to look at the impacts on the devices of the future that will utilize these networks and their capabilities. Within the scope of second-generation networks, the mobile phone has been the predominant device of choice for consumers. Mobile phones have been evolving to support data services via applications such as SMS. However, this is expected to change in the future.

Multipurpose devices that include PDA functionality and support traditional voice services are now becoming available. In addition, capability to transmit still images to other compatible devices is set to take off. These devices, with capability to support graphics with high resolution, color screens, and ability to record images, are begining to utilize packet data networks. Again Japan has been at the forefront of experimenting and deploying such devices. Device manufacturers such as Nokia, Sony, Motorola, Ericsson, Samsung, Handspring, Psion, and Panasonic currently have products on the market with such features. Figure 14–1 shows a picture of some of these devices.

Wireless networks that these devices can access are also evolving. Wireless LANs based on 802.11 standards are becoming more widespread. Bluetooth is increasingly being incorporated into the devices. Hence we can expect to see a wide variety of networks whose scope spans from personal

Nokia 7650

Sony-Ericsson P800

Psion Revo

Figure 14–1 *Devices with cameras, color screens, PDA functionality.*

area networks (PANs) based on Bluetooth to local area networks (LANs) via 802.11 and wide area networks (WANs) supported by WCDMA, cdma2000, and GPRS/EDGE. The number of devices that are not only multi-band but also multi-radio will slowly increase in the future as the costs associated with building such devices keeps going down.

14.3   Enhanced Voice Service

Voice services have been the bread and butter of wireless operators for a long time. Voice as the killer application is expected to continue for quite some time into the future as well. However, there is evolution in terms of enhancements to the traditional voice call. One aspect is that the current circuit switched voice call may be carried over packet networks in the future. Hence the capability to support voice over IP is slowly being developed in 3G networks. One of the key requirements of enabling VoIP is, of course, QoS support. With support for QoS being built into 3G networks, VoIP can be delivered in the near future. VoIP is already utilized in core networks and in enterprises over LANs. However it is not yet a part of the mainstream voice communication technology. End users really do not care about the technology being used to deliver the voice service: what matters to them is the voice quality. With the new codecs such as AMR in 3G networks, voice quality is expected to improve over wireless networks.

In addition to supporting VoIP, the signaling mechanisms used to establish the voice calls are also evolving. The Session Initiation Protocol (SIP), which is developed in the IETF, has a lot of momentum and is included in the standards of 3G networks (both 3GPP and 3GPP2). SIP-based call control for supporting VoIP is expected to be widely available in the next few years. With SIP it is also possible to add new features to the traditional voice calls and create a rich call experience for the end user.

Rich calls can be defined as calls or sessions in which voice or video conversations are supported with concurrent access to data services, such as transferring an image or file or any other value add to the call itself. An example of this is a conversation between two parties that requires both users to take a look at some information on the Web to make a decision or if one user would like to send the other user an image of the location that he is currently at or a music clip from the concert that he is currently attending.

14.4   Presence and Messaging

With approximately 667 million text messages sent across the globe every day, mobile operators have been reaping easy money from SMS (short message service). Today's largely person-to-person messaging market will be one of the main drivers toward increased mobile data adoption, crucial to the future of 3G services. Currently cellular operators in mature markets obtain 5 to 20% of their total revenues from SMS. Experts in the sector forecast that globally messaging revenues will constitute 11% of total cellular revenues by 2006, up from a global average of 2.7% in 2000. The value of the current global SMS market, worth U.S.$13 billion in 2001, will more than quadruple by 2006 to over U.S.$69 billion. Western Europe will be the world's leading market, with total mobile messaging revenues of U.S.$30 billion by the end of 2006, followed by the Asia Pacific region, generating U.S.$22 billion in mobile messaging revenues.

In this framework, the convergence of multimedia applications and the mobile phone is on its way. New applications to replace today's "not-so-successful" WAP interfaces are in the works. Besides SMS, which appeals in large part to young people, new "serious" applications will be enabled with the "always on" 2.5 and 3G mobile network technologies, which will greatly increase the flexibility and usefulness of applications such as mobile banking, entertainment services, and multimedia messaging applications in general.

In this section we provide a description of multimedia messaging applications, focusing on the background of their success and evolution, and describing what will characterize these applications and what types of services are to be expected.

14.4.1   Evolution of Messaging

The Short Message Service (SMS) is a technology that was introduced in the early 1990s when the Internet was still unknown to the general public. SMS can be seen as the starting point of convergence between the Internet and the mobile world. In fact, long before the appearance of the Wireless Application Protocol (WAP) and other ways to access the Internet, wireless users were receiving simple information such as stock quotes, weather, train schedules, flight information, and access to e-mail using SMS. The widespread use of SMS is mainly due to the ability of young people to master the user interface and their desire to communicate cheaply with their friends even in situations where a phone call would not be possible. The popularity of SMS has definitely triggered the general interest in mobile data solutions and has shown to the industry the advantages of "always on" services, setting the stage for more evolved services.

The introduction of the SIM application toolkit standard opened a set of new opportunities: service providers can change or download applications in the wireless device over the air, and the user can be offered a menu-based choice of services, as well as support for new services and advanced security features such as those required for banking applications. However, at first only GSM subscribers could benefit from it and suffered all the inherent limitations of the SMS bearer: for example, limited bandwidth available and short message length.

The effort to overcome these constraints and allow wireless users easier access to Internet content regardless of the wireless technology led to the creation of the WAP standard. However, its popularity is still low, and WAP's true potential will be exploited when 2.5G and 3G packet switched services are introduced on a large scale.

In the meantime, while WAP was being developed, SMS evolved. Proprietary protocols have appeared, such as Nokia's "Smart Messaging," and then standards were formed, such as Enhanced Message Services (EMS). EMS allows simultaneous downloading of ring tones, icons, and text, exploiting the current SMS network infrastructure.

The Mobile Station Application Environment (MMxE) standard, currently being defined by 3GPP, will speed up the convergence between the Internet and the wireless world. MMxE aims at creating a standard environment for wireless applications by defining a Java environment on the phone and incorporates SIM card technology. In addition, MMxE supports standard Internet protocols for transport, security, and applications. Thanks to MMxE, in this environment, the wireless user has new possibilities that are currently available only to laptop and desktop computer users (e.g., download client applications such as interactive games, execute services on remote servers, and interact with another MMxE user in a variety of scenarios). MMxE is a powerful enabling technology for the multimedia message service (MMS) that will support messages combining text, images, sounds, and video clips in a variety of formats. MMS will be the first mobile service to utilize open Internet standards for messaging, such as multipurpose Internet mail extensions (MIME), Simple Mail Transfer Protocol (SMTP), and Hypertext Transfer Protocol (HTTP).

The technology for advanced service and open access to the Internet already exists. Mobile phones can provide streaming video, play music, deliver news and other content, facilitate financial transactions, and provide entertainment, among many other things. However, we need to keep in mind the difference between what these devices can provide and what users actually want. The greater majority of the consumers are not technically skilled to understand the full potential of these new technologies. In order for the new services and technologies to be successful and trigger even more evolution, it is essential to educate users, make them aware of what they can do, and develop services that keep them interested and coming back for more. For this reason, the focus in the wireless community has been on fun, youth, and communities, with an offer of services that are entertaining, interactive, and easy to use. To maintain the success, services must evolve and continually provoke the users' interests and never leave them unsatisfied or bored. Today's youth is the most important part of the market for the evolution of wireless services, since they will drive the convergence revolution, in the same way that they drove the popularity of the early SMS. They grew up with technology, they have seen their world through screens and windows, and they are the early adopters that set new trends. In the future, guys and girls might flirt and date through video calls on their cellular phones. It is easy to foresee that the more these services aggregate people into a wireless community, the more successful they will be.

Although mobile phones have already partially changed the way we interact with others, we can easily foresee that thanks to new capabilities and applications, mobile phones will change the way we live, exchange information, have fun, and interact with other human beings.

Examples of the trend toward mobile messaging and mobile multimedia are the initiative of companies like Nokia and Lycos Europe to work together to develop multimedia messaging services. Lycos Europe recently launched its Mobile Channel, merging its communities with the power of mobile technology. The new channel is currently built around SMS service, and extending Lycos Mobile with new MMS features and MMS content gives the users—in a community environment—an even more exciting experience of informative and entertaining MMS services. Features such as composing multimedia messages out of ready-made Lycos content or personally created images will make MMS more accessible to the consumer.

14.4.2   Toward Multimedia Messaging

MMS is a natural continuation of short message service (SMS) and has capability similar to e-mail. Through MMS, text, photo images, voice, and video clips can be sent from one mobile device to another. Messages are sent to either an MSISDN address (i.e., mobile phone number) or an e-mail address, and MMS messages can be sent to multiple recipients. The receiver is notified of the incoming message with an MMS notification using SMS and needs to retrieve the message from the network.

MMS is a highly appealing service for practical use as well as sharing and having fun. Possible usage situations for the MMS could be sending a love song, a substitute for postcards, or on-the-job usage, for instance, at construction sites, during real-estate dealings, or even with insurance investigations.

MMS is considered the most versatile standardized messaging service to date, including all the features and content types of preceding messaging services. Multimedia messaging service is an open standard supported by 3GPP and WAP Forum and is bearer independent. Figure 14–2 shows the architecture of the MMS defined by 3GPP.

The WAP forum has standardized the MMS architecture. The main components are as follows:

MMS Client is the application in the user's terminal. The client will utilize the general WAP client services like WIM identity. Image and multimedia content rendering is an MMS-specific function.

MMS Relay is the point that the client connects to. The proxy may be integrated with the MMS server.

MMS Server stores the multimedia messages.

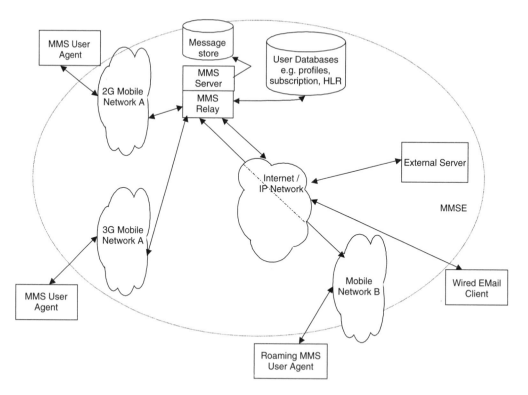

Figure 14–2   *Architectural elements of 3GPP MMS.*

Email Server is the traditional Internet mail service with the SMTP, IMAP, and/or POP interfaces.

Legacy Wireless Messaging systems exist already in the 2G cellular networks. Text messaging with the 2G subscribers will be needed until MMS gains large enough user base.

In the MMS model, an active client can pull messages from the proxy when convenient. The proxy can also push content to the client if such service has been subscribed to. In the low-bandwidth cellular access case, a WAP gateway optimizes the transport between the client and the proxy. The MMS proxy relay forwards client-originated e-mail in the MIME format to the e-mail server with the SMTP protocol. In the downlink direction, the proxy converts MIME to the MMS format. An *X-Mms-* prefix in the MIME header name indicates MMS-specific header field. MMS systems handle all the header fields while non-MMS systems ignore the prefixed ones. The proxy retrieves e-mail with the POP and/or IMAP protocol. The MMS interface between two proxies uses the normal SMTP and its service extensions (ESMTP) for the interconnection. ESMTP is specified in RFC 1869 and RFC 1870.

Both Internet and wireless network addressing are possible with MMS, with *User@realm* address being the familiar e-mail format, whereas wireless network addressing traditionally used PSTN phone numbers to identify a device, with IP addresses as a later addition.

Advanced multimedia messages may contain a significant amount of additional information to present the content in the receiver's terminal. In the browsing context, HTML layout and form commands are the most familiar examples, but voice and video stream synchronization with other simultaneous media requires even more advanced mechanisms. Presentation and rendering capabilities in the receiving terminals vary: Low-end terminals may ignore some of the synchronization and timing information. However, the specification does enable more advanced devices with a large display and high-quality loudspeakers. MMS specification uses Wireless Markup Language (WML) for hypertext sequencing and layout. Synchronized Multimedia Integration Language (SMIL) (based on XML) provides multimedia timing and animation capabilities.

MMS messages carry the content and the presentation language, the latter containing pointers to the multimedia objects in the message. MMS security builds on the underlying WAP and Internet protocols and adopts wireless transport layer security (WTLS) to protect data confidentiality and integrity; a Wireless Application Protocol identity module (WIM) to store sensitive key material and participate in the authentication protocol when setting up a security association; WAP public key infrastructure (PKI) definition to indicate how the Internet PKI standards should be used in the wireless messaging, with the WIM storing the user and device certificates; S/MIME to protect MIME confidentiality and integrity when carried over SMTP; and finally, IPsec to protect the transmission between the servers when application-level security (S/MIME) is not suitable.

14.4.3   Multimedia Messaging Technologies

There are several different technologies for multimedia content transmission, and it is not yet clear which of the technologies best suits which markets. The multimedia messaging technologies currently available are as follows:

- *Enhanced messaging service*: EMS extends the popularity and profitability of SMS by letting subscribers add images, animations, sounds, and style.
- *Smart messaging:* This is a Nokia proprietary system for delivering various kinds of messages from service providers to mobile phone users and between mobile phone users. The most common and popular services so far are the delivery of ringing tones and operator logos.
- *E-mail*
- *Multimedia messaging service*
- *Mobile IM (Instant Messaging):* It is similar to fixed-line services available from providers such as AOL, ICQ, MSN, and Yahoo, and enables subscribers to see via the presence service capability which of their contacts is currently using the service so that they can enter into an exchange of messages.

In the following section some examples of the services that will be available in future multimedia messaging systems are described:

- *Interactive multimedia information retrieval:* This is a device-independent Internet portal that allows to request content with any device and to push immediately generated answers to any user-specified destination.
- *Mobile E-mail:* Makes email accessible from any mobile phone by liberating e-mail access from its dependence on the PC. This enables users to send, receive, and process e-mail messages and personal information no matter where they are.
- *Push proxy gateway:* Enables mobile operators to push information and content (from simple texts to pictures and video clips) to mobile subscribers, without a previous user request and to any mobile device in 2G, 2.5G, and 3G networks.
- *Video messaging:* Allows subscribers to compose video messages using a Web interface on a PC or mobile device.
- *Voicemail information services:* Provides subscribers with easy access to precisely the information they want, when they want it. The service allows operators to deploy information services to offer sub-

scribers 24-hour connectivity to a wide range of information available through the Internet.

14.4.4   Presence Service

The IETF community has recently developed two IP services that are being adopted in wireless networks and have the opportunity to revolutionize mobile services. Instant Messaging and Presence (IM/P) services provide a way to exchange content and user status information inside a user group.

The idea behind these services is that, before the message exchange between nodes, the communicating parties must register their presence information to the presence server. Users can indicate to the presence server their status and "mood" (i.e., whether the user is available to receive incoming communications from all users or only for some user defined groups). At the same time, the user can select whether her presence can be made public or if only a restricted set of other parties can be aware of the user presence. Personal status and "mood" information will tell the possible callers if it is a proper moment to set up a session. Parties interested in the presence information of a given user can request such information when needed or can subscribe with the presence server to be immediately informed of changes in the presence information of the user so that they know immediately when the other party becomes available. Attributes such as location of the user can also be added to the presence service and this would enhance the usefulness of presence service.

SIP (Session Initiation Protocol) is used to support these services. SIP signaling controls the sessions and may contain user payload such as a brief text message or caller's personal information. However, the bulk of the payload should be carried over the normal e-mail, voice call, and Web browsing protocols (i.e., SMTP, RTP, and HTTP). SIP message primitive provides communication via a proxy server or directly between the endpoints in a peer-to-peer fashion. An advanced authentication and authorization mechanism is used to manage the user groups and the visibility of the data, as the presence information is highly private in nature.

Instant Messages and Presence service will become one of the most common services in future networks. 3GPP and 3GGP2 have considered this and included the services as part of their service provisioning mechanisms.

14.5   Web Surfing on the Mobile Internet

The mobile or wireless Internet will be an extension to the current Internet. End users have a certain perception about what Web surfing means today. Users are typically used to large screens and high-resolution graphics. The millions of Web sites on the World Wide Web are typically designed for devices such as traditional notebook and desktop computers. Web sites include images, Javascripts, advertisements, and other extras in addition to the content that the user is interested in. As wireless devices accessing the Internet become significantly larger in number, Web site designers and content providers will start to pay attention to these users and will start to customize the content for such end users. The form factors as well as the capabilities of these devices, which typically would have smaller screens, low battery life, and smaller processors (in terms of MIPS execution), would dictate how content is delivered. The success of I-Mode in Japan can be attributed to various factors, such as its early entry into the market as well as the development of content by more than 4000 information providers. The rapid growth and current penetration of the service has demonstrated the acceptance of data services that have a different look and feel in future networks.

Microbrowsers attempt to emulate the typical or traditional Web browsers that users are familiar with. However, the fact that these devices may in many cases not even have a keypad would require other ways for human–machine interaction. Unless the services and content are made compelling enough by providing intuitive ways of Web browsing and are simple to use, the wireless Internet will be what WAP is. So there is a challenge that faces the wireless Internet.

Languages such as HTML, XHTML, and XML are incorporating features that are capable of indicating the type and capability of a device and content to be adapated dynamically based on this information. As Web browsing via the wireless medium becomes the norm, we can expect to see Web sites that adapt content on the fly.

Various microbrowsers are available today for different operating systems. The Symbian operating system, which is used in many handheld devices including the Nokia Communicator and Psion, includes the Opera microbroswer. A picture of the opera browser on a Psion Series 5 device is shown in Figure 14–3.

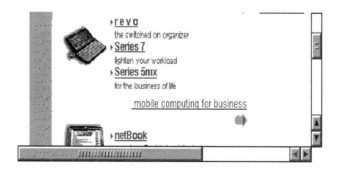

Figure 14–3   *Opera's microbrowser for the Symbian OS.*

Microbrowsers from Microsoft for Pocket PC-based devices are also currently included on devices such as the iPaq from Hewlett Packard.

14.6   Location Services

Location services are expected to be yet another new class of value-added services that are used to some extent in current cellular systems. 3G cellular networks, especially, will make the location services a powerful concept for operators and application service providers by combining the knowledge of a subscriber's up-to-date position being available via the mobile device. In the United States, the Federal Communications Commission (FCC) has mandated that wireless networks provide the capability to track a user's location within 50 to 100 meters in most cases. This service is termed E911. While this is a specific example of location being used for emergency services, the applicability of location information is vast. According to research studies, location sensitive services to wireless mobile users are expected to achieve a penetration of about 30% in five years.

Location information can be used to target advertisements and local information. Currently on the Internet, users have to specify a certain area of zip code in order to obtain information about the surrounding businesses. However, in the case of mobile networks, the network is already aware of the geographical position of users at any time. Various geographical location technologies are used such as GPS (global positioning system), observed time difference (OTD), and triangulation, to estimate the location of a user or device. The location information can be applied to other applications, such as driving directions or local weather. An example of using location information would be a service that provides driving directions to a user. An application server in the network may be aware of traffic conditions on the route that would be optimal for a user who has requested such information. The application server in such a scenario could provide alternate route information as well as information about traffic conditions.

Location information can also be vital to fleet management, thereby creating a more efficient operational system. A call to the taxi Web site can tailor content for subscribers based on the information that is obtained from the application servers in the network. Such specialized services add value to the mobile Internet that is not possible with the traditional way things have been done in the Internet.

Location interoperability between vendors was started as a forum by Nokia, Ericsson, and Motorola. The work of this forum is now continued under the auspices of Open Mobile Alliance (OMA). Details of OMA are provided in Chapter 16.

Location services offer yet another revenue stream for operators and content providers. However, location tracking also raises some privacy issues. It should be possible for users themselves to control and manage access to location tracking information to some extent. Law enforcement agencies can also obtain access to this information, and this is a requirement in most countries around the world.

14.7   M-Commerce

Mobile commerce is yet another new service area that has shown some promise for a while. However, no significant advances in terms of technology or acceptance by consumers have been seen in this area. M-commerce essentially includes doing business and financial transactions via the mobile network. Security is one of the major concerns of anything that deals with financial transactions. Wireless networks are essentially a broadcast medium and hence a cause for being concerned with security. Consumers in the wired world have a false sense of security simply by virtue of having a physical wire as opposed to data being transmitted over ether. Wireless networks have, however, developed sophisticated encryption and ciphering algorithms that will make it possible to carry out financial transactions over the mobile Internet.

M-commerce also includes the capability to make payments using the mobile device. The mobile device with its smart card can be considered as an extension of one's wallet. The use of the mobile phone as a payment instrument to make purchases in the physical world or online is another application of M-commerce. The mobile phone as a wallet is based on existing technologies such as ECML (Electronic Commerce Modeling Language). More information about ECML is at www.ecml.org.

Mobile commerce is still in its infancy, and many problems need to be dealt with, including user perception and technology, before revenues from M-commerce as a service can be expected.

The Mobey forum is a financial industry–driven forum whose mission is to encourage the use of mobile technology in financial services. The URL for the Mobey Forum is http://www.mobeyforum.org.

The Mobile Electronic Transaction (MET) initiative was also intiated by Nokia, Ericsson, and Motorola with the aim of defining a framework for secure mobile transactions. The URL to the MET forum us http://www.mobiletransaction.org.

14.8   Mobile Office

The mobile office is essentially an extension of one's office via the mobile device. Many executives, doctors, engineers, and workers in industries such as finance, health care, and telecommunications feel the need to be connected to their office to access information as well as to be reachable. In the wireline oriented Internet world, VPNs have created an extension to corporate offices by extending the office to the user's home or any location in the world.

Wireless data networks provide employees access to information, enabling them to be productive and effective while away from the office. They can send and receive faxes or e-mail, log onto a company's LAN, search a database for product information, or even exchange computer files. Salespeople can complete sales orders, obtain the latest pricing, or check product availability on their own without requiring a support person at the main office. Field service personnel select work assignments, get directions and service details, check inventories, review parts lists or schematics, and even handle remotely without having to be close to a phone line.

With the increase in bit rates in third-generation wireless networks, we can now expect that users will be connected to the office via their mobile devices. Notebook computers with the appropriate access interfaces, which include 802.11 as well as GPRS, UMTS, and cdma2000, will enable connectivity to the workplace from any place. While it is possible today to achieve the mobile office concept via the Internet, it is limited to places that have Internet connectivity. The capability of being connected via wireless networks from anywhere will make this feature even more enticing and be a revenue source for operators who rely on business customers for a significant portion of their revenues.

14.8.1   Secure Corporate LAN/Intranet Access

In wireless data networks, the air link is encrypted, providing security for confidential data. This enables solutions for securely accessing corporate LANs. Some service providers leverage this capability to provide VPNs to corporate LANs. Using a VPN service or application, employees can browse the company Intranet from anywhere and access all applications. A few applications that may be accessed over such VPN connections are as follows:

* Electronic mail
* World Wide Web (text, graphics, sound, links, etc.)
* Matching databases
* Remote file access
* Multimedia access (sound and video)
* Inventory status in warehouses

Efforts are underway to make the transition from remote access to local access smooth and transparent to the user. An office worker in the near future will have access to wireless data networks that deliver an all-IP, carrier-grade, access agnostic, mobility-enabled core network.

The goal of mobile office–type applications is to provide users with the capability to handle professional and personal business whenever they want and wherever they want. Grabbing a cup of coffee and the Financial Times before boarding the morning train used to constitute the daily routine. While coffee will remain a staple, imagine a commute consisting of activities that traditionally would be done at home or at the office. Accessing the corporate intranet and e-mail, reading the latest industry news, and ordering flowers can be done on the wireless network today. Future applications will be even more dazzling. Order the latest movie release on the way home and it will be waiting on a playback device for immediate viewing. Order the new Lou Reed album and it will play on headphones in real time. Watch video highlights from last night's sporting events, or log onto the live camera at Waikiki Beach. The applications are endless but have one thing in common: a wireless data network that can handle data efficiently.

14.9   Peer-to-Peer Applications: Gaming

Networked games have slowly begun to take shape but are definitely a strong contender in the future. With the increase in the number of broadband connections to end users, the video games industry has started to develop the games that can be played over a network. The video games industry is almost as big as Hollywood in terms of revenue. Currently mobile devices include some form of games on the devices. However, with the networks being upgraded to support packet data services, new types of games are expected to be developed and deployed for these devices and networks.

Games are often focused toward the younger generation. With support from mobile networks and devices, games present an opportunity for both game developers and games services. Games are also considered a big source of revenue in the future for operators. Games can be played between end users or by an user with the network. Online casinos and gambling are other types of applications that will be deployed by operators in order to generate revenue from new services over mobile networks.

Another type of peer-to-peer application is the ability to share music. Napster is a well-known phenomenon. Peer-to-peer applications such as file sharing will also be possible via the wireless IP networks in the future.

14.10   Use of Wireless IP Networks for Telemetry and Telematics

One of the applications that can benefit from wireless data networks is telemetry. An example of this is parking meters throughout a city or electric meters in rural communities. Since the capacity requirements of wireless networks are high and the usage of these resources is based on the time of day, telemetry applications can be designed to use these networks to transmit data about usage, violations, and maintenance during off-peak hours.

Telematics is another application that can use wireless data networks. As automobiles are becoming increasingly sophisticated, they could also be enabled to transmit engine conditions and location information to a monitoring center. This will enable the manufacturer to provide services that can be revenue generating. Many other types of applications can be considered for use. It is easy to imagine a scenario in the near future where the local gas station could be a wireless access hot spot capable of delivering content such as music, video, directions and other information at very high speeds to automobiles which are equipped with devices that can use these services. With the deployment of IPv6, address space will no longer be a concern, and hence it is conceivable that every electric and gas meter could have an IP address and a wireless interface can upload usage information to the utility companies automatically.

14.11   Healthcare Industry

Mobile data services will also be of value in the healthcare industry. Some of the applications that can be considered as being enabled by 3G wireless networks are:

- The ability to monitor patients remotely. Patients can go about their lifestyles while using wireless data transmitters, and the data is then monitored by hospitals and doctors. Medical research also benefits with the ability to monitor patients on a constant basis.
- Doctors can access patient information and records easily from mobile devices and provide prescriptions in emergencies.
- When ambulances or emergency services are requested, location information provided via the mobile device or monitors can be used to direct vehicles and emergency personnel more effectively.
- Doctors can also have access to databases while on the move to check for more information regarding symptoms or research information.

14.12   Summary

The ultimate test of the success of 3G networks will be measured by the number of users that will embrace wireless data applications and services and use them. In order for this to happen, the key enabler is the packaging of applications and presentation of content within an easy-to-use terminal device. This drives more users to use the new services and devices. These enable previously undetermined applications, or sometimes wholly new user needs, to be identified and satisfied, and this process results in the creation of a completely new, previously unknown class of services.

The applications covered in this chapter are only a small set of examples. Many different kinds of applications and services can be developed and deployed over wireless IP networks. The creativity fostered by the Internet in terms of developing new applications will spread to the wireless Internet as well in the near future.

References

MITA, Mobile Internet Technical Architecture by Nokia, IT Press.

Report 11 of the UMTS Forum, Enabling UMTS/Third Generation Services and Applications.

Evolution of IP Wireless Networks

The evolution of the Internet and mobile networks toward the creation of the mobile Internet is driven by technological advances in the field of networking protocols, radio technologies as well as services. The major factors influencing the evolution of the Internet are the pervasiveness of PCs and the established telecommunications infrastructure. As the number of wireless devices capable of accessing the Internet and providing new services that are based on data increases, the networks that are currently focused on delivering voice services will also evolve. Eventually the mobile networks will be a part of the evolving global Internet as any other network today. With the evolution of society toward an information centricity, access to information and services anywhere and anytime will be a key requirement. Devices and networks will evolve to provide the kind of access to information that we have today for a small set of applications such as voice.

The end-to-end architecture of the Internet has been a facilitator in itself and has enabled its extraordinary growth and usage. The architecture of the Internet, has been the driver for the smooth evolution of the core and access networks. Mobile networks have also been evolving in parallel. Growth rates in terms of number of mobile subscribers passed the billion mark in the first half of 2002. It is also expected that the number of mobile users will soon surpass the number of Internet users. The evolution of these two types of networks, which primarily offer different services today, is leading toward convergence and the creation of the mobile Internet.

This chapter focuses on the evolution of the technologies covered in the earlier parts of the book. Evolution of networks from the two major standards perspective, 3GPP and 3GPP2, is considered as well as evolution of 802.11 wireless LANs. Evolution of services in the wireless networks is covered briefly.

15.1   Network Evolution Overview

15.1.1   Fixed Transport Network Evolution

The fixed transport network has been evolving rapidly in the last few years. The optical technology revolution of the late 1990s has resulted in deployment of long-haul as well as metro networks based on wavelength division multiplexing (WDM) and dense wavelength division multiplexing (DWDM) technologies, which has increased the available bandwidth and network capacity to a great degree. Technologies that are having an impact on the transport network evolution include Gigabit Ethernet among others. The increased availability of bandwidth directly translates to lower costs for carrying the bits.

Asynchronous transfer mode (ATM) was predominantly deployed in the backbone networks in the early 1990s. However with the development of multi-protocol label switching (MPLS), the growth of ATM has slowed down and MPLS is now in the process of cohabiting with ATM switches in some places and in many instances replacing it altogether. Technologies such as packet over sonet (PoS) are also changing the way data networks interface to the backbone networks.

One of the major costs of operating a wireless network is the backhaul network cost. Base stations and cell sites need to be connected to a centralized controller. Generally this has been done using T1s and E1s as well as microwave links. With the availability of high-capacity optical networks in metro areas, it is possible that the base stations could be connected to the optical networks directly, and traffic to and from the central controller routed through such networks. Hence, instead of having point-to-point connections between the controller and the base stations, a large number of base stations could be connected to a fiber ring and share the resources of the transport network with other traffic, thereby reducing the cost of the backhaul networks. The availability of technologies such as xDSL will also allow different models and networking technology to be used for the transport networks used by cellular systems. The proliferation of IP will also have an impact on the transport network architectures in the radio network and the core network. Currently these are based primarily on ATM and use dedicated circuits. These may evolve in the future to use packet switched networks and utilize shared networks (as opposed to dedicated circuits) with guaranteed service.

15.1.2   Wireless Network Evolution

On the mobile networking side, third-generation WCDMA technology will dominate the wide area access networks as well as licensed band hotspots. 802.11a and 802.11b wireless LAN technologies provide high data rates (on the order of 11 Mbps and 54 Mbps) and are ideally suited for hotspots such as airports, convention centers, and other public places. New WLAN security standard increases WLAN's significance, especially if the access provider does not have a license to operate a cellular network. Cellular operators are also interested in WLAN technologies and are in the process of building such networks to complement their wide area cellular service. A nominal air interface bit rate of 2 Mbps in WCDMA hotspots is clearly less than WLAN can provide. However, direct bit rate comparison does not reflect the end user experience since WLAN lacks the QoS and smooth handover features that are standard in the WCDMA air interface. Advanced WCDMA radio resource control optimizes the access bandwidth usage, thus lowering operator costs and giving indirect savings to the subscriber.

In the short term, the evolution of wireless networks is based on the technology path chosen. Third-generation license ownership is one of the major control points here (thus the high European auction prices). Existing second-generation GSM, TDMA, or CDMA networks are another crucial factor when selecting a new technology. In the longer run one or two technologies will dominate the market. A small number of technologies can provide better economies of scale than multiple heterogeneous networks. Global roaming and other features are also easier to achieve when only a few interfaces must be matched. UMTS networks, WCDMA radio technology, and global radio band allocation have been major steps toward harmonizing the networks. The IETF Mobile IP working group is attempting to specify a universal mobility management mechanism with IPv6 technology.

Personal area networks (PANs) are an interesting future development. A single node ("personal base station" or "mobile router") passes traffic between the subscriber's personal area and the wide area, which is in the operator's domain. Technically a small-scale gateway between the domains is not that difficult as low-power integrated circuits can do most of the user plane processing, but the deployment scenarios are much harder: PAN management is a totally new issue; how trusted is the mobile router from the WAN perspective (and vice versa), and will the development lead to a peer-to-peer network where WAN has only a minor significance? Bluetooth devices already implement the required radio technology. Several control technologies related to security, QoS, and addressing are still under study in Bluetooth Forum and IETF Mobile ad hoc networks working groups. PAN use cases vary from cooperation of a mobile phone and embedded intelligence in an automobile to mobile phone–wireless earpiece–laptop communication.

15.1.3   Wireless Applications

This book focuses on Internet technologies in wireless networks. Internet and IP networking especially concentrate on carrying messages from the source to the destination. But in the end the applications—mail, news, chat, messaging, Web browsing, presence services—is what subscribers ask for. The applications in turn set the quality and security requirements for the network. So far circuit switched voice has been the dominating application in cellular networks, and data traffic has been transported on top of the circuits. The ratio of voice and data will be reversed, which means that it will be more economical to adjust voice traffic into the packet switched data networks than vice versa.

Unfortunately the applications are the part that is hardest to predict. We have seen this many times: GSM short message service (SMS) is limited to low bandwidth and 160-character messages since it was considered a niche application when design decisions were made. Open System Interconnection (OSI) protocols were an alternative to TCP/IP data networking until the WWW applications termed the latter the definitive winner. Browsing and user experience (graphical user interface included) had the key position here, not the http, ftp, DNS, or IP protocols.

Mobile phones with embedded digital cameras and color displays were launched in 2001. These features in the terminals will enable new services like multimedia messaging (MMS) with mixed data and images. 3GPP selected the IETF Session Initiation Protocol to control IP multimedia services in future mobile networks. SIP is a flexible, text-based signaling protocol for connection setup and teardown. In the IMS model the network holds the connection status for each user. Peer-to-peer connection directly between the hosts (e.g., mobile terminals), is also possible, but it will be a later development when terminals become capable. Even then certain kinds of centralized directories, proxies, and portals will be in place so peer-to-peer is only an additional form of communication between the hosts.

15.2   3GPP Network Evolution

Chapter 9 describes the Release 1999 standard network. The main standardization effort was in the new radio access network and the WCDMA air interface. Release 4 and 5 standards focus on the core network evolution.

15.2.1   3GPP RAN Evolution

Second-generation GSM networks that were introduced in the early 1990s have experienced phenomenal growth over the last decade and have become the predominant wireless technology in the world today, with a market share of 70% or more. While the acceptance and numbers of subscribers in wireless cellular networks has been growing rapidly, the other phenomenon of the 1990s has been the exponential growth of the Internet and the number of Internet users. We have in essence a wireless network that primarily serves voice and messaging (SMS), and the Internet, which is a data-centric network that offers information, entertainment, e-commerce, and a slew of other services. With the natural evolution toward convergence of voice and data networks and the demand for Internet access and data services in wireless cellular networks, radio technologies defined for second-generation digital networks are evolving to accommodate packet data and services based on packet networks.

The initial GSM specifications provided only basic transmission capabilities for supporting data services. Data rates were in the 9.6-Kbps range. Release 96 specified high-speed circuit switched data services (HSCSD). The theoretical limit of HSCSD with 14.4-Kbps channel coding is 115.2 Kbps. However, practical limits allow data rates up to 64 Kbps.

After five years of intense standardization efforts, the result is an evolution path for GSM that is seen to be smooth, competitive, and cost-efficient. The first steps of this evolution were specified in Release 97 standards when GPRS was introduced. GPRS is able to deliver packet data services efficiently over existing GSM networks. The theoretical maximum throughput in GPRS networks is 160 Kbps per mobile station using all eight channels without error correction.

Voice capacity in wireless networks has always been an issue. In order to maximize the ROI (return on investment), operators have been asking for higher voice capacity over the existing spectrum. Adaptive multirate codec (AMR), which is included in Release 98, increased the spectral efficiency and quality of speech services significantly. The AMR codec contains a set of fixed-rate speech and channel codecs in addition to fast inband signaling and link adaptation. It operates in the full-rate and half-rate GSM channel modes.

Enhanced data rates for GDM evolution (EDGE) was introduced in Release 99. EDGE introduced more efficient modulation, coding, and retransmission schemes. The net effect of this was a significant boost to the performance of data services. EDGE as specified will enhance the throughput per time slot of both HSCSD and GPRS. Enhancement to HSCSD is called ECSD (enhanced circuit switched data), and enhancement to GPRS is called EGPRS (enhanced general packet radio service). ECSD in reality is not implemented since EGPRS is a superior mechanism for packet data access. The enhancement is equivalent to tripling the data rates for HSCSD and GPRS. This is accomplished by using 8-PSK modulation in addition to the existing GMSK. EGPRS is built on top of GPRS. One major change in EGPRS over GPRS is the link quality control, which in EGPRS also supports incremental redundancy. EGPRS also includes QoS capabilities that allow support for real-time services as well.

WCDMA was standardized as UTRAN (UMTS terrestrial radio access network) by 3GPP as part of Release 99. Characteristics of WCDMA have been covered in Chapter 9. With WCDMA, bit rates of 384 Kbps and a maximum of

2 Mbps were introduced. With significant gains in capacity, multiservice capability can now be introduced in WCDMA-based networks. Subscribers can have voice and data sessions ongoing at the same time.

GSM/EDGE radio access network (GERAN) has now been standardized as another radio access network for UMTS in Release 5 by 3GPP. With this UMTS now supports two access technologies, namely, UTRAN and GERAN. GERAN supports the same traffic classes as UTRAN and interfaces to the core network via the Iu interface. Hence from an UMTS vision perspective, GERAN provides the same services via the core network as UTRAN.

Another evolution step forward in Release 5 of 3GPP is the standardization of HSDPA (high-speed downlink packet access) for WCDMA. With HSDPA it is now possible to have data rates of a maximum of 10 Mbps on the downlink. The HSDPA concept offers over 100% higher peak user bit rates than Release '99. HS-DSCH bit rates are comparable to DSL modem bit rates. The mean user bit rates in large macrocell environments can exceed 1 Mbps and in small micro cells 5 Mbps. The HSDPA concept is able to support efficiency not only for non-real-time UMTS QoS classes but also for real-time UMTS QoS classes with guaranteed bit rates.

Release 6 of 3GPP, which is expected in 2003, is currently studying the introduction of WLAN technologies based on 802.11 as another access type, in addition to UTRAN and GERAN. Release 6 will primarily focus on services and the IP multimedia subsystem.

Evolution of radio technologies beyond Release 6 is not a working item yet. However, it is expected that as the capacity requirements for voice and data keep increasing, radio technology will keep evolving to meet these requirements. As new spectrum is opened up, new radio technologies will be developed as well in addition to adapting the current technologies for the new spectrum. As UMTS also evolves to the point where radio networks such as UTRAN, GERAN, and WLAN coexist, mobility across these networks in a seamless manner will also become important. It is expected that multimode terminals with capability for any access type will become available. Operators will deploy UMTS networks in a way that makes use of the capabilities of the access networks. Hence WCDMA-based UTRAN base stations will be deployed where capacity for voice and data is high, and GSM/GPRS base stations will be used in less demanding environments. For existing GSM spectrum, EDGE offers a smooth evolution path to support packet data access and new services based on these. So it is very likely that operators who have GSM networks will upgrade via the EDGE route. For new spectrum, WCDMA offers higher capacity, better spectral efficiency, higher data rates, and QoS support. Existing and new operators who have spectrum for WCDMA will deploy such networks on a gradual basis as demand for data services rises.

The term *4G* or *fourth generation* at this time is a marketing term. No specifications as to what exactly 4G means have been defined. The term is generally used without necessarily referring to any spectrum or radio technologies. At the moment it simply means radio networks with data rates that are higher than what current 3G can offer.

15.2.2   3GPP Release 4 Standard

The 3GPP Release 4 standard introduces the possibility to split the mobile services switching center (MSC) to separate control and switching parts. The MSC server implements the call control and mobility management functions of the MSC. The MSC server controls the user plane part of MSC, called media gateway function (MGW). The MGW terminates the user plane transport channels from both the circuit switched (CS) and packet switched (PS) domains. A channel can be an AAL2/ATM virtual circuit or an RTP/UDP/IP media stream. The MGW can also convert between different types of media so that one party of the call may be in the CS domain (AAL2) while the other uses PS domain VoIP (RTP) call facilities. The MSC server controls the switching in the MGW over a MEGACO (ITU H.248) interface. The roots for the MSC server development lie in the voice over IP (VoIP) networking, where similar development has taken place earlier.

The general architecture of UMTS Release 4 is the same with the Release 1999 standard. Access stratum services and functions are the same.

15.2.3   3GPP Release 5 Standard

The 3GPP Release 5 standard introduces the IP multimedia subsystem (IMS) into the UMTS architecture. In Release 5, the access and core networks are like in the Release 4 standard.

The IMS is the service machinery to support IP services on top of the packet switched network domain (Figure 15–1). The IMS services are based on the Session Initiation Protocol (SIP) defined in IETF, and for which 3GPP has defined specific extensions. SIP is used by the user in the terminal to communicate with the network, and for signaling between the IMS network elements. The IMS is mainly involved in service control, whereas the PS core network provides the transport for the user plane payload. The IMS supports VoIP services, presence services, instant messaging, and other IP services.

Release 5 introduces minor modifications to the PS core network, mainly for the support of QoS for IP services and the control by the IMS of QoS provisioning.

The IMS group service and system specification (3GPP TS 23.228) describes the mechanisms to support multimedia services in a mobile environment. The services themselves are not described, but a general framework where the service can be plugged in is given. Internet application development is seen as the fast way to create the services. When the service is attached to IMS, it adds strong authentication and roaming-related functions, which are typically not supported by the service itself.

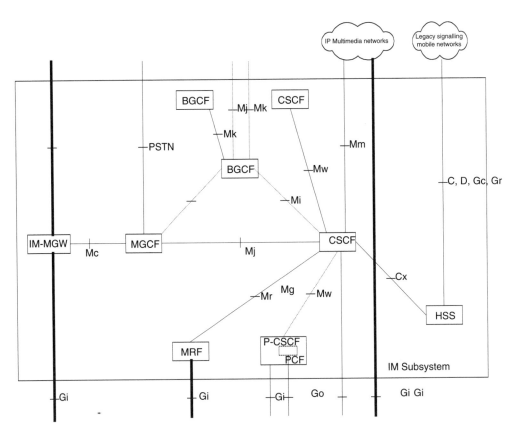

Figure 15–1 *IP multimedia subsystem configuration.*

Call session control function (CSCF) and proxy CSCF (P-CSCF) are the heart of the SIP session management inside the network. The P-CSCF is the mobile subscriber's first contact point for the SIP services inside the visited network. The P-CSCF forwards the SIP signaling to the CSCF in the home network. CSCF verifies the SIP identity with the authentication token from the home subscriber server (HSS), which also generates session-specific cryptographic keys. Service control always takes place in the home network; therefore, the end user has the ability to access the same services and experience the same quality whether the subscriber is roaming in a far-away foreign network or connecting directly to the home network. The IP multimedia media gateway function (IM-MGW) terminates circuit and packet switched media flows and provides media conversion and payload processing in largely the same way as the CS-MGW does in the Release 4 standard. Other elements in the IP multimedia subsystem manage the switching resources.

15.2.4   3GPP Release 6 Standard

Release 6 of 3GPP has many work items for standardization that span the radio interface, radio network, packet core and the IMS. Release 6 is expected to be completed in the second half of 2003. Some of the enhancements for the radio interface in UTRAN are are :

- Multiple input/multiple output (MIMO) antennas
- Terminal power saving features
- Improvements in inter-system and inter-frequency measurments

The transport network in the RAN, which is currently defined as ATM, is also being revised and the possibility of using IP in the RAN is being studied. Some of the other changes in Release 6 will be the support for multicast broadcast and multicast services (MBMS). With MBMS, the operators could deliver services such as advertising to users. MBMS also brings IP multicast to wireless networks. This creates yet another source of revenue for the operators.

Within the core network, the IP multimedia subsystem is being enhanced for the messaging and presence services. Group management within the scope of IMS is also being addressed in this release. Emergency calls in the packet switched network are also being addressed. A feasibility study on wireless LAN and UMTS interworking is in place. Actual inclusion of such a solution is expected in Release 7. Release 6 is also addressing an important issue which is network sharing. Since the cost of deployment of 3G is becoming a limiting factor, network sharing offers a solution by which multiple operators could share a common radio network. Other enhancements will be in the area of QoS for packet services especially services such as streaming audio and video. The open service architecture (OSA) specifications are also being worked on. Enhancements to the Generic User profile, ability to discover terminal capabilities and push services are being added to OSA.

The emphasis is shifting from adding more features to the network architecture to services. There is a far greater need to ensure that services can be developed and deployed in an efficient manner. Also the ability for third parties to provide services to cellular subscribers is becoming more apparent and is being taken into consideration in the evolution of the 3GPP architecture.

15.3   3GPP2 Standard Evolution

Chapter 13 provides the current view of the network architecture for provisioning of IP services. The evolution of the 3GPP2 cdma2000 network will be focused on three main aspects: enhancements to the cdma2000 radio interface, evolution of the core network at the IP transport level, and service evolution.

15.3.1   Evolution of cdma2000 Radio Interface

Unlike other evolutionary paths taken by competing GSM and TDMA technologies that have interim 2.5-generation technologies, with cdma2000 (also called 1xRTT), the third-generation (3G) wireless technology has arrived. However, the performance of the "wireless Web" based on currently deployed 2.5-generation technology, such as GPRS, and 3G technology, such as cdma2000, as well as soon to be deployed 3G technology, such as UMTS, is still a far cry from what subscribers can receive currently over the "wired Web." Wireless industry organizations are working fervently to develop evolutionary paths toward closing of this performance gap.

The marriage of mobile IP with cdma2000 has facilitated a true "always-on" mobile Internet service delivering user mobility anytime, anywhere. However, significant challenges remain before the wireless Internet performance comes close to that of the wired Web. One such challenge is the coexistence of circuit switched voice and packet switched data, resulting in a suboptimal over-the-air access performance for packet data services. The other challenge is seamless merger of an IP-based packet core network into an IP-based access network to create an all-IP network (core and access). In this section we will first briefly review the access technology evolution followed by a review of the underlying network evolution plans.

15.3.2   cdma2000 Access Network Evolution

The evolution of cdma2000 access technology beyond 1xRTT is called 1xEV (Figure 15-2). It is geared toward being backward compatible with current CDMA technologies and forward compatible with each evolution step. 1xEV consists of two distinct but compatible standards using a standard 1.25-MHz carrier:

* 1xEV-DO (1X Evolution Data Only)
* 1xEV-DV(1X Evolution Data and Voice)

1xEV-DO is a companion standard to cdma2000 that enables higher data rates by decoupling voice and data in access network by mandating a separate carrier for packet data. It is designed to be an overlay technology and very suitable for hotspot deployment. However, it is backward compatible and allows hand-offs to a 1xRTT carrier if simultaneous voice and data services are needed. By allocating a separate carrier for data, it is possible to deliver peak rates of up to 2.4 Mbps.

1xEV-DV is the next step in the evolution of the cdma2000 technology and designed to improve system capacity and performance for mixed voice and data traffic. The first release of the standard is currently under review as cdma2000 Release C and was approved in 2002. New concepts, such as fast

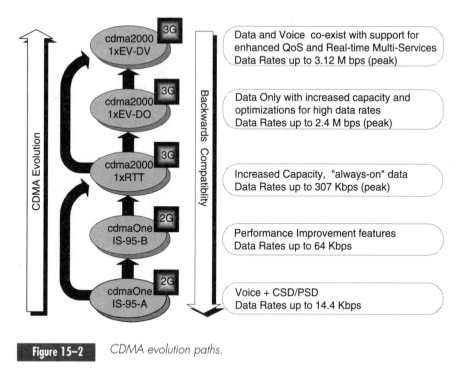

Data and Voice co-exist with support for
enhanced QoS and Real-time Multi-Services
Data Rates up to 3.12 M bps (peak)

Data Only with increased capacity and
optimizations for high data rates
Data Rates up to 2.4 M bps (peak)

Increased Capacity, "always-on" data
Data Rates up to 307 Kbps (peak)

Performance Improvement features
Data Rates up to 64 Kbps

Voice + CSD/PSD
Data Rates up to 14.4 Kbps

Figure 15–2   *CDMA evolution paths.*

cell switching, to facilitate support of real-time applications over the packet data channel are being considered. Increased system data capacity over 1xEV-DO is provided by addition of new packet data states, such as a virtual active state. Allowing independent target FERs for data streams provides enhanced support for QoS. The framework for an all-IP network is being established via IP multicast/broadcast support. It is prudent to note that some key features could be delayed to the next release of the standard.

15.3.3   Evolution of cdma2000 Access and Core Networks to All-IP

In North America many network operators are keen on migrating to an all-IP network in which the core as well as the access network is IP based. The foundation of such a migration is the existing TIA/EIA-41, cdma2000, and IOS standards with support of both circuit and packet switched technologies. 3GPP2 and its organizational partners have recommended a phased approach to achieving the goal of an all-IP network. The phases can either be sequentially evolved or can be a "mix and match" evolution. These proposals have been defined at a high level, and standards activity is in progress to define details. Figures 15–3 and 15–4 depict the current paths of evolving to an all-IP network.

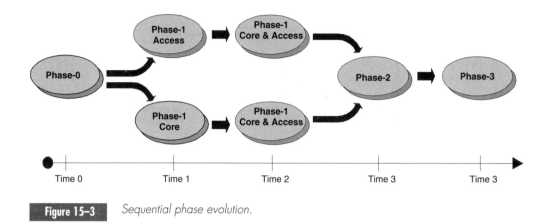

Figure 15–3   *Sequential phase evolution.*

In Phase 0 the legacy core network is defined by TIA/EIA-41, which defines the network functional components, interfaces, and protocols. The packet core is defined by P.R0001, which describes the overall packet architecture with simple and mobile IP as access methods. The access and the radio networks are defined by IOS version 4.x1 and IS-2000. IOS version 4.x1 defines the interface between the circuit switched MAC and BS as well as the packet control function (PCF) and the PDSN, while the IS2000 family of standards defines the air interface.

Phase 1 is the first step toward the evolution into an all-IP network. The main thrust of this phase is the separation of the access and core networks. In the core networks the focus is toward carrying the TIA/EIA-41 operations

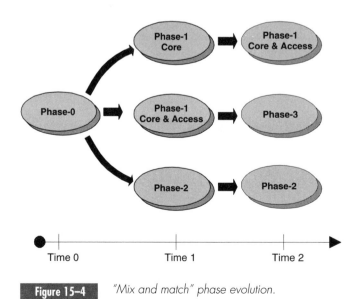

Figure 15–4   *"Mix and match" phase evolution.*

over IP. In the access networks, signaling links wherever possible will be carried over IP while the bearer transport will continue to be based on IOS. The radio interface will remain based on the IS-2000 family of standards.

Phase 2 introduces an IP multimedia domain, allowing VoIP. The core network will transport both signaling and bearer streams over IP and support IP multimedia services. Legacy equipment will continue to use legacy transport mechanisms. On the access side, the separation of the signaling and bearer streams is mandated with the signaling links carried over IP transport. The radio interface would have to be evolved to support end-to-end IP multimedia call control (such as SIP) while at the same time providing support to legacy equipment.

Phase 3 is the culmination of the process of evolving to an all-IP network. The significant achievement of this phase is the extension of IP over the radio interface. The core network will throw off the shackles of legacy non-IP support requirements. IP multimedia will be the network technology with support for enhanced IP multimedia services. The access network too will complete the move to an IP-based transport with support for enhanced service and QoS. The radio interface will move to an IP transport for both signaling and bearer stream.

15.3.4   Evolution of cdma2000 Core Network: The All-IP NAM

The cdma2000 all-IP network architecture model (NAM) represents the model of the target architecture for the evolution of the cdma2000 networks toward an architecture based completely on IP protocols. Evolution of the cdma2000 network has already started in standardization, with small steps taken to improve the functionality of the current cdma2000 network toward the concepts defined in the all-IP NAM. In this section we describe the main features of the all-IP NAM, in order to provide the reader with an understanding of the direction in the evolution of cdma2000 and of the major evolutionary steps.

The all-IP NAM architecture is based on three major protocols:

- SIP (Session Initiation Protocol) for control of multimedia sessions
- DIAMETER for authorization, authentication, and accounting
- Mobile IP, both IPv4 and IPv6 versions, for mobility support in the core network

In the following section, the details of the architecture are described.

ARCHITECTURE MODEL

A set of architectural principles is used in the all-IP NAM architecture. In particular, the architecture derives from the following objectives:

- *Independence from lower layers:* The all-IP network architecture is being designed to be independent of Layer 1 and Layer 2 protocols thanks to the use of IP protocols. The network architecture is also designed to be independent of the access network; therefore, the core network has the ability to support multiple access network technologies (e.g., cellular radio technologies, WLAN, DSL).
- *Phased migration:* The all-IP network architecture is designed to allow for a phased migration of existing networks.
- *Radio efficiency:* The network mechanisms adopted in the all-IP network architecture allow efficient use of radio resources in order to optimize the use of the limited and expensive cellular bandwidth.
- *Improvements of reliability and quality of service:* The all-IP network is being designed to support reliability levels and quality of service equal to or better than those found in legacy networks.
- *User/control plane separation:* The network will permit separate signaling and bearer paths.
- Terminals: the network will support a wide range of terminal types (e.g. voice-only terminals, IP multimedia terminals, laptop computers).
- *IP migration:* The architecture will allow migration from IPv4 to IPv6 and interoperability between IPv4- and IPv6-based networks.

Figure 15–5 provides a simplified representation of the cdma2000 all-IP NAM. In the diagram, only the aspects related to IP and multimedia services are described, whereas aspects related to support of legacy terminals are not represented.

To better describe the cdma2000 all-IP NAM, the following sections describe the principal functionality in the architecture.

ACCESS FUNCTIONALITY

Access functionality provides control and management of access to network resources (e.g., radio bearers, IP bearers), as shown in Figure 15–6. The purpose of access functionality is to hide access-specific aspects to other functionalities. The access functionality contains L2 functions specific to an access technology (e.g., access technology specific authentication and authorization); it receives QoS requests through the network functionality and translates these requests into access-specific QoS requests. The access network, the access gateway (AGW), and the AAA (authentication, authorization, and accounting) support access functionality.

The access network (AN) in cdma200 all-IP NAM performs mobility management functions for registering, authorizing, authenticating, and paging IP-based terminals. The AN supports handoff within an AN and between ANs of the same technology. AN can be enhanced to support handoffs between ANs of different technologies. The cdma2000 AN contains the base station

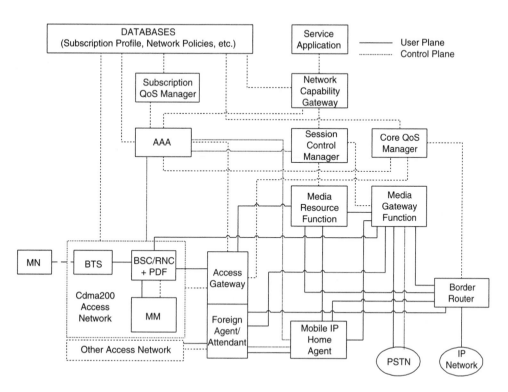

All-IP NAM architecture.

transceiver system (BTS), the base station controller (BSC), the mobility manager (MM), and the packet control function (PCF). In particular, the mobility manager is responsible for handling registration messages from the MS, for establishing of logical bearers through the IP multimedia domain core network, for communicating with the AAA for access network authentication, for authorizing radio link access (multimedia registration, multimedia page response, interradio access network handoff), and for accounting. The packet control function (PCF) is responsible for establishing, maintaining, and terminating Layer 2 connections to the AGW, interacting with PDSN to support dormant handoff, maintaining knowledge of radio resource status (e.g., active, dormant), buffering packets arriving from the AGW when radio resources are not in place or are insufficient to support the flow from the AGW, relaying packets to and from the AGW, and collecting and sending radio link (air interface)–related accounting information to the AGW. PCF behaves very similarly to the PCF in current cdma2000 network.

The AGW supports both the multimedia and legacy MS domains and provides the core network with access to the resources of the access network

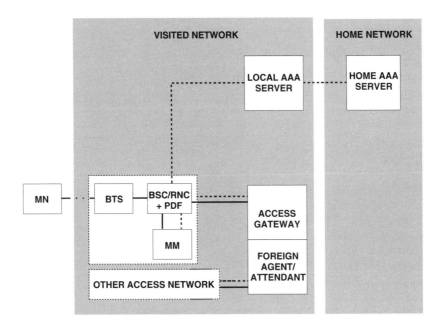

Figure 15–6   *Access functionality.*

(e.g., radio bearers) by presenting a common interface to the specific capabilities, configurations, and resources of the different access network technologies. The AGW supports inter-access gateway handoffs, provides foreign agent functionality (for Mobile IPv4) and/or attendant functionality (for mobile IPv6), and acts as a peer function for link layer termination of the IP traffic between the MN and the network (e.g., PPP). AGW provides the interface to access network functions such as the PCF function, provides access to network-level registration and authentication for the mobile station (e.g., mobile IP registration), and communicates with the AAA for user authentication, access authorization to the core network, and accounting purposes. AGW supports link-layer handoffs between homogeneous access networks supported by the same AGW and may be extended to support link-layer handoffs among access networks of differing technologies when the access networks are supported by the same access gateway. AGW communicates with the core quality of service manager (CQM) for management of core QoS resources, intercepts and processes QoS requests from the mobile station, provides policy decision information to the access network for enforcement within the access network, and enforces policy decisions for authorized services by policing traffic to and from mobile stations as per QoS profile. The QoS allocation requests from the MN are forwarded by the AGW to the CQM for authorization.

The AAA provides IP-based authentication, authorization, and accounting. The AAA maintains security associations with peer AAA entities to support intra- and/or inter-administrative domain AAA functions. AAA provides authentication of terminal devices and subscribers by verifying an entity identity for network access, QoS request, multimedia resource request, or service request, and by providing authentication and/or encryption keys to establish dynamic security associations between network entities. AAA provides authorization of requests for services and/or bandwidth and has access to the policy repository, directory services, subscriber profiles, and device register. AAA provides the authorization decision for services, and bandwidth in terms of whether a user or device is authorized for a particular service, and to what levels a given service may be used. An entity that requests authorization from the AAA entity may receive a set of information that allows it to make further decisions concerning services and/or bandwidth without a new request to the AAA entity (i.e., the requesting entity may be able to cache authorization information from the AAA entity). Cached information may have an assigned expiration time. The AAA entity may send unsolicited messages containing policy decisions to appropriate entities. AAA also performs accounting functionality by gathering data concerning the services, QoS, and multimedia resources requested and used by individual subscribers. Currently, the all-IP NAM utilizes Radius as the AAA protocol and will soon adopt Diameter Mobile IPv4 and Diameter NASREQ application. The service authorization request may be sent to the AAA by access gateway via the CQM (i.e., in case of a request for QoS authorization), or by the session control manager once it has determined the specific service to be provided in the case of a multimedia session.

AAA may provide authorization by providing a set of information that allows other entities to make further decisions concerning services and/or bandwidth without a new request to the AAA entity (i.e., the requesting entity may be able to cache authorization information from the AAA entity). AAA may also send unsolicited messages containing policy decisions to appropriate entities.

AAA also performs accounting functionality by gathering data concerning the services, QoS, and multimedia resources requested and used by individual subscribers.

NETWORK FUNCTIONALITY

The purpose of network functionality is to provide end-to-end IP connectivity between the mobile station (including devices connected to it) and other IP entities in the architecture (Figure 15–7). The access functionality appears to the network functionality as a link layer. The network functionality controls the access functionality through the access gateway-core quality of service manager and protocols/mechanisms such as DiffServ and RSVP. The network functionality is provided through the core QoS manager (CQM), the mobile

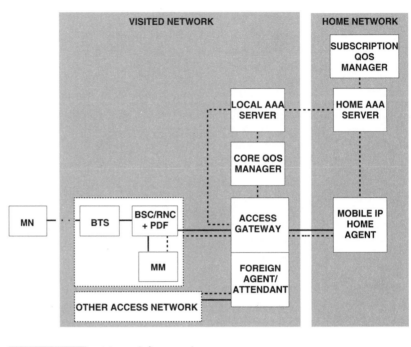

Figure 15–7   *Network functionality.*

IP home agent (HA), the AAA, and the subscription quality of service manager (SQM).

The CQM provides management of core network QoS resources within its own core network necessary to support services to network users. It communicates with the access gateway to provide authorization of resource allocations. The CQM makes policy decisions with regard to use of core network QoS resources within its own network, including consideration of service-level agreements. QoS policy information for network resource utilization may be forwarded to and cached by the CQM. CQM manages resources of the border router and access gateway that handle traffic between low-speed networks (e.g., radio access network) and the high-speed backbone core network.

The mobile IP HA provides two major functions, according to mobile IP:

- registering the current point of attachment of the user
- forwarding of IP packets to (and from in the case of mobile IPv4) the current point of attachment of the user

The HA accepts registration requests using the mobile IP protocol and uses the information in those requests to update internal information about the current point of attachment of the user (i.e., the current IP address to be used to transmit and receive IP packets to and from that user). The HA interacts with the AAA to authorize mobile IP registration requests from mobile nodes. The HA also interacts with the access gateway to receive subsequent mobile IP registration requests. The HA may interact with several network entities in performing its work of forwarding IP packets to the current point of attachment of the user.

The SQM provides management of QoS resources on a per subscription basis for users subscribed to the home network. AAA interrogates SQM to authorization allocation of resource for a given subscriber based on policy rules defined by the user subscription and current allocations already made with respect to that subscription. SQM keeps track of QoS allocated in the core network on a subscription base.

MULTIMEDIA SERVICE APPLICATION CONTROL FUNCTIONALITY

The multimedia service application control functionality implements the call control and services/applications that provide the multimedia services.

The multimedia service application control functionality is access independent and represents an abstraction above the network plane. The network functionality provides end-to-end IP connectivity to the multimedia control functionality by ensuring that IP packets are routed correctly and the necessary QoS is available, so that these entities may communicate directly. For example, a SIP client in the MN may communicate with SIP servers (SCMs) in the network, assuming the SIP client has obtained knowledge about the IP address to use.

The multimedia service application control functionality is supported by the multimedia client and/or applications in the MN, the network capability gateway (NCGW), the session control manager (SCM), the AAA, and the service applications. Figure 15–8 depicts the multimedia service control functionality.

The service applications provide value-added network-based services for wireless subscribers. These services may be accessed via the network capability gateway or accessed directly from the user's MN. Service applications may reside inside or outside of the operator's network (e.g., operator applications or Internet applications). Service applications may access network resources (e.g., session control manager, position server) for functionality needed during service logic execution. These service applications use standard APIs (e.g., open service architecture [OSA] API) supported by the NCGW. The APIs allow access to service applications during SIP sessions and allow service applications to access resources in the network (e.g., position server, SCM, AAA) as required for service logic execution. Service applications that reside outside of the wireless network operator network may also access private databases, SIP or http servers, and other functionality on equipment provided by a third party. Service applications (e.g., hosted on

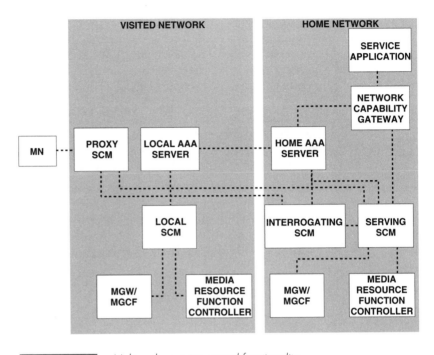

Figure 15–8   *Multimedia service control functionality.*

equipment in the Internet or a private network) may also not use network resources other than for bearer management.

The NCGW provides access to network resources needed during service
application execution. The interface toward the service application uses API
interfaces such as Open Service Architecture (OSA). The interfaces toward
other network entities use the relevant protocols. The NCGW, in conjunction
with AAA and the position server (for position-related requests), is responsible for guaranteeing proper authorization for access to resources.

The SCM establishes, monitors, manages, and releases multimedia sessions and manages the user's service interactions. The SCM is responsible for
managing the allocation of required resources such as announcement servers,
and multiparty bridges, for maintaining knowledge of session states and
user's service precedence, for providing session state information to the authorization function as needed, for supporting the decision-making responsibilities of the authorization function while allowing the authorization function
to remain stateless relative to the subscriber's open sessions, and for performing session processing tasks (e.g., network selection) required for session
completion.

As can be seen in Figure 15–8, the functionality of the SCM in a roaming
situation is split between the visited network and the home network. The SCM

function in the home network is responsible for multimedia session control and IP service control and may be further divided into an interrogating-session control manager and a serving-session control manager for load sharing and/or hiding of the internal network structure to other networks, or for allocation of a serving SCM close to the mobile station. The interrogating SCM would in such a case be the entry point to the network, responsible for locating the serving SCM serving the user, while the serving SCM is the entity actually keeping the session state. The SCM function in the visited network proxies requests from the mobile station to an SCM in the home network and returns responses from the home network (proxy session control manager); it allocates local resources and provides access to local services (local session control manager); and it supports emergency calls (emergency-session control manager). The proxy SCM is adopted only in case of SIP sessions, as seen in Figure 15–8.

SCM communicates with AAA for two reasons: to support authorization/authentication for users, and to establish secure communications with other SCM entities (e.g., through the passing of addresses and security tokens). Through the AAA the SCM uses information from various databases (e.g., subscriber profile) and invocation of various services applications to determine the exact service being requested.

The media gateway (MGW) is responsible for converting the media, which is typically voice, between the CDMA network and the PSTN. For calls originating or terminating in the PSTN, the MGW plays the role of media converter. The media gateway control function (MGCF) is responsible for translating the signaling between SIP an ISUP, as well as managing the assignment of trunks and circuits on the PSTN interface of the MGW. The MGCF interfaces to PSTN signaling on one side which uses ISUP and the SCM on the other side (CDMA network) which uses SIP as the signaling protocol for session setup. The MGCF interface to the session control manager is for communicating session control information (e.g., via a protocol like SIP).

15.3.5 Future Evolution of cdma2000 Core Network

Two main threads will characterize the evolution of the cdma2000 network to an all-IP NAM and the future evolution of the all-IP NAM:

- Evolution of the IP transport infrastructure
- Evolution of service provisioning

When operators propose new service requirements, the all-IP NAM will be modified in terms of network functionalities and protocols to satisfy such requirements. Evolution of service provisioning is described in following sections.

The main evolution regarding the IP transport infrastructure will be the adoption of mobile IPv6. Adopting mobile IPv6 in the all-IP NAM implies a set of changes in terms of protocols and functionalities in the network. In fact, with mobile IPv4, either Radius or Diameter MIPv4 are used in the network to provide user authentication, authorization, accounting, and support of IP mobility. The mobile IPv4 network model identifies the foreign agent function and defines the mechanisms for a mobile node to register with the network. However, the network model for mobile IPv6 does not foresee a foreign agent and does not define any registration protocol between the mobile node and the network. The mobile IPv6 network model uses instead an attendant functionality in the default router: In the All-IP NAM, the attendant is located in the AGW. The attendant should have a function similar to the foreign agent, but the mobile IPv6 signaling is not directed to the attendant. In fact, whereas in mobile IPv4 registration request messages allow the mobile node to register with the network, obtain authorization to access network resources, and indicate to the home agent the current point of attachment, mobile IPv6 defines only a way for the MN to communicate to the home agent and correspondent nodes the current point of attachment to the network in terms of a care-of address through binding update messages. Therefore, a registration/authorization protocol between the mobile node and the network (in this case, the attendant in the AGW) is needed in order to allow mobile nodes to obtain authorization to gain IP connectivity and access network resources.

In order to adopt mobile IPv6 in the all-IP NAM, the following mobile IPv6-related protocols are needed:

- Diameter mobile IPv6 application, to support mobile IPv6–specific mechanisms for authentication, authorization, and mobility support.
- A registration/authorization protocol between the mobile node and the attendant in the network.

Two main paths can be identified for the evolution of all-IP NAM from mobile IPv4 to mobile IPv6:

- Direct adoption of Mobile IPv6: In such a scenario, mobile IPv4 support is replaced with support of mobile IPv6 and the adoption of mobile IPv6-related protocols.
- Support of IPv6 mobility through mobile IPv4 is adopted first.

In the second scenario, IPv6 is provided to mobile nodes as a service over mobile IPv4, therefore enabling mobility of IPv6 nodes. This is similar to the support of IPv6 in UMTS, where IPv6 is a service provided to the user and mobility is supported through UMTS-specific mobility mechanisms. The drivers behind the adoption of this additional steps in the evolution of the 3GPP2 network architecture will be the ability to support IPv6 mobility with minimal changes to the network (i.e., addition of NATs, network address translators) while allowing operators deploying a mobile IPv4 All-IP NAM to reuse completely the investment. Such a scenario becomes plausible if the growth of data services will not justify large investments in network equipments.

Operators may see the direct adoption of mobile IPv6 as a dangerous and costly disruption, since it will require operators already deploying a mobile IPv4 all-IP NAM network to modify network elements in order to support mobile IPv6 and the related protocols. Therefore, the direct evolution to mobile IPv6 may be problematic from a political point of view. However, the evolution to mobile IPv6 will be justified in case of significant growth of data services, since the adoption of IPv6 and mobile IPv6 allows operators to deploy a more efficient network architecture.

In conclusion, the steps in the evolution of cdma2000 that will actually take place in the next years are dependent mainly on the market thrust toward data and multimedia IP services.

15.4   Wireless LAN 802.11 Evolution

802.11-based wireless LAN networks are gaining in popularity and being deployed on a wide scale. The lure of high-speed and low-cost wireless Internet access is an enabler in itself. The other primary drivers for this phenomenon are as follows:

- Ease of deployment
- Cost of equipment
- High data speeds
- Unlicensed spectrum

802.11 access points and networks are primarily being deployed in home networks and communities, enterprises of all sizes, and public hotspot areas such as airports, hotels, and convention centers.

As the number of users with laptops and PDAs grows, access to the Internet via these hotspot networks will increase. Notebook computer manufacturers have begun to incorporate wireless LAN functionality into computers. Some of the newer PDAs are also beginning to incorporate 802.11b functionality as a standard feature.

15.4.1   Wireless LAN Technology Evolution

From a technology evolution perspective, 802.11 technology has come a long way. From the 2-Mbps standard to the 11-Mbps standard (802.11b) to 45 Mbps (802.11g) and 54 Mbps (802.11a), the increase in the data speeds has been impressive. Access points and interface cards based on 802.11a are already becoming commercially available.

Some of the Operators Providing Public WLAN Access

Boingo Wireless
Hereuare Communications
Wayport
Sonera
Telia
Jippii Group Oyj
mm02
NTT Docomo
Voicestream Wireless
Skynett Global

What is the future for an increasingly popular technology? Market pressures are forcing vendors and operators to increase the bandwidth/data rates offered by wireless LANs as well as provide enhanced security. In order to achieve even higher data rates, on the order of 100s of Mbps, new coding schemes, error correction, and operating frequencies will be developed. Antenna technology will also help resolve deployment issues that are currently faced in real life networks.

One of the drawbacks of the current 802.11 systems is the lack of security. As has been described in the chapter on 802.11, WEP is a nonstarter for securing networks. This is being worked on in the IEEE by Task Group i, and a more secure solution is expected to be standardized in the near future. The Advanced Encryption Standard (AES) is expected to be standardized for securing the air interface. The work on security is being done in Task Group I of the IEEE 802.11 work area.

Current 802.11 networks do not support quality of service. In order to support real-time services such as voice and video, QoS will be a requirement. Work on QoS is currently being standardized in Task Group E.

Current WLAN networks allow a user to move within the same subnet. However, movement across subnets will be a requirement in the near future. One solution to address such mobility is based on the use of mobile IP. We can envision the use of mobile IP on top of wireless LAN networks to provide seamless mobility across subnets of WLAN access networks.

15.4.2   Wireless LAN Service Evolution

Wireless LAN service in the enterprise is becoming more accepted. IT departments recognize the vulnerability of WLAN security based on WEP. Hence they have resorted to other means of securing networks deployed within the campus. One such means is to use a virtual private network (VPN) solution.

The WLAN access points are deployed outside a VPN gateway and hence are not directly connected to the enterprise LAN. Users gain access to the enterprise LAN over a VPN that is between the terminal/device/notebook computer to the VPN gateway and that allows valid users access to the LAN. Since all the data traffic is now carried over the VPN tunnel (which is IPsec secured), the threat of snooping on the air interface is mitigated. Other solutions for securing include proprietary ones such as Cisco's Lightweight Extensible Authentication Protocol (LEAP) for enhanced security.

15.4.3   Operator Wireless LAN

Traditional cellular operators are beginning to deploy WLAN networks on a nationwide basis. Some examples include Voicestream's wireless LAN network in the United States and mm02's plans for deployment in the United Kingdom. WLAN access points are generally deployed in hotspot areas such as train and bus stations, airports, cafes and restaurants, stadiums, and shopping malls. These networks are referred to as public wireless LAN or operator wireless LAN networks. In order to access these networks, subscribers need to have a subscription to the service and authenticate themselves before access is allowed. The ISP model has used authentication mechanisms and protocols based on Radius for this purpose. Nokia has also developed a solution that allows the users to authenticate themselves using a SIM (subscriber identity module). Since many mobile users already have a subscription for their mobile telephones with an operator, the same subscription can be used to access these WLAN networks. A view of the architecture that utilizes the GSM network's SIM-based authentication infrastructure for WLAN access is shown in Figure 15–9.

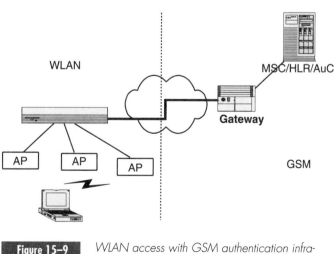

Figure 15–9   *WLAN access with GSM authentication infrastructure.*

The benefits of such a solution to operators are manyfold and include the following:

- Subscriber management and billing based on the GSM SIM
- Leveraging global GSM roaming capability via the GSM roaming agreements
- Cellular operators becoming wireless ISPs by offering WLAN coverage to their existing subscribers
- A secure mechanism for authenticating users

End users benefit from the fact that they do not need to have multiple subscriptions for different services. Their existing GSM subscription with an operator will allow them to access WLAN networks provided by the user's service provider or by any other operator who is also a GSM operator with whom the user's service provider has roaming agreements.

15.4.4   WLAN Service as Another Access Technology in 3G

802.11-based networks are now being considered as another access type for 3G networks. In the UMTS architecture the two access technologies that are specified today are the UTRAN and GERAN. 3GPP is currently working on specifying WLAN as another access type as well. With the introduction of WLAN as another access type, users will be able to access the same services that they are used to from their mobile phone/terminal when using the WLAN medium. This work is expected to be completed in the R6 specification of 3GPP.

15.5   Evolution of Bluetooth

The interesting aspect of Bluetooth technology is that it has attracted manufacturers from varied industries, including automobiles, computing, communications, digital photography, and handheld devices. Currently there are numerous manufacturers developing Bluetooth products such as PC cards and adapters for use in laptops, PDAs, and in PCs. The next step would be to integrate Bluetooth into mobile phones, PDAs, laptops, headphones, and home gateways connected to the Internet. The usability is further extended in automobiles and appliances.

On the technology front, Bluetooth SIG continues its specifications development in enhancing the technology and its usage scenarios. In future releases, the SIG is planning to include a specification for higher data rates (between 2 and 10 Mbps) to support multimedia applications that require higher bandwidth. At the time of this writing, the SIG has announced two new wireless advancements from their working groups that address the needs of mobile phone users. The Car working group within SIG has announced that the new hands-free profile will enable hands-free use of mobile phones in automobiles. Second, the Imaging working group announced the introduction of the new Imaging profile for use in wirelessly transmitting digital images.

In addition, a printing profile is being specified to allow devices to issue wireless print commands to the Bluetooth-enabled printer. Recently, a new profile called the Bluetooth Extended Service Discovery Profile (ESDP) for Universal Plug and Play™ (UPnP™) was introduced that defines how devices with Bluetooth can use the Service Discovery Protocol initially to discover other devices that support UPnP services and retrieve information about these services.

With current capabilities and future technology developments, Bluetooth technology will become more ubiquitous than it is today.

15.6   Service Evolution

Service provisioning in wireless networks is evolving differently for mobile operators, ISPs, and corporate networks.

15.6.1   Service Evolution in 3GPP

Service control has been an integral part of the 2G cellular networks and provides functionality similar to the Intelligent Networks (IN) in fixed networks. Service control is related to controlling the use of network resources as per the user communications, available application services, and subscription agreements. In GSM, the service control functions are implemented as a variation to IN called Customized Applications for Mobile Network Enhanced Logic (CAMEL). CAMEL provides network features and capabilities so that roaming subscribers can utilize the operator service even when roaming outside the home network. Service control in 3G networks has taken precedence due to higher costs in obtaining 3G licenses. Hence, mobile operators must provide more revenue-generating and value-added services (VAS) beyond traditional voice services like IP real-time multimedia services.

Although service control in 3G networks is an evolution of CAMEL, one of the important aspects introduced is the concept of virtual home environment (VHE). VHE allows subscribers the flexibility and convenience to access the home operator services irrespective of where the subscriber may be roaming and even with different terminals. VHE allows subscribers to create a personal service environment (PSE) in the home network and provides access to same services, configuration settings, and perception as if subscribers are in the home network at all times. Within the VHE concepts, a toolkit was introduced so that the network functionalities can be utilized by means of an open standardized API support in the form of middleware from external application servers. The API shall provide an extensible and implementation-independent approach to support subscriber call control, supplementary services, and service capability discovery functions. In addition to OSA, the VHE can be implemented by use of other tools like CAMEL, MEXe, and USAT. UMTS Release 99 specifications included the VHE/OSA concept for CS services. However, the service control for IMS services has been evolving in the recent UMTS Releases 4 and 5.

For 3GPP, service provisioning is evolving toward the support of most IP services through the IMS (i.e., through a SIP infrastructure). This includes not only voice over IP, but presence services, instant messaging, and streaming services. This is true of course only for services provided by the mobile operator, whereas users can still access services available over the Internet (e.g., multimedia streaming).

Presence service architecture has been introduced in UMTS Release 6. Figure 15–10 shows the architecture that is under discussion. The presence information of the user maintained in the presence server is collected through HSS and S-CSCF together. Other interested parties, called watcher applications, can query the user presence information through standard interfaces.

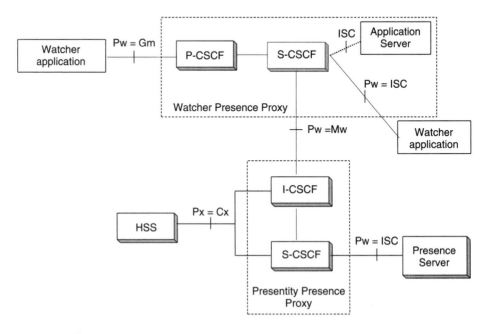

Figure 15–10   *Presence service architecture in 3GPP Release 6.*

15.6.2   Service Evolution in 3GPP2

In 3GPP2, the all-IP NAM has introduced a high-level view of the type of services that should be supported by cdma2000. Recently, service provisioning in 3GPP2 has been evolving toward the concepts of the Internet Multimedia Subsystem defined in 3GPP. Several manufacturers and carriers are working toward the adoption of the same concepts and solutions defined in 3GPP, with the intention to provide a common set of services and service machinery for both 3GPP and 3GPP2 networks.

For ISPs, service provisioning is evolving to consider a large variety of services, with focus on supporting multimedia applications. It is to be expected that the service model adopted by ISPs will be different from the one adopted by traditional mobile operators as 3GPP and 3GPP2. ISPs have traditionally been providing access to the global Internet and providing a somehow limited set of specific services, maintaining the focus on allowing subscribers access to services available over the Internet.

Recent years have seen the expansion of corporate networks through VPNs and the support for remote access, wherein users can access with security tunnels the services and resources of the home corporate network. In a way, VPNs allow a mobile subscriber to be connected directly to the home corporate network independent of the actual point of attachment to the IP networks. VPNs can be supported through mobile wireless networks, and this allows corporate networks to provide to their users the same set of services independent of the location of the users. This model seems to be very beneficial for corporate users and for the corporation itself, while mobile operators benefits from the use of transport resources.

15.7   Summary

In this chapter we have described how networks that provide IP services are evolving. We described the generic evolution of wireless networks and described how 3GPP networks and 3GPP2 networks are evolving. We also described how WLAN is evolving and what will be the applications for this technology. Finally, we briefly discussed service evolution.

References

Geoffrey A. Moore, *Crossing the Chasm: Marketing and Selling High-Tech Products to Mainstream Customers,* HarperBusiness, 1999.

Heikki Kaaranen et al., *UMTS Networks: Architecture, Mobility and Services,* John Wiley & Sons, Inc., 2001.

3GPP TS 23.002 V4.4.0, "3GPP Release 4 Standard."

3GPP TS 23.002 V5.5.0, "3GPP Release 5 Standard."

H. Holma et al., *WCDMA for UMTS: Radio Access for Third Generation Mobile Communications,* John Wiley & Sons, Inc., 2001.

J. Rosenberg et al., "SIP: Session Initiation Protocol," Internet Engineering Task Force *RFC 2543,* 2001.

C. Perkins, "IPv4 Mobility," Internet Engineering Task Force *RFC 2002,* May 1995.

P. Calhoun, and C. Perkins, "Mobile NAI Extension," Internet Engineering Task Force *RFC 2794,* March 2000.

IP Network Architecture Model for cdma2000 Spread Spectrum Systems, 3GPP2 TSG-N, January 2002.

P. Calhoun et al., "Diameter Base Protocol," Internet Engineering Task Force Working Group draft-ietf-aaa-diameter-09.txt, March 2002.

P. Calhoun. and C. Perkins, "Diameter Mobile IPv4 Application," Internet Engineering Task Force Working Group draft-ietf-aaa-diameter-mobileip-09.txt, March 2002.

P. Calhoun et al., "Diameter NASREQ Application," Internet Engineering Task Force Working Group draft-ietf-aaa-diameter-nasreq-09.txt, March 2002.

S. Faccin, "Diameter Mobile IPv6 Application," Internet Engineering Task Force draft-le-aaa-diameter-mobileipv6-01.txt, November 2001.

The Official Bluetooth Homepage—*http://www.bluetooth.com.*

Standards Bodies and Their Roles in the Future

The path to success for wireless IP is facing many challenges. There is a challenge not only in solving technical problems (e.g., how to transport multimedia using IP over wireless links), but also in dealing with regulatory issues (e.g., spectrum allocation) in different parts of the world. At the same time, there is a challenge in finding applications and services that will provide inevitable value to mobile users and thus will create an unavoidable need for wireless IP. Most of the technical problems can be solved by industry collaboration through different standards bodies. A standardized solution would also help to reduce cost for consumers.

In this chapter we review some of the important standards bodies that will play a critical role in the future of wireless IP networks. We focus on three main wireless areas: cellular or wireless wide area networks (WWANs), wireless local area networks (WLANs), and wireless personal area networks (WPANs).

Beside standards bodies, there are many important industry fora, special interest groups, and consortiums that have made extensive contributions in the development of wireless IP. Some of the examples are 3G.IP (www.3gip.org), IPv6 Forum (www.ipv6.forum), UMTS Forum (www.umts-forum.org), World Wide Web Consortium (www.w3c.org), Wireless Multimedia Forum (www.wmmforum.com), Wireless Fidelity Alliance (www.wi-fi.org), and Bluetooth SIG (www.bluetooth.com). In this chapter, we limit the discussion to 3GPP, 3GPP2, IETF, IEEE 802, Bluetooth SIG and open mobile alliance (www.openmobilealliance.org). These standards bodies and fora were selected based on their relevance to the contents of this book.

16.1   3GPP

The European Telecommunication Standards Institute (ETSI) pioneered the concept of "Partnership Project" in telecommunications by establishing Third-Generation Partnership Project (3GPP) in December 1998. 3GPP was initiated as a global initiative for a single globally common 3G standard. However, different cellular operators in the three largest telecommunication market sectors—America/South Korea, Japan, and Europe—went in their own ways in determining the choice of technology. 3GPP was able to attract a large portion of the cellular market by providing both TDMA- and CDMA-based solutions. It is expected that almost all of the existing GSM-based networks will evolve into 3GPP-based solutions. Some of the IS-136 operators (e.g., ATT Wireless Systems) have also adopted 3GPP-based solutions. The scope of 3GPP is to produce globally applicable technical specifications and reports for 3G systems based on evolved GSM core networks (CNs) and the radio access technologies (RATs) supported by the CN. For the evolved CN, 3GPP has produced specifications for the general packet radio service (GPRS) system. For the RAT, it has produced specifications for enhanced data rates for GSM evolution (EDGE) and wideband CDMA (WCDMA) technologies.

3GPP is a collaboration agreement that brings together a number of telecommunications standards bodies, which are called organizational partners (OPs), for developing specifications for wireless packet networks. The current OPs are the Association of Radio Industries and Businesses–Japan (ARIB), China Wireless Telecommunication Standards Group (CWTS), ETSI, T1, Telecommunications Technology Association–Korea (TTA), and Telecommunications Technology Committee–Japan (TTC). 3GPP has also included industry fora and consortiums as market representation partners (MRPs). Some of the MRPs are 3G.IP, Global Mobile Suppliers Association (GSA), GSM Association, IPv6 Forum, UMTS Forum, Universal Wireless Communication Consortium (UWCC), and WMF. They provide guidance to the process so the standards meet the market requirements for services, features, and functionality.

The functional organization of 3GPP (Figure 16–1) consists of a project coordination group (PCG) that administers the work of technical specifications groups (TSGs). PCG is composed of OPs and MRPs. There are five TSGs, each with an area of responsibility. The TSG core network (TSG CN) is responsible for the specifications of the CN part of the system. Some of the important areas covered by TSG CN are user equipment, CN Layer 3 radio protocols (call control, session management, mobility management), signaling

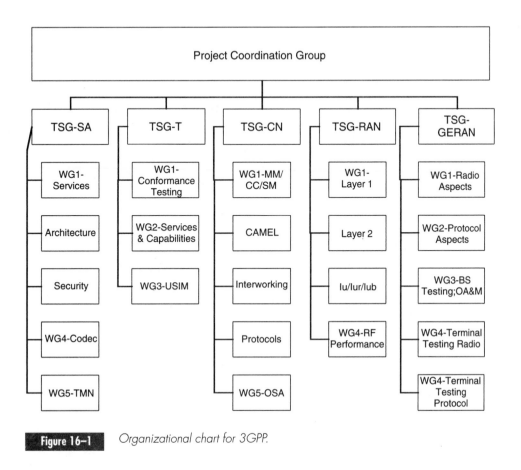

Figure 16-1 *Organizational chart for 3GPP.*

between the CN nodes, interconnection with external networks, O&M (Operation & Management) requirements, and mapping of QoS. TSG GSM/EDGE radio access network (TSG GERAN) is responsible for the specification of the radio access part of GSM/EDGE. It covers radio interface protocol layers, OA&M specifications for the RAN nodes, internal (Abis, Ater) and external (A, Gb) interfaces, and conformance test specifications for GERAN base stations and terminals. TSG radio access network (TSG RAN) is responsible for definition of the functions, requirements, and interfaces of the UMTS Terrestrial Radio Access network (UTRAN). It covers radio interface protocol layers, OA&M requirements, access network interfaces (Iu, Iub, and Iur), and conformance test specifications for base stations. TSG service and system aspects (TSG SA) is responsible for the overall architecture and service capabilities of the system. This includes charging, security, and network management aspects of the system. TSG terminals (TSG T) is responsible for specifying terminal logical and physical interfaces, terminal capabilities, and terminal performance/testing.

Each TSG has divided its responsibilities in a set of working groups (WGs); detailed technical work takes place in the WGs. TSG-CN has the following WGs:

- TSG CN WG1 defines the terminal to CN Layer 3 radio protocols (call control, session management, mobility management, etc.). For example, CN1 addresses SIP call control and SDP protocols for the IM subsystem.
- TSG CN WG2 is responsible for the customized applications for mobile network enhanced logic feature (CAMEL); this feature provides the mechanisms to support the same services independent of the serving network.
- TSG CN WG3 specifies the bearer capabilities and the interworking functions toward both the UMTS terminal and the terminal equipment in the external network. It is also responsible for end-to-end QoS.
- TSG CN WG4 specifies supplementary services, basic call processing, mobility management within the CN, and bearer-independent architecture. CN4 also specifies the mobile-specific protocol specifications within the mobile CN.
- TSG CN WG5 is responsible for the interfaces specific to the UMTS Open Service Access (OSA) and is used to facilitate service implementations. CN5 develops application programming interfaces (APIs) for the OSA.

TSG-GERAN has the following WGs:

- TSG GERAN WG1 is responsible for the radio frequency aspects of GERAN, radio layer 1 specifications, internal GERAN interface specifications, and the specification of GERAN radio performance and radio frequency system.
- TSG GERAN WG2 is responsible for protocol above the physical layer and the interfaces between them.
- TSG GERAN WG3 develops the conformance test specification for GERAN base stations and works on the O&M requirements and specifications for all GERAN nodes.
- TSG GERAN WG4 works on the conformance test specifications for testing of radio aspects of GERAN terminals.
- TSG GERAN WG5 works on the conformance test specifications for testing of all the protocols and services above Layer 2 for the GERAN terminals.

TSG-RAN has the following WGs:

- TSG RAN WG1 works on the physical layer of the radio interface for UE and UTRAN.

- TSG RAN WG2 is responsible for the radio interface architecture and protocols above the physical layer. It also works on the radio resource control and management procedures.
- TSG RAN WG3 is responsible for the overall UTRAN architecture and the internal and access interfaces.
- TSG RAN WG4 works on the RF aspects of UTRAN. For example, it looks into the minimum requirements for transmission and reception parameters.

TSG-SA has the following WGs:

- TSG SA WG1 works on the services and features for 3G. The group sets requirements for the overall system and provides this in a high-level description, which is expanded by the other groups.
- TSG SA WG2 is in charge of developing the architecture of the 3GPP network, based on the requirements by SA1. SA2 identifies the main functions and entities of the network and also the interfaces of the entities.
- TSG SA WG3 is responsible for the security of the 3GPP system. SA3 is responsible for the security implications of new services.
- TSG SA WG4 deals with the specifications for speech, audio, video, and multimedia codecs. It also deals with quality evaluation, end-to-end performance, and interoperability aspects for the codecs.
- TSG SA WG5 specifies the management framework and requirements for management of the 3G systems.

TSG-T has the following WGs:

- TSG T WG1 works on the conformance test specifications for the radio interface. T WG1 is organized in two subgroups: RF subgroup and signaling subgroup.
- TSG T WG2 is responsible for the services and capabilities to be delivered on 3GPP terminals and ensuring that terminals meet the 3GPP objectives. In general, the group is responsible for terminal-based applications, features, and interfaces.
- TSG T WG3 is responsible for the subscriber identity module (SIM), which is used by 2G systems, and the USIM (universal SIM), which is used by 3GPP systems. It is not responsible for the security algorithms (developed by SA3).

3GPP has already accomplished a lot in its endeavor to provide IP on cellular networks. It is consistently working toward evolving its network and radio technology to an all-IP paradigm. There are still open issues and unfinished tasks, which are scheduled and being sought in the next releases. 3GPP is working with IETF to utilize IP expertise in solving issues for its all-IP network. In addition, radio is being evolved to support faster data services. The partnership project is already using synergy from its OPs. 3GPP is looking into bringing IP transport inside the RAN. This, among other benefits, would help in reducing the cost of infrastructure by using the economy of IP technology. Faster downlink data transfer is also under development, and high-speed downlink packet access (HSDPA) is being specified for this purpose. If in the future a widely used application demands a faster uplink data transfer, then 3GPP needs to add that work item to its task list. 3GPP has selected SIP as session control protocol in the Internet multimedia subsystem (IMS). However, there are many tasks related to SIP that need completion. Some of these tasks stem from the specific requirements of cellular telephony (e.g., support of SIP-based supplementary services, support of SIP-based emergency calls). Some of the tasks stem from the narrow bandwidth of cellular (e.g., support of SIP compression). Further improvement in QoS is also desired, such as support for end-to-end QoS. There is also a task for WLAN and UMTS interworking; this would allow a cellular subscriber to access a high-bandwidth WLAN. Support of multimedia services (e.g., video conferencing, video streaming) is also in the list of work items.

16.2   3GPP2

The Third-Generation Partnership Project 2 (3GPP2) is a collaborative effort for generating 3G specifications for providing high-speed IP-based mobile systems. It was established for developing global specifications for network evolution from ANSI/TIA/EIA-41 to 3G, and global specifications for the radio transmission technologies supported by ANSI/TIA/EIA-41. 3GPP2 is mainly supported in North America, China, Japan, and South Korea and continues to play a dominant role in bringing IP technology to these cellular markets. 3GPP2 was born out of the International Telecommunication Union's (ITU) International Mobile Telecommunications-2000 (IMT-2000) initiative for providing high-speed data over the wireless network.

Although discussions did take place between ETSI and the ANSI-41 community to consolidate collaboration efforts for 3G, in the end it was deemed appropriate to establish 3GPP2 as a parallel partnership project. However, ETSI (3GPP Secretariat) is an observer in 3GPP2, and TIA (3GPP2 Secretariat) is an observer in 3GPP. In addition, the groups collaborated through seminars to address interworking of the CN and radio access technologies between these two projects. These bridges have helped to foster openness, cooperation, and goodwill among the participants of each project.

3GPP2 is a collaborative agreement between telecommunications standards development organizations (SDOs), which are called organizational partners (OPs). The five officially recognized OPs are: ARIB, CWTS, TIA, TTA, and TTC. 3GPP2 requires that a participating individual member company be affiliated with at least one of the OPs. 3GPP2 has market representation partners (MRPs) such as CDMA Development Group (CDG), and IPv6 Forum. They provide guidance to 3GPP2 so the specifications meet the market requirements for services, features, and functionalities.

The functional organization of 3GPP2 (Figure 16–2) consists of a steering committee (SC), which manages the overall work process and adopting the technical specifications. The SC is composed of OPs and MRPs. The work of producing technical specifications is done by five TSGs. The TSGs meet, on average, ten times a year to produce technical specifications and reports. Each of the TSGs is comprised of representatives from the individual member companies. TSG-A deals with the access to network interface specifications (e.g., A interface). It also covers Abis and BSC to BTS interface specifications. TSG-C specifies cdma2000 air interface specifications. It also covers base station performance, channel codec, and conformance test specifications. Together, TSG-A and TSG-C are responsible for the radio access networks based on cdma2000. TSG-N specifies Layer 3 protocols for mobility management, call control, and other CN protocols and functionalities. It also covers wireless intelligent network (WIN) services. TSG-P works on wireless packet data interworking. It is responsible for data services and applications. TSG-S is responsible for the services and systems aspects, including the overall architecture, security, and OA&M aspects. TSG-S is responsible for defining the high-level requirements and network architectures required to support the future wireless Internet.

3GPP2 has also achieved a lot in solving technical issues for bringing IP to the cellular users. TSG-P, along with the other TSGs, is active in pursuing an all-IP network for cdma2000 users. There are still open issues and work items that need to be completed. Some of the issues and work items are common with 3GPP (e.g., high-speed downlink data enhancements). The 3GPP2 all-IP network architecture model uses IETF-defined protocols, so necessary

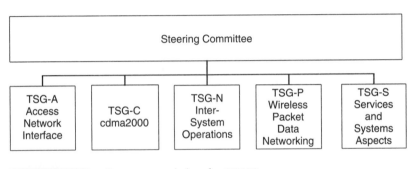

Figure 16–2   *Organizational chart for 3GPP2.*

collaboration between these two standards bodies is necessary for timely delivery of the solutions. 3GPP2 still needs to support IPv6, to offer the benefits of IPv6 (e.g., more address space). The 3GPP2 wireless data network uses mobile IP for mobility; any delay in mobile IPv6 work is also going to delay support of IPv6 in the network. Development of cdma2000 single-carrier evolution for data and voice (1x-EV-DV) is still in progress. This work is highly desired for high-speed downlink packet access. Support for end-to-end QoS is also another open work item. 3GPP2 also needs to work on support of IP broadcast and multicast services. This may involve modifications in the air interface functions and protocols. Currently, there is no IP transport in the cdma2000 RAN. IP transport in the RAN is also another initiative toward all IP. 3GPP2 needs to provide support for IP multimedia applications, such as video streaming and video conferencing. In summary, there are plenty of tasks that need to be accomplished. 3GPP2 is going to serve as a platform for all the cdma2000-based operators to finish those tasks. The market is dynamic and the applications are evolving, and this may change the priority of tasks in the journey toward all IP.

16.3   Internet Standard Bodies

The architecture, maintenance, interoperability, and evolution of the Internet are made possible by the standards bodies that are shown in Figure 16–3.

The Internet standards bodies are organized under the umbrella of the Internet Society (ISOC). The society's mission statement is to assure the open development, evolution, and use of the Internet for the benefit of all people throughout the world. The ISOC is the organizational home of Internet standards. The body acts as the final point of appeal in the Internet standards process. The ISOC is a nonprofit, nongovernmental, international, professional membership organization.

The Internet Architecture Board (IAB) is responsible for defining the overall architecture of the Internet, providing guidance and broad direction to the IETF. IAB members provide vision and direction to the development of the Internet architecture. The IAB also serves as the technology advisory group to the ISOC and oversees a number of critical activities in support of the Internet. IAB members are elected by a nomination committee, and the normal term for an IAB member is two years. The IAB is also the point of appeal regarding any disputes over the standards process and interpretations of the IESG.

The Internet Engineering Steering Group (IESG) is responsible for technical management of IETF activities and the Internet standards process. As part of the ISOC, it administers the process according to the rules and procedures that have been ratified by ISOC trustees. The IESG is directly responsi-

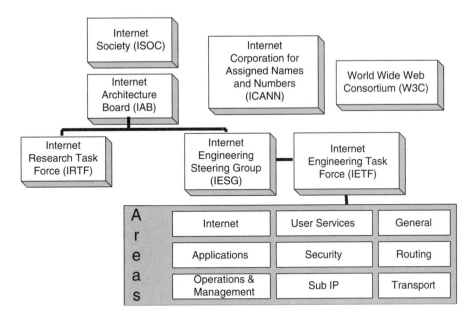

Internet
Society (ISOC)

Internet
Corporation for
Assigned Names
and Numbers
(ICANN)

World Wide Web
Consortium (W3C)

Internet
Architecture
Board (IAB)

Internet
Research Task
Force (IRTF)

Internet
Engineering
Steering Group
(IESG)

Internet
Engineering Task
Force (IETF)

A r e a s	Internet	User Services	General
	Applications	Security	Routing
	Operations & Management	Sub IP	Transport

Figure 16–3 *Bodies defining and maintaining the standards for the Internet.*

ble for the actions associated with entry into and movement along the Internet "standards track," including final approval of specifications as Internet standards. IESG members who are also elected by the nomination committee with two-year terms are involved in the development of the standards process and are responsible for providing direction to the various work groups, reviewing and approving Internet drafts as RFCs, and approving new work groups proposed in different areas.

The Internet Engineering Task Force (IETF) is the main protocol engineering and development arm of the Internet. The working of IETF is discussed further in Section 16.3.1.

The Internet Research Task Force (IRTF) tackles the research problems of the Internet. Unlike the IETF, which deals with protocols and issues that directly impact the Internet today and over the short term, the IRTF looks at the Internet from a research perspective and deals with issues that may impact the Internet in the longer term.

The Internet Corporation for Assigned Names and Numbers (ICANN) was formed as a result of the Internet becoming separated from the NSF. ICANN is responsible for the creation and maintenance of domain prefixes and assignment of port numbers and protocol type numbers. This function, which was earlier performed by IANA (Internet Assigned Numbering Authority), is now taken over by the ICANN.

The World Wide Web Consortium (W3C), which was created in 1994, develops interoperable technologies (specifications, guidelines, software, and tools) to lead the Web to its full potential as a forum for information, commerce, communication, and collective understanding. W3C defines the standards for the Web. It has developed widely used protocols, such as HTTP and XML.

More information on the standards bodies can be found at the following Web sites: www.ietf.org, www.irtf.org, www.isoc.org, www.iab.org, www.iana.org, www.icann.org, www.w3.org.

16.3.1   IETF

The working and structure of IETF is different from a telecommunication standards body, such as 3GPP and 3GPP2. It is not driven by industry leaders, does not require membership or dues, and is open to any interested individual. This actually benefits the industry by opening up the platform for good ideas and opinions. At the same time, it makes the development of an open protocol slower compared to a telecom standards body.

The actual technical work of the IETF is done in its working groups (WGs), which are organized by topics into several areas. There are eight different areas in the IETF: application area, internet area, operations and management area, routing area, security area, sub-ip area, transport area, and user services area. Each WG has a charter and a set of work items. One chairperson (sometimes two), manages the WGs. The area directors (AD), who are collectively called IESGs, oversee the WGs. The WGs or areas are also overseen by the Internet Architecture Board (IAB), which is responsible for providing architectural oversight and focuses on long-range planning and coordination among the various areas. When members are interested in starting a new WG, they can form a "Birds of a Feather" (BOF) session. This is taken from the saying, "Birds of a feather flock together." If the BOF gathers sufficient interest and is thought to be working on a useful and solvable problem, a WG is formed.

WGs do most of their work using the e-mail distribution list. They meet three times a year for face-to-face meetings. Usually, a participant submits an Internet draft (ID) containing a solution for any of the WG's work items. The ID is discussed and its contents are agreed on by rough consensus. A WG may merge multiple solutions for different issues or the same issue into a WG ID. When all the issues are addressed, the WG chair calls for a last call for comments on the WG ID. After the comments are successfully addressed, the ID is sent to the IESG. The IESG also issues the last call for comments on the ID, but from all IETF participants. After all the comments are considered, the draft is sent to the request for comments (RFC) editor for publication as an RFC. RFCs are permanent IETF publications available as specifications to the users.

Since the advent of 3GPP and 3GPP2, the cellular industry has shown interest in IETF. The main reason is to reuse the Internet standards unchanged as much as possible. At the same time, the cellular industry desires to work with the IETF community to get solutions of the issues related to IP over wireless. One such example is the development of the radio network to packet data serving node (R-P) interface protocol for 3GPP2 with the Mobile IP WG. IETF formed liaisons with both 3GPP and 3GPP2. The initial reluctance was mainly the IETF working philosophy of honoring individual contributions instead of having an organization-coordinated contribution. The collaboration between 3GPP/3GPP2 and IETF is necessary for developing specifications for IP wireless networks. At the same time, adaptation of Internet protocols by a huge number of cellular devices will also be a success for IETF. The collaboration will bring about knowledge sharing on both sides. IETF WGs will benefit from radio knowledge, so they can consider that in the evolution of Internet. 3GPP/3GPP2 will benefit from the network knowledge and can thus design radios that will work best with IP protocols.

Considering that WLAN technology is similar to Ethernet, it is fair to say that wireless LAN was always in consideration as a link technology to the IETF community. The Bluetooth Special Interest Group (SIG) has already held few BOFs in IETF. Bluetooth is an IP-based ad hoc personal area network (PAN) technology. (It is the objective of the BOFs to get leverage from the IETF expertise to accelerate the design of Bluetooth IP networking.)

In addition to the liaisons and BOFs, there is a lot of focus inside IETF on developing protocols/recommendations that are also friendly to different wireless technology. Individuals from 3GPP, 3GPP2, Bluetooth, and the WLAN industry are working in different WGs to get solutions that would help in bringing IP to their technologies. Examples of such WGs are Performance Implications of Link Characteristics (PILC), Seamless Mobility (SEAMOBY), Session Initiation Protocol (SIP), Mobile Ad-Hoc Networks (MANET), Mobile IP, Zero Configuration Networks (ZeroConf), and Robust Header Compression (ROHC). This trend will increase due to the open nature of IETF.

16.4   IEEE 802

The Institute for Electrical and Electronic Engineers (IEEE) is a well-recognized body that was founded in 1884. The IEEE is a global technical, professional society serving the public interest and members in electrical, electronics, computer, information, and other technologies.

The IEEE, which is based in the United States sponsors more than 300 conferences each year, including technical conferences, workshops, professional/careers/technical policy meetings, and standards working group meetings. In addition, the IEEE is involved in almost 200 "topical interest" meetings, either as consultants to the technical program or as nonfinancial partners.

The IEEE standards process consists of more than 30,000 volunteers and a Standards Board. IEEE is responsible for creating standards for the very popular local area networks (LAN) standards, such as 802.3 (also known as Ethernet), IEEE 802.5 (token ring), and 802.11 (wireless LAN).

The standards process begins with the submission of a Project Authorization Request (PAR) to the Standards Board. According to IEEE, a PAR is the means by which standards projects are started. PARs define the scope, purpose, and contact points for the new project. If the Standards Board approves the PAR, then the standards process is initiated by the creation of a standards working group. The members of the standards working group are volunteers and may or may not be members of the IEEE.

The members of the IEEE working group create a draft standard. This draft is reviewed by a balloting group of IEEE members for review and approval. The constitution of the ballot group consists of standard's developers, potential users and others having general interest.

Once this process is completed, the Standards Board conducts a review of the Final Draft Standard for the approval. Standards are typically reviewed once every five years for revision.

One of the standards of interest to us is the IEEE 802 family, which is formally referred to as the IEEE 802 LAN/MAN Standards Committee. According to the IEEE, the IEEE 802 LAN/MAN Standards Committee develops local area network standards and metropolitan area network standards. The most widely used standards are for the Ethernet family, token ring, wireless LAN, bridging and virtual bridged LANs. An individual working group provides the focus for each area. IEEE 802 family standards and documents cover layers 1 and 2 of the OSI reference model.

Let's review some of the key documents and task groups with respect to the 802 and specifically the 802.11 family:

- IEEE 802: This provides Overview and Architecture
- IEEE 802.1: This document along with IEEE 802 provides the scope of work for 802 standards.
- IEEE 802.2: It specifies Logical Link Control (LLC) layer. LLC creates a glue that binds the Medium Access Control (MAC) and Physical (PHY) layer.
- IEEE 802.11: This standard specifies MAC and PHY layers. The layers are specified on a 2.4GHz operating frequency with data rates of 1 and 2Mbps. It provides two options for the modulation technique:

frequency hopping spread spectrum (FHSS) or direct sequence spread spectrum (DSSS). Since the approval of the initial 802.11 standard, the IEEE 802.11 WG has made several revisions through various task groups. These groups enhance portions of the 802.11 standard. A suffix of an alphabet, such as 802.11a and 802.11b, represents a task group.

- IEE 802.11a: This PHY standard specifies WLAN operation in the 5GHz band using orthogonal frequency division multiplexing (OFDM). 802.11a supports data rates ranging from 6 to 54Mbps.
- IEEE 802.11b: This PHY standard enhances the initial 802.11 DSSS to include 5.5Mbps and 11Mbps data rates in addition to the 1Mbps and 2Mbps data rates. 802.11b provides the higher data rate by using CCK (Complementary Code Keying), a modulation technique that makes efficient use of the radio spectrum. Compliance with 802.11b is also the basis for the Wi-Fi certification.
- IEEE 802.11c: This standard contains information to ensure proper bridge operations. It is useful for the product developers for developing the WLAN access points.
- IEEE 802.11d: This defines PHY requirements to satisfy regulatory requirements within different countries. This is especially important for operation in the 5GHz bands because the use of these bands differ widely from one country to another.
- IEEE 802.11e: This is refining the IEEE 802.11 MAC specifications to improve Quality of Service (QoS) for better support of audio and video applications.
- IEEE 802.11f: This is specifying an inter access point protocol to support the 802.11 distribution system functions, e.g., user roaming.
- IEEE 802.11g: This task group is extending 802.11b PHY to increase data rate to 54 Mbps, while operating in the 2.4GHz band. 802.11g decided to use OFDM instead of DSSS as a modulation technique.
- IEEE 802.11h: This task group addresses the requirements in Europe for reducing the interference in the 5 GHz band. Satellite communications is the designated primary user in 5 GHz band.
- IEEE 802.11i: This task group is defining enhancements to the MAC layer for enhanced security. It is exploring stronger encryption techniques.

The task groups e, f, g, h and i are setting the stage for the next generation WLAN. QoS work from 802.11a will provide better usage of the resources and improved user perception of the wireless IP services. 802.11f will allow user roaming from one access point to another, thus potentially can increase offered services and WLAN usage. 802.11g is increasing data rates to 54 Mbps in the most popular and globally available band, i.e. 2.4 GHz. This technology will be beneficial for improved access to fixed network LAN and inter-network infrastructure. It will also enable creation of higher performance ad-hoc networks. 802.11h provides dynamic channel selection (DCS) and transmit power control (TPC) for devices operating in the 5GHz band (802.11a). In this way it avoids interference with the primary user (satellite communications) of 5GHz in Europe. It creates additional mechanisms for indoor vs. outdoor channel selection. It will likely become the successor of 802.11a. 802.11i is actively defining enhancements to the MAC Layer to enhance the security of the data exchanged over the air link. 802.11's optional encryption standard, Wired Equivalent Privacy (WEP), is the existing available security mechanism. This uses static encryption keys and does not have key distribution management. 802.11i will incorporate 802.1x that provides a framework for authenticating and controlling user traffic to a protected network. 802.1x provides dynamically varying encryption keys. It ties a protocol called Extensible Authentication Protocol (EAP) and provides multiple authentication methods, such as token cards, Kerberos, certificates, and public key authentication. 802.11i will use a stronger encryption algorithm such as Advanced Encryption Standard (AES). In summary, 802.11 task groups are exploring solutions for providing higher speed access, reduced interference, better quality management, strong security, and user roaming.

16.5   Bluetooth

Bluetooth is a major initiative for low-cost, short-range wireless technology developed by the big leaders in the computing and telecommunications industry. Originally formed in February 1998, it is not directly connected to any standards body like the 3GPP, IEEE, or ITU. The independently operated consortium, called Bluetooth SIG, is largely comprised of 3Com, Agere, Ericsson, IBM, Intel, Microsoft, Motorola, Nokia, and Toshiba as promoter companies who are actively involved in the development of the Bluetooth specifications. Additionally, there are hundreds of associate and adopter member companies. Associate and adopter members are allowed to use the specifications and the Bluetooth brand. At present, the total number of member companies exceeds 1400.

Although Bluetooth SIG is an incorporated company by itself, it is primarily a volunteer organization run by participants from the member companies. These individuals form a number of working groups that focus on the specific areas, such as requirements, specifications development, qualification, and marketing. Bluetooth SIG is also responsible for conducting interoperability testing events to ensure strict adherence to the qualification procedures and testing of Bluetooth products for the participating members. The latest version (Version 1.1) of the Bluetooth specifications was released in early 2001. But the effort continues to enhance and extend the technology for wider applications, usage models, and markets.

The Bluetooth specifications include a complete definition of wireless products ranging from link-layer to application-layer aspects for Bluetooth products. The link layer defines the operation of Bluetooth radio in the 2.4-GHz unlicensed ISM band that employs spread spectrum and frequency hopping. The application-layer specifications support a wide variety of application functions for the Bluetooth products and their interaction between Bluetooth products and with the lower layers. Member companies can download the latest Bluetooth specifications at http://www.bluetooth.com/dev/specifications.asp. The Bluetooth specifications are organized into the following components: a core specification and profiles definitions.

- **"Specification of the Bluetooth System—Core,"** *Bluetooth SIG* **Version 1.1, February, 2001**
  Requirements for components such as the radio, baseband, link manager, and the service discovery protocol, transport layer, along with interoperability information regarding different communication protocols.
- **"Specification of the Bluetooth System—Profiles,"** *Bluetooth SIG* **Version 1.1, February, 2001**
  Higher-level protocols and procedures required to implement user-level functions using Bluetooth technology. In the latest release, new profiles for printing, imaging, automotive, and networking applications were added.

The IEEE initiated an interest in similar technology and formed a working group within the 802 standards committee in early 1999 and named it WG15. The newly formed IEEE 802.15 group formed a charter for wireless personal area network (WPAN) and solicited proposals for a draft standard. But Bluetooth SIG was the only respondent. Even though the Bluetooth specifications do not meet the complete requirements of the IEEE 802.15 charter, it was accepted with some arrangements on the use of the specifications. Presently, IEEE 802.15 and Bluetooth SIG are working together to develop the standard based on the Bluetooth specifications.

Bluetooth SIG has held two BOFs in IETF. But the technology itself is mainly for Layer 2 and has not gained much interest in the IETF for mutual work.

Bluetooth SIG continues its specifications development in enhancing the technology and its usage scenarios. In future releases, the SIG is planning to include a specification for higher data rates (between 2 and 10 Mbps) to support multimedia applications that require higher bandwidth. At the time of this writing, the SIG has announced two new wireless advancements from their working groups that address the needs of mobile phone users. First, the Car working group within SIG has announced a Hands-Free profile. The Hands-Free profile is a definition for how Bluetooth wireless technology will enable hands-free use of mobile phones in automobiles. Second, the Imaging working group announced the introduction of the new Imaging profile for use in wirelessly transmitting digital images.

In addition, a Printing profile is being specified to allow devices to issue wireless print commands to Bluetooth-enabled printer. Recently, a new profile called the Bluetooth Extended Service Discovery Profile (ESDP) for Universal Plug and Play™ (UPnP).was introduced that defines how devices with Bluetooth wireless communications can use the Bluetooth Service Discovery Protocol initially to discover other devices that support UPnP services and retrieve information about these services.

Wide adoption and acceptance of Bluetooth technology due to its current capabilities will drive the evolution of Bluetooth to define more capabilities and new applications in the future.

16.6   Open Mobile Alliance

The Open Mobile Alliance (OMA) was formed to promote global user adaptation of mobile services and applications by ensuring seamless interoperability. It was established on June 12, 2002. The work done by the Open Mobile Architecture and WAP fora laid the foundation of OMA. Later on Location Interoperability Forum (LIF), SyncML, Multi-Media Messaging Services Inter-Operability (MMS-IOP), Wireless Village, and Mobile Wireless Internet Forum (MWIF) joined the alliance by consolidating their efforts with the OMA. These fora were working individually in the same problem space of mobile services and applications. The LIF is promoting and working industry common solutions for the location based services. The SyncML is working on specifying an open standard for establishing a protocol between devices, applications and networks to ensure a consistent set of data available on any device or application at any time. The MMS-IOP is facilitating and coordinating MMS interoperability testing and problem solving. The Wireless Village is specifying the Internet based mobile instant messaging and presence services, all fully interoperable and leveraging existing web technologies. The MWIF was specifying an open mobile wireless and Internet architecture that is independent of the wireless access technology. OMA harmonizes all these efforts and provides a common platform for the development of all these mobile services and applications.

OMA is developing global open standards for services and applications independent of underlying wireless access technology, e.g. cdma2000, and

WCDMA. It intends to provide seamless inter-technology and inter-generation roaming for services and applications across the globe. OMA has achieved its first milestone by developing specifications for OMA Download Feature Set. The specification enables distribution and download of content data to mobile devices independent of vendor and content. It is an over the air protocol and features enhanced download reliability. The specification also provides protocols for associating Digital Rights Management (DRM) with content. DRM allows control of use and distribution of media content.

OMA is a new organization compared to the other organizations discussed in this chapter, such as 3GPP, and 3GPP2. They have taken a mission that is very much needed to promote data services on wireless. OMA could play a key role in promoting the data over wireless in the future. The mobile services and applications is an important part of the wireless data industry, since it has direct interaction with the end users. Development of this part can help boost wireless data usage. Currently, OMA is working on simplifying data application and content development for a mobile user. This includes work on the specifications related to the MMS. It is looking into providing a global standard for email notification on the wireless devices. OMA is working on script language for browsing environment. It is also working on the implementation of interoperability process and testing between its members.

16.7   Summary

This chapter has provided an organizational view of 3GPP, 3GPP2, IEEE 802, Bluetooth, and OMA. It has also described some of the mutual work between these organizations. It highlights some of the in-progress work from these standard bodies. The development in the organizations are going to play a prominent role in the future for the wireless IP networks.

References

3GPP Web site, www.3gpp.org

3GPP2 Web site, www.3gpp2.org

IETF Web site, www.ietf.org

IP Network Architecture Model for 3GPP2 Spread Spectrum Systems, 3GPP2, August 2001

S. Harris, RFC3160, The Tao of IETF, August 2001.

K. Rosenbrock et. al., RFC3113, "3GPP IETF Standardization Collaboration," June 2001.

S. Bradner et. al., RFC3131, "3GPP2 IETF Standardization Collaboration," June 2001.

Standards specifications in 802 family, IEEE, http://standards.ieee.org/cgi-bin/status?802

Open Mobile Alliance Web site, www.openmobilealliance.org.

Index

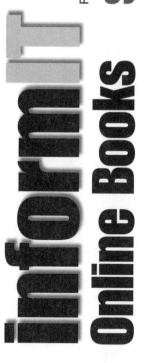